NEW MEXICO - *A History of Four Centuries*

The Author

WARREN A. BECK became interested in writing a history of New Mexico while teaching in Eastern New Mexico University at Portales. He is a graduate of Wayne State University, and his Ph.D. is from Ohio State University. He now teaches Latin American and Southwestern history in Orange State College, Fullerton, California.

NEW MEXICO

A History of Four Centuries

By WARREN A. BECK

UNIVERSITY OF OKLAHOMA PRESS : NORMAN

Library of Congress Catalog Card Number: 62–16470

COPYRIGHT 1962 BY THE UNIVERSITY OF OKLAHOMA PRESS,
PUBLISHING DIVISION OF THE UNIVERSITY.
COMPOSED AND PRINTED AT NORMAN, OKLAHOMA, U.S.A.,
BY THE UNIVERSITY OF OKLAHOMA PRESS. FIRST EDITION.

Dedicated to the memory of my brother Eldor

Preface

THIS HISTORY of New Mexico is intended for readers who want a brief, yet reasonably comprehensive treatment of the development of the state. The narrative begins with a presentation of the geographical setting and its impact upon those who have made New Mexico their home. The story goes back to the time of the Spanish *conquistadores*, treats the Indian and Spanish heritage and the coming of the Anglos. Finally, it is an attempt to evaluate the meaning of the "new" New Mexico that has emerged in the second half of the twentieth century.

Most writers on New Mexico have been concerned with special themes. Some have been intoxicated with the Indians of both the remote past and the present. Others have made the Spanish heritage and the impact upon it of the entrance of the Americans the focal point of their attention. Still others have made frontier life and the "wild west" environment their special field of study. Too many writers have been apologists for the unique characteristics of New Mexico and have been unduly eager to defend the state from its outside critics. This author is wedded to no central theme in preparing this work. History tells its own story, and the story of the development of New Mexico through more than four centuries is alone important enough to tell.

Those readers who feel that this work may in some instances be critical of the course of New Mexican history are reminded of the words of Philip D. Jordan, who warns that "state history is not an exercise in local pride and puffing." Several years' residence and teaching within the borders of the "Land of Enchantment" have served to make this author just as enthusiastic a booster of his adopted state as many native-born enthusiasts. Therefore, careful efforts have been made to attain historical objectivity, and some New Mexicans may feel that these attempts have been too scrupulous.

The preparation of this work has placed the writer in the debt of countless people. Naturally, all who have written about the state have been of assistance. The authors of scholarly articles, especially those appearing in the *New Mexico Historical Review*, have made a most worthwhile contribution. Also, the students who have prepared theses and dissertations have greatly aided this work. Giving generously of their time to this project have been the library staffs of Eastern New Mexico University, the State Museum of New Mexico, the University of New Mexico, and the Huntington Library of San Marino, California.

Grateful acknowledgment is made to the many individuals who have aided with their time and talents. Professor Byron Gordon of the department of geography at the University of New Mexico read the chapters on land and mining and made many helpful suggestions. Professor Ira C. Ihde of Eastern New Mexico University read the entire manuscript for criticism. Professor Robert C. Olson, also of Eastern New Mexico University, gave valuable assistance on grammar and literary style. Paul Horgan, of Roswell, contributed material on current musical developments in New Mexico, and Roland Dickey offered information about the University of New Mexico Press, which he directs. The staffs of the Division of Government Research and the Bureau of Business Research of the University of New Mexico made available much material concerning recent political and economic history.

Warren A. Beck

Fullerton, California
April 2, 1962

Contents

Illustrations

xi

Maps

NEW MEXICO - *A History of Four Centuries*

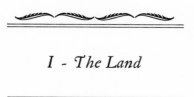

I - The Land

THE NAME NEW MEXICO was first used by the explorer Antonio de Espejo in his description of the land north of Mexico in 1583. Its use represented the hope of the Spaniards that this new land would be similar to Mexico itself as a source of great treasure in minerals. Throughout Colonial times other European cartographers as well as the Spaniards used this name to apply to the vast area of what is today the southwestern United States and northern Mexico. It was inevitable that such an extensive region should have indefinite boundaries.

Today the state embraces an area of 121,666 square miles, making it the fifth largest state in the Union. However, its water area is only 155 square miles, making it the smallest state in this respect. It is located between 103 and 109 degrees west longitude and 32 and 37 degrees north latitude. Except for the slightly panhandled effect of the southwest corner, the state is almost a perfect rectangle. It measures 390 miles from north to south and 350 miles from east to west. New Mexico has no natural boundaries, its limits having been set by man. It is bounded on the north by Colorado, on the east by the tip of Oklahoma and by Texas, on the south by Texas and Mexico, and on the west by Arizona.

Terrain

The most striking quality about the land of New Mexico is its great diversity. Few other areas in the world of comparable size have as many variations in topography. The *Llano Estacado* contains some of the flattest land found anywhere, and some of New Mexico's mountains are as rugged as any in the world. In some parts of the state snow-capped peaks thrust heavenward with all of their majestic beauty, pine forests and lush grasslands abound, and mountain streams laden with fish wend their way toward the plains below. But in other areas of the state there are vast regions which have no surface streams, where even cactus struggles to survive in the blazing sun of the desert sky or among the lava beds. The diversity of New Mexico is well illustrated by the fact that of the seven life or crop zones found in North America, six appear within the state boundaries.

To a geologist, the state of New Mexico must come somewhat close to being a mixture of paradise and hell. It is a geologist's paradise because few other states possess a more remarkable array of varied features. On the other hand, the very presence of rocks that range from the old crystalline and igneous materials to quite recent sedimentary rocks and alluvial deposits makes more difficult the task of exploration and classification that confronts the geologist. This is more evident when one considers the multiplicity of forms in which these rocks are found in New Mexico. As one authority laments, within the state there is a "long sequence of geological events which are as yet only imperfectly known."[1]

The presence of fossils and marine deposits such as the sedimentary rocks, gypsum, and potash salts are ample evidence that the state was submerged beneath the sea. The fact that these deposits occur at different levels is evidence that this submergence may have been repeated several times in the geologic past. The lava flows in various parts of the state are indicative of an age of volcanic activity. In fact, one of the finest displays of volcanic necks in the world exists in the Mount Taylor–Río Puerco region. The abundance of metamorphic rocks bespeaks geologic age. Many varieties of minerals have been found in the state.

Just as the land of New Mexico was periodically submerged beneath the sea in the geologic past, so also was the land raised at inter-

[1] State of New Mexico, *Seventh Biennial Report of the State Engineer, 1925–26,* 82 (hereafter cited as *Seventh Report*).

4

vals. Today, the diversity of the topography of the state is largely due to the elevation of the mountainous areas so far above the adjacent terrain. Because of this elevation, the mountains receive more moisture than the surrounding area. Because the mountains are steep, the streams that make their way down from them are laden with silt and with debris that has been weathered away. Once a stream reaches more level ground, its velocity is reduced, and its ability to carry silt and debris in suspension is likewise reduced. Therefore, the load is dropped in a fan-shaped deposition which ultimately may extend for miles. This process is similar to that by which delta plains are built up at the mouth of a river. Ultimately, these fans coalesce so that a vast area is built up composed of the debris washed down from the mountainside. Naturally, such a region is subject to continued erosion by streams traversing it.

This, then, is the manner in which the plains constituting the eastern third of the state were formed. However, the origin of the western two-thirds is more complex. For here there exists a complicated history of lava flows, faulting, and erosion cycles. In many areas, the San Agustín Plain, for example, there is no exterior drainage. Thus, in periods of heavy rainfall an inland lake may be formed. Such enclosed valleys are called bolsons, of which there are many in New Mexico. Many of them support good stands of grass and have great commercial value. Others are covered by a layer of salt or gypsum when the water evaporates, causing the soil to remain sterile. This is true of the White Sands region.

Then, too, the eroding of the mountains has created the fertile lands along New Mexico's rivers. Depending upon their width, these river valleys have been the most valuable areas of the state because of the ready availability of irrigation water to go with the rich alluvial soil. Unfortunately these ribbons of rich soil cling precariously to the banks of streams and have frequently been destroyed by the very force that created them. The Río Grande has always been plagued by such devastation, having suffered a total of sixteen major floods during the past eighty years. The Red River Canyon was at one time a fertile green valley lined with truck farms. In a few hours a flash flood took away houses, fences, corrals, and orchards. Only a few rock houses stood as mute reminders of a more prosperous past. Worst of all, the fertile land deposited through the centuries was washed away.[2]

In general, the state slopes southward and eastward. The elevation at Farmington in the northwest corner is 5,305 feet, while at Jal in the southeast it is 3,000 feet. Eighty-five per cent of the state lies in an altitude of over 4,000 feet, and much of that between 5,000 and 6,000 feet. The highest mountain peak in the Sangre de Cristo Range is over 13,000 feet. New Mexico's mountain ranges and major divides run in a north-south direction, but with some variations.

Physiographically, New Mexico is included in three of the eight divisions in the United States. The Great Plains Province with its three sections, Raton, Pecos Valley, and the High Plains—covers the eastern third of the state. The Southern Rocky Mountains Province lies in the north-central part of the state. The Colorado Plateau Province occupies a vast area of New Mexico. This more complex province embraces the Navaho and Datil sections in the northwest and the Basin and Range Province and, with its two sections, Mexican Highland and Sacramento, occupies the southwest and central portion of the state.[3]

The Raton Section of the Great Plains is a part of the High Plains area, which was once approximately contiguous to the mountains on the west. Further erosion has materially altered this area of alluvial origin. Today, the more prominent features of its topography are high mesas and buttes, vast dissected plateaus, deep picturesque canyons, and volcanic cones. These scenic features, which seem partially to jut out of the ground, were formed because igneous rocks are not as susceptible to erosion as the fluviatile mantle.

The Pecos Valley Section includes the headwaters of the Canadian as well as the Pecos River. The area was created from the High Plains by erosion. It is probable that the *Llano Estacado*, or Staked Plains, once extended across what is now Pecos Valley, a troughlike depression bounded on the west by the mountains of the Basin and Range Province and on the east by the bluffs of the *Llano Estacado*.

[2] J. W. Wilferth, "An Economic History of Harding County, New Mexico" (M.A. thesis, New Mexico Normal University, 1933), 16.

[3] The physiographic subdivisions are taken from Nevin M. Fenneman, *Physiography of the Western United States*.

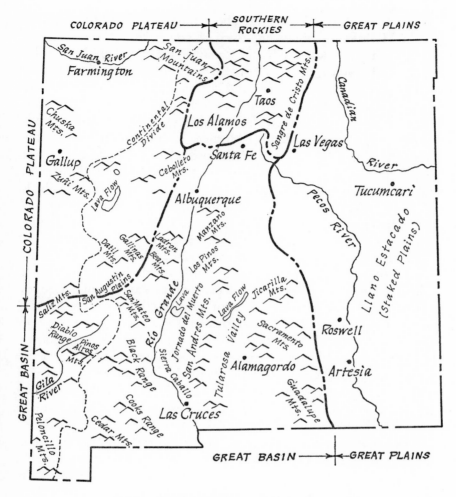

Physiographic Features of New Mexico

The *Llano Estacado* includes about thirty thousand square miles of the High Plains, about one-third of which lies in New Mexico. It is bounded on the north by the Canadian River and on the west by the Pecos.[4] Much of this area "is as flat as any land surface in nature."[5] Because of this lack of relief and scarcity of water, early settlers avoided the area. In fact, there is a myth that the name *Llano Estacado* originated when men drove stakes into the ground as landmarks. Actually, according to Herbert E. Bolton, the name came from the Spanish designation of the palisaded area lying to the east which looks like a stone fortification from a distance.[6] However, all of this area is not flat. There are ravines which were once the beds of now extinct streams, as well as hills made by wind erosion. Interesting features of the *Llano Estacado* are the many saucerlike depressions varying in diameter from a few rods to several miles.

The Southern Rocky Mountains Province is located in the north-central part of the state, extending south a little beyond Santa Fe. This is the highest and most rugged part of the state. The upper slopes of the mountains give evidence of comparatively recent glacial action. Cirques (or glacial amphitheaters) are cut into the bases of the higher ridges.[7] Mountain streams, coniferous forests, snow-capped peaks, and deep river canyons make this an area of great scenic beauty. The Sangre de Cristo Range marks the eastern edge of the province. Beginning west of the Río Grande and near the southern tip of the Rockies lie the Jemez and Nacimiento Mountains, which are similar in structure to the Sangre de Cristos but lack the grandeur.

The Colorado Plateau Province has two sections in New Mexico, the Navaho and the Datil. The first of these takes its name from the Indian reservation which has been its main economic function. It occupies the extreme northwestern corner of the state, near Gallup and east about seventy-five miles from the Arizona state line. The distinctive features of the landscape are young plateaus, rock terraces, dry washes, and mesas. Canyons are shallow because the area

---

[4] Walter Anderson Browne, "The Llano Estacado: A Geographic Interpretation" (Ph.D. dissertation, George Peabody College, 1935), 4–6.

[5] Fenneman, *Physiographic Regions*, 14.

[6] Bolton, *Coronado, Knight of Pueblos and Plains*, 243.

[7] George W. James, *New Mexico: The Land of the Delight Makers*, 304.

8

lacks rainfall. Included in this section are the San Juan Valley and the Chuska Mountains. The Datil section lies directly south of the Navaho and is especially distinguished by extensive lava flows and volcanoes and volcanic necks. Most of the area is covered with lava at least in places. "It is scattered about as if the molten stuff had been dashed over the country from a titanic bucket, and lies like great inky slops over the brightly colored soil and clays."[8]

The Mexican Highland of the Basin and Range Province is featured by several narrow isolated mountain ranges of partially dissected block mountains, some of which are of volcanic origin. The mountain ranges are separated by broad arid basins, about half of which are closed. The principal ranges are the Sandia and Manzano east of Albuquerque; the San Andreas and Caballos between Socorro and Las Cruces; the Magdalena and San Mateo west of Socorro; and the Mogollon near the Arizona border. Among the most important basins found in this section are the Tularosa, Jornada del Muerto, Plains of San Agustín, and the Deming Plain.[9]

The Sacramento Section lies between the Mexican Highland on the west and the Pecos Valley to the east. It is three hundred miles long and is nowhere over seventy miles wide. The Sacramento Ranges include the Jicarilla, Sierra Blanca, Sacramento, and Guadalupe Mountains. All of these ranges are similar in that they slope gently eastward and are plateau-like, although they are naturally dissected. As in the case of the Mexican Highlands, the section is featured by bolsons, the most important of these being the Estancia Basin. This area was originally an extensive lake with shore features comparable to Lake Bonneyville in Utah.

⌒ *Vegetation* ⌒

The vegetation of the state can be classified into six zones: Lower Sonoran, Upper Sonoran, Transition, Canadian, Hudsonian, and Arctic-Alpine. The sequence is from warmest to coldest areas and from driest to wettest. Since in New Mexico altitude is of greater

[8] Quoted in Fenneman, *Physiographic Regions*, 318.
[9] *Ibid.*, 383.

importance than latitude in accounting for climatic differences, the sequence is altitudinal, as in the tropics.[10]

The *Lower Sonoran* is the zone of mesquite and black grama grass. It is found in the Río Grande Valley below Socorro, in the Pecos Valley up to Santa Rosa, and in most of the southwestern part of the state. Usually at altitudes below 4,500 feet, this zone permits more grazing than is possible at higher elevations. In area it embraces about 19,500 square miles. Because of the long frost-free period, the fertile soil, and the high temperatures, this is the most important agricultural zone. Enough water is available here for grazing and some agriculture.

The *Upper Sonoran* is a zone of blue grama and buffalo grass, the piñon, and the juniper. Most of the plains, foothills, and valleys lying above 4,500 feet are included in this zone. It embraces about three-fourths of the area of the entire state. Because of the vast region included within this zone, there is considerable variation in the vegetation. At the lower altitudes within this zone vegetation is very scanty, showing the result of arid conditions. At the higher altitudes of the Upper Sonoran zone (8,000–8,500 feet) a better stand of grass, sagebrush, piñons, junipers, and some trees are found, showing the obvious effect of more rainfall.

The *Transition* zone covers about 19,000 square miles and is identified with the yellow pine. It is found on the middle mountain slopes of the high ranges at altitudes of 7,000 to 8,500 feet on the northeast slopes and 8,000 to 9,500 on the southwest slopes.

The *Canadian* is the zone of blue spruce and Douglas fir. Embracing about 4,000 square miles, it is found at altitudes of 8,500 to 12,000 feet. It is the most humid area of the state, and its rain or snowfall feeds the streams that irrigate the more arid regions. There is also some lumbering in this region.

The *Hudsonian* is a zone of dwarf spruce. It occurs in a narrow scrubby timberline belt around the higher peaks, above 11,000 feet. It covers only 160 square miles in New Mexico, and its only commercial use is summer pasture for sheep. The *Arctic-Alpine* is the

[10] The basic source for this section is Vernon Bailey, *Life Zones and Crop Zones of New Mexico.*

treeless zone of the low and hearty alpine plants identified with the Arctic tundra. It is found as a cap on the highest peaks and is important only because it frequently retains snow until late summer when it is most needed in the dry valleys below.

~~~ *Water* ~~~

To the historian the importance of natural features lies in their effect on man's activities. Within New Mexico the prime natural determinant has been water. Without water, the richest soil or even gold mines have been useless. With water the state could become a veritable Garden of Eden. With water some portions of the state have become that.

Historically then, water has played a vital role in the development of New Mexico. One explanation of the decline of the ancient Indian civilizations is the destruction of their water supply. Until improved technology made possible the exploitation of the ground water, about 1900, man's use of New Mexico was largely limited to the valleys of the five main rivers and some of their tributaries. The only exceptions were the occasional cases of the nomadic Indians who could live in the arid regions of the state as long as they knew where water could be found. The Apaches, though badly outnumbered, held the United States Army at bay for years by the simple process of polluting the wells.

The major rivers of New Mexico are the Río Grande, Pecos, Canadian, San Juan, and Gila. These are listed in the approximate order of their economic significance. The first of these is the most important. In fact, to some mistaken observers, the history of New Mexico can be told in the story of the Río Grande.

From source to mouth the Río Grande travels some eighteen hundred miles, placing it among the great rivers of the world. In the United States only the Mississippi and the Missouri are longer. Rising in southwestern Colorado, the river enters New Mexico near the small town of Costilla and then flows southward across the state until it leaves just above El Paso. The river was probably formed when the debris from the surrounding mountains filled a series of seven basins

11

so that the Río Grande could then cut its way basin to basin.[11] The river channel is still hemmed in by mountains which are closer on the east than on the west. The alluvial plain that has made possible man's use of the river varies in width from a few feet in the northern part of the state to one to five miles on either side of the river in the southern part of the state. This plain was formed when the river overflowed its banks, depositing the material carried in suspension. Unfortunately, this deposition has continued in some places until the river at high water is above the surrounding plain. The result has been disastrous floods and waterlogging of the irrigated soil.[12]

The Indians were irrigating in the Río Grande Valley when Coronado made his way northward in 1540. The ruins of ancient villages and canals indicate that irrigation was probably practiced here more than a thousand years ago. Throughout the Spanish and Mexican eras, man's use of New Mexico was limited to the Río Grande and the valleys of its tributaries. Helping to concentrate the Spaniards in this area were the presence of the Pueblo Indians, who provided needed labor, and the fact that the Río Grande was readily accessible to Mexico. In addition, the hostile Indians and the lack of engineering knowledge necessary to obtain water elsewhere were factors in causing the concentration of white settlements in this area.[13] A slow but steady increase in irrigation took place after 1850, with the maximum use being reached in 1880. From that date the trend was downward. The too-frequent floods with their resulting destruction and waterlogging of lands caused much irrigated acreage to go out of production.

The first serious attempt to harness the waters of the Río Grande took place with the building of the Elephant Butte Reservoir near Truth or Consequences. Completed in 1915, this reservoir impounds water to help meet seasonal irrigation needs as well as to store water for year-round use. In addition to controlling floods, this huge lake, forty miles long and three miles wide, is an important recreation center for water-starved New Mexicans. Caballo Dam, along with

11 Fenneman, *Physiographic Regions*, 390.

12 See Rufus H. Carter, Jr., "An Historical Study of Floods Prior to 1892 in the Rio Grande Watershed, New Mexico" (M.A. thesis, University of New Mexico, 1953.)

13 Joseph Miller, ed., *New Mexico: A Guide to the Colorful State*, 21.

a complex system of flumes, siphons, and several hundred miles of main channels, supplements the main dam and provides for the irrigation of the Mesilla Valley.

In 1925, the Middle Río Grande Conservancy District was organized to control floods, provide more irrigation water, and install a drainage system to help regain some of the waterlogged land above the Elephant Butte Dam. By erecting dams, mainly on the tributaries of the Río Grande, and by building levees along the main streams, much has been done in New Mexico's battle with its "Great River."[14]

The Pecos River lies east of the Río Grande and follows a course approximately parallel to it. As previously mentioned, the Pecos has cut its way through the High Plains, forming a troughlike impression. Most of the flood-plain valley is an alluvial-filled basin. Its soil is highly productive when irrigated, but, unlike the Río Grande, the Pecos Valley has no long record of use by men. In 1888 a private company sought to exploit the potentially rich area by building a series of canals and dams. Several disastrous floods convinced the investors that this was a project too big for private capital. In 1904 the federal government took over the project. Today, three dams control the Pecos. One is upstream of Lake Alamogordo (north of Fort Sumner), and the other two are near Carlsbad. More than 25,000 acres of land have been reclaimed by the project, some near Fort Sumner, but most of it in a ham-shaped area about the city of Carlsbad.

The Canadian River arises on the eastern slopes of the Sangre de Cristo Mountains and flows almost due east. The Canadian has cut a valley as much as one thousand feet deep in the plateau through which it travels. This depth is approximately maintained as the river cuts its way across the High Plains. Except for a few primitive attempts at irrigation, very little use was made of this valley, other than for grazing, until recently. Conchas Dam was authorized as a federal relief project in 1935 and completed in 1940. It has made possible the irrigation of some 39,000 acres around Tucumcari.

[14] Allan G. Harper, Andrew R. Cordova, and Kalervo Oberg, *Man and Resources in the Middle Rio Grande Valley;* C. T. Pease, "Report on Floods and Drainage at San Marcial, New Mexico" (unpublished manuscript, 1925; Huntington Library, San Marino, California).

The San Juan River flows southwest from Colorado. Thirty miles after the stream enters New Mexico, its course changes westward for 124 miles before leaving the state. The valley formed by the San Juan is one to four miles in width and has fertile river bottom lands along its course. There is sufficient water available for irrigating many thousands of acres. Unfortunately, surrounding benchlands are difficult to irrigate successfully because of their shale origin. Even the fertile flood plain lies in small blocks which necessitate the construction of long and expensive canal systems. One observer claims that with its two most important tributaries, the Animas and the La Plata, the San Juan has approximately 70 per cent of the surface water supply found in New Mexico.[15] The projected Navaho Dam will soon convert these potential acres into fertile farmland. Unlike the Pecos and the Canadian, the San Juan was probably the site of Indian civilization before the coming of the white man.

The Gila River rises in the high Mogollon and Black Range Mountains of southwestern New Mexico. It flows in a southwesterly direction across Grant and Hidalgo counties, draining some 6,100 square miles before reaching the Arizona line. In the first 70 miles from its source the river flows through a narrow canyon, making irrigation possibilities meager. However, where the river valley widens at Cliff to as much as a mile in width, irrigation is feasible. Some 8,000 acres are now in cultivation, and current surveys have been made to investigate the possibilities of increasing the arable acreage. The ruggedness of the terrain has thus far made it impractical to divert the water to the Lordsburg area, the closest region of fertile land. Also, the flow of the stream is so undependable as to make such planning unwise. The frequent floods which plague the Gila have earned it the reputation of being "the world's muddiest river."[16]

The almost complete dependence of man upon the rivers of New Mexico has ended in the twentieth century. The techniques of pumping the underground water have kept pace with the indispensable work of the geologist. By 1955, there were about 576,000 acres of

[15] Robert W. Duke, "Political History of San Juan County, N. M. 1876–1926" (M.A. thesis, University of New Mexico, 1947), 4. *Fourteenth and Fifteenth Biennial Reports of the State Engineer of New Mexico*, 152.

[16] *Seventh Report*, 93; *Eleventh Biennial Report of the State of New Mexico*, 191. For more on the Gila River see Ross Calvin, *River of the Sun*.

land irrigated by ground water, or roughly 66 per cent of the total irrigated area of the state. The use of ground water doubled between 1950 and 1955 and quadrupled between 1940 and 1955. Further underground water surveys now in progress will undoubtedly increase this figure.[17]

⌇ *Climatic Factors* ⌇

The diversity noted in the topography of New Mexico is likewise reflected in its climate. The mean annual temperature for the state is about 53 degrees F. but varies as much as 26 degrees at different stations.[18] The variations are mainly due to the difference in latitude and altitude. Some of the stations at lower altitudes in the southern part of the state have July averages similar to those of South Carolina or Georgia, which lie in approximately the same latitude. For example, Carlsbad (elevation, 3,120 feet) records a July average of 81.7 degrees Fahrenheit and Hobbs (elevation, 3,600 feet) has a July average of 79.2 degrees. Deming (elevation, 4,331 feet) in the southwestern corner of the state records a July average of 80.2 degrees, whereas Silver City (elevation, 5,595 feet) only a short distance away has an average of 74.9 degrees for the same month. The effect of altitude upon temperature is readily noted by comparing the July average of Santa Fe which is 69.2 degrees (elevation, 6,996 feet) with that of Santa Rosa (elevation, 4,616 feet) which is 77.5 degrees. The January averages are: Carlsbad, 43.9 degrees; Hobbs, 41.1 degrees; Deming, 41.5 degrees; Silver City, 35.7 degrees; Santa Fe, 29.4 degrees; and Santa Rosa, 39.7 degrees. The continental position of New Mexico plus the arid condition of the atmosphere causes a great variation of the temperature between night and day.

Statistics, of course, fail to tell the full story of climate. A hot, muggy day in Washington, D. C., where the temperature reaches

---

[17] *Twenty-Second Biennial Report of the State Engineer of New Mexico,* 93.

[18] This section on climate is based upon information released by the various Weather Bureau stations of the United States Department of Commerce, material contained in *Biennial Reports of the State Engineers,* special reports of the State Engineer's Office, and general studies on climate.

15

only 90 degrees Fahrenheit but then falls to only 75 degrees at night may be far less desirable for human habitation than Carlsbad, where the temperature may soar to 100 degrees during the day but then may fall to 65 degrees at night. Similarly, the January temperature in Detroit may range between 35 degrees Fahrenheit and 25 degrees for a single day whereas at Santa Fe it may go as low as 0 degrees and as high as 60 degrees. In both instances the statistical average might be the same, but the sensible temperature (that temperature which people feel) may be quite different. One of the prime determinants of the sensible temperature is the amount of moisture in the air. Evaporation involves the expenditure of energy and takes place more readily when the air is hot and dry. In the case of the human body, evaporation involves taking much sensible heat from the body surface, and cooling results. The more evaporation, the more the body will cool. When the air is hot and damp, there can be little evaporation, and thus little cooling of the body. Consequently, the air becomes oppressive to human beings. Conversely, there is little evaporation in cold-dry air because air at low temperature cannot hold much water vapor. In addition, because cold, dry air is not a good conductor, the body doesn't lose as much heat by conduction as it does when the air is cold and damp, damp air being a good conductor. Thus, severe cold in winter is much less chilling when the air is dry than when it is damp. So "dry" heat and "dry" cold can be tolerated with much less discomfort than when the air is moist. New Mexico, having the lowest average humidity of any state, has a pleasant "sensible" temperature.[19]

The thermal milieu has a direct and considerable impact on vegetation and agriculture. Average dates of killing frost set the limits for the period of safe plant growth and are thus a decisive factor in

[19] Robert DeCourcy Ward, *The Climates of the United States*, 282. Either it has been getting warmer in New Mexico or Barreiro was exaggerating in 1831 when he wrote: "The largest streams are congealed to their very beds and the ice takes on such solidity and thickness that well-loaded wagons . . . may cross on it. . . . In the cow-houses the milk congeals almost on issuing from the cow's udder and one can carry it in a napkin to melt it in the house." But after describing such intense cold, he still found the climate of New Mexico "truly healthful." Antonio Barreiro, *Ojeada Sobre Nuevo-México*, trans. and ed. by Lansing B. Bloom, Historical Society of New Mexico *Publications in History*, V, 11–12.

the choice of crops and in the sequence of farming activities within a given area. In general, the growing season (i.e., the frost-free period) varies between 148 and 216 days. The variation is, naturally, caused by latitude and altitude. Fortunately, the longer growing season is normally found in areas under irrigation while shorter seasons occur where they can only influence the grassland.

Precipitation is the other important component of climate; and here is where New Mexico is deficient, the average annual precipitation being only fifteen inches. When one considers that some of the mountain areas have up to twenty inches per year, this means that some parts of the state have very little. In general, precipitation is the greatest in the eastern third of the state and diminishes westward. Along the Texas line it varies from twelve inches at Hobbs to seventeen at Portales and fifteen inches at Clayton. In the Río Grande Valley and in the western portion of the state the average is usually eight to ten inches. This figure is naturally exclusive of the mountain areas, where the precipitation is much greater. Such a pattern is followed because the source of most New Mexico moisture is the Gulf of Mexico, and the farther one goes from that body the less the precipitation.

But rainfall statistics do not always tell the full story. When the moisture is received, in what form, and its regularity are most important. Fortunately, 70 to 80 per cent of the state's precipitation occurs from June to September, during the growing season, when it will do the most good. Unfortunately, like most steppe or semiarid climatic regions, New Mexico's rainfall is notoriously unreliable. The pattern of recent drought suggests that throughout the history of the area comparable dry cycles have been the principal plague of the land. At some stations, as little as one-fourth of the normal rainfall has been received during recent years. Sometimes parts of the state have suffered catastrophic drought the very year that they received rainfall in excess of their average of seventeen inches. The following year, when precipitation fell to less than eight inches, the dry farms and grasslands had adequate rainfall. The reason for unpredictability is simply that rainfall frequently occurs in torrential downpours, as in most semiarid regions. Several inches may fall in a single day, leaving the land flooded and crops seriously damaged.

17

Naturally, if the showers occur more frequently, a greater benefit results, even if much less moisture is recorded. One of the greatest problems of dry-land farming is that the delay of spring rains prevents seed germination and frequently makes replanting necessary.

The precipitation in the state is derived from local high-intensity storms of relatively short duration. Such storms occur when a warm air mass heavily laden with moisture is suddenly forced upward. As the air mass expands, it cools at higher levels, its moisture condenses, and then precipitation results. Hence, these showers are usually extremely local. Farms only a few miles apart may show radically different amounts of rainfall received in the same thunderstorm. With such a deficiency in moisture, it is only natural that irrigation from the streams and ground waters should have played such a vital role in the history of the state.

Snow falls in every part of the state. The amount varies with latitude and elevation from two to five inches in the Río Grande Valley up to three hundred inches in the mountains. About three-fourths of the annual stream flow originates in the forest and grassland regions above 8,000 feet where the snowfall is more than half the annual precipitation. The accumulation of snow in the mountains largely determines the amount of water available for irrigation during the growing season. The amount of snowfall, like the summer rains, varies drastically from year to year. Several years may intervene between major snowstorms in areas where the altitude is low. The prevalence of high winds whipping the snow about creates storms which are almost as truly blizzards as those of the Dakotas. The small amount of moisture within the snow reduces its value as precipitation.

The lack of precipitation, though the most serious, is not the only defect in New Mexico's climate. Second only to drought as an objectional factor is the wind. In most of the state an average annual wind velocity of more than twelve miles per hour is common. In March, the windiest month, velocities up to fifty miles per hour are quite frequent. The presence of ocean-like trade winds so far inland is due to the dry, rarified atmosphere which is subject to sudden, drastic changes in temperature. Besides, the vast level surface permits the wind free play.[20]

18

The light soil, lacking in moisture, is easily picked up by the high winds, thus causing disagreeable dust storms. In the spring these storms frequently last for days, causing much destruction. Even at noon, driving with headlights on is sometimes hazardous because of the limited visibility. Nor is it uncommon to see road graders used to clear the sand drifts from the highway just as if they were snow.[21] The blowing sand has a cutting effect that is destructive to paint on frame houses and automobiles. It drives its way at the most tightly closed structures, and many housewives have taken out as much as two gallons of sand a day. An early traveler uttered a common complaint: "The dust penetrates everything. You eat it, you drink it, you breathe it, you wear it like a coating, and the last handkerchief at the bottom of the box in your trunk is gritty and smells of alkali."[22] Besides being disagreeable for human beings, such winds also destroy crops by increasing the rate of evaporation and thereby lessening the effects of available moisture.

Another objectionable feature of New Mexican weather is the hail. As one authority points out, "The maximum frequency of hail during the frostless season is seen to occur over the Great Plains and Rocky Mountains region."[23] This includes all of New Mexico except the southwestern corner. Although hailstorms are local in character, many a farmer who has considered himself fortunate in having enough moisture for his crops has seen them ruined by hail. If we are to believe Castañeda, the chronicler of Coronado's expedition, the hail of New Mexico is exceptional in size. "One afternoon a great cyclone began of furious wind and hail. And in a short time there fell such a quantity of hailstones, as big as bowls and even bigger, and as thick as raindrops, in places they covered the ground to a

---

[20] Ward, *Climates of the United States*, 156.

[21] Following is one impression of a typical New Mexican duster experienced near Tucumcari: "We couldn't see across the highway. The wind shouted and rocked the car and slammed great handfuls of dust and gravel against the car. It sounded like a hailstorm. . . . The sand poured across the highway, covering the center stripe one moment, uncovering it the next, like waves breaking on a beach and receding. . . . Headlights loomed eerily out of the abrasive fog." *Amarillo* (Texas) *Daily News*, February 28, 1956.

[22] Susan E. Wallace, *The Land of the Pueblos*, 142.

[23] Ward, *Climates of the United States*, 336.

depth of two or three spans and even more. The hailstones destroyed many tents and dented numerous houses. Many horses were bruised, and all of the pottery and gourds of the army were broken."[24] Along with the aridity, hail and wind are just two more features that made New Mexico's climate less desirable than it might otherwise have been.

Restrictive Natural Influences

Dominating the history of New Mexico is one salient fact: it is a state in which Mother Nature has been niggardly with her gifts. The extent to which the natural deficiencies of the area restricted development of the Indian civilization before the coming of the palefaces must remain a matter of speculation. The deficiencies apparent since the advent of the Spaniards have been easy enough to recognize. They vary from the most obvious one of the lack of rainfall to the less apparent ones of extreme isolation, the lack of navigable rivers, the lack of timber in much of the state, and, until recently, the paucity of valuable minerals.

From the beginning of the colonial period, New Mexico was isolated. Remote from Mexico City and lacking gold and silver to whet the appetite of the Spanish crown, it remained a stepchild. Had it not been for the missionary zeal of the Franciscans it probably would have been abandoned to the Indians after the Oñate expedition as being unworthy of colonization. As it was, those who made their way northward soon found themselves engaged in a bitter struggle for survival in an inhospitable world where the very elements seemed to be in conspiracy against man. The eternal problem of water prompted these early settlers to remain along the Río Grande or its tributaries. Just as Santa Fe soon found itself isolated by distance and rigorous travel conditions from Mexico City, so in time the small river settlements also found themselves cut off from the capital city of the province.

Some scholars contend that isolated communities cut off from civilization are not progressive. It is maintained that "the antiquated

[24] Bolton, *Coronado*, 263–64.

customs are preserved long after they have been forgotten elsewhere. Local dialects persist. Education is backward, the percentage
of illiteracy is abnormally high, and inbreeding is common. Professional and artisan classes are almost completely absent. And such
people must be practically self-sustaining: they must make or produce almost everything that they use—implements, furniture, clothing, and food."[25] So it was with the New Mexicans. Removed from
the outside world and soon caught up in a grim struggle for livelihood in a restrictive agricultural environment, new ideas from outside
were not only shut out, but unwanted as well. The customs of the
New Mexican, his language, his technology, and his social mores
remained those of sixteenth-century Spain. The Penitentes are a
graphic example of this attempt to preserve the ways of by-gone
centuries. The coming of the merchant caravans, the railroads, and
the Anglos in the nineteenth century began the breakdown of the
centuries-old geographic isolation of New Mexico. Improved roads
and the motorcar are in the process of completing it in the twentieth
century.[26]

The natural geographic isolation of New Mexico was intensified
by the absence of navigable streams. In the eastern United States,
navigation played a vital role in the early history, but not so in the
Southwest. The Río Grande was useless, even for canoes. Laborious
overland transportation was the only means to reach a destination.
Lack of timber in most of the state was a serious handicap before
the coming of the railroads, there being no streams to float timber
of the mountains down to the lowlands.

The most restrictive natural influence, of course, is the lack of
water. Many New Mexicans feel that this problem has been largely
conquered today. The many projects to irrigate and the rapid ex-

[25] C. Langdon White and George T. Renner, *Human Geography: An Ecological
Study of Society*, 336.

[26] This transition in New Mexico is well discussed in George I. Sanchez, *Forgotten People: A Study of New Mexicans;* Arnold L. Rodriguez, O.F.M., "New
Mexico in Transition," *New Mexico Historical Review*, Vol. XXIV (July, 1949,
and October, 1949) (hereafter cited as NMHR). John C. Russell, "State Regionalism in New Mexico" (Ph.D. dissertation, Stanford University, 1938); Paul A. F.
Walter, Jr., "A Study of Isolation and Social Change in Three Spanish Speaking
Villages of New Mexico" (Ph.D. dissertation, Stanford University, 1938).

pansion of the use of ground water appear to be a just basis for their optimism. Yet they ignore the fact that there never has been a civilization built on irrigation that has lasted any appreciable period in historical times. The original storage capacity of Elephant Butte Dam has already been decreased one-sixth by silt deposition. And the problem of cleaning sediment in canals remains an acute one. Where ground water is used, there are pumps which are frequently pumping air after being operated for only ten years. The two enemies of irrigation, waterlogging and the alkalinity of the soil, have been past problems of New Mexico, and will continue to reappear.

Science through the development of rapid transportation has destroyed the restrictive influences of New Mexico's geographic isolation. The air conditioner has made it possible to inhabit some of the less desirable parts of the state. Perhaps science can completely solve the problems attendant upon irrigation so that man can truly triumph in his struggle with nature for the control of New Mexico.

II - The Natives

WITHIN THE PRESENT BORDERS of the state of New Mexico the Spaniards found a wide variety of Indian tribes. These varied from the sedentary Pueblos, whose civilization was, in some respects, comparable to that of Mexico and Peru, to the simple nomadic tribes who were in the primitive food-gathering stage.[1]

Recent archaeological discoveries have proved that the state was the site of prehistoric civilizations which may have been the oldest in North America. The unearthing of the remains of the Sandia man and the Folsom man and the interesting excavations in Blackwater Draw (near Portales) are evidence of the presence of man in the area at some point in the geologic past.[2]

The Pueblos

The Indians with whom the Spaniards came into closest contact were found grouped together in tightly integrated communities which the Europeans called "Pueblos" or towns. These natives had probably been living in their current stage of civilization for about

[1] The literature concerned with the Indians of the Southwest is far too voluminous to cite here. The most significant sources are: Hubert H. Bancroft, *The Native Races*, I, chapter 5; Edward Everett Dale, *The Indians of the Southwest;* Clark Wissler, *The American Indian;* Mary Roberts Coolidge, *The Rainmakers: Indians of Arizona and New Mexico*. Also valuable as reference is Frederick Webb Hodge, *Handbook of Indians North of Mexico*.

[2] On early Pueblo history see Harold S. Gladwin, *A History of the Ancient Southwest*, and Edgar L. Hewett, *Ancient Life in the American Southwest*.

five hundred years before the Spaniards came, and there is ample evidence to indicate that their forefathers had settled in New Mexico countless centuries before.

The most significant of the ruins of early native civilizations are those found in Chaco Canyon, at Aztec, and at Mesa Verde, just across the state line in Colorado. It is assumed that the earlier Pueblo Indians were originally nomadic like the other tribes in North America but had banded together in defense against the more war-like natives. One of the larger ruins contained 800 rooms, and an estimated population of some 1,600. The manner of building is ample evidence that protection was what these people sought in their buildings. The periodic abandonment of these communities probably grew out of the fact that drought made it impossible to produce enough corn and beans, the early staples, to support the community. Many were also undoubtedly destroyed by hostile roving tribes.

The Spanish found some twenty such pueblos when they arrived, primarily concentrated in the upper Río Grande Valley. In fact, only the pueblos of Zuñi, Acoma, and Laguna were to be found very far west of that river. These communities varied in size from about 100 people to a probable maximum of 2,000, and perhaps totaled approximately 20,000 souls. Although their habits, customs, and traditions were very similar, these New Mexico Indian families actually had different origins and spoke three distinct tongues: Zuñian, Tanoan, and Keresan.

The Zuñian group consisted of three pueblos in the extreme western part of New Mexico with an approximate total population of 2,500. The other two groups were located in the Río Grande Valley. Of these the Tanoan was the larger, including the five tribes of the Piros, Tiguas, Tanos, Jemez, and Tewas. Although fewer, the Keresans were divided geographically. In the West the Acoma pueblo was a part of this family, while the remainder occupied the region north of where the Río Jemez joins the Río Grande, and were commonly known as the Queres Nation. Language ties meant nothing, and each of the pueblos acted on its own, seldom finding a common cause with the other tribes.

The basis of their economy was agriculture, with the men working in the fields and even weaving blankets, tasks reserved for the

24

women among most North American Indians. Some hunting of rabbits and antelope was practiced, and the eastern tribes even hunted buffalo upon occasion or traded among the Plains Indians for meat. Fish were eaten, another unusual trait, since most Southwestern tribes abhorred fish.[3] Poultry was domesticated and supplemented the diet. Corn, beans, and squash were the principal crops, and efforts were made to raise enough of these so that a three years' supply would be always available, indicating the Indian's dread of what has always been New Mexico's nemesis: the lack of rainfall. Some irrigation was practiced, but the role of the Rain Dance among these tribes indicated that they were largely dependent upon nature for success in the tilling of the soil. Land was held and worked communally, individual ownership apparently being unknown. Despite the fact that the Pueblos have been eulogized as having made a perfect adaptation to the arid climatic conditions of New Mexico, there is little question but that they were declining in population at the time the Spaniards came, and continued to do so until the mid-twentieth century.

The Pueblos were a race of small people, the men seldom exceeding five feet in height and the women usually being only four feet. Their hands and feet were small even for their build. Their even features gave them a generally attractive appearance.[4] Many Pueblo men wore only a breechcloth, adding robes when the weather required. Among the eastern villages buffalo robes were common, but robes usually were woven from cotton or even made of rabbitskin. The women usually wore a woven garment that reached from the shoulders to the knees, being fastened over the right shoulder. Moccasins protected the feet. Pottery-making was highly developed, but basket-making was not important.

The complex interrelated nature of the government, social, and religious organizations has made full understanding of Pueblo life very difficult. Secular and religious activities are so inextricably mingled that the outsider has not yet arrived at a complete understanding of their society, especially because the Indian is reticent concerning such affairs. Like most primitive people, the Pueblo tribes

[3] Wissler, *The American Indian*, 242.
[4] Bancroft, *Native Races*, I, 529.

25

worshiped that which they could not understand. A vast storehouse of legendary lore was built up to explain the origin of the Indians, what happened after death, the nature of the seasons, why misfortune befell people, and this even extended to the worship of the mountains as well as various birds and animals.

The force of religion was so strong that planting, cultivating, harvesting, and even hunting and making war were dominated by religious rites. The kiva, the ceremonial chamber, was about thirty feet in diameter and was partially recessed into the ground. It was usually located in the courtyard and was the center of extensive religious rites. The designs in basketry, on pottery, and in weaving were usually connected with some aspect of religious symbolism, although, in general, the artistic expression of the Indian was crude and primitive.[5]

Religion was indeed so potent a factor in the natives' lives that it would be fair to describe their form of government as theocratic. The fact that the governor and many other officers of the pueblo were elected every year has prompted many mistaken observers to conclude that here "the people rule," and that in the American Southwest was to be found the first true expression of Democracy.[6] Ignored is the fact that the chief priest was elected for life and most of the authority remained in his hands, few being brave enough to challenge the leadership of the religious. Socially, the Pueblos were a matriarchy with descent being through the mother. When a man married, he joined the family of his wife. The basic unit of the pueblo was the family. The clan may have had some significance in earlier times, but in more recent years it largely existed for ceremonial reasons.

The buildings created by the Pueblo Indians represent an able adaptation to the need for defense, to climatic conditions, to the resources of the land, and to their peculiar social organization. Usually built of adobe or stone, these communal dwellings consisted of four rectangular buildings in the form of a hollow square. It was most common for them to be four rooms in width on the ground floor, and one on the fourth floor. The buildings were terraced from

[5] Charles F. Coan, *A History of New Mexico*, I, 23.
[6] Hewett, *Ancient Life in the Southwest*, 69–71.

the court toward the outer wall. The rooms were usually eight by ten feet, the pueblos themselves varying in size from two hundred to four hundred feet square. Because of precautions for defense, there were no outlets on the ground floor, so first-floor rooms were usually used as storehouses. Access to the building was by means of ladders, which could be withdrawn from story to story as necessary. Most doors and windows were small, again for reasons of defense and also because of the lack of transparent material, and lintels were used above them.[7] Heating was by means of circular fire pits, and most of the furniture was very primitive.

Compared to the surrounding nomadic tribes, the Pueblos were not considered warlike, although the Spaniards were to find that they were fully capable of fighting upon occasion. Like many sedentary groups beset by warlike nomads, the Pueblos used guile and hypocrisy as their first weapons of defense. They would display friendliness toward an intruder until they were sure they could master him. They made it a practice to try to side with the warring element that was the strongest, but would desert if the other side gained the advantage. These traits were to be evident many times in dealing with the Spaniards, especially at the time of the 1680 uprising, when they attempted to lay the blame elsewhere.

~~ The Nomadic Tribes ~~

Far more troublesome to the Spanish conquerors of New Mexico than the sedentary Pueblo Indians were the several nomadic tribes that roamed the area of the state.[8] These roving bands were from the Athapascan and Shoshoni Indian families. Of the latter group, the Comanches were the most important, the Utes being mainly a Coloradan tribe that only occasionally made forays southward. Far more

[7] Coan, *History of New Mexico*, I, 26–28.
[8] There is much material on the nomadic tribes in Barreiro, *Ojeada Sobre Nuevo-México;* Pedro Bautista Pino, "Exposición sucinta y sencilla de la provincia de Nuevo México," translated in H. Bailey Carroll and J. Villasana Haggard, eds., *Three New Mexico Chronicles;* and Ferdinand Andrews, "The Indians of Arizona and New Mexico" (unpublished manuscript, Huntington Library, San Marino, California).

important were the Athapascans or Apaches. Though linguistically similar within the tribe, the Apaches were broken into some twenty subdivisions, these subdivisions in turn divided into bands, and the bands into families. For the purposes of clarity, only the most important subdivisions will be considered: the Navaho-Apaches, the Jicarilla Apaches, the Mescalero Apaches, and the Apaches proper. Considered as Apaches proper are those tribes which are frequently referred to as western Apaches because they inhabited the southwestern corner of the state, frequently extending the domains of Apachería southward into Mexico and westward into Arizona.

Though dissimilar in many respects, all of the nomadic tribes had certain things in common. In general, they spurned the cultivation of the soil practiced by the Pueblos, being interested in obtaining a living by hunting, or by stealing when there was nothing to hunt. Most of them disliked fish. Originally, stronger tribes pushed them southward into the less desirable lands found within the boundaries of New Mexico. Even after their arrival, there were constant fluctuations in the particular areas in which they tended to roam. For example, the Apaches were at one time located in the northeastern part of the state. But the fierce Comanches pushed them southward and westward, with one branch of them, the Jicarillas, retreating into the northern mountains of the state.

By the beginning of the nineteenth century the areas in which each of these tribes roamed were vaguely defined. The Navahos were in the western part of the state as far north as the San Juan Valley, extending eastward to the Pueblo settlements near the Río Grande, westward into Arizona to the Hopi pueblos, and southward to the Zuñi Mountains. As previously noted, the Apaches were to be found in the southwestern part of the state, but there were many exceptions. Occasionally they roamed far into Texas, south into Mexico, westward into Arizona, and even eastward into the plains. Driven from the plains by the Comanches, probably at the beginning of the eighteenth century, the Jicarilla Apaches had retreated into the mountains of northern New Mexico, and the Mescalero Apaches were largely to be found near Sierra Blanca and the Sacramento Mountains. Far more clearly defined was Comanchería. The land claimed by the Comanches was not often invaded because they were among the most competent warrior groups in North America, and easily the best in the Southwest. Hence, no other tribe dared challenge their control of a particular area. Within New Mexico they were the masters of everything east of the Pecos River and north to a line just east of Taos on into Colorado.

People throughout the world who inhabit marginal lands are famed for their warlike proclivities. Mother Nature, niggardly in her gifts, drives such people to work out an adjustment to their environment that will enable them to exist. So, like the nomadic tribes of the steppe country of Asia, the Bedouins and Arabs, and many people in other places, these Indian tribes evolved cultural conditions to suit their habitat. There was little land worth cultivating, and the nomads, except for the Navahos, disdained farming; though capable of tremendous bursts of energy when on the hunt or a raiding expedition, they viewed with contempt most physical labor.

The society of these nomadic Indians was geared to the needs of warfare. They lived for the hunt and the warpath; a man who had not stolen a horse or scalped an enemy was not worthy of association with the rest.[9] Like their counterparts in other parts of the world, they were primitive savages, having little in the way of religious or artistic expression. What little government they had was built around a warrior chieftain who was capable of leading them to victory in battle. Seldom was rank hereditary, leadership going to the warrior who was most distinguished by the number of his slaves and the value of his other property.[10] The rampant individualism of the natives was difficult to check, and a war chief had trouble in getting his following to accept him, even on the field of battle. In peacetime there was no governmental structure worthy of the name, and thus there was no way to correct individual wrongdoers, a fact which helps explain much of the misunderstanding with the whites when Indians violated treaties.

The most important factor making possible the adaptation of the nomadic tribes to the vast land areas of the Southwest was their use of the horse. Afoot, the Indian was a furtive and pitiable figure, all but helpless in the vastness of the land in which he found himself. On

9 Quoted in C. L. Sonnichsen, *The Mescalero Apaches*, 7.
10 Bancroft, *Native Races*, I, 508.

horseback his whole world changed. At first the Indians probably used the Spanish horses for meat, but they soon discovered their greater importance as a means of transportation. As a result of their raids upon the Pueblos, the Navahos were probably the first tribe to utilize the horse.[11] More than likely, it was about 1650 before the Indians obtained enough animals that they could be described as having a horse culture. The uprising of 1680 likewise increased the availability of horses among the tribesmen.[12]

A horse greatly increased the mobility of the Indian and made possible his dependence upon the buffalo on the plains, and also made him an enviable warrior. Suddenly, the area in which a tribe could roam increased from perhaps one hundred miles to more than one thousand miles, thus extending the area in which food could be found and making it easier to obtain a livelihood. Relieved of some of the pressure of food-hunting, the Indian was now free for the more pleasant activity of warfare.[13]

The Apaches

To the early Spaniards, grouped as they were along the banks of the Río Grande and its tributaries, the Apaches appeared to be more numerous than all of the other Indians of New Spain. Their raids on the established settlements, as well as on the road which links Santa Fe to the Mexican capital, made them the most feared of all the tribes. Father Benavides said with considerable justification, "This entire nation is so warlike that it has proved to be the crucible of Spanish valor."[14] In spite of their dread of them, the Spaniards were to hold the Apaches in the highest esteem.

Though of medium height, the Apaches were among the more attractive Indians. They had high cheekbones, well-formed noses, and firm-closed lips. Their hair was permitted to fall to the shoulders

[11] Alpheus H. Verrill, *The American Indian: North, South, and Central America*, 308.

[12] Ernest Wallace and E. Adamson Hoebel, *The Comanches*, 38.

[13] Paul I. Wellman, *Glory, God, and Gold*, 155.

[14] Alonso de Benavides, *Benavides Memorial of 1630*, trans. by Peter P. Forrestal, 42.

but was trimmed in front at the level of the eyebrows. The legendary endurance of the lean, supple, and sinewy body of the Apache was held in awe by their bitterest enemies.

One trait that all who came into contact with them noted was the Apache emphasis upon telling the truth, a characteristic which the Caucasian had good reason to recognize. Their great intelligence, their quick perception, and their primitive instinct was also admired. Their absence of pity and their prowess as warriors was acknowledged, but not, for obvious reasons, admired. Their dwellings, as befitted nomads, were simple circular shacks, called wickiups. They were made by thrusting poles into the ground, bending them inward until they met, and then weaving brush or branches into the framework, or using bark or deerskin to cover the whole. When the Apaches moved, these dwellings were simply burned. Their food was varied, with mule meat and horse meat being most important. They ate almost all other kinds of flesh with the notable exceptions of bear meat, pork, turkey, and fish. In lean times they subsisted on roots, berries, nuts, acorns, and similar fare. Their clothing was exceptionally simple.

Polygamy was practiced, a warrior having as many wives as he could afford. Socially and economically the family was the basic unit among the Apaches, with each family group being bound together by rights and duties that were formal and well defined. As was customary among the southwestern Indians, the home of the mother was the center of the family, with the husbands dwelling in the maternal camp. The unit of organization larger than the family was the local group, frequently made up of several affiliated families, though blood relationships were not necessary. Such leadership as existed in the local group was elective and constantly changed. The next highest organization was the band, which existed primarily for the purpose of hunting, raiding, or making war. The final unit of organization was the tribe, usually very ill defined. Differences between such tribes usually occurred in peculiarities of speech as well as distinctive matters of dress or decoration.

To exist in the dry land area in which the Apaches lived, it was necessary to migrate seasonally. During the summer, the Apaches stayed in the mountains hunting the deer and elk near the streams and eating the fruit and berries to be found there. But when winter came, they made their way to the surrounding lowlands, where it was warmer.

The Apache is a classic example of excellent adaptation to a harsh environment. Like the xerophytic plants of the desert, which drive their root structure deep in order to obtain water, his powers of endurance, his ability to live off the land, and his skill in eluding pursuers all went to make him one of the toughest human organisms the world has ever seen.[15]

Besides making baskets and doing some beadwork, the Apache seemed to have been devoid of any desire to create things of beauty. His was an art of war, and at this he was a master. Among the Apaches, study of color was for the purpose of better being able to conceal themselves on a raid. Their social mores, as well as their political and economic institutions, rested upon a military foundation. The suitor who was best able to furnish a maid with an ample supply of stolen horses and cattle, as well as trinkets and other items, was most in demand. The man who could excel in warfare or in theft was looked up to as a person of accomplishment. From infancy, the boy was trained for the highest calling in life, that of the warrior.

The Apache had much the same attitude toward his vocation as a Prussian officer. It was a business, not a romantic interlude. It was a job to be done, and with the least amount of fanfare. For this reason the Apaches looked with contempt upon those who engaged in unnecessary acts of daring and seemed to have never developed a code of bravery. They were far more interested in the booty of war, than its glory. Their lack of pity and their legendary cruelty were more the result of their businesslike attitude toward the vocation of war than of any inculcated tradition. The enemies they slew were dispatched in the line of duty, much as an executioner does his work. For almost three hundred years, until the Americans were finally to crush them in the late nineteenth century, the Apaches were to be the scourge of the Southwest, "the Huns of the New World."

An interesting branch of the tribe were the Mescalero Apaches.[16]

[15] Frank P. Lockwood, *The Apache Indians*, 41–54. Also valuable is John C. Cremony, *Life Among the Apaches*.

[16] This tribe is definitively treated in Sonnichsen, *The Mescalero Apaches*. In

They were so named because, although their economy was comparable to the other tribes, the mescal was their staple food. Hence the name Mescalero, meaning "mescal maker." A big desert plant, the mescal belongs to the agave family and abounds in the foothills on the lower mountain slopes where the sun, soil, and altitudes are just right for its growth. In May or June, the women went out to gather the raw mescal, sometimes traveling many miles to find a good supply. An earthen pressure cooker was used to process the pulp of the plant, making it a syrupy mess, much of which was eaten as a part of the harvesting ceremony. Most of it was dried on a flat rock and was used as sort of a "C-ration" for the rest of the year. In addition to this emphasis upon mescal as food, the Mescaleros were also more interested in agriculture than the western Apaches, and their habitat was somewhat different.

One Apache group, the Jicarillas (which means "basket-makers"), was not accorded the respect given to the other branches of the tribe. When their brothers were driven southward and westward by the advent of the Comanches the Jicarillas had retreated into the mountains of northern New Mexico. From these retreats they lived primarily by raiding the surrounding Pueblo Indians or Spanish. They were described as being indolent and cowardly, and were accused of having been corrupted by intermarriage with the Utes. Occasionally, when they believed the Comanches to be out of the way, they would venture back into their original plains habitat to hunt buffalo.[17]

The most important Apache group were the Navahos, who have dominated western New Mexico for centuries. Although linguistically and in many other respects a part of the Athapascan family, this is a tribe that has virtually developed a distinct culture of its own. The Spanish first referred to them as Navaho Apaches, and in the colonial period the two terms were used interchangeably so that it is frequently difficult to tell which the observer had reference to. The

addition see Alta Mae Tate, "History of the Mescalero Apache Indian Reservation From the Time of its Establishment to 1954" (M.A. thesis, Eastern New Mexico University, 1955), and T. T. McCord, Jr., "An Economic History of the Mescalero Apache Indians" (M.A. thesis, University of New Mexico, 1946).

[17] George Garry Kahl, "The Apaches in New Mexico: 1846–1861" (M.A. thesis, University of California, Berkeley, 1928), 76.

reason for the Navahos' split with their Apache brethren is not known, but one authority suggested that the Apaches were ejected by the Navahos because of "their mischief-making proclivities and excessive turbulence."[18]

When the Spaniards arrived in New Mexico, the Navahos, along with other tribes of the Plains Apaches, carried on an extensive trade with the Pueblo Indians. Hides, dried meat, and tallow were exchanged for the maize, cotton blankets, and other goods of the sedentary Indians. This important commerce was continued during the Spanish era, although it was frequently disrupted by warfare. The conflict between the Spaniard on the one hand and the Navaho and his brother Athapascan on the other grew out of the age-old conflict between the nomad and the oasis dweller. It was made far more bitter in New Mexico, because the white man attempted to impose his civilization upon the freedom-loving Indians. In order to convert the nomadic tribes to Christianity it was first thought necessary to force them to give up their nomadic ways and live like the Pueblo tribes. This the roving Indians would not do, nor did they understand the God of the white man. Their primitive minds could not penetrate the subtleties of the message brought by the friars, particularly when the Spaniards made a regular practice of seizing their children to be sold into slavery.[19]

Thus, the seventeenth century was one of constant warfare between the Navahos and the Spaniards. The hostility of the Navahos and other Apache groups towards the intruders into their homeland consistently endangered the Spanish hold on New Mexico. In addition to regularly plundering the resources of the white man and his Pueblo subjects, the Navahos were a thorn in the flesh in other ways. Their tribe provided a place of refuge for the dissatisfied Pueblo Indians, who became unhappy under the blessings of Spanish rule and longed for the freedom enjoyed by their heathen brethren. Hence, many backsliding converts to Christianity fled to the Navaho

[18] Lockwood, *The Apache Indians*, 4.

[19] Sources on the Navahos consulted were Ruth Underhill, *The Navajos,* and Mary and Dane Coolidge, *The Navajo Indians.* See also Jack D. Forbes, *Apache, Navaho, and Spaniard;* Forbes effectively proves that the Spaniards were more to blame than the Athapascans for the period of warfare.

strongholds, where they doubtless encouraged the depredations upon the Pueblos and the whites.

The Navahos also encouraged the Pueblo tribes to revolt against their oppressors. There is no question that they collaborated with other Athapascans to incite the Pueblo Indian uprising of 1680. Perhaps fear of retaliation by the Spaniards caused the Navahos to flee their usual haunts near Jemez, ultimately taking refuge in Canyon de Chelly.

For over a century they virtually remained lost to the world, secure in what they believed to be an impregnable fortress. Though small in numbers when they fled, their raising of corn and their peaceful attitudes rapidly increased the size of the tribe. They became virtually a sedentary people raising corn and tending flocks of sheep.

The devotion to pacific pursuits did not last indefinitely, however. Perhaps because of increased population pressure, or for other reasons, the Navahos again began raiding in the late eighteenth century. With a safe base of operations, they roamed far and wide, trading as well as raiding. In addition to picking up the ideas and customs of the people with whom they traded, their practice of gathering in slaves from the Pueblos, and even from the Plains Indians with whom they were at war, was ultimately to cause the Navahos to be a virtual synthesis of the culture of all tribes. They were truly a sedentary nation that was nomadic and a nomadic nation that was sedentary.

Because of their readiness to borrow the ideas of others and put them to good use, as well as their industrious habits, most observers looked upon them as the finest of their race, one claiming that "they are certainly the noblest of the American aborigines."[20] Unlike the other Apaches, the Navaho men tilled the soil and were not above working at the most menial of tasks.

Corn was their principle staple, but they also cultivated fields of melons and vegetables, and even were known to have orchards of apples, pears, peaches, and plums. The sheep, goats, and horses they stole from the Spaniards and the Pueblo Indians were put to good use. Because they were excellent herdsmen, their flocks of animals

[20] Quoted in Kahl, "The Apaches in New Mexico," 12.

35

grew rapidly. They learned the art of weaving fine woolen blankets from the Pueblos, doubtless with the unwilling assistance of women slaves captured in their frequent forays, and ultimately were to be famous for their success at this craft. Their flocks freed them from most of the danger of periodic famine and doubtless accounted for their rapid growth as a tribe. Their horses provided them with the means of trading and raiding over vast expanses of territory.

In appearance, the Navahos are generally considered to be the most handsome of all of the southwestern Indians. The men are usually tall, and the women, though much shorter, have far more natural grace and dignity when young than do their sisters of the other tribes. Their ceremonial dress has long been distinguished by its rich colors and its elaborate silver and turquoise ornamentation. In most respects, the Navahos have taken the art of the Pueblos and vastly improved it.

The dwellings of the Navahos were the hogans which still dot the landscape of western New Mexico. They were built of wood and stone, but in order to weatherproof them, they were coated with earth, thereby giving them their hivelike appearance. There were three types of hogans: the regular dwelling, the ceremonial lodge, and the sweat house. In summer, an ordinary brush and pole tipi was used, especially when the Indians were following the flocks to greener pastures.

Their religious belief represents a superb example of acculturation. They have superimposed much of the Pueblo creed and ritual upon the more primitive Athapascan beliefs. Like the Pueblos they have elaborate rites for every phase of life, and especially to accompany the growing season. But in borrowing from the Pueblos, they have not surrendered the complete control of their tribe to the theologians. Their creation myth is quite similar to that of the Apache, and according to some there is striking similarity to comparable Mongolian beliefs.

In brief, then, the Navaho could be said to have attained the most advanced state of civilization of all of the nomadic Indians, and in very many respects was superior to the Pueblo. His economy was certainly the most stable. To the Navaho, war was an avocation rather than a vocation, a means whereby a man supplemented his income instead of being his whole life, as it was to the Apaches. But this does not mean that the Navahos were not effective warriors. They were to harass the Spaniards mercilessly at the close of the eighteenth century and were to wreak havoc upon Mexican, Spanish, and American settlements until they were subdued in 1864.

～ *Comanches* ～

Fortunately for the white man, the Comanches had not yet made their appearance in New Mexico when the Spaniards first arrived. If they had, the whole history of the early period might well have been different. Exactly why or when the Comanches left their home in Wyoming to come southward is not known. Their stature as warriors makes it highly unlikely that they were driven out. They must have made the move through choice alone.

In appearance, the Comanches certainly did not look like superb warriors. The men were short with a tendency toward corpulence, and had the widest faces of any of the Indians of the Southwest. Their women were in general unattractive and, because of the rugged life they led, aged prematurely.[21] But mounted on horses these odd-looking little men were even more feared than the little bowlegged Huns of Roman times. Superb horsemen, they have been dubbed "the Cossacks of the plains" or even the "Arabs of the prairie—the model of the famed Thessalian Centaur, half-horse, half-man, so closely joined and so dexterously managed that it appears but one animal, fleet and furious."[22] Even the renowned Apaches, the implacable enemy of the Comanches, were no match for them in battle. Using the horse to optimum advantage (in fact, they were nicknamed "the horse Indians") they harassed the Spaniards throughout the eighteenth century and at the height of their power boasted that "the only reason they allowed Spanish and Mexicans to remain in New Mexico, Texas, and northern Mexico, was to raise horses for

[21] An excellent source on the Comanche is Wallace and Hoebel, *The Comanches.*
[22] Quoted in *ibid.,* 49.

them."[23] In the nineteenth century they were to be the terror of the Santa Fe Trail.

The Comanches being Plains Indians, their dwelling place was the tipi, which could be easily and quickly moved from camp to camp to suit the needs of the hunt or the raid. The buffalo was the economic basis of their existence, and they wasted no part of the slaughtered animals. Hair, skin, flesh, blood, bones, entrails, horns, sinews, kidneys, liver, and even buffalo chips were all utilized. But the horse was to be indispensable to the Comanches, and they prized him above all else. They roamed the entire Southwest in search of horses, catching wild animals when necessary, but preferably stealing them from the white man. Their knowledge of the horse was the most extensive of all tribes and even included selective breeding. A man's wealth was calculated by the number and quality of horses that he possessed, and as horse thieves the Comanches had no peers. A highly successful warrior might own fifty to two hundred animals.[24]

Even the Apaches, famed as warriors, did not attempt to fight from horseback, but preferred to dismount and to battle on foot. The Comanches not only preferred being mounted when they fought, but were most effective when mounted.

As nomads who moved about within a vast area, the Comanches had little time to think or develop a distinctive religion or governmental traditions. In this respect they were probably more primitive than the Apaches.

[23] Quoted in Wellman, *Glory, God, and Gold*, 155.
[24] Wallace and Hoebel, *The Comanches*, 39.

III - Exploration and Conquest

THE EARLY DESTINY of New Mexico was determined by the course of Spanish history in the early sixteenth century. For the pent-up energies that Spain had expended in the reconquest of the Iberian Peninsula needed release in other areas once the Moors had been defeated. The Western Hemisphere provided the outlet for the national drive that had been built up in the long struggle to reclaim their lost homeland, and New Mexico was to be in the backwash of the tidal wave of conquest that extended Spanish control over the New World.

By 1500, Spain, in many respects, represented the finest ideals of medieval civilization. The fight against the Moslems had kindled a crusading spirit which expressed itself in terms of a fanatical religion and a fervent patriotism. To spark the campaign against the Moors, the Church had made it into a holy crusade, thus firing the religious enthusiasm of the people. To gain further adherence for the crusade, the property of the enemy was parceled out among the land-hungry Spanish nobles. An essential part of any conquest is the military, and the soldier of Spain was elevated to a commanding social position.[1]

Thus, with the discovery of America, there were many Spaniards eager to find new worlds to conquer. Large numbers of soldiers were available for adventures across the ocean with the expectation that fame and fortune would be theirs. Clergymen who had been enthu-

[1] Bailey W. Diffie, *Latin-American Civilization*, 34.

siastic over the prospect of saving souls during the Moorish Crusade were now eager to direct their talents towards saving the heathen red men from eternal damnation.

The dynamic Hispanic culture, represented by only a few thousand soldiers, priests, and adventurers, quickly overran the Indian civilization of America. Younger sons destined for a position of inferiority in Spain suddenly became important and wealthy individuals as a result of this conquest. Even those from the lower classes, some reputed to have been illiterate swineherds, found gold and honor in America. Wealth beyond the wildest dreams of man was suddenly made available. Hence, it was little wonder that the exploits of Cortés, Pizzaro, and others whetted the appetites of adventurous Spaniards. Men used to a pattern of fabulous success were convinced that a pot of gold was awaiting them, likewise, at the end of the rainbow. Fantastic stories of wealth circulated through all of the Spanish colonies in the New World. The wilder the tale, the easier it was to believe. Hearty men clad in coats of mail, armed with the primitive weapons of the early sixteenth century, plodded through the mosquito-infested lowlands, crossed the arid wastelands, or climbed icy mountains in search of more wealth, which they assumed was readily available. Equally as important as the gold they expected to find would be the recognition in titles and the consequent elevation in social stature home in Madrid. They were usually accompanied by zealous men of God whose rewards would be in the hereafter, for having saved the souls of the savage.

Out of this perpetual quest for "Glory, God, and Gold" came the exploration and ultimate conquest of New Mexico. As early as 1530, Nuño de Guzmán, the governor of Nueva Galicia, had heard stories from the Indians of the fabulous seven cities of Cíbola, which lay across the trackless wastes of northern Mexico. This was reputed to be a land wherein the streets were paved in gold, and the natives had so many diamonds and other valuable minerals that they could hardly carry their ornaments around with them. The Indians who early discovered the insatiable Spanish taste for precious metals found that they could curry favor with their masters by concocting such stories, and they usually grew with the telling. Although

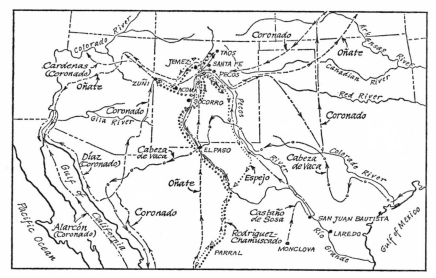

Routes of the Spanish Explorers

Guzmán outfitted an expedition, he was unable to go to this fabulous land.[2]

⤖ *The Odyssey of Cabeza de Vaca* ⤖

The first authentic information about New Mexico was brought to the Spaniards as a by-product of the attempt to settle Florida. Pánfilo de Narváez, an early antagonist of Cortés, led an expedition into Florida in 1528. There, difficulty with the Indians led to abandonment of the project. About 250 men built horsehide boats and set

[2] The Seven Cities of Cíbola that the early Spaniards were seeking was a legend, perhaps of Portuguese origin, dating back to 1150. In that year the Moors captured the city of Mérida, Spain, and among the Christians fleeing from the Moslem conquerors were seven bishops and their congregations. They were supposed to have sailed away westward, finally landing on some beautiful island. There, they burned their ships and founded Seven Cities that ultimately became great and wealthy towns. Hence, many explorers sought their location in the New World. Cleve Hallenbeck, *Land of the Conquistadores*, 17–18.

41

sail westward, hoping to return to the Mexican settlements. They were shipwrecked near the present site of Galveston, and most of them were either drowned or provided a new item on the menu of the local Indians.

Only four escaped: Cabeza de Vaca, Dorantes, Castillo, and Esteban, a Moorish slave of Dorantes. For a time the four men were scattered among various Indian tribes, finally being thrown together in 1533. At first they were probably slaves, but later both Cabeza de Vaca and the Moor, Esteban, developed a following as medicine men, becoming famous among the natives for their marvelous cures.

In 1534, the four castaways were finally able to escape from the Indians and to make their way westward through the trackless wilderness. They crossed the *Llano Estacado*, went up the Pecos River for some distance, and then, striking westward, crossed the Río Grande some distance above the present site of El Paso.[3]

Ultimately reaching the Spanish settlements, Cabeza de Vaca and his companions told stories about large settlements of people who lived in permanent dwellings and who gave evidence of considerable wealth.[4] Most important, Vaca reported "many fine signs of gold, antimony, iron, copper, and other metals." Such stories were most welcome to the ears of those who yearned for more Indians to plunder, and who had visions of finding natives with as much gold as the Aztecs had originally possessed.

The Journey of Friar Marcos

The Viceroy of New Spain, Antonio de Mendoza, wanted Vaca and his companions to go as his agents and conquer the territory that they

[3] Bolton, *Coronado*, 10. Just who was the first white man to put foot in New Mexico is only one of many points in the state's history that remains controversial. This writer accepts the conclusion of Professor Bolton that it was Cabeza de Vaca. However, another competent authority on New Mexican history concludes that "Friar Marcos was indisputedly the first white man to set foot on the soil in New Mexico." From Percy M. Baldwin, "Fray Marcos de Niza and His Discovery of the Seven Cities of Cíbola," *NMHR*, Vol. I (April, 1926), 193.

[4] The standard source on Vaca is still Morris Bishop, *The Odyssey of Cabeza de Vaca*.

had reported on, but Vaca had visions of obtaining backing from Madrid for an expedition on his own. In any event, the stories of the castaways opened entirely new horizons to the north that had to be acted upon.

The Viceroy selected one Friar Marcos de Niza to make an exploratory trip to the region. Having been present when Pizzaro conquered the Incas in Peru, this clergyman had additional adventures in the isthmian area, and was reputed to have walked from Guatemala to Mexico. The fact that he had already packed more adventure into his life than most men ever see did not deter the indomitable friar, and his real claim to fame was yet to come.

Accompanied by Esteban, the Moorish slave, many Indian companions, and an escort of soldiers, Friar Marcos made his way northward. His instructions from the Viceroy were the usual official ones concerning treatment of the Indians: they were to be treated fairly, and under no circumstances were slaves to be taken. He was admonished to observe the people, check on the fertility of the soil, the climate, the trees and the plants, to make notes on domestic and wild animals, but, above all, to observe the presence of precious stones and metals.[5]

Esteban was sent on ahead to act as an advance party. It was understood that if the Moor located an important settlement, he was to send messengers back to the main group. A unique communication system was arranged, it being agreed that if anything of interest was encountered, a cross the size of a hand would be sent. The size of the cross was to be greater depending upon the significance of the discovery. Only four days after the Moor had pushed on ahead, the friar was overjoyed to welcome Esteban's Indian messengers burdened with a cross "as high as a man," indicating the great importance of the discovery.[6] In addition, an Indian who was familiar with Cíbola accompanied the cross and told Friar Marcos of the great size and wealth of the fabulous seven cities that lay only thirty days' march in the distance.

Instead of waiting for the clergyman and his party to overtake him as he was supposed to do, the Moor pushed on, sending native

[5] Baldwin, "Fray Marcos de Niza," *NMHR*, Vol. I (April, 1926), 197–200.
[6] *Ibid.*, 205.

messengers back urging the main group to hurry and catch up with him. More than likely, Esteban was taken in by the stories the Indians told him of great wealth just ahead, and seeing an opportunity of making a name for himself, he violated the friar's instructions. He pushed on until he reached Cíbola, where disaster awaited him. Esteban had on his previous sojourn among the Indians used a gourd rattle to good effect to convince them that he was a medicine man. However, the natives that he met this time were not to be so easily misled. In addition, they frowned on Esteban's liberties with their women. Therefore, they killed the Moor and many of his Indian companions.

This setback did not halt the friar's explorations, at least according to his story. He pressed on until he came within view of the fabled cities of Cíbola. The fact that these legendary seven towns turned out to be a miserable collection of mud huts does not indicate that the friar was telling the truth. Nor was the large amount of gold that he observed adorning the Indians ever found.

More than likely, the imaginative clergyman never got beyond the present international boundary line. It has been rather conclusively proved that he did not have enough time to make all of the journeys that he so glibly relates. Perhaps there was more read into his report than was actually there. Maybe even the Viceroy was involved in a plot to justify further exploration to the north and simply wanted Friar Marcos "to deliver" the kind of information that would lead to a general expedition.[7] Perhaps it would be fairer to designate the good friar as the first of a long line of enthusiastic Chamber of Commerce boosters for the fortunes of New Mexico.

~ The Coronado Expedition ~

In many respects Francisco Vásquez Coronado was the epitome of all that was fine in the Spanish nobleman of the day. A dashing individual whose bravery was never questioned, respected by friend and foe alike, he also had the natural talents for leadership frequently lacking. More important, he had influential friends, both in Mexico

[7] Hallenbeck, *Land of Conquistadores*, 21.

and in Madrid, to endorse his capabilities. Finally, Coronado was selected to lead the ill-fated expedition because he was able to finance it.[8]

It was easy to get followers for such an activity because the Spanish conquest was first of all a business enterprise. Those who supported the expedition financially naturally expected to make money out of it. Even the lesser soldiery were to be included in the spoils that came from the conquest of a new area. Their wealth did not come in gold or silver; it would come in land, properly equipped with Indian slaves to work it for them. Most of the money for Coronado's expedition came either from his wife or from the coffers of the Viceroy Mendoza.

In all, Coronado had under his command 336 men equipped with 559 horses, and some 100 Indians. They drove a large group of cattle and sheep along with them for food. This was also to be a missionary as well as a business enterprise. Consequently, several members of the clergy accompanied the expedition "so that the conquest may be Christian and apostolic, and not a butchery." Naturally, the most important among the clergy was Friar Marcos.

As the expedition proceeded northward, there was ample evidence that the reports of the friar had been greatly exaggerated. The desolate nature of the country made it difficult to obtain food, and the Indians were not as friendly as the friar had contended they were. Of more importance, the clergyman's classic geographical error, which had placed Cíbola near the head of the Gulf of California, made it impossible for Coronado to obtain supplies from his accompanying naval expedition. Even in light of the geographical information of that day, this was a stupendous mistake and can only be explained on the basis of Friar Marcos' wild tales, rather than as a simple error.

Proceeding up the coast of what is today western Mexico, Coronado discovered that the pace of the full expedition was too slow. Therefore, with an advance guard of about fifty men, accompanied by Friar Marcos, he set out to reach the heralded wealth of Cíbola

[8] Bolton, *Coronado*, 73. Professor Bolton's study is the most complete. Also consulted were A. Grove Day, *Coronado's Quest*, and George P. Hammond and Agapito Rey, eds., *Narratives of the Coronado Expedition, 1540–1542.*

as soon as possible. Coronado's route took him through southeastern Arizona northward to about where Highway 66 lies now; he then turned eastward.

In only a short time, from April to July, the advance guard were able to make their way to the "Seven Cities of Cíbola." There, their disappointment was to be boundless. For instead of streets gleaming with gold pavement and wealthy Indians adorned with precious metals and stones, they found six miserable hovels, populated by Indians who barely had enough food to subsist. These Zuñi Indians at first resisted the Spaniards, but after a brief skirmish they submitted. Here the explorers awaited the main body of the expedition.

In his dispatches to Viceroy Mendoza, Coronado described the poverty of the area, stressing the absence of gold, silver, and precious stones. Naturally, Friar Marcos received much blame for his previously exaggerated reports.

Although the initial disappointment to Coronado and his men must have been great, they were not ones to give up. Exploratory expeditions were sent to neighboring pueblos searching for evidence of wealth. One of these found the Grand Canyon, while others encountered the Pueblo Indian towns at Acoma and along the upper Río Grande.

Impressed by the greater availability of food among the Río Grande Indians, Hernando de Alvarado, one of Coronado's lieutenants, sent messages requesting the leader to transfer his base of operations there for the winter of 1540–41.

Meanwhile, Friar Marcos had returned home "because of ill health." (It is not clear whether his health was impaired by his sudden unpopularity.) En route he had given orders for the main body of troops to follow Coronado, except for a small body that was to go westward to keep a rendezvous with the fleet and obtain needed supplies. However, the fleet under Alarcón had left beforehand, and they were sent only to obtain a message, and thus no supplies.

After exploring eastward as far as the plains country around the Canadian River and encountering buffalo in the process, Alvarado returned to the Pueblo of Cicuyé. It was here that the explorers were finally to have their flagging hopes revived. For a Pawnee Indian slave whom the Spaniards called El Turco (because he looked like one) told them the kind of stories their ears longed to hear. Taking a page from the book of the imaginative Friar Marcos, El Turco told of a fabulous Indian country called Quivira lying to the east where the Indians not only paved the street with gold, but also made water jugs of that most common metal. El Turco explained his own lack of ornamentation by insisting that the Cicuyé chief, Bigotes, had taken his gold bracelets.

When the Indian chief denied this story, he was tortured in an effort to get it out of him. He failed to tell the Spaniards what they wanted to hear, but the Spanish mistreatment of the chief infuriated the Indians. In addition, the natives had become restless as a result of the Spaniards' taking their food and, reportedly, bothering their women. This made necessary a campaign of chastisement in order to convince the savages who was their master.

In the spring of 1541, Coronado pushed eastward in search of the rich city of Quivira with the imaginative Indian El Turco to guide him. As they made their way over the high plains, the Spaniards began to suspect that they were again being misled. Adding to their suspicions was the report of another Plains Indian named Isopete, who had consistently branded the stories of El Turco as false and who had described the Indians of Quivira as they actually existed.

In July, 1541, Coronado finally came upon the heralded Quivira, near the present site of Lyons, Kansas. Bitterly disappointed in finding only Indians living in grass huts, the Spaniards promptly sent El Turco to join his ancestors, a harsher fate than the lying Friar Marcos had enjoyed.

Coronado made some exploration in the region, and in his reports stressed that the land held excellent promise for the future, emphasizing that the soil was excellent and would grow most of the crops found in Spain. Unfortunately, he likewise reported that there was no gold or silver available, and hence the Spaniards were to pass up the agricultural potentialities of Kansas.

Although rumors circulating among the Indians of white men in the area excited Coronado, he was not to learn that De Soto's expedition was only a short distance away. Returning to his headquarters base in New Mexico by October, the leader prepared for further explorations. Unfortunately, Coronado was injured in an accident, and his illness led to the abandonment of the expedition. Plagued with the weakening effects of a painful head injury, their disappointed leader led the would-be *conquistadores* homeward, where Coronado was to face a far different reception from that accorded him when he had left two years earlier.

For the expedition that had set out with such high hopes, and which had been so costly in terms of money and lives, was a dismal failure. And Coronado was to suffer the barbs and misfortunes of all those who failed in such undertakings. His sin lay in his inability to bring back packloads of precious metals. The debacle of the Coronado expedition was to cool the enthusiasm of the Spanish leaders for further explorations to the north, so New Mexico was to remain an unwanted area depicted as desolate and useless for many years to come.

The Chamuscado-Rodríguez Expedition

The failure of the Coronado venture northward was not the only reason for Spanish neglect of the land to the north. The outbreak of the Mixtón War ravaged the frontier of New Spain for many years, and before the hostile Indians were suppressed, whole provinces were virtually depopulated.[9] This revolt of the natives prompted the Spaniards to be careful about building settlements that were too remote from the population nucleus. There was too much danger that they could be wiped out by hostile natives. Furthermore, the discovery of rich silver mines at several points in New Spain kept the Spaniards occupied.

In order to obtain workers for these mines, many slave-hunting expeditions constantly expanded their areas of search outward, gathering in the reluctant Indians for the necessary labor in the white man's mines. Such practices were, of course, illegal, but rather generally engaged in. The slave hunters brought stories of the lands lying to the north that again excited the imagination of the Spaniards.

[9] The story of the Mixtón War is ably related in Arthur S. Aiton, *Antonio de Mendoza, First Viceroy of New Spain.*

It is quite unlikely that the information gathered by Coronado was even available in 1580, at least to the frontier settlements.

One Agustín Rodríguez, a Franciscan lay brother, proposed a missionary expedition into the strange land, about which consistent rumors continued to circulate.[10] It was necessary for the clergy to take the initiative in such an activity because the Spanish crown, seeking to curtail the activity of the slave hunters, looked with displeasure on expeditions of the kind led by Coronado. Hence, permission was obtained for what was to be ostensibly an opportunity to save the souls of the heathen Indians.

The total party consisted of three friars, nine soldiers led by Francisco Chamuscado, and nineteen Indians. They took with them an appropriate number of horses as well as livestock for food. They also had a generous supply of trinkets to use as gifts to the Indians in an effort to win their favor.

Leaving Santa Bárbara, on the Mexican frontier, on June 5, 1581, the small party made its way down the Conchos River to the Río Grande. They then went upstream through the open country until they reached the first Indian pueblo near what is now Socorro. They probably went as far north as the Taos region. In addition, they went into the plains area beyond the Pecos River, encountering buffalo. Retracing their steps, they then went westward as far as Acoma and Zuñi.

Although the Indians frequently gave signs of unfriendliness, they were won over by a combination of intimidation and the liberal distribution of gifts. That such a small body of men could wander with impunity through the vast Indian country is alone ample testimonial to their diplomatic skill. Unfortunately, all of the Indians were not as friendly as they appeared to be. When Father Juan de Santa María left the company and set out alone, seeking to chart a different route to Mexico, he was murdered by hostile natives. And when the soldiers decided to return home, Fathers Rodríguez and López elected to remain behind, and were also soon to find the martyrdom they sought.

The remainder of the party returned home in April, 1582, with

[10] J. Lloyd Mechem, "The Second Spanish Expedition to New Mexico," *NMHR*, Vol. I (July, 1926), is a full treatment of the Chamuscado-Rodríguez Expedition.

Chamuscado dying en route. Thus, the small group was able to do approximately what Coronado's large and expensive expedition had accomplished earlier. One of their members, Hernando Gallegos, was to compile a complete record of the journey, including much valuable information about the land, the inhabitants, and its potentialities.

One authority suggests that this expedition was "as adventuresome as any undertaken by Gilbert or Raleigh." Although this may be a bit of an exaggeration, the exploits of Rodríguez and Chamuscado were doubtless to pave the way for the ultimate settlement of New Mexico. Perhaps also the expedition had been instrumental in naming the land Nuevo México.[11]

The Espejo Expedition

The Franciscan brethren of the two friars who had been left behind demanded that a rescue group be sent northward. During its preparation, news came that one of them had been killed, but the party was outfitted nevertheless.[12] The clergy were eager to get on with the rescue and were unwilling to wait until the civil authorities had unraveled "the requisite yardage of red tape."[13] that so plagued the Spanish colonial administration.

To the aid of the Franciscans came one Antonio de Espejo, a wealthy rancher who happened to be at Santa Bárbara. Espejo offered to form and finance the necessary rescue party. It is assumed that his reason for doing so was to escape punishment for having killed one of his ranch employees. It was common for Spaniards to flee to the frontier region and remain out of circulation until the wrath of the king's peace officers had subsided. Perhaps Espejo

[11] Hubert H. Bancroft, *Arizona and New Mexico*, 91.

[12] Rudolph Levin Dalager, "The Espejo Expedition in New Mexico, 1582–1583" (M.A. thesis, University of Southern California, 1929); J. Lloyd Mechem, "Antonio de Espejo and his journey to New Mexico," *Southwestern Historical Quarterly*, Vol. XXX (October, 1926); Diego Pérez de Luxán, *Expedition into New Mexico Made by Antonio de Espejo 1582–1583*, trans. and ed. by George P. Hammond and Agapito Rey.

[13] Mechem, "Antonio de Espejo," 119.

would win enough wealth and lands for the crown that the king would be willing to forget his past misdeeds.

Espejo's later claim to have had official authority to lead such a venture is probably false. The lieutenant governor of Nueva Viscaya had in fact granted the authority to one of the Franciscan friars, and it was only after the expedition was under way that Espejo was elevated to its leadership.[14] With only two friars and fifteen soldiers and a few Indian servants, the group set out, following a route similar to that of the preceding party. Once they learned that both of the friars they had come to rescue were dead, many wanted to return at once. However, Espejo was able to hold most of the group together and continue his explorations for gold, doubtless the motive that had prompted his generosity in the first place. During the winter of 1582–83 this small group of men was to go up the Río Grande, visit the various pueblos in that area, and then a party of only nine men under Espejo probably went as far west as the present site of Prescott, Arizona. Occasionally, they were called upon to fight the hostile Indians, and one time six Spaniards counted an estimated force of two thousand natives against them. Part of the group returned home down the Río Grande while Espejo and his following went eastward and returned down the Pecos River and then turned southwestward to the Río Grande.

Espejo came back to his point of departure in New Spain on August 10, 1583, after having been gone exactly nine months, during which he covered at least 3,500 miles. Upon his return Espejo wrote a grandiose account of the new lands which he saw and addressed it to the king hoping to obtain authorization for the exploration and Christianization of the provinces. He greatly exaggerated the resources of the country, estimating that there was a native population of 250,000 awaiting the message of the Roman Catholic faith. More important than the opportunity for missionary work were the descriptions of the Lake of Gold, which attracted a lot of attention among the mining elements of Mexico.

For unknown reasons, the petition of Espejo was not acted upon by the crown, and his proposal to colonize New Mexico was per-

[14] *Ibid.*, 119.

51

mitted to die, but it was only to be a few years before another was to be commissioned to make the conquest.

⟵ *The Oñate Conquest* ⟶

Indirectly influencing the future development of New Mexico was the Spanish belief that Sir Francis Drake, while on his around-the-world voyage (1579–82) had found a passage through Asia homeward. This prompted the crown to order the viceroy of Mexico to make a contract with some individuals leading to the settlement of the lands lying to the north, it being assumed that New Mexico was close to the bay area.[15] As a result, several applicants for the honor came forth, in addition to Espejo. One of these, Gaspar Castaño de Sosa, even led a group of colonists up the Río Grande and briefly made a settlement near the present site of Santo Domingo. Unfortunately, when his request for authorization was turned down, he was returned to New Spain to answer for having moved too quickly, and his colony was abandoned.

The task of the final conquest of New Mexico was to be given to Don Juan de Oñate.[16] The reason for the selection undoubtedly lay in the fact that his father was a wealthy Zacatecas mining man. In addition to the obvious influence of his father and his brothers, Oñate was married to a granddaughter of Cortés, whose own family was one of the most noted in New Spain. Finally, Oñate had the support of his four famous nephews, the Zaldívar brothers, two of whom were to be trusted lieutenants in the conquest. To these significant family connections were also added many influential friends.

The contract granted Oñate by the crown provided that he raise a force of two hundred men and supply them with the necessary live-

---

[15] Herbert E. Bolton, *The Spanish Borderlands*, 169.

[16] George P. Hammond, *Don Juan de Oñate and the Founding of New Mexico;* Beatrice Quijada Cornish, "The Preliminaries to the Oñate Expedition Into New Mexico" (M.A. thesis, University of California, Berkeley, 1915); Juan de Montoya, *New Mexico in 1602: Juan de Montoya's Relation of the Discovery of New Mexico,* trans. and ed. by George P. Hammond and Agapito Rey. Of considerable interest is the epic poem describing the conquest, Gaspar Pérez de Villagrá, *History of New Mexico,* trans. by Gilberto Espinosa.

Wheeler Peak

Kuaua Pueblo ruins near Bernalillo

Taos Pueblo

Acoma Pueblo

Inscription Rock

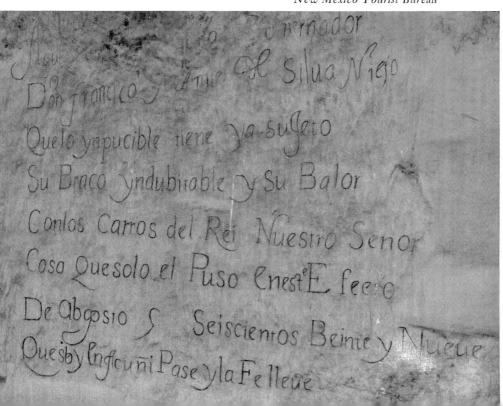

New Mexico *Magazine*

A Mescalero Apache tipi of the old days

Photograph by Milton Snow, U.S. Indian Service

An early Navaho forked-stick hogan

A Navaho chant. Sitting on a sand painting, a Navaho woman and her child receive strength from the spirits.

American Museum of Natural History

Santa Fe, 1846

Santa Fe, 1895

Fort Defiance, New Mexico Territory, about 1860

A typical New Mexico fort

From Parker, Annals of Old Fort Cummings

An Indian and his oxcart

New Mexico stage line

stock, farm implements, and other merchandise needed for one year. Obviously, it took a wealthy man to fulfill such a requirement, and many of the applicants failed in this respect. In return for the investment, Oñate was to receive the title of governor, a salary of 6,000 ducats a year, certain tax exemptions which included a reduction of the royal fifth to only a tenth for a time, the right to give the title of *Hidalgo* to his followers for five generations, and by implication, the right to grant lands and the use of native labor.

Although it was assumed that the basic objective would be the exploitation of the rich mines that Espejo had discovered, provision was included in the contract for the conversion of the natives to Christianity. When the contract was nearing consummation in the fall of 1595, a change of viceroys occurred in New Spain. Because of this upheaval, the would-be conqueror of New Mexico became involved in the intricacies of colonial politics. Other applicants sought to make a stronger bid and replace Oñate. A three-year delay in the final authorization to proceed with the conquest followed, costing Oñate large sums of money and endangering the project from its very inception.

It was not until January, 1598, that the expedition finally was on the move for the promised land to the north. Officially, it consisted of 129 soldiers, 83 wagons, and 7,000 head of stock. There were also eight priests and two lay brothers to convert the heathen. The total number of settlers has never been established, but it is usual to describe the group as totaling 400 men, 130 of whom had wives and children with them. Naturally, no one bothered to count the Indians who accompanied them.

The party followed the Conchos River for a short distance, but then struck northward on a more direct route, reaching the Río Grande south of El Paso, the site of this city being reached on May 4, 1598. Because the colonists moved very slowly, as it was necessary for the livestock to graze along the way, Oñate took thirty soldiers and pushed on ahead.

This advance party followed the Río Grande and visited the various Indian pueblos from below Socorro northward. As he proceeded, Oñate took possession of the territory with the elaborate ceremony the Spaniards had developed. Through his interpreters the explorer explained in speeches to the natives that the king of Spain owned all of the territory and they must submit to his rule. If they would only do so, they would be protected from their enemies in this world, provided for, and, more important, be assured of an easy transit into the glorious life to come. Undoubtedly sincere attempts were made to explain the rule of Spain as well as Christianity, but there is little question that most of it was beyond the comprehension of the natives. What they did understand was that if they refused to go through the ritual of submission described, the Spanish soldiers were capable of compelling a reconsideration of their decision. This threat was probably more meaningful to the Indians than that of eternal damnation if they refused the rites of the church.

In July, Oñate established a headquarters at San Juan, near the junction of the Río Grande and the Río Chama. Some time later this capital was moved westward to San Gabriel. Using this site as a base, the explorer or his lieutenants, usually the Zaldívar brothers, Juan or Vicente, fanned out over New Mexico in all directions. In a short time the energetic leader had traversed the ground explored by his predecessors. He was seeking the same thing that they had sought, precious metals, and his search was to be as futile as theirs had been. Wherever they went, they followed the established ritual of obtaining the submission of the natives and then of promptly requisitioning supplies from them, a practice which inevitably brought trouble.

But Oñate was to have far more difficulty with his own people than he was to encounter from the Indians. Like their English counterparts in Virginia, the followers of the Spanish explorer were more interested in wresting the plates of gold which were reputed to have adorned the pavements of native villages than they were in wresting a living from the inhospitable environment in which they found themselves. The colonists were, from the very first, embittered by the poverty-stricken appearance of the natives. Not only were they not arrayed in plentiful supplies of gold ornaments, but neither were there precious metals to be easily mined. Worse yet, it was obvious that food was going to be scarce. Those who accompanied Oñate had done so, not to establish a long-range colony in a wilderness, but

54

rather to get rich quick. The money that they had borrowed on their possessions in New Spain, or from friends or relatives, constituted to them a stake in a gambling enterprise. And when they saw that the chances for success were not promising, many were ready to leave for home at once.

As early as August, 1598, a group of such malcontents were to plan desertion and a return to New Spain. The plot was discovered in time to be checked, but the threat of such action was to hang over the expedition continuously.

Complicating matters for the leaders was the fact that they were there to Christianize the Indians, and they had to limit the exploitation of them. This meant there had to be some restrictions upon the seizure of Indian food supplies and upon forced native labor. Oñate was caught between the clergy, who favored the position of the Indian, and those Spaniards who were prepared to exploit them ruthlessly. It was a dilemma that was to plague the governors of the province incessantly, and was to remain one of the primary problems of colonial days.

At first the Indians had been cowed into submission by fear of the strangers with their horses and firearms, and perhaps also by their tactful initial approach. However, as time went on, the requisitions for food supplies caused restlessness among the natives. Then closer contact with the white man helped dispel some of the initial fear and prompted some natives to believe that with their numbers they could easily overwhelm the handful of Spaniards in their midst.

The Acoma Indians were to provide the Spanish invaders with their most severe test. Their pueblo was built on a large white rock which towered 357 feet towards the sky. Because the path to the top consisted of small holes hewn in the rock, it was virtually impregnable, and had been so considered by the neighboring tribes. On an inspection tour to the west in the fall of 1598. Oñate himself very narrowly escaped assassination at Acoma when he was in too much of a hurry to investigate a kiva where natives waited to kill him.

According to Villagrá, the poet-historian of the Oñate conquest, there were two factions among the Acoma Indians, one advocating friendship with the Spaniards and the other favoring their extinction.

Disaster befell the Spaniards when Juan de Zaldívar accompanied by eighteen men was making his way westward to join the commander on an exploratory trip to the sea.

On December 4, 1598, the small Spanish party stopped at Acoma to obtain food. The Indians tricked them into accompanying them to their storehouse, ostensibly to procure provisions. During this effort the Spaniards were divided, and while they were in a very narrow place near the cliffs, the Indians attacked. Thirteen of the party were killed, and it was miraculous that any escaped; the seven who did jumped onto the cliffs below.

The setback at Acoma was disastrous for the Spanish forces in New Mexico in many ways. The thirteen lost men could ill be spared from the limited manpower available. In Juan de Zaldívar, the commander had not only lost one of his most competent officers, he had also lost his nephew and a trusted friend. Many faint-hearted colonists looked upon this reversal as an excuse to return to New Spain. The loss in manpower, and the consequent fear of further Indian trouble, was to make it difficult for Oñate to carry on as much exploration and search for treasure as he had planned.

The challenge presented by the Acoma Indians could not be overlooked, for other Indians were doubtless prepared to follow their resistance and thus make the position of the Spaniards untenable. Hence Oñate received the approval of the clergy to carry on a military campaign against them. Responsible for its prosecution were Vicente de Zaldívar, the brother of the slain officer, and some seventy men.

When this small force put in an appearance on January 12, 1599, and demanded that the Indians submit and turn over to the white men those guilty of the earlier crime, the Acomas looked at them with ridicule. They doubtless considered the soldiers crazy to attempt to attack their impregnable fortress with so few men. The number of Indian warriors available is estimated as high as three thousand, but no figures are reliable. Zaldívar's attack was based upon a frontal assault, by which he hoped to cause the natives to concentrate their strength at one place and leave other points undefended. Zaldívar himself led a squad of eleven men up the deserted side of the cliff, gaining a foothold at the top. During the night, the Spaniards prepared a beam to be used in bridging the deep gorge separating them from the Indians on the other two parts of the mesa making up the Acoma Pueblo. Thirteen Spaniards had crossed the gorge in the attack, when the beam was pulled away. Villagrá leaped across the eighteen-foot chasm and restored the beam, allowing the other soldiers to cross over. When artillery was brought up, the Spaniards slowly but surely gained the upper hand. Perhaps of as much assistance to the Spaniards as the artillery was the apparition of St. James riding a white horse and using a terrible sword in behalf of the Christians.

In two or three days' fighting, some six or eight hundred natives were killed at Acoma, with the Spaniards suffering no losses. Critics of Oñate contend that the natives attempted to surrender, but Zaldívar would not permit that. The pueblo was completely destroyed and some six hundred Indians taken captive. Some escaped with only twenty years of slavery ahead of them, whereas many of the warriors had a hand or foot cut off.[17]

The lesson taught the Acoma Indians was not lost upon the other natives. As this pueblo was considered impregnable, the others doubtless questioned whether they had a chance against the Spaniards, despite the fact that they badly outnumbered them. The Indians were so completely cowed by the ease and completeness of the Spanish victory that it was 1680 before the pueblos were to challenge Spanish rule again.

The battle with the Acomas surely had its influence upon Oñate's message to the viceroy dated March 2, 1599. In this document Oñate showed that he understood what appealed to the Spanish authorities. He stressed the richness of the vast area yet to be explored, emphasizing the great wealth available in gold and silver, as well as the pearls to be found. He also stressed the further opportunity for conversion among the Indians. What Oñate wanted was reinforcements for this tiny colony, for without them he was virtually helpless. In response to his plea, a force of seventy-three soldiers made their way northward in August of 1600, reaching Oñate's camp on Christmas Eve.[18]

[17] Hammond, *Don Juan de Oñate*, 112–23.
[18] *Ibid.*, 130.

Despite the reinforcements, conditions remained severe for the handful of struggling colonists. Continuous prospecting within New Mexico failed to divulge any riches, the Spaniards missing the gold not very far from them near Santa Fe, near Taos, and in the Red River area. It became increasingly difficult to forage food from the natives, who were hard pressed to feed their Spanish masters. The discontent among the settlers reached a point where drastic measures were necessary in order to control it. Oñate ordered the slaying of one of his captains, Aguilar, who had been a perpetual troublemaker; but the immediate reasons for the execution have been obscured. When others attempted to leave for New Spain, they were accused of treason and their leaders executed. Naturally, such repressive actions increased the already extensive unrest among the struggling colonists.

In an effort to quiet the discontent. Oñate decided on an exploratory expedition eastward to Quivira, that graveyard of the high hopes of Coronado. Wealth not having been found on an earlier westward trip, this was virtually the last hope. Between seventy and one hundred men set out in June, 1601, and after a journey to central Kansas returned to New Mexico in November, 1601, having been no more successful than Coronado had been.

During Oñate's absence, most of the colony had deserted. Peñalosa, whom Oñate had left in charge, permitted the malcontents to organize a desertion. The ringleaders were those who had set out with substantial fortunes and had already lost them in New Mexico and wanted to return to New Spain as soon as possible. These included most of the soldiers. Added to the settlers who left were the clergy, who lamented the fact that their task of conversion was made more difficult by Oñate's repressive measures. However, some of the colonists who remained behind later testified that most of the difficulty experienced by the clergy in their efforts to convert the natives arose from their own laziness, stressing the fact that one father who discharged his obligations properly had enjoyed much success. As one soldier put it, " 'If the padres had fulfilled their duty the Indians would all have been Christians by this time.' "[19]

Regardless of the reasons, the weary soldiers on their return from

[19] *Ibid.*, 149.

Kansas found only some twenty-five Spaniards waiting to greet them. Oñate's attempt to overtake the colonists and force them to return was unsuccessful. This desertion was to mark the beginning of the end for New Mexico's conqueror.

The many enemies back in Mexico, jealous when Oñate had originally been appointed, now became most vociferous in their denunciations of him. When news of the measures used against the Acoma Indians had reached the Viceroy, that official had discussed the matter before the *Audiencia* of New Spain. The cruel punishment and the destruction of the pueblo must have been shocking news. No action was taken at the time because Oñate was not present at the affair, and it was feared that open discussion might discourage the whole New Mexico enterprise.[20] The desertion and news of the drastic measures used to control the New Mexico colony prompted a complete review of the whole project. It was decided that the land and its inhabitants were too poor to justify further expenditure and, because Oñate was not financially able to carry the responsibility, the attempt to colonize New Mexico should be abandoned. This recommendation went to Madrid, where it was concurred in by the crown. After an expenditure of more than 400,000 pesos by Oñate and considerably more by others in the attempt to colonize New Mexico, the decision was to permit the area to return to its previous primitive state.

That this decision was never carried out was a direct result of the dilemma faced by the royal officials concerning the disposition of the converted Indians. As it was estimated that there were more than two thousand such natives, it would be difficult to move them to New Spain. Hence, it was finally decided to turn the colony over to the crown as a mission station with control in the hands of the clergy, the entire area being converted into a *custodia*, with the military there only to protect the missionaries.

As dissatisfaction continued to mount over Oñate's conduct of affairs in New Mexico, the commander sought for some major deed which would recoup his waning prestige. Like other Spanish colonial officials, he was convinced that if he could only accomplish the original objective of his mission, the finding of wealth, the com-

[20] *Ibid.*, 126.

plaints of the colonists would be satisfied, and the king, obtaining his share, would find little fault. Taking a small band of only thirty soldiers, Oñate left San Gabriel on October 7, 1604, and went all the way westward to the Colorado River and thence south to the Gulf of California. He and his followers returned to their home base on April 25, 1605.

But this last effort was to be in vain. In spite of the fact that they gathered much valuable data, precious minerals eluded their grasp. Thus Oñate's fate was sealed. He was later to be tried for the crimes committed during his conquest, the most significant being the harsh measures against the Acoma Indians and the execution of many persons who had attempted to leave the colony. Ultimately, New Mexico's conqueror was to be tried and convicted along with many of his leading officers for a wide variety of crimes. But the most important crime Oñate had committed in the eyes of Spain's rulers was one he was never tried for: that of failing to duplicate the feats of Cortés and Pizzaro in finding Indians of sufficient wealth to swell the bottomless coffers at Madrid.

IV - The Seventeenth Century

ONCE IT HAD BEEN ESTABLISHED that New Mexico was not a land either of great mineral wealth or of significant agricultural potential, Spain's interest in the area lagged. Between 1609 and 1680 Spanish control could be described as essentially a holding measure. Responsibility for administration of the province passed into the hands of the crown, and its main reason in remaining along the Río Grande was to protect the converted Indians. For this purpose the missions were of fundamental importance, and during the period cited above, it is estimated that their maintenance probably cost Madrid more than one million pesos. This was a very considerable sum for that time, and when one adds to that the cost of the civil and military installations, some idea of the Spanish interest in the religious motive during the colonial period is obtained.[1]

Without seeking to depreciate the importance of this religious motive however, it would be unfair not to mention the fact that Spain's support of its "white elephant" in New Mexico was influenced by another factor. This was the fact that as long as there was a Spanish force in the area, Madrid retained a claim to the vast country lying to the north. As France, England, and even the Netherlands had already challenged Spain's exclusive control in the Western World, it is possible that the interest in supporting the mission stations was to retain a claim to the vast unknown areas lying north of New

[1] France V. Scholes, "The Supply Service of the New Mexico Missions in the Seventeenth Century," *NMHR*, Vol. V (January, 1930; April, 1930; October, 1930), 114. Professor Scholes in a series of scholarly monographs has exhaustively examined the seventeenth century in New Mexico.

Spain. No attempt was made to define the limits of the province of New Mexico, and in general it included most of what is now the western United States. Any setting of boundaries to an area whose limits were not known might endanger future claims.[2]

At best, the Spanish hold on this vast area was a tenuous one, and if other European nations had been in a position to enter the region, the Spaniards would have found it difficult to keep it. One authority maintains that in 1617 the number of Spanish soldiers and settlers was only forty-eight,[3] though this figure could very well be in error. Friar Benavides, who was to contribute much valuable information on the status of the colony in 1628, claimed that it had a Spanish population of fifteen hundred. Regardless of the size of the settlement, the distance of more than fifteen hundred miles to Mexico City, much of it through wastelands frequented by hostile Indians, was in itself enough to make administration both costly and difficult.

The first royal governor of New Mexico, Don Pedro de Peralta, arrived in the province in 1609 with instructions to seek a more suitable location for the headquarters of the province. The new capital was founded at Santa Fe, probably in the spring of 1610. The reason for this location was doubtless first of all defense, as the new capital was centrally located among the pueblos along the Río Grande, most of them being within a radius of fifty to seventy-five miles. In addition, it was easily accessible from the north via the Española Valley, and from the south via Santa Fe Creek. Easy access was likewise gained both to the east and to the west. The attractiveness of the Santa Fe Basin, the availability of water and arable land, as well as open fields in which horses could maneuver in the event of warfare, were all factors in the location of Santa Fe.[4]

The Mission Supply Service

Connecting the tiny village of Santa Fe with the outside world was

[2] France V. Scholes, "Civil Government and Society in New Mexico in the Seventeenth Century," *NMHR*, Vol. X (April, 1935), 71–72.

[3] Bancroft, *Arizona and New Mexico*, 159.

[4] Irene Alma Moke, "Santa Fe, New Mexico: A Study in Urban Geography" (Ph.D. dissertation, University of Nebraska, 1935), 117–119.

one of the most unusual trading arrangements the world has ever known, the mission supply service.[5] Originally organized in 1609 and reorganized in 1664, this service was intended to provide only for the missions of New Mexico, but in actual practice it handled most of the commerce of New Mexico in the seventeenth century.

A caravan was supposed to make the trip every three years, but frequently four and even five years intervened before such trips were made. Originally made up at Mexico City, the caravans followed a route that took them through Zacatecas, Durango, Parral, and then along the Río Grande. The journey took five to six months, with approximately the same length of time being utilized in Santa Fe to distribute the cargo and make necessary repairs, and then another six months for the return, a total of one and one-half years being considered standard for the round trip.

The caravans were to consist of thirty-two wagons, which were probably four-wheel affairs, each capable of carrying about two tons and normally pulled by a team of eight mules. In appearance, they were doubtless similar to those later used in the Santa Fe trade, but perhaps were cruder in construction.

On the northward trip, the goods carried consisted largely of mission and church supplies. These would include hardware for the missions as well as essential materials for the altar and clothing for the missionaries. Quite frequently, various items of luxury goods would also be included.

On the return trip from New Mexico, the goods carried were normally staples, consisting mostly of hides, piñon nuts, and *mantas*, or blankets. Later in the century, flocks of sheep raised at the missions were driven with the caravans southward to be sold to the miners of New Spain. Another staple "export" of New Mexico is frequently overlooked by historians: the Indian slaves that were driven along with the flocks of sheep to be likewise sold to the miners.

As there was no other formal system of transportation, the mission supply caravan became Santa Fe's link with the civilized world to the south. Settlers and new groups of friars, as well as public servants, accompanied the caravan because of the safety it insured,

[5] In addition to the treatment of the supply service by Scholes, see Max L. Moorhead, *New Mexico's Royal Road: Trade and Travel on the Chihuahua Trail.*

since it was usually guarded by a small detachment of soldiers. Without such a supply service and the competent Franciscans who administered it through most of the century, Spain's holding operation in New Mexico might not have been successful.

The Church and State Conflict

But the real story of the history of New Mexico in the seventeenth century is that of the bitter, and sometimes violent, conflict between the church and state for supremacy.[6] In general the issues at stake in this controversy grew out of the conflict of religious and economic motives which existed in all of colonial Spanish America. Since the Dominican friar, Las Casas, had written his famed attack upon the Spaniard's mistreatment of the Indians, the church had attempted to defend the native from the cupidity of the white man. Hence, the conflict between church and state in New Mexico during the seventeenth century was but a part of the larger struggle. It was more bitter in this province than elsewhere for two reasons: isolation made difficult the enforcement of Spanish laws relative to the treatment of the natives, and in the poverty-stricken land Indian labor was virtually the only source of wealth.

At his best, the exaggerated individualism of the average Spaniard made it extremely difficult to govern him. At his worst, proper restrictions upon his conduct were all but impossible. The extreme isolation of New Mexico made the province a haven of refuge for social outcasts from the outlying mining camps of New Spain. Making more difficult the control of Spain's remote colony was the fact that the political administrators of New Mexico too frequently were themselves outcasts, some of them arriving at Santa Fe with forged documents, and others, like Peñalosa, being disreputable adventurers. Laws passed by the Council of the Indies in Madrid were most difficult to administer among such people.

In this environment, the most competent governors found it difficult to carry out the laws. The secular Spaniards backed the gov-

[6] France V. Scholes, "Church and State in New Mexico in the Seventeenth Century" (Ph.D. dissertation, Harvard University, 1943).

ernors in their quarrel with the clergy when it was in their own best interest, but they turned on the civil authorities whenever it seemed they could gain an advantage from such action. The governors, as well as most of the other political administrators, viewed their positions as an opportunity to enrich themselves, and, as Indian labor was the only real source of wealth, they did so by exploiting the natives. This exploitation was accomplished by measures which included slave raids against the nomadic tribes, compelling the Pueblo Indians to tan hides, weave *mantas* and blankets, and making them forced laborers. Because they looked upon the natives as a source of their own enrichment, the governors could not be expected to be in sympathy with the ideals of conversion held by the church. Such an attitude on the part of the governors led inevitably to conflict with the clergy, which was heightened by the fact that many of the political leaders openly ridiculed the practices of the church as well as its authority.

Making more difficult the position of New Mexico's governors was the fact that, like most of Spain's administrators, they had to face a *residencia* at the end of their term in office. In theory, this was an opportunity for the citizens openly to express their feelings about the outgoing administrator before impartial judges prepared to render a decision. In practice, the *residencias* were held by the new governor and were opportunities for enemies made while in office to even the score with the departing official. Even the most competent administrators discovered that it was far safer to use bribery to obtain a favorable *residencia* than to rely upon the irresponsible justice of Spanish law. For several of New Mexico's governors of the seventeenth century died in prison after having all of their wealth, frequently attained before their appointment, taken from them.

Even if the governors had attempted to treat the Indians fairly, they were forced to recognize the economic interest of the Spanish settlers in their exploitation. Indian slave labor was widely used, being justified on the grounds that the nomadic savages would be Christianized during such service. Doubtless some of the Spanish slave-gathering expeditions provoked the Indians to war and thus furnished an excuse to obtain more slaves. More common as a source of Indian labor was the *encomienda*. This was a system whereby natives were assigned for the purposes of necessary labor to certain Spanish settlers. Their status was comparable to that of the serfs of the Middle Ages who did labor for the feudal knights so that the warriors would be free to fight. In return for this native labor, the *encomendero* was expected to furnish so many days of military service as well as to provide for the conversion of the natives to Christianity and to protect them from want. Abuses within the system were common.

Making the Spanish population more difficult to manage was the fusion with the Indians. The contact between European and native was more than just a blending of race to produce the *mestizo;* it was actually a fusion of cultures. Ample evidence exists that the Spanish women, particularly through contacts with their Indian servants, rapidly assumed many of the basic beliefs and superstitions of the natives.[7] Naturally, a full understanding of this influence is not possible. But as one authority puts it, "It is a well-established fact that the impact between advanced peoples and those culturally backward, though hard on the characters of both, is likely to be more disastrous to the former than to the latter."[8]

In New Mexico, as well as other parts of Spanish America, the work of converting the natives to belief in Christianity was made very difficult by the bad example set by many Spaniards. To the Indians, the word "Christian" became synonymous with someone who came to kill and plunder them, seize their women, or sell them into slavery. Some Indian tribes welcomed the priests but warned them not to bring any Christians with them. Indians in Mexico who understood the teachings of Christ decided that the Spaniards must not be called Christians because they did not act like Christians; instead, they called them *Castiltecas.*[9]

The Franciscans, charged with the administration of the New Mexico missions, had good reason to resent the interference of the Spanish laity with their attempt to convert the Indians. The zealous missionary, eager for favor in this world and the next as a result of the

[7] France V. Scholes, "The First Decade of the Inquisition in New Mexico," *NMHR*, Vol. X (July, 1935) 216.

[8] Mary W. Williams, *The People and Politics of Latin America*, 229.

[9] Diffie, *Latin-American Civilization*, 256.

number of souls he had been able to save, viewed the Spanish settlers as his bitter enemies because their attempts to exploit the native interfered with the work of conversion.

Most of the Franciscans who labored in the vineyard of seventeenth-century New Mexico were worthy followers of the Saint of Assisi. Their devotion to the cause of Christianity must continue to command admiration and respect. Many of these friars sacrificed promising careers within the order in Spain or Mexico, as well as the relative ease and comfort of life in civilization, to convert a new and inhospitable people to the faith. Some sought and obtained the martyr's crown. To others, the only reward was the extension of the kingdom of God, and for most of them that was enough.[10]

Unfortunately, all of the Franciscans who came to New Mexico were not saints. Some were unworthy of the habits they wore, while others were mere restless troublemakers. But their major failing as a group was their undue insistence upon the privileges and immunities of their clerical status. Although the clergy were frequently correct in vigorously maintaining their position of defending the Indians and criticizing the abuses of the Spanish officials and settlers, there is ample evidence to indicate that the Franciscans were unduly sensitive concerning trivial matters and were frequently not only involved in, but started, quarrels for no good reason.[11]

Violent name-calling, plotting, slander, and petty treachery can be understood when engaged in by lay officials, many of whom were soldiers, even if such conduct cannot be justified. When clerics, especially those belonging to the Franciscan order, engaged in similar practices, it can be neither understood nor justified.

To a certain extent, the struggle for political supremacy between the clergy and the governor could be classed as an economic conflict. Many times the Indians whom the governor or the Spanish settlers wanted to use for their own purposes were kept busy by the missionaries. As long as the natives were employed building churches or engaged in the immediate support of them, there was little cause

---

[10] France V. Scholes, "Church and State in New Mexico, 1610–1650," *NMHR*, Vol. XI (January–October, 1936). Also Vol. XII (January, 1937) and Vol. XI (July, 1936), 324.

[11] *Ibid.*, Vol. XI (April, 1936), 165.

for complaint. The settlers noted, however, that most of the natives' time was employed attending the herds and flocks owned by the clergy, tilling their fields, or in some other activity that would benefit the clergy. The Franciscans were accused of becoming rich, even by New Mexico's standards of the day. Their control of the mission supply system made it possible for the clergy to get their raw material to Mexican markets and import finished articles, some of which could be classified as luxury items.

Justifying their employing the natives in non-spiritual capacities, the Franciscans stressed that whatever wealth they accumulated was utilized in improving the work of the kingdom of God, principally by beautifying the places of worship. The possession of large herds and flocks was defended as necessary to protect the natives in time of drought. Naturally, such a long-range view was not readily acceptable to the settler who found his pasture increasingly infringed upon by mission livestock, nor did the Spanish laity recognize the fact that the Franciscans were not living lives of luxury as a result of the riches they were able to amass.

The quarrel between church and state began in the first administration, about 1610, and grew in intensity until it verged on civil war by 1650. After that date it continued, but with less danger to the Spaniards than before. The extent of the conflict varied greatly, depending upon the character of the governor and the particular friar who was the supervisor of the Franciscans, there being no secular clergy in New Mexico.

Governor Peralta, whose administration began in 1609, was an able administrator and did his best to moderate some of the abuses in the treatment of the Indians. But the Spaniards had to eat, and as a result the Indians were frequently placed upon the most meager rations. The labor of the Indians was also forced, to enable the Governor to build the necessary structures in the new capital at Santa Fe.

Taking charge of the missions in 1612 was Friar Ordóñez. An arrogant and intolerant man, Ordóñez was convinced that all civil authority must be under himself. He was so disliked by even his own friars that one of them reported that his original credentials were forgeries. In any event, Ordóñez presented to Governor Peralta an order from the viceroy permitting the departure of all soldiers and

68

colonists who wanted to return to New Spain. Such a step doubtless weakened New Mexico, and this order is believed by many to have been likewise a forgery.

Ordóñez took every opportunity to interfere with the civil functions of the Governor, and when Peralta insisted on conducting the duties of his office, he was excommunicated. In July, 1613, the Governor took a shot at Ordóñez (he missed). Anyone who attempted to defend the position of Peralta was liable to excommunication. The situation becoming intolerable, Peralta determined to go in person to Mexico, but en route he was arrested by Ordóñez, who invoked the authority of the Inquisition. The many bitter accusations the clergyman sent his superiors in Mexico City led to the replacement of both Ordóñez and Peralta.

By 1618, the population of New Mexico was perhaps at its lowest point. Conditions were not helped by the appointment as governor of Juan de Eulate. The new leader had been a military official who had seen service in the campaigns in Flanders and was notorious for his tactlessness and his irreverence. Like his predecessors, he looked upon his appointment as a reward for previous services and an opportunity for personal profit. Unlike them, his contempt for not only the church officials but for everything about the church, including its ceremonies, was most flagrant. He abused and insulted the friars at every opportunity and refused to encourage their missionary efforts. Of course, it is always questionable whether the governors were as bad as they were depicted, as most of the charges were registered by the clergy.[12]

A new governor, Felipe de Sotelo, who took office in 1625, was an entirely different type of person. He did have difficulty with part of the population, but there was a brief truce in the struggle between the executive and the clergy. Credit for this doubtless rests with the character of the new clerical leader, Friar Alonso de Benavides. Benavides was not only an accomplished scholar who wrote one of the finest reports on colonial New Mexico,[13] he was also an able administrator who was dedicated to the mission work. He was too busy traveling, inspecting the already established missions, and

12 *Ibid.*, Vol. XI (April, 1936), 146–47.
13 See note 14 in Chapter II above.

aiding in the development of new fields to be concerned about the trivial questions that too many of his fellows were to take up during the century. It was unfortunate that there could not have been available more clerical leaders of his caliber.

There followed a series of governors, most of whom were accused of forcing the Indians to work for them and of engaging in illegal trade. Luis de Rosas, governor from 1637 to 1641, is described as one of the most interesting of all the men who ruled New Mexico in the seventeenth century. Another vigorous, two-fisted soldier type, Rosas was ill suited for the kind of civilian administration necessary in New Mexico.[14]

Rosas got into trouble with the clergy from the very beginning of his term when he refused to use the *residencia* of his predecessor as a means of proving the opinions of the clergy. His enemies were later to claim that he accepted a bribe, which was not unlikely. Apparently a better businessman than some of his predecessors. Rosas virtually acquired a monopoly of the trade of the province and compelled most of the Indians to work for him.

The usual charges and countercharges made their way southward to Mexico City, with both factions claiming to be right. Unfortunately, there was to be more than words hurled in this controversy. A showdown occurred when one of the Governor's friends, a Sebastián de Sandoval, was assassinated, two friars being implicated. When a clergyman permitted Sandoval to be buried in holy ground, he was arrested by the Inquisition and held until the governor forcibly rescued him.

The clergy were able to obtain the support of some of the soldiers who disliked Rosas' arbitrary administration. This faction fortified themselves at the clerical headquarters at Santo Domingo and openly challenged the Governor. The cold war continued for over a year, with both sides dispatching the usual accusations to the authorities in Mexico City, and awaiting results. In the spring of 1641, both Governor Rosas and the clerical official were removed from office. But the Inquisitor conducting the investigation took only evidence to justify the clerical position, so Rosas appeared in a sorry position. Although the incoming governor soon died, the anti-Rosas group

14 *Ibid.*, Vol. XI (October, 1936), 297.

was in complete control in Santa Fe. Finally, one of Rosas' enemies, named Ortiz, charged Rosas with intimacies with his wife and led a group which assassinated Rosas. The charges were doubtless fabricated for the purpose.

Engaging in wordy conflicts was one thing; assassinating the king's former governor was something else again. Echoes of the conflict in New Mexico soon reached all the way to Madrid, and orders were given that the affair he promptly investigated. A new governor, Alonso Pacheco, reached Santa Fe in the fall of 1642. He had secret instructions to punish those guilty of the murder of Rosas and sufficient authority to get to the root of the trouble.

At first the new governor was friendly with all of the various factions. Apparently this was only until he had been able to gather the necessary evidence. Finally, in July of 1643, he executed eight soldiers who had been ringleaders in the preceding revolt. A general amnesty to the minor offenders made it possible for the Governor to gather full information on the plot. The alienation of the clergy that resulted from such extreme measures was intensified when Pacheco insisted upon the interment of Sandoval in the church cemetery. So ended the Rosas conflict, which narrowly missed resulting in civil war.

A succession of governors in the 1640's and 1650's continued the struggle. As a result, many of the Pueblo Indians became increasingly dissatisfied, some even deserting for a time and joining the Apaches. Peace reigned from 1656 to 1659 primarily because the Franciscan *custodio*, Friar Thomas Manso, had his brother appointed governor. Perhaps the authorities at Mexico City had arranged this to spare themselves the virulent dispatches that were regularly coming from Santa Fe.

The conflict was renewed in 1659 when the new governor, Bernardo López de Mendizábal, and the new head of the Franciscans, Friar Juan Ramírez, were appointed. Each of these men was talented, hotheaded, and convinced that his own particular side was right. The two men had come to New Mexico in the same supply train and had begun their wrangling over authority en route. During the trip, ten new friars, seeing what was before them, decided to return home.

The new governor got off on the wrong foot by arresting Manso, the former governor, who had many friends in the colony, especially among the clergy. The usual charges were made against Mendizábal, accusing him of maltreatment of the Indians; apparently he was an able businessman who had most of the pueblos working in his business enterprises. In addition, he was accused of being irreligious and of showing disrespect for the church.

Mendizábal died before the full hearing could be completed before the Inquisition, but the case against his wife, Doña Teresa, was continued, and its discussion shows the depth to which the clergy were prepared to go to make a case against their adversaries.

Doña Teresa was accused of Jewish inclinations because of her custom of bathing and changing linen on Fridays. In addition, she had the horrible habit of primping on Saturdays, as if specially celebrating that day "which the dead law of Moses orders to be observed." Special emphasis was placed on the fact that the Governor and his wife liked to sleep alone in their bedrooms. One of the most significant charges against Doña Teresa was that she read a book in a foreign tongue, and was even heard to laugh as she did so. The book in question was Ariosto's *Orlando Furioso*. The Governor's lady had been reared in Italy, had learned the Italian language, and delighted in reading works in it.

In her defense before the Inquisition, Doña Teresa prepared a lengthy document which answered the various charges leveled against her. So effective was her defense that it greatly strengthened her case. But for the historian she laid bare the details of life and society in New Mexico in the mid-seventeenth century. She mentioned by name more than seventy-five persons and gave reasons why they were her enemies. She discussed the local jealousies, the petty crimes, the carousing activities of many citizens, with considerable emphasis upon their marital infidelities. If Doña Teresa's account is accurate, life in Santa Fe, especially in the governor's palace, must have been most turbulent and trying.[15]

The next governor was to be easily the most controversial man of the century, Don Diego de Peñalosa, whose administration lasted

[15] France V. Scholes, "Troublous Times in New Mexico, 1659–1670," *NMHR*, Vol. XII (April, 1937; October, 1937), Vol. XV (October, 1940), 381–85.

from 1661 to 1664. Endowed with unlimited confidence in his own ability and possessing an attractive personality, he had held several posts in New Spain before his appointment as governor. It is alleged that he was a fugitive from justice from Peru.

What is important here is that the struggle with the clergy was renewed by him. He probably profited personally from the sale of his predecessor's property as well as trying to engage in as much trade as he could. The breach with the clergy came into the open when he arrested Posada, who was the *custodia* as well as the Inquisitor of New Mexico. As he got into more difficulty, Peñalosa sought to improve his position by presenting the story of an expedition to Quivira, which he represented himself as having made, but it probably was one of Oñate's accounts.

Ultimately, Peñalosa was convicted by the Inquisition, forced to do penance in Mexico City, and then banished from New Spain. In an effort to get even with the Spanish authorities, he tried to interest the English in a scheme to capture New Mexico. When that was unsuccessful, he went to France. The stories that he told Louis XIV may have been a factor in launching the explorations by La Salle.

The long period of controversy between the clergy and the governor had undermined Spanish authority among the natives. Unrest among the pueblos was common during the middle years of the century and increased in intensity. This restlessness was undoubtedly made worse by the raids of the Apaches, who became more daring as the Spaniards failed to punish their aggressions. The stage was being set for an effort on the part of the Indians to drive the hated white men out of New Mexico.

The Pueblo Revolt

By 1680, the Spanish population of New Mexico was estimated to be 2,800, which was concentrated along the upper Río Grande or its tributaries. The number of Christianized natives living in the various pueblos is usually set at 16,000,[16] whose spiritual needs were admin-

[16] One authority puts this figure as high as 35,000. José Manuel Espinosa, *Crusaders of the Río Grande*, 19.

istered by thirty-two Franciscans. Few in numbers, the white population was at the mercy of the Indians in the event there was any concerted effort to drive them from the province. Between 1645 and 1675 there were many uprisings of restless natives, all of which were put down rather easily but not without considerable bloodshed, which increased the already existing antagonism toward the oppressors.

The weakness of these sporadic outbursts on the part of the Pueblo Indians convinced the Spaniards that the natives were incapable of co-operating in an all-out assault against them. In this respect, the Spaniards had long been favored by the antipathy of one pueblo for another, as well as the conflict between the nomadic and sedentary Indians. But it was recognized by some that Spain's authority in New Mexico had reached desperate straits. Slowly but surely the Indians had become bolder in their challenges to Spanish rule. Such daring increased as a result of drought and famine and the continual depredations by the Apaches. Friar Ayeta asked of the crown in 1675 that steps be taken at once to strengthen the military defense of the province. He requested fifty additional soldiers and a requisite amount of equipment for the purpose.[17]

Many early historians of New Mexico have claimed that the immediate cause of the native uprising in 1680 was resentment of the Indians over having to work in the Spanish mines. One of them even repeats a legendary tale that the caving in of the shaft of a silver mine which buried alive a large number of Indians was "the last straw" which precipitated the revolt.[18] If there was any mining at all in the province in 1680, it was on such a small scale that it could have had little to do with the uprising. The fact that forced labor in the mines had created so much Indian unrest in other parts of Spanish America doubtless accounts for the desire to blame the 1680 uprising upon it.

It is never possible for the historian to fix the cause of major occurrences with absolute certainty. Rather, significant upheavals in history are the outgrowth of various, and sometimes contradictory, events. The revolt of the Pueblo Indians of New Mexico was a result of a growing antagonism toward the totality of Spanish rule. The

17 Scholes, "The Mission Supply Service," *NMHR*, Vol. V, 401–402.
18 L. B. Prince, *Concise History of New Mexico*, 110.

fact that it was brewing for fourteen years before it broke out and was carefully planned for five years immediately prior to 1680 is sufficent indication of the long-range forces at work.[19]

To a large extent, the control of such a small number of Spaniards over the more numerous Pueblos was a result of several factors: need for protection from hostile tribes, fear of or respect for the religion of the Spaniards, the existence of a food supply in time of need, and fear of what the Spanish military force would do to them if they failed to comply. Hence, the effectiveness of Spanish rule depended upon internal harmony within the colony so that these factors which held the natives in check would always be present. "Seventy years of controversy had made the province a house divided against itself," and reconciliation came too late to save the house.[20] In the factional dispute between church and state, the natives found themselves in a position similar to that of a child who lacks direction because his parents cannot make up their minds about the policy that should be followed. The constant bickering made impossible any intelligent or long-range plan so far as the natives were concerned. Policies started by the governor were countermanded by the clergy, and vice versa. Natives treated to the spectacle of clergymen berating the Spanish political authorities ended by losing respect for both. The dread of Spanish arms slowly faded and, unfortunately, respect for the religion of the Spaniards likewise diminished.

Even if one assumes that the Spanish administration of the province was completely harmonious throughout the seventeenth century, it is still possible that the Indians would have risen against their white masters. For the real cause derived from a basic antagonism on the part of the natives toward the Europeans' attempt to force them to adopt an entirely new civilization. As has been pointed out, religion was so important to the Pueblo Indians that the shamans or medi-

[19] See Charles W. Hackett, ed., *Revolt of the Pueblo Indians of New Mexico;* by the same author, "The Revolt of the Pueblo Indians of New Mexico in 1680," *Texas State Historical Quarterly,* Vol. XV (October, 1911) (hereafter referred to as Hackett, "Revolt of the Pueblo Indians") and "Retreat of the Spaniards from New Mexico in 1680, and Beginnings of El Paso," *Southwestern Historical Quarterly,* Vol. XVI (October, 1912).

[20] Scholes, "Troublous Times," *NMHR,* Vol. XVI (October, 1941), 327.

cine men virtually regulated their institutional life.[21] Despite vigorous efforts, the Spaniards were unable to eradicate the tendency of the Pueblos to cling to their heathen religious practices. Natives had been hanged, flogged, and tortured in an effort to stamp out such practices, but to no avail. The influence of the old ways, especially the power of the medicine man, continued. It is quite clear that so far as the religion of many natives was concerned, the beliefs, practices, and ritual of Christianity had simply been superimposed upon the existing faith. Later investigations have agreed that the primary reason for the uprising was religious resentment.[22]

Not to be overlooked as a cause of the revolt was the force of a dynamic personality embodied in the Indian Popé, a medicine man from San Juan. He apparently fancied himself as the man who could unite all of the Indians against the Spaniards. Undoubtedly, some of his contacts with the white men, perhaps while a prisoner, aided him in formulating an over-all plan which would gain the adherence of the superstitious natives. The planning was definitely that of a Caucasion and perhaps was suggested by Popé's understanding of Spanish tactics.

Forced to flee to Taos because it was more remote from Spanish control at Santa Fe, Popé claimed a divine message from three infernal spirits. It was one of these divine messengers who suggested the knotted rope to represent the number of days before the revolt.

For five years this cagey Indian leader laid his plans. A series of secret meetings of the chiefs and medicine men of the northern Pueblos was held, with the planning being entrusted only to the most important leaders. Tradition has it that Popé murdered his own son-in-law, fearing that he intended to betray the plotters to the Spaniards. The plans called for all of the Indians to arise at an agreed-upon time, to seize the arms of the unsuspecting white men, and kill every one of them, only sparing the more attractive young women. Escape was to be blocked by an Indian force which would cut off anyone fleeing southward along the Río Grande. Plans were made for the Mansos Indians in the El Paso area to slaughter any Spaniards

<hr />

[21] See page 26 above.

[22] Bancroft, *Arizona and New Mexico,* 174; Hackett, "Revolt of the Pueblo Indians," 98.

that might escape that far. Finally, the Indians planned to completely eradicate all evidences of the presence of the hated Pale Faces by destroying the churches, the buildings the Spaniards had built, and other trappings of the white man's civilization.

August 13, 1680, was the date agreed upon for the simultaneous uprising of the Pueblo Indians, who were to be joined by their hereditary enemies, the Apaches.[23] The knotted cord was circulated among the Indians with each knot representing a day remaining before the time of attack.[24]

The Spaniards learned of the plot on August 9 through three different sources—one of them the confession of a friendly Indian,[25] another, messages from friendly Indian chiefs, and a third, the capture of two messengers who confessed the projected revolt.[26] Unfortunately for the Spaniards, they had heard the cry of "wolf" too many times. The extent of the native uprising was not recognized in time for proper safeguards to be taken, and Governor Otermín wasted precious time when he might have been able to check the revolt before it was under way. It was not until the twelfth of August that the gravity of the situation was realized and steps were taken to issue warnings.

Meanwhile, with the capture of his messengers, Popé ordered the revolt to begin at once, and the first hostilities did occur on August 9. How so many events could have transpired on one day and messages could have been sent from Santa Fe to Taos fast enough to prompt action on the same day is not clear. It is known that the Indians used relay runners to carry news from one pueblo to another. More likely, however, would be the use of prearranged smoke sig-

[23] Though many have questioned whether the Apaches were originally a party to the uprising, there is no question that the Pueblos had the support of at least one Athapascan group in the planning of the revolt. See Forbes, *Apache, Navaho, and Spaniard*, 178.

[24] Some authorities claim that Popé's messengers carried two knotted cords, one to indicate whether or not the pueblo would participate in the uprising or preferred to remain neutral. See Hallenbeck, *Land of Conquistadores*, 146. Hackett discounts this theory and contends that smoke signals were to be used to commit a Pueblo to the attack ("Revolt of the Pueblo Indians," 104).

[25] Ettie Miriam Healey, "The New Mexico Missions in the Middle Eighteenth Century" (M.A. thesis, University of California, Berkeley, 1922), 13.

[26] Hackett, "Revolt of the Pueblo Indians," 132.

nals, this being the most plausible explanation of the ability of the natives to strike so quickly after their plans were revealed.[27]

By the time the Governor did act, most of the destruction had already occurred. From Taos to Isleta, with the exception of Santa Fe, the countryside was devastated and depopulated. The *estancias* and haciendas, once the homes of prosperous Spanish settlers, had been completely destroyed and the inhabitants mostly murdered. A total of approximately 400 Spanish men, women, and children were killed, including clerics. Only a few settlers were warned in time to make their way to the safety of Santa Fe. Some of the messengers dispatched by the Governor to warn the people were themselves slain.

Finally realizing the seriousness of the revolt as the reports of his scouts filtered in, along with intelligence from friendly Indians, Otermín prepared the defense of Santa Fe. The citizens were concentrated in a fortified section of the town and the supply of weapons distributed among the able-bodied men. There were probably about 1,000 Spaniards in Santa Fe at this time, of whom about 150 were capable of military service.

The siege of Santa Fe began the morning of August 15 when the first detachment of the Indians arrived. An integral part of Popé's plan was for all of the tribes of the northern pueblos to concentrate at Santa Fe after completing the chores of destruction in their assigned areas. Thus, they could all be together for the final extermination of the hated white man. The natives informed Otermín that all the Spaniards except those at Santa Fe had been killed and offered him the alternative of choosing a red cross or a white cross. If he accepted the white one, the Spaniards would be permitted to depart in peace; but if he accepted the red one, there would be war to the end. The Governor ignored the ultimatum.

The siege continued, with the Spaniards concentrated in the royal buildings and the natives firing the outlying houses. On the nineteenth the Indians were able to cut off the water supply, thereby making the position of the Spaniards untenable. On the morning of the twentieth Otermín led a force of about 100 men in an attack upon the savages, and claimed to have killed 300 of them, with a loss of

[27] Hallenbeck, *Land of Conquistadores*, 147.

only five from his ranks. Considering the fact that 100 Spaniards were fighting 3,000 Indians, this constitutes a major victory.

From captives in this battle, the governor was able to discover the full extent of the uprising, as well as the fact that a large number of refugees were gathered at Isleta. This prompted the withdrawal from Santa Fe on August 21, the survivors, numbering just over 1,000, taking only what few personal effects they could carry, since there were not enough horses to carry many supplies. As they left, the Spaniards expected to be attacked momentarily. However, remembering their encounter the day before, the Indians were ready to let them go in peace.

While Otermín and the refugees from Santa Fe were making their way slowly southward, another body of Spaniards was attempting to meet the problem presented by the Indian revolt as best they could. On the twelfth of August, the Governor had ordered Lieutenant-Governor García, stationed at Isleta with approximately 40 soldiers, to come to the aid of Santa Fe. García never received the message, and if he had, he would have been unable to carry it out. The small Spanish garrison kept the Indians at Isleta from joining the revolt and made this pueblo a center of refuge for survivors fortunate enough to reach it.

When the revolt began García was forced to act on his own. Attempts to communicate with Santa Fe having failed, he sent a small force up the Río Grande and rescued many Spaniards who had been able to escape the initial attack. In addition, this group was able to get news of the pillage and destruction which had been caused by the depredations of the native warriors. A total of about 1,500 Spaniards soon reached the safety of Isleta.

On the fourteenth, Garcia called a meeting of the Spanish settlers, soldiers, and missionaries to help him decide what should be done. They believed themselves to be the only Spaniards alive in the province, for not until August 20 did refugees from Taos report that fighting was still going on at Santa Fe. With only eight days' supplies for 1,500 people, short of munitions and with the Indians at Isleta becoming restless, the group decided to retreat down the river until they met the mission caravan.[28] It was García's intent to use this shipment of supplies to refit his forces. Then, after providing a place of refuge for the women and children, he planned to return northward to search for whatever Spaniards might still be alive. In spite of later charges of desertion against him, the decision was wise.

It was not until September 3 that the Governor and the refugees from Santa Fe reached Isleta. There they learned for the first time that a large number of Spaniards under García were very much alive, and the Governor sent a messenger after them. The lieutenant-governor promptly returned to meet Otermín, who first accused him of desertion but finally admitted that his decision to leave had been proper. On September 13 the two refugee groups were joined and totaled 2,520. Fortunately for the refugees, the mission supply wagons they met carried enough food to prevent absolute starvation.

The expatriates finally made their way to a place near the present city of El Paso, thus managing to retain a toe-hold in New Mexico. Within a matter of only a few days the work of almost a century in New Mexico was lost. The treasure that Spain had spent to hold the territory and to convert the Indians was wasted. More important, the efforts of countless clergymen to carry on their work was lost, and those who had tried to settle the inhospitable land had been stripped of their personal possessions.

The extent of the Spanish setback is difficult to assess. It was natural for the authorities to want to depreciate the losses because they would be held responsible. Hence, the figure of 400 slain may be in error. Although it was claimed that the two parties of refugees originally totaled 2,500, when Otermín again counted them, there were only 1,936 refugees. This total included some 317 Indians, the latter having fled with the Spaniards. Of this group only 155 were men capable of bearing arms. The obvious question is, what happened to the rest of the party? It is possible that they simply fled southward for safer places in northern Mexico or perhaps they died between the two counts or even the first accounting could have been in error.[29] Actually, the full story will never be known.

[28] Hackett, "Revolt of the Pueblo Indians," 146–47.
[29] Hackett, "Retreat of the Spaniards," *Southwestern Historical Quarterly*, Vol. XVI (October, 1912), 268–69.

V - Spanish Rule

AT THE END OF 1680, the Pueblo Indians of New Mexico were free of their Spanish masters. The remnants of what had once been Spain's settlers in her northernmost province were now huddled together near the modern city of El Paso, awaiting an opportunity to escape to the more pleasant regions to the south or to return to their former homes to the north. As the region they occupied was possibly a part of the province, it is inaccurate to conclude that the natives had been able to drive the Spaniards completely out of New Mexico. Instead they had only forced them from the Pueblo Indian country.

Although the Spaniards had lost a battle, they had no intention of giving up the war. Even if the province had been a constant drain upon the royal treasury and a source of constant bickering and conflict between royal officials and clergy, even if it had failed to contribute to the coffers of the Spanish crown, the officials at Madrid had no intention of leaving the Indians in charge. That they did not can be accounted for largely on the basis of their interest in saving the souls of the converted Indians who were left behind. Consigning these well-meaning aborigines to hell-fire and damnation through no fault of their own was something which the Spanish crown was not prepared to do. Less altruistic motives for the decision to regain all of New Mexico can be found in the continual fear that France might move into the political vacuum of an unoccupied New Mexico, and from such a vantage point threaten the safety of New Spain itself, as well as Spanish possession of all of the lands westward to the Pacific. Then, too, the blow to Spanish pride as a result of such a setback could not be tolerated. Finally, the fact that many strong individuals among both clergy and laity were desirous of regaining the lost province undoubtedly influenced the decision of Madrid to renew the struggle for control of New Mexico.

The Reconquest

It was, however, to be some thirteen years before the reconquest of the upper Río Grande area was to be accomplished. Actually, Governor Otermín had seriously considered returning to Santa Fe as soon as the women and children in his group had been safely settled. The council which Otermín had called decided that the condition of the horses, the lack of munitions, and the fatigue of the men precluded any immediate attempt at reconquest in October of 1680. The decision was to postpone the return, and it did not imply a surrender of the northern area to the savages.[1]

An attempt was made to keep together the Spanish fugitives from New Mexico, including some 1,946 soldiers, servants, women, children, and Indian allies, in the expectation that they would soon be returning to their former homes. Their place of refuge, the first real Spanish settlement in the area, was located at San Lorenzo, near present El Paso. Crop failures, continual raids by hostile Indians, and fading hopes that there would soon be a return northward rapidly decimated the group, and by 1684 the total population had been reduced to 1,030.[2] Nevertheless, the settlement survived, and was ultimately to furnish the nucleus that would resettle the Santa Fe area. The length of time it was to take to return to the abandoned

[1] Hackett, "Retreat of the Spaniards from New Mexico," *Southwestern Historical Quarterly*, Vol. XVI (October, 1912) 269–70. See also Anne E. Hughes, "The Beginnings of Spanish Settlement in the El Paso Area," University of California *Publications in History*, I, and Vina Walz, "History of the El Paso Area" (Ph.D. dissertation, University of New Mexico, 1951).

[2] Espinosa, *Crusaders of the Rio Grande*, 20. This is the most scholarly work on the reconquest, but of considerable value also are Clara E. Kyle, "The Reconquest of New Mexico, 1680–1698" (M.A. thesis, University of California, Berkeley, 1924), and Jessie Bromilow Bailey, *Diego de Vargas and the Reconquest of New Mexico*.

areas of the province gradually gave to San Lorenzo a permanence ultimately recognized by the crown.

The initial effort to return Spanish rule to the Santa Fe area was made by Governor Otermín. The expedition, which got under way on November 5, 1681, was composed of 146 soldiers and 112 Indian allies, with a large number of horses, carts, and mules. On the third day out from El Paso, a halt was called in order to make a careful inventory of men, arms, horses, and supplies. This had not been possible earlier because men were continually deserting.[3] Perhaps Otermín was interested in recording the information in order to stress the weakness of his forces, thereby giving himself an excuse for the failure of his projected mission even as it was under way.

The entire venture turned out to be a dismal failure. Sent out ahead as an advance group was a party led by Juan Domingo de Mendoza. This officer took a short period of time to visit several pueblos, burning them and destroying their food supply, which the Spaniards could have used. Unfortunately for the Spaniards, when Mendoza faced a large group of warriors ready for battle, he accepted their protestations of repentance and permitted them to go free. Had he been firmer in dealing with this group, the entire reconquest may have been quickly consummated.

Wherever the Spaniards went, they promised pardons for those Indians who would repent of their sins and promise to abide by Spanish rule. There is little question that many Indians accepted such amnesty only awaiting the opportunity to turn against the Spaniards. Both Mendoza and Otermín apparently were more interested in surveying the damage of the uprising and making copious reports on it than they were in subduing the Indians. At any rate, they decided to return southward at the earliest possible opportunity. One of Otermín's officers argued that the food destroyed could have fed the Spaniards all winter and that both of his superiors really did not want to fight. It was contended that twenty Spaniards were the equal of a thousand Indians anyway. Regardless of the reason, Otermín abandoned the northern country and retreated southward in late December, 1681. Because the Indians of the Isleta Pueblo had been

[3] Hughes, *Beginnings of Spanish Settlement*, 315.

83

the first to accept the return of the Spaniards, they feared reprisals: therefore, they petitioned for the right to accompany the Spaniards on their retreat, some 385 of them making the journey.[4]

During the period of the El Paso settlements and the exile from northern lands, governors of New Mexico were regularly appointed. Domingo Jironza Petriz de Cruzate succeeded Otermín as governor in 1683 and until 1689 retained the office, except for a short period of suspension, perhaps 1686 to 1688, when Pedro Reneros Posada was governor. Most of the time of these administrators was taken with repelling the Indians preying upon the El Paso settlements and administering the problems thereof. Apparently, little opportunity was left to plan the return to Santa Fe. In 1688, Cruzate did lead a small force northward and fought the Indians at Zía Pueblo. Though outnumbered about ten to one, the Spaniards sacked and burned this pueblo, killing an estimated six hundred natives and taking some seventy more prisoners to be sold as slaves. The harsh defeat inflicted upon the Indians here lessened their ardor for fighting the Spaniards and later made easier the task of Governor Vargas.

Don Diego de Vargas, the hero of the reconquest of the pueblo country, was the scion of an illustrious Spanish family distinguished by centuries of service to both church and crown. In many respects, Vargas represented the noblest ideal of the medieval Spanish knight. In him were embodied the religious fervor of Spain's reconquest of the peninsula against the Moors, the desire to do valorous deeds on the field of battle so as to be worthy of his knightly calling, and an unbelievable energy and strength of character. His courage was so great that at times it verged on the foolhardy. In his dealing with the New Mexican natives, he was at one and the same time a suave diplomat, a decisive military leader, and a resourceful and experienced campaigner. Though always ready to fight, Vargas preferred to win his point by diplomacy. Unfortunately, this man was also to be capable of implacable cruelty toward the Indians, a trait that was to prove costly to the Spaniards in the long run. Even with this failing, Don Diego de Vargas deserves to rank with Coronado as one of the noblest Spaniards in the history of New Mexico.

[4] Most accounts give the number of Indians at Isleta at this time as 1,511, but there is a good possibility that there were less than 500.

With all of these qualifications went the added one of a considerable family fortune, most of which was to be spent in the ensuing
campaign for the control of the lost province. This wealth, added
to his previous experience in various capacities on the frontier, made
Vargas an excellent choice for the difficult task ahead. Appointed
governor and captain-general in 1688, Vargas did not arrive at El
Paso to take up his duties until February 22, 1691.

The enthusiasm that he brought to the task was necessary, for he
was immediately to encounter many setbacks. He discovered the El
Paso colony in deplorable condition. Plagued by unfortunate weather, the continual raids of hostile Indians, and frequent desertions
from their numbers, the group was in no condition to return to
Santa Fe. Those who were eager to reclaim their former lands to
the north lacked sufficient money and equipment to prepare for the
expedition. The new governor was forced to spend lavishly to obtain
the necessary supplies, as well as to recruit soldiers and settlers, before he was prepared to depart.

Impatient to be on with the difficult task and desirous of winning
laurels on the field of battle, Vargas set out from El Paso on August
21, 1692, with a small force of only sixty Spaniards and one hundred
Indians. He left instructions for a detachment of fifty additional
men to join him as soon as possible. When one considers that he was
entering an area populated by twenty-five to thirty thousand Indians,
it was obvious that his force was not excessive for the task at hand.

The Governor's strategy was planned so as to use his small force
with maximum effectiveness. On reaching the pueblos, the Spaniards
intended to lay siege, preventing the escape of any of the inhabitants.
Orders were given that no one should open fire on the Indians without Vargas' express orders. The Governor was then to have everyone sing praises to the Blessed Virgin five times. Next, the missionaries would try to persuade the Indians to re-enter the fold of the
church and again become vassals of the Spanish crown. Should the
Indians accept, the priests would absolve the people of their sins and
baptize the children who had been born since the missionaries had
left. It was hoped that if this tactic worked at one pueblo and that
if the Indians would accept the pardon offered, others would quickly
follow suit and the conquest would be a bloodless one. However,

Vargas was prepared to attack the besieged pueblos and use whatever force might be necessary.[5]

This bold campaign was aided by conditions among the Indians themselves, who discovered that almost a century of Spanish rule could not be as easily obliterated as they had thought. One might destroy the outward trappings of Christianity, but many of the teachings of the friars lingered, and many Indians found it difficult to return to their previous savage state. Then, too, Popé had so copied the ways of the white man that he fancied himself the absolute sovereign of all of the pueblos. At first he had been followed willingly in the flush of excitement after the ouster of the Spaniards, but it was soon discovered that his arbitrary and oppressive rule was even worse than that of the white man. He wreaked vengeance upon those who would not obey his every whim, exacted a heavy tribute for himself and his followers, and even selected the most beautiful women for his pleasure.

The spirit of co-operation manifested by the Indians in the 1680 uprising disintegrated once the Spaniards, the common foe, were no longer on the scene. By 1692 the Pueblo Indians had divided into several factions. The neighboring Apache tribes were also divided, with some groups allied with the various Pueblo divisions. It was usual for these splinter factions to be at war with one another. By moving swiftly, Vargas was able to reconquer most of the province before the Indians could again unite.[6]

Finding the pueblos along the Río Grande abandoned, the Indians having fled, Vargas and his party continued to Santa Fe. Arriving after dark before the town, now occupied by Tano Indians, who preferred the white man's former habitation to their own pueblos, the Spaniards had a difficult time convincing the natives that they were truly who they claimed to be. After lengthy and involved negotiations that could easily have erupted into hostilities with disastrous results for the Spaniards, Vargas was finally able to convince the Indians that it would be wiser to submit than fight. Perhaps the

[5] Espinosa, *Diego de Vargas*, 25–30.

[6] Bancroft, *Arizona and New Mexico*, 184–86; Forbes, *Apache, Navaho, and Spaniard*, 237–38.

display of the banner of the Blessed Virgin, the cross, and frequent invocations of the Blessed Spirit convinced the natives that the God of the white man was far more powerful than their own pagan deities. Vargas later confessed that he had given up hope of convincing the natives to surrender without a fight, and that if he had had the fifty additional soldiers (who were en route at the time), he would have attacked.[7] Such a move could have been disastrous and changed the whole course of the future campaign against the Indians.

Shortly after the victory at Santa Fe, Don Luis Tupatu, a former lieutenant of Popé and still one of the more influential Indian chieftains, arrived in Vargas' camp to offer his allegiance. His adherence to the Spanish cause was perhaps the decisive factor spelling success, for he not only raised a force of friendly Indians to aid the Spaniards, but brought much valuable intelligence about the other pueblos.

Having the initial advantage, Vargas was not one to lose it. In a vigorous four months' campaign he was able to restore twenty-three pueblos to Spain's empire and to the Christian fold. All of this was accomplished without wasting a single ounce of powder or unsheathing a sword. Some 2,214 Indians, mostly children, were baptized.

Accounting for this remarkable success was the very daring of Vargas in taking such a small group of men into hostile Indian country, especially that of the western pueblos, and by such action effectively intimidating the Indians. On several occasions some of the pueblos were prepared to rise against the Spaniards, but luck, fear of retaliation, and division among the Indians enabled Vargas to win all of them to the banner of Spain.

Having at least obtained the tacit submission of the pueblos, Vargas retraced his steps to El Paso to prepare for the actual colonization. After the usual delays, it was September, 1693, before some eight hundred settlers, a large number of livestock, and the necessary paraphernalia for settlement were gathered together and the expedition started northward. When they reached the upper Río Grande area, friendly Indians warned Vargas that preparations were being made to attack the settlers. In fact, since Vargas was to receive almost continual reports of such plotting, the Indians must have prepared

[7] Espinosa, *Crusaders of the Rio Grande*, 67.

many times for action, but their inability to co-operate with each other and, perhaps, their lack of competent leadership prevented them from taking the drastic step of an open assault.

The harshness of a Santa Fe winter and the lack of food finally forced matters to a showdown that led to conflict in December, 1693. The question was strictly one of survival. The Spaniards were dying of both hunger and privation and longed to occupy the more comfortable dwellings of Santa Fe. They looked upon the heathen occupants as usurpers and argued that Vargas waited too long in driving them out. As for the Pueblo Indians, who were not warlike by nature and disliked fighting if they could possibly avoid it, they found themselves in a position whereby the Spaniards were exacting most of their food from them and now were prepared to deprive them of what they considered their homes. Hence, the fighting was well-nigh inevitable.[8]

The battle was of short duration. As usual, the Spaniards were successful. Some eighty-one Indians perished as a result of the fight. Unfortunately, seventy of these were executed after they had surrendered. Some four hundred were seized as slaves. Thus, Vargas had fought his first battle for the reconquest of New Mexico and had won the fortified center at Santa Fe, the traditional capital.

It was, however, to be a dearly won victory. The harsh penalties meted out to the Indians who had surrendered convinced many of the pueblos that a like fate awaited them. A rumor circulated that the Spaniards planned to kill all of the Indian chiefs. As pueblo after pueblo arose to challenge Spanish rule, Vargas marched with rapidity from one to another during 1694, until the Indians had again been subdued. Two years of truce resulted, to be broken in 1696 when, probably driven by the desperation of famine, the Indians revolted once more. But again, Vargas, with his small army, was equal to the occasion and was able to quell the Pueblos so completely that they never again were to challenge Spanish rule effectively.

Once the Indians were pacified, the Spanish settlement took on a more permanent character. The small initial group was augmented by the arrival of perhaps 230 additional settlers in 1694. Slowly but

8 *Ibid.,* 156.

88

surely the numbers grew, and Spanish *estancias* and haciendas again made their appearance along the upper tributaries of the Río Grande. Livestock multiplied in number, but the colony was continually plagued by a lack of supplies and equipment. The extension of Spanish rule, as well as the re-establishment of mission stations, was halted during the uprising of 1696, only to be renewed after that conflict.

As for Governor Vargas himself, his reward for having spent most of his own fortune and having performed such valuable service to the crown was to receive the ingratitude frequently meted out to political servants of Spain. He was replaced by Don Pedro Cuberó in 1697. Vargas was the object of the usual accusations made against Spanish governors of the day: cruelty to the natives and engaging in commerce for his own enrichment. Ultimately, the man who had so valiantly reconquered New Mexico was cleared of these charges and reappointed for a second term as governor, only to die in 1704.

General Characteristics of the Eighteenth Century

The historian Bancroft claims that "from 1700 New Mexico settled down into that monotonously uneventful career of inert and non-progressive existence which sooner or later is to be noted in the history of every Hispano-American province."[9] Such an observation may be unfair, but it was certainly true that between the reconquest of Vargas and the entry of the Americans there was little of significance happening in the province. The seemingly uneventful existence of New Mexico during this period resulted more from its agrarian characteristic than from any intent of the Spanish crown. Remote from the main centers of population, the settlers were compelled to eke out an existence tilling the fields or tending their flocks. Such activities were in themselves uneventful, but it is questionable whether the gradual development of an agrarian society deserves to be termed non-progressive. Along with the gradual growth of the Spanish community, there was a similar slow but steady development

[9] Bancroft, *Arizona and New Mexico*, 225.

89

of the mission work among the natives. The story of eighteenth-century New Mexico, then, concerns these missions and the various threats to the Spanish settlements. The first of such threats was posed by the encroachments of the French; and perhaps of more significance in the long run were the almost continual raidings by the nomadic tribes, which increased as the century progressed.

The Missions

The Indian mission was a significant vehicle by which Spain sought to hold her outlying possessions.[10] Usually established at the sites of Indian pueblos, though not always, the missions were not only centers for keeping the natives within the church, but also a means by which they could be held under Spanish rule.

The center of all missions was the church. Frequently these were impressive structures, when one considers the wilderness in which they were found. All had the necessary equipment for the proper observance of the sacraments, such as altars for the celebration of mass, a vestibule for the confessional, and proper vestments for the friars, usually brought in from the old country. Some had well-executed statues, fine oil paintings, and even frescoes. On the other hand, the poverty of the area or the ravishes of the hostile natives sometimes reduced the church to a mere shed.

Each morning the bell was rung to call the people to prayers, instruction, or mass. Each had his designated place, with the married couples sitting together, the women being separated so as to prevent their gossiping. The girls were seated on the left side and the boys on the right. Careful preparations were made to see that all were in attendance and that proper order was kept.

One of the most vigorous criticisms leveled against the Franciscans during the eighteenth century concerned their failure to teach the Indians the Spanish language and their own inability to learn the native tongue. It was argued that this made it impossible for the Indians to understand religious instruction and the confessional.

[10] Herbert E. Bolton, *Wider Horizons of American History*, 118.

Authorities vary widely as to the extent of this deficiency, but more than likely few natives really understood Spanish. Another deficiency was failure to use the sermon as a means of instruction in the faith.

Supporting the missions economically were the surrounding fields. These differed in fertility and crops, depending upon the conditions of the soil and their location within the province. Normally they were irrigated in order to insure a good yield. Wheat, corn, and beans were the basic crops. Most friars tried to vary the fare of their charges by raising fruit, and numerous references are made by travelers of the period to the orchards of peaches and apricots. Cotton was likewise raised where the climate would permit. Each mission had its own flocks of sheep, and some had herds of cattle and hogs. Land, which the Indians were obligated to work, was set aside for the support of the clergy. Some authorities contend that the Indians performed this work voluntarily and gladly,[11] while others are of the opinion that the padres had great difficulty getting the Indians to assist them.[12] More than likely conditions varied, depending upon the particular friar and the particular pueblo.

The complaints of the missionaries about the continuation of pagan practices by the Indians indicated that the Franciscans were never able to instill completely in their charges an understanding of the basic tenets of Christianity. All attempts to eradicate the ancient dances, some of which shocked the taste of the clergy, failed. When one considers the fact that these friars were forced to live alone among the savages, removed from contact with their fellow Spaniards and, more important, their fellow clergymen, it is miraculous that they were as successful as they were. Frequently, the missions constituted little islands in the midst of a vast wilderness, cut off for long periods of time from contact with the outside world. It was not unusual for the priests to complain bitterly that they could not celebrate mass because the wine or the host was not available,

[11] Henry W. Kelly, "Franciscan Missions of New Mexico, 1740–1760," *NMHR*, Vol. XV (October, 1940), 65; also Vol. XVI.

[12] See Francisco Atanasio Dominguez, *The Missions of New Mexico, 1776*, trans. and ed. by Eleanor B. Adams and Fray Angelico Chavez. Also of interest is Ellie Miriam Healey, "The New Mexico Missions in the Middle Eighteenth Century."

shipments from civilization having failed. In 1776 twenty priests had to minister to 18,261 Indians, hardly an adequate number for the task at hand.[13]

Even assuming that the Franciscan missionaries of the eighteenth century had lost much of the ardor that had distinguished the work of earlier members of their order and that many looked upon assignment to New Mexico as an exile to a wilderness and only went about their duties perfunctorily, the clergy were still superior to the Spanish laity in talents, character, and respect for the duty to which they were called. The eighteenth century did not see a renewal of the open conflict that had marked relations between church and state during the preceding century, but there was still controversy. Perhaps the absence of open struggle is evidence that the Franciscans lacked the dynamic characteristics of an earlier day or that either of the two factions was so completely in control that there was no room for dispute. As during the preceding century, the work of conversion of the Indians was seriously hampered by continued maltreatment of them by the Spanish officials. The governor and most of his lieutenants looked upon their positions as an opportunity to improve their financial position, and, as native labor remained the only kind of economic wealth available, it was exploited. Many devices were contrived to compel the Indians to furnish hides, woven goods, and even livestock to the governor. One of the cruelest forms of exploitation was forcing the Indians to do a week's labor in Santa Fe. Having to come long distances, through all kinds of weather, they frequently underwent unbelievable hardships in order to fulfill this obligation.[14]

Considering the maltreatment of the natives by professing Christians, it is amazing that the clergy were as successful with their converts as they were. The only area in which the Franciscans could be accused of complete failure was their efforts to Christianize the nomadic Indians. Several attempts were made to lure these savages from their native haunts and to have them settle at some designated point, for it was believed that such tactics were necessary if they were to

[13] *Ibid.*, 217.
[14] Healey, "New Mexico Missions," 27; Kelly, "Franciscan Missions," *NMHR*, Vol. XV (1940), 74.

be controlled. Lack of success caused the Franciscans to lose enthusiasm for the project. However, the threat by the more dynamic Jesuit Order to move into the adjoining fields prompted them to continue their efforts. In fact, the Jesuits were warned that they would all be slain if they tried to invade the Moqui field because only Franciscans were welcome there.[15]

Franciscan efforts among the Navahos were to be a complete failure. At first some success was achieved because the friars brought gifts with them, and converts were gained (perhaps something like the "rice Christians" gained in China at a later date). The response of the Navahos to the sincere efforts of the clergy indicated the inability of the Indians to grasp the significance of the Christian religion. They replied to entreaties to come to the pueblo by saying "that they could not become Christians or stay in one place because they had been raised like deer, that they would give some of the children who were born to have water thrown upon them and that these as believers, might perhaps build pueblos and have a father, but that now they did not desire either fathers or pueblos."[16]

In spite of this significant failure, the Franciscan missions continued as outposts of Spanish civilization. Although their work was not spectacular, it was accomplished in days of untold difficulties, in spite of the indifference of the civil authorities and the indifference of the natives themselves, and, more significantly, in the face of frequent and costly raids by hostile Indians, a difficulty which became greater as the century progressed.

The Indian Threat

The eighteenth century did not witness an uprising of the scope of that of 1680,[17] although it was marked by the savage raids of the hostile nomadic tribes. In some respects, however, the problem was

[15] Healey, "New Mexico Missions," 25.

[16] Kelly, "Franciscan Missions," *NMHR*, Vol. XV (1940), 65.

[17] In 1705 the Spanish settlers were thrown into panic when a knotted cord was found at Zuñi. Many assumed that it heralded another attempt by the natives to drive them out. Helen Haines, *History of New Mexico from the Spanish Conquest to the Present Time, 1530–1890*, 112.

to be more difficult of solution because the Indians who attacked the Spaniards did not retire to their settlements to await retaliation. The nomadic Indians, mounted on swift horses, struck the Spanish settlements and missions, leaving death and destruction in their wake. They would then disappear into the vastness of surrounding New Mexico. An entirely new style of warfare had to be developed before they could be contained. Unfortunately, the Spanish forces in New Mexico lacked the necessary mobility to meet the challenge, few of the soldiers even having horses and the colony without leaders competent to handle the changed situation.

The cause of most of New Mexico's trouble during the eighteenth century was the Comanche migration southward. By 1706 this most warlike of all Plains tribes began driving the Apaches out of the northeastern part of the province. By 1746 the Comanches were undisputed masters of the eastern plains regions, having driven their hereditary enemies, the Apaches, westward and southward. Hence the Spaniards were forced to fight the Comanches and the Apaches, as well as the Utes and the Navahos on occasion.

The Comanches were either at war or at peace with the Spaniards in New Mexico depending upon which course was most advantageous to them at the time. Hardly a decade passed without their making a raid upon one of the Indian pueblos, Spanish *ranchos*, or even populous settlements. Though usually enemies, the Comanches could also be friends.[18] During their periods of good behavior they came to the Taos Fair bringing with them some of their loot in the form of livestock, Indian slaves, or other goods to be traded for Spanish wares.

When not trading with the Comanches, the Spaniards were engaged in trying to exterminate them. In 1717 an expedition led by Don Juan de Padellao handed the tribe a crushing defeat. A similar setback was meted out in 1747. A consistent campaign against the Comanches was difficult to conduct because many Spanish settlers desired periods of peace so that they could trade with them. In addition, it was not always certain who was responsible for the outrages supposedly committed by the Comanches, for the wily Apaches, along with other tribes, littered the trail with Comanche gear after

18 Dominguez, *Missions of New Mexico,* 252.

raiding the white settlements. Thus, it was not always clear which tribe was guilty. More important was the fact that the presence of the warlike Comanches in the Plains established an effective buffer between the Spanish hold in New Mexico and the French far to the east. Hence, a complete removal of this hostile tribe might not be in the best interest of Spain.

Once Louisiana had been transferred to Spanish ownership in 1762, this reason for not crushing the Comanches was removed. A change in policy was carried out with the threat of force combined with a proffer of peace. In 1779, Governor Juan Bautista de Anza led a combined Spanish and Indian-ally force against the Comanches, inflicting heavy damage upon them as well as killing their chief.[19] Efforts to convince the Comanches that they should forget their nomadic ways and settle down like the Pueblo Indians and be converted to Christianity were all failures. But the threat of force coupled with friendly overtures kept the Comanches friendly with New Mexico until the late nineteenth century. The Comancheros, the Spanish-speaking traders, were always free to come and go, even in the midst of the bloody campaigns against the Texans and the frontier settlements.[20]

The Apaches were more implacable enemies of the Spaniards than were the Comanches. The various tribes which made up this vast nation consistently raided the frontier settlements, killing or taking as many captives as possible, driving off livestock, and spreading fear and devastation wherever they rode. Their area of attack included the northern states of Mexico as well as the western part of the province. The rugged terrain they infested made it difficult for Spanish punitive expeditions to get at them. There were attempts on the part of the zealous friars to convert these Indians, and the Apaches displayed some interest in the white man's religion whenever the Spaniards acted as though they intended to carry the war to them or if the Comanches became too great a threat to them.

Spain had stationed in New Mexico only eighty troops, and most of these were household servants at Santa Fe. Few of them had either the equipment, the leadership, or the initiative to carry out a deter-

[19] Bancroft, *Arizona and New Mexico*, 264.
[20] Wallace and Hoebel, *The Comanches*, 289.

mined campaign against the Apaches. They usually lacked horses that were equal to any belonging to the Indian tribes, and their small pay provided little incentive to risk their lives. More often than not, their food and the meager pay they received were reduced through the graft of the local authorities. Scattered along the fifteen-hundred-mile frontier which the Apaches consistently attacked were several presidios commanded by Spanish captains with small forces under them. They too were ineffective in handling the Apache menace.

As the raids became increasingly destructive and more daring, it was obvious that Spain had to act to control the Apaches, for their very rule in the area was in danger. Between 1775 and 1790, the vacillating attitude of Spain was ended, and a determined effort was made to control the Apaches since it was deemed impossible to convert or destroy them. To carry out this difficult task, Spain was fortunate in having a series of competent military men, including General Don Hugo O'Conor, who initiated the campaign between 1775 and 1777. He was relieved by Don Teodoro de Croix, with the work being completed by Governor Don Juan Bautista de Anza.

The campaign was relatively simple in that it consisted mainly of chasing the Apaches into their retreats, destroying their camps, and fighting them wherever possible, killing as many as possible. As they were driven from their home stamping grounds, the Apaches were forced to flee to the plains country, where they were put upon by their hereditary enemies, the Comanches. Recognizing that the Spaniards were determined to crush them, the Apaches again became interested in conversion and in settling down like Pueblo Indians. They even joined the Spaniards in a campaign against the Comanches. Treaties were signed between the Spaniards and the Apaches, but they were to be no more effective than those with the Americans almost a century later. The way of life of the Apache was such that he had to be completely defeated before he would change. Thus, because of the expense and other frontier problems, Spain was not prepared to wage the kind of campaign necessary to humble the nomadic warriors. However, from 1790 to 1810 the Apaches were relatively quiet, limiting their depredations along the border more than at any time in preceding history. It was during this time that mines were opened, ranches were built, and much constructive work along the frontier was accomplished.[21]

The French Intrusion

Alarming the Spanish settlements in New Mexico far more than the threat of the hostile Indians was the persistent fear of a French invasion during the eighteenth century. Throughout the long period of domination in the Western Hemisphere, Spain had consistently to fight the French and the English, as well as the Dutch, to maintain control of her holdings in the western hemisphere. Fear that the French were prepared to take over the northern outpost was very real and greatly concerned officials at Santa Fe, although there was never any actual possibility of such a venture by the French.[22]

As early as 1695 reports reached Vargas that traders from New Orleans had penetrated the wilderness uncomfortably close to New Mexico. These reports were carried by Apaches, who hoped to obtain help from the Spaniards against their foes, who had been armed with French rifles. Such rumors continued to circulate, and every decade was to be marked by a virtual panic over an impending French invasion. It was not until 1762, when the Louisiana Territory was turned over to Spain, that this threat was removed.

An expedition commanded by Pedro de Villasur was sent out in 1720 to investigate the truth of these usually exaggerated reports. A force of some forty soldiers accompanied by perhaps sixty Indians went northeastward from Santa Fe looking for the French intruders. Accompanying the group as interpreter was Jean de l'Archévèque of Santa Fe, who was reputedly one of the slayers of La Salle and could have been a fugitive from French justice. In August this expedition was attacked by a force of Pawnees and, except for about a

[21] Lockwood, *The Apache Indians*, 18–28.

[22] The story of the French threat to New Mexico is told in Henri Folmer, *Franco-Spanish Rivalry in North America, 1542–1763*. Also Henri Folmer, "French Expansion Toward New Mexico in the Eighteenth Century" (M.A. thesis, University of Denver, 1939) and Lelia Kearney, "French Intrusion into New Mexico after the Pueblo Revolt of 1680." (M.A. thesis, Catholic University, 1939).

dozen survivors, was completely destroyed. The Spaniards claimed that the French directed the Indian attack, but verification of the charge is lacking.[23]

During the 1720's France made an effort to reach New Mexico. The reasons for this action stemmed from disappointment with the Louisiana Territory. The bursting of the Mississippi bubble showed that quick fortunes were not to be made in this vast wilderness. In an effort to derive some gains from their possession of Louisiana, the French turned their longing eyes toward the Spanish colonies. The mirage of wealthy Spanish gold and silver mines was a primary factor behind such interest. Then, too, the French were accomplished traders, and they believed that a profitable commerce could be developed between the French outposts and Santa Fe.

Attempts to establish such trade were a dismal failure in 1724 and again in 1739. Handicapping the initial efforts was the fact that the geography of the area was little understood; for example, one French party believed that New Mexico could be reached by ascending the Missouri.

In 1748, Comanche traders at Taos reported that the rifles they carried had recently been purchased from French traders.[24] For the next ten years several parties of Frenchmen made their way either to Taos or to Santa Fe with goods to be traded. Some of these unfortunate businessmen were arrested and sent south to Mexico and had their merchandise confiscated. But the official records probably do not tell the full story. It can be assumed that Spain's attempts to close the border to such trade were unsuccessful and that a sizable quantity of contraband goods found its way to the Taos fairs as well as the markets at Santa Fe. Bribing Spanish colonial officials was never difficult, and the need of the isolated province for the wares of the French was so great that the officials either looked the other way or, more likely, participated in this contraband trade to their own profit.

Spain's interest in halting the activities of the French traders stemmed first of all from the exclusive economic policy exercised

[23] Folmer, *Franco-Spanish Rivalry*, 282–83.

[24] This alarmed the Spaniards, for they took great care to keep firearms away from the Indians.

by Madrid throughout the colonial period. Trade was a monopoly held by carefully selected merchants who paid dearly for the privilege and therefore believed they were entitled to be free from outside competition. Besides, the French led all Europeans in their ability to get along with the Indians, principally because of their readiness to accept the savages for what they were, and not interfere with their primitive existence. The Spaniards feared that the hostile Indians, either armed with French weapons or directed by the French themselves, would increase the already existing difficulty with the nomadic tribesman. Once Louisiana had been ceded to Spain, the French threat to New Mexico, such as it was, was ended.

The Colonial Economy

At the end of Spain's rule in New Mexico, most of the people continued to be engaged in the difficult task of wresting a living from the soil. The self-sufficient economy was built around the raising of crops in the valley lands through irrigation. They consisted mainly of corn, wheat, and beans. Sheep were the most important type of livestock, with both wool and animals being shipped southward to the Mexican markets. What little manufacturing existed was for domestic consumption.

As is usual in such an isolated community, trade was the primary economic activity. During the eighteenth century the annual fair at Taos, held in late summer, was the most important activity of the trading world. This small village became the center of trade because its location was easily accessible through the valleys in several directions, and also because trade there could be carried on without the official scrutiny existing at Santa Fe.

Attending these fairs were the Pueblo Indians, the Spanish settlers from the surrounding areas, and even the hostile Plains Indians, who took time out from lifting Spanish scalps to do business with their possessors. The Indians brought hides, captives, and stolen livestock to trade for the necessary knives and horses and a wide variety of trinkets.

The merchants of Chihuahua, who had gained control of the

former mission caravans about the middle of the century, dominated the commerce of New Mexico in the eighteenth century.[25] Their annual caravans brought the goods to be bartered at Taos and returned with the raw materials of the province. Their monopoly enabled them to engage in sharp practices which oppressed the inhabitants in the frontier settlements. The report in 1804 emphasizes the disadvantage of the province when its exports were valued at only $60,000 while its imports totaled $112,000, leaving a trade balance against the area of $52,000.[26] The disadvantage suffered by exchanging raw materials for finished goods was aggravated by a clever and unscrupulous manipulation of the current monetary unit on the part of the merchants.[27]

[25] Moorhead, *New Mexico's Royal Road*, 41.
[26] Twitchell, *Leading Facts*, I, 475.
[27] Moorhead, *New Mexico's Royal Road*, 50–51; Bancroft, *Arizona and New Mexico*, 278.

VI - Enter the Americans

As THE NINETEENTH CENTURY BEGAN, Spain's precarious hold in New Mexico was fast drawing to a close. Titular ownership soon was to pass to Mexico, but there was only to be a pause until the westward sweep of Manifest Destiny would bring the Anglo-Americans into possession. Spain had long feared the acquisitive habits of the Americans and had employed various techniques to keep them out. An important reason for the tranfer of title to the vast Louisiana territory to Napoleon in 1800 was the hope that the more aggressive French might set up an effective buffer zone that would protect Spain's empire. Unfortunately, Spain was thwarted in this effort, and Americans were soon coming westward.

A basic conflict existed between the Americans and the Spaniards regarding the use that should be made of the frontier. Developed through the centuries as the English moved westward from the Atlantic seaboard, the Anglo-American philosophy stressed the role of the individual in the new land, granting him complete license to exploit the frontier for his own enrichment. The Spaniards, on the other hand, had long accepted a frontier philosophy which subordinated the individual to the state. In theory, at least, the role of Spain's pioneers was not to enrich themselves but to assist in creating a strong nation and a powerful church. In the American Southwest these two philosophies were to lock horns, and the issue was never in doubt. The triumph of the American frontiersman over the Hispanic world was well-nigh inevitable.[1]

[1] Ray Allen Billington, *The Far Western Frontier 1830–1860,* 1.

101

The acquisition by the United States of the Spanish Southwest, including New Mexico, was a direct result of increased information about the area at the beginning of the nineteenth century. First calling attention to the area around Santa Fe was to be the expedition of Lieutenant Zebulon M. Pike, 1806–1807. But the real interest of the Americans was to be economic, and Pike's entrance was followed by numbers of eager fur trappers called "mountain men." Finally, the Santa Fe trade was virtually to make the area an economic satellite of the United States before actual possession was gained by force of arms.

⟶ The Pike Expedition ⟵

The year 1806 was one in which the eastern seaboard of the United States was paying considerable attention to Spanish America. Rumors of filibustering expeditions against Madrid's holdings in the New World filled the air, and one such effort actually got under way. Francisco de Miranda sailed from New York in an effort to drive the Spaniards from his native Venezuela. The lack of success in this venture did not deter further plotting, and one aspect of the infamous Burr conspiracy was the promise to bring riches to the plotters by despoiling Spain's empire in America. The intrusion of Lieutenant Pike into New Mexico was a by-product of the Burr conspiracy and was probably intended as an effort to lay the groundwork for a further filibustering effort.[2] The young army officer, made famous by this unlawful intrusion, was an unwitting accomplice of the treacherous General Wilkinson. This infamous officer having lost confidence in Burr, had decided to betray his co-conspirator. Accompanying Pike was a Dr. John Hamilton Robinson of Virginia, who was ostensibly along for the purpose of collecting a debt in Santa Fe for a merchant. His presence in the party is enigmatic, but the young physician may have had secret instructions from

[2] The most up-to-date study of this famous conspiracy is Thomas Perkins Abernathy, *The Burr Conspiracy;* standard for Pike's role are Elliot Coues, ed., *The Expeditions of Zebulon Montgomery Pike,* and W. Eugene Hollon, *The Lost Pathfinder: Zebulon Montgomery Pike.*

Wilkinson to reveal the details of the Burr conspiracy to the Spanish officials. The fiction of debt collection was created in order to protect Dr. Robinson from being held as a spy in the event war had broken out between Spain and the United States over the Sabine River boundary controversy.

That Wilkinson had other motives besides the secret instructions carried by Robinson was evidenced by the briefing he gave Lieutenant Pike. The young lieutenant was warned always to move with the greatest circumspection and to avoid any clash with the enemy. The small number of men in his unit naturally made it impossible for him to fight to protect himself. Had he been captured, he was to have explained that he was on his way back to Natchitoches but, being uncertain of the geography in the area, had lost his way.[3] More than likely Pike's venture, carried out with the authority of General Wilkinson, was intended to gather information about the area in anticipation of either the success of the Burr conspiracy or war between Spain and the United States.

While Pike was making his way slowly westward across the plains country in the summer of 1806, the Spanish learned that such an exploring party would soon be entering their territory. This resulted in the expedition of Melgares, a Spanish officer, eastward on the plains in an effort to find Pike. But the American party was late in getting started, so was not intercepted. Pike made his way westward, met with a number of tribes of the Plains Indians as he went, and informed them that the United States controlled the area. Going up the Arkansas River, he reached the peak which ultimately was to bear his name and then proceeded southward into New Mexico despite the hardships of winter travel in the snow-covered mountains. Once he passed the Sangre de Cristo Range, there was little question that Pike knew he was in Spanish territory. It is difficult to believe that Pike could have mistaken the Río Grande for the Red River as he later claimed. Perhaps the wily Wilkinson wanted him to erect a fort within Spanish territory as a basis for United States claim to the area in the event that war with the Spaniards did come.

In February, 1807, the small group of Americans constructed a blockhouse on the Río Grande near the mouth of the Río Conejos.

[3] Abernathy, *The Burr Conspiracy*, 121–23.

In the meantime, Dr. Robinson left for Santa Fe, supposedly as a debt collector. A Spanish force from Santa Fe was sent out to escort the Americans to the capital. After their capture, Pike and his friends virtually became prisoners of war, but they were treated with so much politeness and care that their status remained in doubt. The Lieutenant's efforts to get rid of his papers failed, and they were seized by Governor Alancaster. As a result, Pike and his men were forced to go to Chihuahua, where they were ultimately released and sent overland back to the United States.

An examination of the Lieutenant's papers convinced the Spanish governor that the object of the expedition, despite its small size, was to claim all the territory drained by the tributaries of the Mississippi River and to try to get control over the Indians living within this region. The fact that Pike had built a substantial blockhouse and had flown the Stars and Stripes over it lends credence to this supposition. Unfortunately, no historian has yet been able to unravel completely the ends of the Burr conspiracy. Hence it is difficult to fathom exactly what General Wilkinson had in mind and the role that Dr. Robinson was to play in the Burr affair.

Irrespective of the motives of the Pike Expedition, its results for the future of New Mexico were most significant. Pike was a very competent observer and, in publishing the journal he kept on his travels, was to be the first of many Americans to tear aside the shroud of mystery that had long enveloped the Spanish Southwest. The information (and misinformation) the young officer collected publicized this strange land, with its different population and unique manners and customs, shortly after the Lewis and Clark Expedition had aroused a great deal of curiosity about the Northwest. There is little question that the publicity attendant upon Pike's efforts ultimately attracted many more Americans to New Mexico and played a significant role in the Anglo-American conquest.

The Mountain Men

After Pike had shown the way, several Americans, between 1807 and 1821, attempted both to trade with the isolated province of New

Mexico and to trap in its streams. In general, these efforts were futile, as the Spanish continued to take necessary safeguards against an influx of Americans.

In the year 1821 a combination of circumstances led to a changed atmosphere. First of all, the success of the revolt in Mexico meant that Spain's authority was ended. And Mexican officials were to prove far less competent in halting the inroads of Anglo-Americans than Spain, perhaps because the government at Mexico City was unable even to give the little support extended when the Spaniards were in control.

The whims of Dame Fashion made more difficult the task of the officials at Santa Fe and increased the flow of Americans into the Southwest; for in the 1820's a well-dressed gentleman, if he would be properly dressed, had to wear a tall beaver-skin hat. As the skins of this animal were selling at six to eight dollars apiece and were much in demand, trappers and traders pushed their way westward, scouring the Rocky Mountains for beavers, and naturally came into what was then the Mexican Southwest.

These trappers or mountain men, as they were called, were the precursors of the ultimate floodtide of American immigration that swept over all of Spain's possessions in the American Southwest. They were men of all races, types, and cultural backgrounds, bound together by one thing: fascination with the wild, free, and irresponsible life of the trapper. Some were well educated, while others were illiterate frontiersmen, typical of those who had steadily pushed the fringes of civilization westward from the Atlantic seaboard. Through the books, letters, and even oral reports carried by these men, the rest of the United States was to learn rapidly about the West. And once fashion had changed and the supply of beaver had been depleted, the mountain men turned their talents and knowledge of the vast area to other pursuits.

The saga of these mountain men is not one that, strictly speaking, belongs to the history of New Mexico alone, for the entire West was theirs to roam. Originally, their base of operations was at Taos. But the trapping parties that set out from that point might operate along the Gila River or, finding beaver scarce along that stream, might decide to try their luck along the San Joaquin, Sacramento, or

American rivers in California. Some parties actually operated along these rivers and also added the Grand, Green, Snake, and Columbia on the same expedition.[4]

The beaver, the economic object of these men, was found throughout the West. His natural habitat was along the waterways that were lined with the cottonwood, willow, birch, and aspen which were his main supply of food. Unlike his counterpart in the lake country, the mountain beaver lived in burrows along the banks. Traps were normally placed in the shallow water near the entrance to the burrow. The bait, a pleasantly scented secretion of the beaver's castor gland, was suspended from a leaf directly above the trap. In its eagerness to obtain the bait, the animal would walk directly into the trap and be drowned by the weight of it. The traps were set in the evening and the catch raised at dawn.[5]

Absent from the fur industry in the Southwest were the large companies that dominated the trapping of the Northwest and the northern Rocky Mountain area. Those who sought the beaver along New Mexico's mountain streams were usually the most rugged individuals of the American frontier, frequently starting out with a small supply of salt, gunpowder, a knife, a gun, and the necessary traps. These men lived off the land. Sometimes they had the backing of entrepreneurs who were prepared to advance them the necessary supplies for a part of the catch. In some instances, partnerships were formed, and even small companies; but, in general, the mountain men were on their own.

The trapper's year began in the spring, as soon as the thaws began, and continued until late June, when the beaver began to shift. Then, with their pack animals laden with their catch, they made their way to the trading point in July. Within New Mexico this was usually Taos or Bent's Fort, which was located near the present site of La Junta, Colorado. The catch was traded for the needed supplies for

4 Robert Glass Cleland, *From Wilderness to Empire: A History of California,* ed. by Glenn S. Dumke, 74. The most complete study of the mountain men is Robert Glass Cleland, *This Reckless Breed of Men: The Trappers and Fur Traders of the Southwest;* of value also is Stanley Vestal, *Mountain Men,* and John E. Sunder, *Bill Sublette: Mountain Man.*

5 Hiram Martin Chittenden, *The American Fur Trade of the Far West,* I, 809–10.

the coming year, and then the trapper sought release from his precarious existence in whisky, gambling, and women. After a brief period of debauchery, the trappers rested from their revelry until fall, when the hunt was again renewed. During the winter some trappers lived with the Indians, where they commonly had native wives. Many preferred the more civilized Taos, and this community gradually became a haven for the mountain men.

In following such a yearly routine, the mountain men were forced to adjust to the wilderness in order to survive. Frequently, trappers were the victims of accidents caused by their horses' stepping into a hole, by a rock slide, or even by drowning. More often, they were at the mercy of hostile Indians, especially as they were busily engaged in the early-morning ritual of skinning beaver. Only a little less dangerous than the savages were the grizzly bears which abounded in the Rockies. These animals frequently attacked the trappers, and many a mountain man, fortunate enough to escape from such an event, bore the scars of a fight with a grizzly for the rest of his life.[6]

To survive such an arduous life, the mountain men were forced to adapt to the primitive environment in which they lived and worked. In this process they retrogressed in civilization until they took on the attributes of the savages so completely that they became more Indian than the Indians themselves. Some were even reputed to have engaged in cannibalism. They quickly learned to move as silently as the red man. They were superb fighters, and many were adept at scalping the foe they had slain. Ultimately, they ate like the Indians, talked like the Indians, and developed the same primitive savage outlook towards human life.[7]

The appearance of the mountain man was as distinctive as his way of life. Through long exposure to the sun his skin was as dark as that of the Indian, and his physical features were rough. His hair was long, coarse, and bushy, dangling about his shoulders. His fringed clothing was buckskin. Normally, he wore deerskin moccasins. About his waist was a belt that held a skinning knife, pistols, and a bullet pouch. Upon the mountain man's head was a cap of skin decorated with an

---

[6] Jedediah Smith, one of the most famous of the mountain men, lost an ear in an encounter with a grizzly. Cleland, *Reckless Breed of Men*, 59.

[7] Billington, *Far Western Frontier*, 49–53.

animal's tail or braided horsehair. About his neck he usually carried a sack with pipe, tobacco, awl, bullet mold, and other such wilderness necessities.[8]

The exploits of the mountain men soon captured the imagination of the entire nation. Tales circulated in the East concerning their return to savagery and their legendary exploits. More than any other pioneers, they came to personify man's adjustment to the frontier. Included in their ranks were some of the most important men in American history. The first of these was Kit Carson, a legend in his own lifetime. Of only lesser importance was James Ohio Pattie, who left a significant story of his activities; Ewing Young, Jim Bridger, Jedediah Smith, and the three groups of brothers, the Bents, the Sublettes, and the Robidoux.

To such men the laws forbidding foreigners to enter New Mexico to engage in trapping or trading were made to be broken. As early as 1817, under the Spanish government, members of a party led by Auguste Chouteau and Jules de Mun of St. Louis were arrested and charged with various crimes. Their catch, valued at $30,000, was seized, and they spent some time in jail. It was customary for either the Spanish or Mexican officials to accuse the trappers of being members of a gigantic American conspiracy to seize the territory.

In the 1820's, when beaver trapping was at its peak, more Americans entered New Mexico. It was claimed that these trappers took beaver skins valued at $100,000 a year out of the province. Laws prohibiting such activity by foreigners were ineffective, since it was very easy for Americans to enter into partnership with pliable natives or even to take spurious citizenship themselves.

Mexican officials were really afraid that the beaver would soon be extinct. Their complaints, along with those of Mexicans who envied the profit of the Americans, resulted in a formal protest from Mexico City to the Secretary of State.[9] But without adequate cavalry to patrol the frontier, the Mexican officials, thus unable to enforce the laws, were helpless before this first American invasion.

The fur trade began abating of its own accord in the 1830's. By

[8] *Ibid.*, 49; Cleland, *Reckless Breed of Men*, 20–21.
[9] Thomas M. Marshall, "St. Vrain's Expedition to the Gila in 1826," *Southwestern Historical Quarterly*, Vol. XIX (January, 1916), 256–58.

this time beaver became extremely scarce, having been trapped indiscriminately for so long. Trappers continued to search the remote corners of the mountains, but with limited success. Added to the decline of the beaver was the change in fashion. The growing importation of silk from the Orient led to a gradual emphasis upon such material for men's hats, and the tall beaver hats were soon out of style. By 1840 the mountain men had all but lost their economic importance.

The short space of twenty years in which the beaver trappers roamed the Rockies was brief, but the heritage of the legendary men of the mountains was great. They had explored every corner of the vast mountain country, and many would soon be employed as guides to lead the long wagon trains of settlers westward to the gold of California or the farms of Oregon. Many of these mountain men would ultimately attain fame as military scouts in the campaigns against the Mexicans and the Indians. Some, like Charles Bent, would even be selected for vital roles in the new country that was being created by the Americans. Long before the era of trapping was over, large numbers of the mountain men had found their way into the Santa Fe trade, or were engaged in similar pursuits. Those living in Santa Fe and Taos were to provide a welcome nucleus around which American support could be built.

～ The Santa Fe Trade ～

The mountain men who wandered over every crook and cranny of the mountain vastnesses of New Mexico were but the prelude to the larger intrusion of Americans. The trappers showed the way to the traders who were soon to follow in large numbers.[10] The coming of the American trader into New Mexico grew directly out of the publicity given Pike's description of the area. Enterprising frontier businessmen were more than willing to do something about the high prices and lack of consumer goods the American officer noted at Santa Fe.

Attempts to engage in trade while Spain was still in control failed,

[10] *Ibid.*, 260.

with several American traders suffering considerable loss in their efforts to encroach on the precincts of Spain's monopolistic economic practices. It was not until 1821, when Mexico had attained its independence from Spain, that the American traders were successful. Having long suffered because of the extortionate practices of the Chihuahua merchants, which brought a large imbalance of trade to the Santa Fe area as well as depriving the people of many basic products, the inhabitants of the region were just as eager to trade with the Americans as the latter were to trade with them.

When the trade did begin, it was the result of an accident. One William Becknell of Franklin, Missouri, outfitted a trading expedition to the Indians. While within Mexican territory, the Becknell party encountered a troop of Mexican soldiers. Fear that they would suffer the fate of previous traders was soon eased when the soldiers greeted them with enthusiasm, informed them that Mexico was free of Spanish rule, and invited them to take their goods to Santa Fe.

Becknell returned home in January, 1822, heavily laden with gold, silver, and furs. The extent of his profit is not known, but one of his townsmen realized a return of $900 on a $60 investment in the venture.[11] Such returns were enough to prompt others to accept the invitation of the governor of New Mexico for traders to come to Santa Fe. Consquently, beginning in 1822, the official trade got under way.

Three expeditions went out a year after Becknell's initial success, the most important of which was a second trading venture by Becknell himself. Besides proving that money could be made from continuation of the trade, Becknell mapped a new route which eliminated the hazardous mountain trails. Of more importance, he demonstrated that wagons could be used effectively to haul cargo across trackless prairies, replacing pack animals and thus increasing the size of the load and the variety of merchandise that could be transported. In 1824 the twenty-five wagons that left Missouri were laden with $35,000 worth of merchandise, which was sold for $190,000 in

[11] Billington, *Far Western Frontier*, 26; Josiah Gregg, *Commerce of the Prairies*, ed. by Max L. Moorhead, is still the standard source on the Santa Fe trade. Fortunately, it has been supplemented by a number of monographs on various phases of the trade.

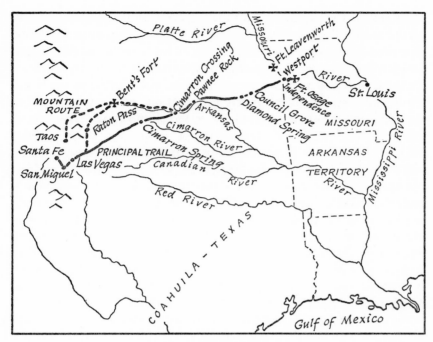

The Santa Fe Trail

gold, silver, and furs. The profit of 300 per cent after transportation costs acted as a magnet to draw in scores of traders. After 1825, however, the margin of profit was rapidly reduced. The number of men engaged in the trade and the volume of goods carried was simply too great for the tiny village of Santa Fe, with its population of 4,000, or even of the total province with its approximate population of 44,000, to absorb. After 1826 profits usually averaged 10 to 40 per cent, but there were also years of loss on account of damage to goods or Indian attacks.[12]

At first those who engaged in the Santa Fe trade did so on a relatively small scale. Farmers would mortgage their land, or pool their resources with their neighbors, to outfit a single wagon and load it with perhaps one thousand dollars' worth of goods. As the trade flourished, such small operators found it difficult to compete because

[12] Billington, *Far Western Frontier*, 36.

111

they lacked the capital to buy merchandise, and businessmen controlling several wagon loads of goods came to dominate the trade. But there always seemed to be a large number of independent proprietors eager to try their success in the trade.

An astonishing variety of merchandise was carried in the Santa Fe trade. Virtually every article found in one of the general stores of the frontier was loaded on the wagons and headed westward. About half of the merchandise was cotton goods,[13] the remainder usually consisting of hardware items, various kinds of costume jewelry, and a wide variety of other consumer goods. One example of the sort of unique demand for American goods which existed was empty bottles. Indians preferred bottles to money in trade for their produce, and were willing to pay up to half a dollar apiece for them. Hence, traders were able to provide liquid refreshment on the long journey by buying liquor in Missouri, drinking the contents, and then trading the empty bottles for goods worth more than the initial cost of the liquor.[14] Most of the merchandise taken into New Mexico was obtained at first from the storehouses of Missouri, but as the trade increased in scope, enterprising wholesalers went to New York City to make their purchases.

The wagons employed in the trade were of several makes, but were usually of the Conestoga type. The first ones used were manufactured in Pittsburgh and sold for about two hundred dollars each. They were distinguished by their long, sagging bed and outward-sloping sideboards and tailgate. These features were intended to settle the cargo at the center. Large hoops were used to hold the canvas covering that would protect the cargo from the elements as well as increase the size of the load. The white canvas and the red and blue framework of the wagons made a diverting sight on the prairie. Mackinaw blankets were also used to protect the cargo, and could thus be smuggled through customs for later sale without duty.

After the Mexican War most of the vehicles were made in St. Louis and were called "Murphy wagons." These were larger than the earlier wagons, usually being three feet wide and up to sixteen

[13] Gregg, *Commerce of the Prairies,* 80.
[14] Susan Shelby Magoffin, *Down the Santa Fe Trail,* ed. by Stella M. Drumm, 153.

feet long, and had rear wheels about five feet high. The iron tires were four inches thick, making it possible to carry loads of more than three tons. Most of the wooden parts were made of oak with the points of strain reinforced by iron. In spite of their sturdy manufacture, many of the wagons broke under the strain of the difficult journey. Despite the fact that extra wagon tongues and axles were carried, the Santa Fe trail soon was littered with the remnants of wagons that failed to complete the journey. Once the upland area was reached, where the atmosphere was very dry, considerable difficulty was encountered because the wood dried out so fast that iron tires fell away from the wheels and boards warped and cracked. It was common to sell the wagons either in Santa Fe or at Chihuahua, as many of them were unfit for the return journey.

Oxen, mules, and horses were all used to pull these giant trading vehicles. Oxen were most common simply because many were available in Missouri. They were placid beasts which did not get excited, even in the face of Indian attack. Unfortunately, they were poor grazers, and many of them succumbed when the short-grass area was reached. Besides, the oxen had delicate feet, and many of them could not stand the rough terrain. Many traders preferred mules because these beasts were far more hearty than oxen. But they, too, had their failings, the most important of which was readiness to stampede in time of storm or Indian attack. It was common practice for the wagons to go out pulled by two or three yoke of oxen and to return with ten or twelve span of mules, the latter animals being easier to obtain in New Mexico.

The westbound caravans outfitted at Franklin, Westport, or Independence, Missouri, in the spring. They started out as soon as there was sufficient grass to sustain the animals. Each proprietor would usually set out with his own wagons until he reached Council Grove. There, animals were rested and needed repairs made on the wagons. From this point the traders traveled in a single caravan so as to have protection from the Indians, and to provide for defense, a captain of the caravan was elected, with regulations and guard duty being established. When Indian country was reached, the wagons marched in four columns abreast so as to shorten the long line that would otherwise exist and to make it possible quickly to form a square for reasons of defense against attack.[15] Most difficult of the approximately eight hundred miles from Missouri to Santa Fe were the fifty-eight miles from the Arkansas River to the Cimarron, since this area was without water.

The first settlements that were reached were at the present site of Las Vegas, New Mexico. Before arriving at Santa Fe, the traders encountered the customs agents, who supposedly came out to escort the caravan in. Actually, the purpose was to arrive at an understanding about tariff duties. Josiah Gregg, the leading authority on the early Santa Fe trade, suggests that the following arrangement was made: The customs duties collected were divided, one third going to the officers, another third being retained by the merchants, and the remainder going to the government.[16] Out of the estimated $50,000 to $80,000 customs duties collected, approximately one-half were known to have been diverted to the customs officials.[17]

One trader contended that Governor Armijo frankly told the traders that he and his officials were engaged in stealing but that the Americans had no complaint because "we do all of the stealing and divide with you, giving you much of the largest share of the booty."[18]

As they neared Santa Fe, the wagoners put on their best clothing and scrubbed themselves up to be presentable. Even the animals caught the excitement of the moment. Crowds of people gathered shouting, "*Los Americanos!—los carros!—la entrada de la caravana!*" Employees soon began relieving the tension of the ten weeks' hazardous journey from Missouri by tasting the excellent assortment of debauchery offered at Santa Fe. But the merchants had to sell their wares before they could celebrate.

Normally, merchandise was sold wholesale to local Mexicans or traders who came up from Chihuahua to buy at Santa Fe. Later, a practice developed whereby some of the Missouri traders went into partnership with Santa Fe residents and virtually set them up in the retail business. This was done to escape the restrictions upon foreign-

[15] Gregg, *Commerce of the Prairies*, 72.

[16] *Ibid.*, 79.

[17] *Ibid.*, 336.

[18] Ralph Paul Bieber, ed., *The Papers of James J. Webb, Santa Fe Trader, 1844–1861*, 274.

ers. Once the goods were disposed of, after a rest of four or five weeks, the return journey was made. The first of September was a normal time of departure, for it was necessary to get home before the snow came or, as Gregg suggests, to save homes mortgaged to start the traders on their journey.[19] The return trip was frequently made in as little as forty days, as the wagons were usually lightly loaded, the cargo consisting of furs, gold, or silver.

The hazards of the trip were many. Animals frequently stampeded for no reason at all, or were driven off by Indians. Many a load of merchandise was lost when one of the cumbersome wagons capsized, spilling its cargo out over the prairie or emptying it into one of the streams. Frequent rain or hail storms likewise took their toll. But the most frightening danger was Indian attack. Such attacks were always feared, although actually more men died from accident than were killed by the savages. In 1829 an appeal was made to the government for a military escort for the Santa Fe caravan. Washington officials, not understanding the terrain of the land, ordered Major Bennett Riley and four companies of the Sixth Infantry to accompany the caravan. Riley was successful in protecting the traders until they had passed into Mexican territory. Unfortunately, he and his group had to await the return of the caravan, and while they waited, they were constantly harassed by the Indians and, being on foot, were unable to protect themselves. Their plight and subsequent report were sufficient finally to convince the skeptical that a mounted force was absolutely necessary in contending with the Plains Indians, who used the horse effectively. Thus was begun the United States Cavalry.[20]

The impact of the Santa Fe trade upon New Mexico was of both immediate and long-range significance. The once isolated settlements practically went through an economic revolution. Not only were consumer goods now available, along with an outlet for their own produce, but New Mexicans soon entered into the trade themselves. They bought goods from the Americans and took them southward, ultimately invading many of the more important northern

[19] Gregg, *Commerce of the Prairies*, 213.
[20] Willis Boldt Hughes, "The Army and Stephen Watts Kearny in the West, 1819–1846," (Ph.D. dissertation, University of Minnesota, 1955), 152.

115

Mexican cities. For some time Santa Fe was port of entry for the trade of much of the Mexican territory, with large caravans being assembled there, thence making their way southward to Chihuahua or westward to California.[21] During the first decade (1822–32) of the Santa Fe trade, one-fifth of the total value of the cargo went southward (about $19,000 worth). During the following eleven years more than one-half of the average cargo was sent southward.[22] In addition to supplying the markets of Chihuahua and California, the Santa Fe trade provided the New Mexico authorities with most of the revenue they had available to operate their province.

Unfortunately, the Santa Fe trade brought friction between the Americans and the New Mexicans. Much of this ill feeling came from the traditional Spanish fear of interlopers, foreigners, and Protestants. Many incidents occurred wherein the persons or property of the Americans were attacked. A constant source of annoyance to the American traders was the capricious manner in which the laws were enforced. The men were granted a license to do business by Mexican officials, and when these men died or were replaced, the incoming officials would frequently decide that the original license was in error and solve matters by seizing the goods in question and holding the Americans for crimes. As the caravans neared Santa Fe, the traders never knew whether the customs fees were going to be modest or exorbitant, the amount frequently being decided by the current status of the local treasury or the immediate needs of New Mexico's governor. It was inevitable that Americans, used to the consistent operation of Anglo law, should violently object to such discrimination.

But the friction was not all caused by the New Mexicans. Most Americans were Protestants, with the intolerance of the day toward the Roman Catholic faith, and seldom missed an opportunity to display it. Frequently, Americans sometimes deep in their cups, attacked or even murdered innocent Mexicans. On the other hand, the resentment against the traders was sometimes not their own fault. For

21 The definitive work on the Chihuahua trade is Moorhead, *New Mexico's Royal Road*, while the development of the California trade is well told in Cleland, *Reckless Breed of Men*, Chapter 7.
22 Moorhead, *New Mexico's Royal Road*, 77.

example, the fear caused by the ill-fated Texan–Santa Fe Expedition in 1841 and the subsequent Texas reprisals caused all Anglos to be suspected of conniving to seize the province. And after what had happened with the secession of Texas, Mexican authorities perhaps had good cause to fear the number of Americans who were moving into New Mexico. The attempts to cut off the Santa Fe trade grew out of this fear. But New Mexico needed American goods too badly for such embargoes ever to be effective.

Many Americans who entered New Mexico as a result of trading activities, such as Colonel James Magoffin of Kentucky, became Mexican citizens, frequently taking Spanish wives and accepting the ways of the land. In general these Americans provided a welcome group around which the ultimate seizure of Mexico's territory in the Southwest could be effected. Thus, the Americans entered New Mexico to trade, but ultimately remained to take over.

Though located in southeastern Colorado on the upper Arkansas River, Bent's Fort was of far-reaching importance in the history of New Mexico between 1832 and 1852. It was intended simply as the trading center of the firm of Bent, St. Vrain and Company, but in practice it became much more than that.[23] Heavily fortified and almost impregnable against the attacks of hostile Indians, it became a haven of safety for travelers on the Santa Fe Trail and a place of refuge for friendly Indians. To the Mexican officials at Santa Fe, the fort was depicted as the center for those who smuggled contraband into the province, the place where hostile Indians obtained the firearms used in raiding unprotected settlements, and, most important, the center of an American conspiracy against New Mexico. The fact that General Kearny stopped there while on his invasion indicates that the Mexican fears were not completely unfounded.

Much of the distrust toward Bent's Fort stemmed from the fear of the strength of the trading company, which had tremendous influence and a strong following among the native New Mexicans as well as the Indians. The leaders of Bent and St. Vrain, Céran St. Vrain, Charles Bent, and William Bent, had all begun their careers as typical mountain men. Having more competence and more busi-

[23] David Lavender, *Bent's Fort*, and Ina Wilson Cason, "The Bent Brothers on the Frontier" (M.A. thesis, University of New Mexico, 1939).

117

ness ability than others, they became traders. For business reasons St. Vrain became a Mexican citizen, as did many other trappers and traders. Even so, the Mexican officials at Santa Fe always, perhaps justly so, suspected that the Mexican citizenship attained did not buy the loyalty of these men and they remained at heart Americans. Charles Bent and St. Vrain married Mexican women at Taos, as did Kit Carson and countless other mountain men, while William Bent married a Cheyenne woman. Such marital ties increased the direct contact the Americans had with the native elements, as well as aiding the retail store that Bent and St. Vrain established in Taos. And, as the Americans became part of the closely knit Mexican families, the Mexican authorities had every reason to question whether or not they would some day become so powerful within New Mexico that they could not be dislodged.

The Mexican War caused an almost complete collapse of normal trade on the Santa Fe road. But the needs of the military led to the continuation of the caravans. Once the war was over the old trade was renewed, along with regular passenger service utilizing stagecoaches. By 1860 nearly seventeen million pounds of freight had gone over the old trail. The business employed approximately 10,000 men and needed 6,100 mules, 28,000 oxen, and 3,000 wagons to service it.[24] After the Civil War was over, the trade continued to flourish, and in some years four or five million dollars' worth of goods were sent out from Missouri. Such goods continued to be largely manufactured items for consumer purposes, for which New Mexico exchanged hides, skins, and wool. Gold and silver were also shipped from time to time, but the balance of trade remained against New Mexico. Fortunately, just as in Spanish times, this deficiency was made up largely through the money brought into the territory by the army. The coming of the railroad shortened the trail and moved the eastern terminus farther westward, until finally in 1879 the railroads invaded New Mexico and the picturesque Santa Fe trade was over. But in its heyday it had served as an important means by which the Americans were able to enter New Mexico.

[24] Cleland, *Reckless Breed of Men*, 146.

VII - The Time of the Gringo

WHILE THE INCOMING AMERICANS were in the process of making a tremendous impact upon the economy of New Mexico, the pattern of Manifest Destiny was unfolding on a national level. As President Polk, having ably sensed the temper of the American people in the election of 1844, cast covetous eyes towards San Francisco Bay, the isolated and relatively insignificant territory of New Mexico loomed large in the American timetable. The dynamic and expansive force of Manifest Destiny made American occupation of the Río Grande area well-nigh inevitable. As one author suggests, it was "the time of the gringo."[1]

Mexican Rule

Making easier this inevitable triumph of the Americans was the in-effectiveness of the government at Mexico City in its administration of Santa Fe and its environs. Even compared to the neglect under Spanish rule, the Mexicans were less effective. Because of the hostility towards the Spaniards, even most of the remaining Franciscan missionaries were driven out, leading to a lamentable decay of the spiritual life. Militarily, protection from the hostile Indians and possible American invasion was provided by a military force that seldom exceeded one hundred. Usually there was no revenue provided from Mexico City to maintain the area; the taxes from the Santa Fe trade

[1] Elliott Arnold, *The Time of the Gringo.*

119

provided what little funds that were available. There was no administration of justice "because there is absolutely no one who knows how to draw up a verbal process, to conclude a defense, nor to fill the office of Attorney General."[2]

Politically, New Mexico was a province until 1824, when it was made a territory. In 1836 it became a department and remained so until the end of Mexican rule. Even so, the boundaries were never adequately defined, possibly because Mexican authorities didn't consider the area worth more attention. What little government that existed was largely in the hands of an appointed *jefe político* or governor. There was a provision for an elective body, which was usually nonexistent.[3]

One of the dominant and interesting individuals during the brief era of Mexican rule was Manuel Armijo, governor for much of the period. It was Armijo who feuded with the Missouri traders over the payment of duties. Also governor at the time of the ill-fated Texan–Santa Fe Expedition, he was held responsible for the atrocities associated with it. Hence, most Americans bitterly hated Armijo. They nicknamed him "his obesity," and early writers tended to follow the unflattering picture of the Governor painted by Gregg and Kendall. The story of how the Governor got his start in life was told in many versions. Mainly, he was represented as having stolen sheep from his employer when he was a young man to build up his own flocks initially, supposedly stealing the same animal thirteen times. On another occasion Armijo was accused of having disguised himself as an Apache to steal a flock of sheep being sent southward to market. The phrase "it is better to be thought a brave man than really to be one" was likewise attributed to him and was used to prove his cowardice. He was depicted as having almost every vice known to man.[4] In any event, he was able to accumulate a substantial fortune in land and mercantile interest.

However, another American trader, James J. Webb, gives us a more flattering picture of the controversial Governor Armijo. Webb agreed that he was naturally irritable, sometimes overbearing, but

[2] Barreiro, *Ojeada Sobre Nuevo-México*, 39.
[3] *Ibid.*, 27–28; Bancroft, *Arizona and New Mexico*, 316.
[4] Ottamar Hamele, *When Destiny Called*, 92–93.

that allowance had to be made for his humble origins.[5] Actually, a man like Governor Armijo must be considered as a typical *caudillo* of his day and judged accordingly. He was certainly a better type of person than Santa Anna, who was currently running Mexico. Allowance must be made for the Governor's difficulties with the Missouri traders, for they were not an easy group to get along with or to administer taxes upon. Further, the atrocities committed upon the survivors of the Texan–Santa Fe expedition were attributed to a subordinate and not to the Governor himself.

The Revolt of 1837

In 1837 the northern Pueblo Indians arose in revolt for reasons that have never been satisfactorily explained. The attacks of the hostile Comanches, Navahos, and Apaches continued to make the sedentary Indians restless and dissatisfied with the ineffectiveness of Mexican rule. This dissatisfaction may have been the basic or long-range factor influencing the uprising, but there were other more immediate causes. The New Mexicans had been used to administering their own affairs, especially collecting the revenue of the Santa Fe trade. In 1835, Albino Pérez was appointed governor and was resented because he was an outsider. Furthermore, a reorganization of government within Mexico took place and a system of collection of direct taxes was inaugurated that was bitterly resented. Difficult to gauge, but perhaps of most importance as the cause of the revolt, was the intense partisanship of New Mexican politics. Manuel Armijo was displeased over his removal as a custom-house official and was not a man to accept such a setback without objection. Within Taos, Padre Antonio Martínez had already developed a reputation as a champion of the people, and thus could be expected to lead the campaign against the direct-taxes burden that the poorer people would be expected to bear.

It is contended, though without historical verification, that Armijo and Martínez together plotted the revolt, meeting several times to effect the final form that it would take. Gregg is the principal author-

[5] Webb, *Santa Fe Trade* 274–75.

ity for Armijo's complicity,[6] and although it is not possible to prove the precise role of either man, one writer states that "Don Antonio's words and actions prove that he was substantially in sympathy with the grievances of the people."[7] It is even suggested that the two men used Penitentes in developing the plot.[8] If Armijo and Martínez were involved, as seems likely, there is little doubt that the friar became unhappy with the turn of events and that Armijo waited an opportunity to turn matters to his own advantage.

The immediate cause of the revolt in July, 1837, was a debt-collection problem. Suit was brought to collect a debt of one hundred pesos, and when judgment was given for the defendants, who were relatives of the *alcalde*, an appeal was taken to the prefect to set aside the finding. The people assumed that the appeal would be granted and that this would be a great injustice. So, with the cry of "taxes, taxes," a mob gathered, indicating that the objection was really against any form of taxation. Soon large groups of Pueblo Indians formed and began marching on Santa Fe. Governor Pérez gathered a force of about 150 militia, including some Pueblo Indians, and marched to meet the insurgents. The Governor's forces were defeated in the ensuing battle and forced to flee. The rebels captured Pérez along with a number of his associates and murdered them.

While the citizens of Santa Fe waited with horror, anticipating a general massacre, about two thousand Indians gathered before the capital on the ninth of August. Especially concerned were the American traders. However, since the Indians were relatively orderly, they may have been controlled from somewhere. They elected a Taos Indian, José González, as governor, reappointed Indians to most governmental posts, and seized the property of the former political figures.

On the eighth of September Armijo raised a force and marched on the capital. His position was vastly strengthened by the arrival of approximately three hundred troops from Chihuahua. Ultimately, the government forces met the rebels in January, 1838, defeating

[6] Gregg, *Commerce of the Prairies*, 95.

[7] E. K. Francis, "Padre Martinez: A New Mexican Myth," *NMHR*, Vol. XXXI (October, 1956), 268.

[8] Harvey Fergusson, *Rio Grande*, 192.

them and executing González and his leaders. It is not known whether Armijo was angry because the Indian was elected governor in his stead or whether he simply awaited an opportunity to turn against his former confederate. As this uprising occurred just after the Texans had rebelled, many Mexicans assumed that it was the Americans who were behind it and were the real leaders of the Indians. This mistaken impression was strengthened when the Indian rebels denied allegiance to Mexico and proposed sending a deputation to Texas asking for protection.[9]

⟶ The Texan–Santa Fe Expedition ⟵

The Texan–Santa Fe venture in 1841 is a controversial incident in New Mexican history. New Mexican writers have depicted it as a diabolical plot on the part of the greedy Texans to enslave them. Most Texas authorities contend, however, that it was but a simple trading expedition. Perhaps there is an element of truth in both versions, with the commercial aspects of the venture being the most important phase.[10]

This ill-fated venture was a project of the fertile imagination of President Mirabeau B. Lamar of the Republic of Texas. Instead of waiting passively for admission to the Union, Lamar headed a group who believed that the future of Texas lay in remaining independent and staying out of potential quarrels over slavery and the tariff within the United States. Under his administration recognition from France

---

[9] Gregg, *Commerce of the Prairies*, 93–96.

[10] Basic contemporary accounts are George Wilkins Kendall, *Narrative of the Texan Santa Fe Expedition;* Thomas Falconer, *Letters and Notes on the Texan Santa Fe Expedition, 1841–1842,* ed. by F. W. Hodge. The most recent secondary account is Noel M. Loomis, *The Texan–Santa Fe Pioneers.* See also Wm. C. Binkley, "New Mexico and the Texas–Santa Fe Expedition," *Southwestern Historical Quarterly,* Vol. XXVII (October, 1923); Thomas Maitland Marshall, "Commercial Aspects of the Texan Santa Fe Expedition," *Southwestern Historical Quarterly,* Vol. XX (January, 1917); Gilbert Roy Bode, "The Life and Times of George Wilkins Kendall," (M.A. thesis, University of Texas, 1932); H. Bailey Carroll, "The Route of the Texan–Santa Fe Expedition" (Ph.D. dissertation, University of Texas, 1935). The Texas point of view was obtained from Stanley Siegel, *A Political History of the Texas Republic 1836–1845.*

and England had been obtained, and Lamar was now looking forward to creating a third great republic in North America with boundaries extending from the Gulf of Mexico to the Pacific Ocean and embracing the Mexican holdings in the Southwest. Such a project was popular in Texas, with many people believing that the citizens around Santa Fe were clamoring for an opportunity to join the Lone Star Republic. And with the upper Río Grande area under the sway of Austin, it would be simple to use it as a "key to unlock the valuable country of California on the shores of the Pacific Ocean."[11] The recent Indian revolt doubtless strengthened the already existing belief that the New Mexicans would welcome the Texans. Finally, the reason for the first move westward to the Río Grande rested upon the tenuous claim that Texas had upon the territory, principally as a result of the treaty signed by President Santa Anna of Mexico.

But before such lofty ambitions could be realized, Lamar had to do something about the sad plight of Texas finances. Conditions were so bad that it was rumored that the fuel bill for the capitol building was not even paid. The public debt was more than seven million dollars, and there was not even money to pay the interest on it. Foreign commerce having collapsed as a result of the panic of 1837, the Texans looked with envy upon what they considered to be the profitable Santa Fe trade. Lamar believed that Texas would be able to take some of this trade away from the Missourians and that such trade might provide an opening wedge for Texan occupation of the area. In addition, the President had visions of trade contacts with Cuba. Perhaps the opening of the trade to Santa Fe would result in Texas' taking over the markets at Chihuahua, and the gold and silver of that area would then flow to Austin. The interest of early French traders, as well as frequent suggestions that Spain establish a trade overland from Texas to Santa Fe, indicates that Lamar's ideas were not completely visionary.

President Lamar had urged such a trading expedition to Santa Fe as early as 1839, but it was not until 1841 that he was able to raise the money to finance the projected expedition. With Texas newspapers openly discussing the proposed venture, it is patently stupid

[11] Quoted in Binkley, "New Mexico and the Texas–Santa Fe Expedition," *Southwestern Historical Quarterly*, Vol. XXVII (October, 1923), 89.

to label it a plot, for had it been one, it would hardly have been publicized so extensively. Had this been intended as a military conquest, even a man like Lamar would not have sent 400 men to conquer a province of 57,000. The evidence is overwhelming that the venture was intended only as a trading expedition, but that if the people of New Mexico were as desirous of political relations with Texas as had been reported, an attempt would be made to take over the area. And, as one authority puts it, "in 1840–41 a large part . . . of the people of New Mexico were yearning with the fever of the possibility of commercial and political relations with Texas."[12]

News of the projected Texan commercial invasion of Santa Fe circulated widely in Mexico City, and steps were taken to halt it. After all, since the Texan declaration of independence had not been recognized by Mexico, a state of war continued to exist. Under such circumstances the Texans were not welcome anywhere within Mexico, let alone at Santa Fe. Especially was this true because the attitude of the New Mexicans was considered to be favorable to the Texans, at least in Mexico City. Hence, Governor Armijo was warned to permit no contact with the Texans at all and to meet them at a distance from the settlements in order to keep people from co-operating with the invaders.

To Governor Armijo, the threat of a Texan invasion was a golden opportunity to create a "red herring" and redeem his waning popularity. To this end, he kept up a steady barrage of warnings to Mexico City accompanied with pleas to increase his military strength. At home he laid plans for defense. One Antonio Sandoval was ordered to watch for intrigue among the Pueblo Indians, and Juan Felipe Ortiz, a priest, was assigned the task of working up fear among the people that the Texans would destroy their religion. Provisions were made to have a party of troops ready on short notice, and two scouting parties were sent out to the east. The Governor's exaggerations of the purpose and strength of the Texans were intended to lay the foundation of an Armijo legend. After all, being a great war-

---

[12] Marshall, "Commercial Aspects of the Texan Santa Fe Expedition," *Southwestern Historical Quarterly*, Vol. XX (January, 1917), 249. There was even speculation that Austin might someday become the center of a profitable trade between Cuba and Santa Fe.

rior who has saved his country has always been an advantage to a politician. But there is no evidence existing that the Governor intended to fight the Texans if he could get out of it.

Fortune smiled on the enigmatic Armijo. The Texans were to be conquered not by the meager military resources available, but rather by the 1,300 mile inhospitable journey through a waterless land of every conceivable kind of terrain, and infested with Indians. Carlos, a Mexican guide, and an Italian named Brignoli had deserted the Texan expedition and made their way to Taos with information about the sad plight of the group. Taking advantage of the disordered conditions of the Texans, as well as their divided command, Armijo was to use the treachery of William T. Lewis to good advantage. The latter was offered safe conduct and money if he would co-operate with the Mexicans. Lewis was able to convince his fellow Texans that there were several thousand Mexican troops ready to fight, instead of a few hundred natives armed with spears and bows and arrows.[13]

This surrender to Armijo's inferior force constitutes one of the blackest marks upon Texas military prowess and certainly is in marked contrast to the valor displayed at the Alamo and San Jacinto. After the treacherous massacre at Goliad, Texans were not supposed ever to be taken alive by the Mexicans. Apparently the surrender took place because of the belief that after all it was a commercial venture and therefore there was nothing to fear. Of more importance was the fact that the Texans were without adequate provisions, horses, and ammunition, and although they believed that one Texan was equal to ten Mexicans in a fight, even if they won the battle it would be impossible for them to escapt alive across the inhospitable wastelands which they had just traversed. Hence, they permitted themselves to be duped by the treachery of one of their members and the false promises of Armijo.

Even allowing for exaggeration on the part of Kendall, the main narrator of events on this expedition, the treatment accorded the Texans was among the most bestial ever meted out in the history of warfare. Many of the prisoners were shot down in cold blood, others were cruelly tortured, and most of them were forced into a death

[13] See Loomis, *Texan–Santa Fe Pioneers*, 156–59, for an analysis of Lewis' conduct.

march southward apparently as dreadful as the march of Bataan. Once they were in Mexico, they were chained and forced to engage in the most degrading labor.[14] Having had very little success against the Texans on the field of battle, the Mexican authorities were going to make the most of this glorious success and through their treatment of the prisoners let everyone know that Mexicans were, after all, superior to Texans.

The failure of the Texan venture was probably caused by the confusion of motives from the very beginning of the project. If it were going to be a military venture, adequate preparation and secrecy should have gone into it. As such precautions were not taken, it is reasonable to contend that the expedition was primarily a commercial project. The Texan–Santa Fe pioneers consistently suffered from the lack of leadership. The Texans, notorious for their lack of discipline, needed a strong leader like Sam Houston, and this they lacked. This deficiency was reflected in the initial failure to start the expedition before the grasslands had begun to dry. Many members actually considered the venture a lark instead of a serious and difficult undertaking. In the midst of unlimited supplies of buffalo meat, bears, and hogs, the men insisted upon eating from their scanty stores of beef, and their leaders permitted them to do so. Competent guides were not provided, hence there were many mistakes in choosing the route to be followed. The distance and hardships encountered from nature were far more extensive than planned for. But perhaps the greatest mistake of the expedition was the failure to realize that, with a virtual state of war existing between Texas and New Mexico, they would not be welcome at Santa Fe and that the authorities would at least take some steps for defense.[15]

The heritage of the Texan–Santa Fe fiasco was to linger. The resulting military conquest had enabled Governor Armijo to increase in stature among the natives. The barbarous cruelty exacted upon the helpless prisoners angered the Texans, but the Republic of Texas was in no position to do anything about it. Furthermore, this success apparently determined Mexico upon a more aggressive attitude

[14] For one account of the treatment accorded the Texans see Falconer, *Letters and Notes on the Expedition*, 215.
[15] Loomis, *Texan–Santa Fe Pioneers*, 114.

toward the Texans and resulted in the beginning of an attempted reconquest in 1842. In that year, Mexican forces captured San Antonio
and plundered the town before they were driven off. In addition,
Corpus Christi was seized by a Mexican force. Such measures forced
President Houston, who had succeeded Lamar, to send two retalia-
tory forces against the Mexicans. One of them was to seek vengeance upon Santa Fe.[16] This force, under Colonel Jacob Snively,
was to number 800 men. One John McDaniel, a Texas captain, recruited a number of men among the riffraff along the Missouri frontier. In April of 1843, this group attacked and plundered the caravan
of José Antonio Chávez from Santa Fe, within United States territory, and murdered the leader. Ultimately, those guilty of the crime
were tried and punished by United States courts. Meanwhile, Colonel Warfield, with a party of perhaps only 20 men from Snively's
command, raided the village of Mora, killing five Mexicans and driving off livestock. During their retreat they were attacked by a larger
force, lost most of their horses in the process, and were forced to
seek refuge at Bent's Fort. There they joined Colonel Snively's force,
composed of about 180 men, many of whom had been recruited with
promises of one-half of all of the plunder obtained in New Mexico.

In June of 1843, Snively's forces encountered an advance guard
of Mexicans on the Santa Fe trail, and in the ensuing fight killed 18
of them, capturing about 80 more. Governor Armijo, who was
camped about 140 miles away at the time of this battle with a force
of about 500 men, fled in terror as soon as he learned the Texans
were near. Perhaps a little care on the part of Snively's forces would
have enabled them to capture Armijo. The forces under Snively met
a detachment under Captain Cooke of the United States Army, who
disarmed the Texans, thus ending the campaign.

One unfortunate aspect of the Texan raids into New Mexico was
the fact that the natives at Mora were antagonistic toward Armijo,
as were also many of the Pueblo Indians. One story has it that the
Indian detachment defeated by Snively had to be tied to their horses
to keep them from deserting until they were out upon the plains.[17]
Naturally, this friendliness toward the Texans was replaced with

16 Billington, *Far Western Frontier*, 140.
17 Ralph Emerson Twitchell, *The Leading Facts of New Mexico History*, II, 86.

enmity. Then too, the murder of Chávez, a prominent Santa Fe citizen, did little to aid the Texans' cause.

The Americans Take Over

The long-heralded war between Mexico and the United States became reality in the spring of 1846. The expansionist drive of Manifest Destiny was undoubtedly the primary cause of this conflict, but long-standing difficulties between the two nations arising from Mexico's inability to maintain an orderly government was likewise an important factor. War clouds had been forming since March, 1845, when Mexico had broken off diplomatic relations following the annexation of Texas by the United States. During the following year, before the actual outbreak of hostilities, American traders and trappers acted as ill-disguised war agents at Santa Fe. These men convinced many of their native business associates and friends that resistance to the United States Army would be futile and, of more importance, that they personally, as well as the province, would profit from the American action. Attempts were made to lessen the fears that the Americans would suppress Roman Catholicism, a point which both Spanish and Mexican officials had stressed to create fear of the aggressive northerners.

The capture of New Mexico figured in President Polk's expansion plans mainly because it was on the path to California. To effect its capture, an army was organized at Fort Leavenworth under Stephen Watts Kearny, soon to be elevated to the rank of brigadier general. After ten years in the West, Kearny had already become legendary, and his skill and fame as a leader was so extensive that men fought to fill the ranks of the invading army. Along with the raw frontiersmen recruited for the venture, Kearny had at his command about 300 army regulars, most of them veterans of western duty.

Rumors reached Kearny that an army of 3,000 men was being sent northward from Chihuahua to aid in the defense of Santa Fe, thus making necessary a prompt movement to effect the invasion before these reinforcements could arrive. On June 26, 1846, the first detachments made their way westward, accompanied by the necessary supply trains. As one soldier said, "As far as the vision can penetrate the long files of cavalry, the gay fluttering banners, and the canvas-covered wagons of the merchant train glistening like banks of snow in the distance, might be seen winding their tortuous way over the undulating surface of the prairies."[18] Kearny's army probably had about 1,700 effective fighting troops, the exact number varying widely because detachments came and went.

After leaving Fort Leavenworth, the first stop of the invading army was at Bent's Fort, 565 miles westward, which served as a rendezvous for all of the other groups. Here the men rested, caroused, and prepared for the coming invasion. Most of the command was composed of hearty frontiersmen who were short on discipline and very difficult for officers to handle, but long on horsemanship, raw courage, and an ability to use firearms. One of the men in Kearny's command, Ebednego Smith, composed a number of little ditties for the soldiers' sake which well represent the mood of the troops.[19]

While the Americans were getting ready for the final invasion of New Mexico, Governor Armijo and the officials at Santa Fe were kept well informed of what was transpiring, either through friendly American traders or their own scouts. In June, riots had threatened in Santa Fe when the natives were warned that the Americans would deprive them of their religion, their possessions, and even take their women and brand them like cattle. The Governor had stopped a threatened assault on the American citizens, but most foreigners lived in dread of such a pogrom.

Exactly what went on in the mind of Governor Armijo and the

---

[18] John T. Hughes, *Doniphan's Expedition*, 14–15.

[19] These songs usually reflected the forces of Manifest Destiny and the contempt of the Americans for the Mexicans:

> *Old Colonel Kearney, you can bet,*
> *Will Keep the boys in motion,*
> *Till Yankee Land includes the sand*
> *On the Pacific Ocean.*

> *Oh, what a joy to fight the dons,*
> *And wallop fat Armijo!*
> *So clear the way to Santa Fe!*
> *With that we all agree, O!*

> (From Hamele, *When Destiny Called*, 24.)

men around him is outside the realm of the historian, for the essential documentary information is not available. But official information is available which hints at transactions which are left undefined. Hence, some conjecture is necessary to recreate what did happen.

Manuel Armijo had always been distinguished as a braggadocio. He had never effectively led troops in battle and was widely suspected of being a coward personally. The best defense of New Mexico had been the inhospitable plains, which had served so effectively in checking the Texan–Santa Fe Expedition. Now, the force that was coming was far more formidable than any in the past. In fact, Kearny would release the Mexican scouts captured after treating them fairly and filling them with much exaggerated information so that they could quickly convey it to Santa Fe, thus increasing the already multiplying fears of Armijo. As rumors of the invasion continued to grow, the Governor made the usual bombastic appeals to the people to fight to the death for the fatherland, their religion, their homes, and all that was dear to them against the encroachment of the barbarian Americans. Such propaganda had little influence upon the natives, who had had many business dealings with Americans, and, more than likely, the Governor was issuing the pronouncements more for the record than for any practical purpose. That Armijo contemplated flight is suggested by the fact that he dissolved his business partnership with Albert Speyer, with whom he was engaged in the Santa Fe trade, at the first rumor of an American invasion.[20]

In fairness to Armijo, it should be noted that he only had between 200 and 300 ill-equipped regulars. To this group he was able to add approximately 2,000 militia, most of them Indians who frequently lacked firearms. There was every reason to believe that the militia would run at the first sign of a fight. The point at which Santa Fe would have to be defended was Apache Canyon, lying a short distance to the east. Here the Santa Fe trail wound through a narrow passage in the mountains, where a small group of men could effectively block an entrance. Invasion by other routes was virtually im-

[20] The atmosphere in Santa Fe at this time is recreated by the following novelists because they are free to utilize legends and are less concerned with accuracy than is the historian. See Elliott Arnold, *The Time of the Gringo,* and Ruth Laughlin, *The Wind Leaves No Shadow.*

possible with a wagon train because of the nature of the mountain passes. Had Armijo made a stand at Apache Canyon, the entrance of the Americans could have been delayed and the position of Kearny's army, because of the lack of water, could have been most hazardous. In any event, there would have been little doubt about the outcome. The Americans undoubtedly would have lost many men in forcing the canyon, or they would have sent a party over the mountains to attack the defender's rear.

The character of New Mexico's governor was well known to the American traders, and one of them, James W. Magoffin, was determined to take advantage of it. Magoffin had been for many years engaged in the Santa Fe trade, was married to a Mexican woman, and, as an Irish Catholic, mixed easily with the native populace and was extremely popular. After visiting President Polk and Secretary of War Marcy, Magoffin joined Kearny's army with special instructions. From Bent's Fort the wily Irishman was sent out with a detachment of twenty troops under Captain Philip St. George Cooke on a secret mission under a flag of truce. Armijo hospitably received his old friend Magoffin and Captain Cooke, even entertaining them lavishly. At a secret meeting late at night Magoffin apparently convinced Armijo that resistance was useless and that he would be doing a service to his people by not fighting. One unprovable legend has it that a heavy satchel of gold was turned over to the Mexican governor during the course of this conference.[21] When Colonel Diego Archuleta, one of Armijo's younger officers, held out and wanted to fight, Magoffin promised the Colonel an opportunity to control a new state west of the Río Grande, as the United States only claimed the area east of that river.[22]

Meanwhile, Kearny's army had left Bent's Fort heading southward through Raton Pass accompanied by former mountain men and traders who acted as scouts and spies. Armijo did go through the motion of leading his army out to Apache Canyon, but when a

[21] Colonel Magoffin later claimed $50,000 from the United States but was able to collect only $30,000. Bancroft, *Arizona and New Mexico*, 412.

[22] Magoffin either did not know of Kearny's instructions to continue on to California and to claim all of the area westward to the Pacific or deliberately misled Archuleta. Cooke to Magoffin, February 21, 1849, in Susan Shelby Magoffin, *Down the Santa Fe Trail*, 264–65.

Christopher "Kit" Carson

Archbishop Lamy

Four Men of Nineteenth-Century New Mexico

Charles Bent

James Henry Carleton

Navaho weaver

Tom Burnsides, Navaho silversmith

Ready for the roundup

Driving cattle

Sheep grazing near Shiprock

Early irrigation well

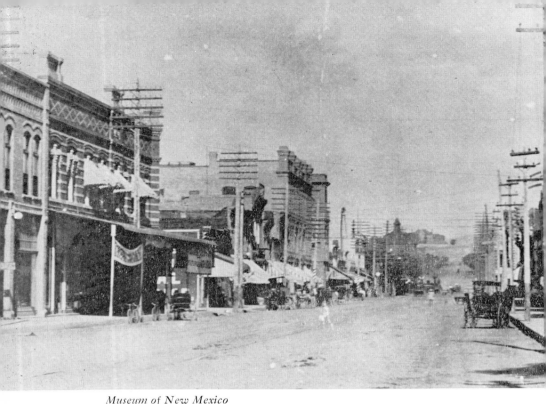

Albuquerque, about 1891

Portales, about 1910

Interior, Trampas Church

Albuquerque Chamber of Commerce

Santo Domingo Church

dispute occurred with his officers over the nature of the defense to be used, he seized it as an excuse to retreat. The Governor returned to Santa Fe, pausing only to complete some necessary business, and then fled southward to Albuquerque and ultimately to Chihuahua. On August 17, Kearny's army arrived at Apache Canyon, found the area deserted, and marveled at their good fortune in not having to attack such a natural fortress. One soldier added that "had Armijo's heart been as stout as the walls of rock which nature gave him to aid in defense of his country we might have sought in vain to force this passage."[23] Santa Fe was captured by the Americans late in the afternoon of August 18, with the formal surrender taking place amid the usual ceremonies the following day.

On this occasion General Kearny repeated the promises already made at the small villages to the east, wherein he committed the Americans to protect the New Mexicans in all respects and guaranteed them freedom of religion and the other advantages of United States citizenship. Every effort was made to allay the suspicions and distrust of the people. Local officials were frequently kept in their posts after taking an oath of allegiance. Thus, New Mexico had been invaded and captured without firing a shot.

Having completed one part of his instructions with so little effort, General Kearny prepared to leave Santa Fe as soon as possible and assist in the conquest of California. In order to accomplish this, he organized a civil government, appointed Charles Bent as acting governor, and authorized Francis Preston Blair, Jr., who was attorney general, to draw up a code of laws for the territory.[24] The heads of the Indian pueblos hurried to Santa Fe to swear allegiance to their new leader, and it looked as though there was no reason for Kearny to tarry any longer in New Mexico, especially while an opportunity for attaining new military honors existed. Therefore, on the twenty-fifth of September the General set out with most of his regular army for the West Coast.

[23] Frank S. Edwards, *A Campaign in New Mexico with Colonel Doniphan*, 44–45.

[24] Blair was a member of a distinguished political family. His father, Francis Preston Blair, Sr., was on intimate terms with both President Jackson and President Lincoln. His brother, Montgomery Blair, was postmaster general during the Civil War. This Blair, whose career took him to New Mexico, served in Congress from Missouri and was later an officer during the Civil War.

❧ *Another Taos Uprising* ❧

Despite the surface appearance of acceptance of the Americans by most of the people, it was going to be necessary to shed blood before the rule of the United States would be firmly established. As Colonel Doniphan correctly pointed out, "A people conquered but yesterday, could have no friendly feeling for their conquerors, who have taken possession of their country—changed its laws and appointed new officers, principally foreigners."[25] And beneath the façade of profound peace there was deep unrest and resentment toward the invaders that was about to express itself in a general revolt.

A variety of factors doubtless caused the general dissatisfaction with the political change. Men such as Diego Archuleta and others who had expected to obtain political positions with the coming of the Americans were disappointed and hoped to improve their own lot through overthrowing the intruders. Many of those antagonistic toward the Americans had always resented the disgraceful nature of Armijo's surrender and its implications that Mexicans were cowards. Erroneous reports of victories to the south doubtless encouraged many natives to seek redress in the situation and get even with the Americans. The natives, especially those from the better classes, would not have been human had they not resented the overbearing, rowdy, and insulting Americans, who lost no opportunity to show their contempt of the "greasers." Frontier militia may have been effective when there was a fight on, but the men were very difficult to control and discipline during a period of peace. After General Kearny left for California, Colonel Doniphan and his troops were frequently out in the Indian country, and in December started for Chihuahua. The plotters were convinced that the small number of Americans remaining could be easily overwhelmed. The leaders of the projected revolt had good reason to believe that they would have the support of the lower-class native elements, both Mexican and Indian, because their lot had been most difficult as a result of the hard times accompanying the war; after all, the Americans had not brought more food for the people.[26]

[25] William E. Smith, *The Francis Preston Blair Family in Politics.*
[26] *Ibid.*, 25–27.

The leaders of the revolt were Tomás Ortiz and Colonel Diego Archuleta. Added to this group were several members of the Pino family and some of the Armijos from Albuquerque, along with several clergymen. In the last group were Father Antonio José Martínez, Father J. F. Leyba, and the Reverend Juan Felipe Ortiz. Most of these men were related by marriage, and though the case against the clergymen was never proved by United States authorities, there is little question about the extent of their complicity.[27]

As early as October 20 the Americans were alerted to a possible uprising and were kept in a constant state of readiness. For several weeks modified martial law was in existence around Santa Fe, and every attempt was made to be ready for action. However, as it was difficult to keep the restless Missouri volunteers consistently alert for a fight and then not have one, the strict discipline was relaxed. On November 20 correspondence addressed to the former governor, Manuel Armijo, was intercepted which pointed out that the United States troops in New Mexico were so widely scattered that any assistance from the south would make possible an insurrection. The drilling of troops by the Mexican leaders went on in secret, and gunpowder was obtained for the coming fight.

Plans for the uprising were crystallized in a series of secret meetings held in Santa Fe during December. The first date, December 19, was later changed to Christmas Eve because it would be easier for a large number of New Mexicans to assemble at Santa Fe for worship services.[28] The conspirators planned to kill Colonel Price and Governor Bent, the American leaders, and in the confusion drive out or kill the remaining soldiers.

The conspiracy collapsed when some of the members made the fatal error of letting women know about their plans. Someone warned the Americans, and protective measures were taken, with most of the ringleaders being captured.

The ease with which the Americans had uncovered the plot lulled them into a sense of false security. Governor Bent issued a proclamation on January 5, 1847, telling the people what had happened and pleading with them to continue to support the new govern-

[27] Ralph Emerson Twitchell, *Old Santa Fe*, 276.
[28] Garrard, *Wah-to-yah and the Taos Trail*, 29–30.

135

ment. Convinced that there was no longer anything to dread, Governor Bent and a group of his friends then left Santa Fe for their homes at Taos for a visit with their families. Though warned of possible danger, the Governor refused a military escort, not believing that anyone would harm a man like himself who had been living in New Mexico for almost twenty years. This failure to gauge the people's real sentiments was to cost Charles Bent his life.

On January 19, 1847, an uprising occurred in Taos in which Bent was brutally murdered and scalped by a group of Indians and Mexicans led by Pablo Montoya and Tomasito. The Governor refused to listen to all requests to flee, feeling that it would be disgraceful for him to act like Manuel Armijo and still refusing to believe that anyone would harm him. In addition to Governor Bent, five other men of importance were slain by the revolutionists in Taos. At approximately the same time seven more Americans were murdered at Turley's Mill in the Arroyo Hondo, and possibly another seven in the town of Mora. Americans living on outlying ranchos or traveling along the Santa Fe Trail were likewise killed by Mexicans or Indians.

Most writers of New Mexico history contend that the Taos uprising was an outgrowth of the earlier plot at Santa Fe and was carefully planned in advance. Evidence to substantiate this point of view is lacking, and Bancroft is probably correct when he states that "it does not clearly appear that the Taos outbreak had been definitely planned in advance."[29] More than likely, the outbreak at Taos resulted when the ignorant natives listened to the exaggerated charges of Pablo Montoya, "the self-styled Santa Anna of the north," and Tomasito, the Taos Indian leader. The chance for booty probably was as good a motive as any for the people to break through the thin layer of civilization in which they had been encased and return to their primitive state.

Lending support to the theory that the Taos outbreak was more the result of spontaneous combustion than long-range planning was the role of the controversial local leader, Padre Martínez. There is little question that Martínez was originally involved in the Santa Fe plot, but it is highly dubious that he had anything to do with the Taos affair. In fact, his control of the people in Taos was so extensive that

[29] Bancroft, *Arizona and New Mexico*, 432.

if long-range planning had been involved, he would inevitably have been aware of it. In addition, Martínez was far too practical a politician not to realize what would happen to the natives after an orgy of killing. Nor was the character of the man such that he would have either encouraged or permitted the revolt to get under way if he could have prevented it.[30]

News of the Taos uprising reached Colonel Price at Santa Fe on January 20 through the interception of messages calling upon the natives to revolt in that area. A request for reinforcements was sent to Albuquerque, and Price prepared to lead an expedition to Taos. The whole force consisted of 353 men, including a company of Santa Fe volunteers under the command of Captain Céran St. Vrain. In the latter group were included many former mountain men and, ironically enough, several Mexicans who had only recently been released from jail as a result of the December plot against the Americans. This was to be their first opportunity to prove the allegiance they had sworn to the United States, and most of them were to prove worthy of the trust placed in them. Additional reinforcements from Albuquerque were to swell the total to 479 men.

They marched northward through heavy snow and the bitter cold of the high mountains. On the twenty-fourth of January the revolting army, 1,500 strong, was encountered, and the battle of La Cañada was fought, with Price winning a decisive victory. On the twenty-ninth another battle was fought, with the rebels being forced to flee to Taos, where they entrenched themselves within the pueblo. The troops laid seige February 3 and 4, their artillery having a difficult time against the thick adobe walls. Before the battle was over, the American force lost 7 killed and 45 wounded, while the Indians were estimated to have lost 150 killed before they surrendered. Except for the battle at Mora, which destroyed the town, and a few other scattered incidents, the defeat of the Taos rebels brought the revolution to a close.

In accordance with the traditions of Anglo-Saxon justice, the lead-

---

[30] Blanche C. Grant, *When Old Trails Were New: The Story of Taos,* presents the orthodox position that Padre Martínez masterminded the uprising. Francis, "Padre Martínez," *NMHR,* Vol. XXXI (October, 1956), denies the complicity of the controversial clergyman.

ers of the uprising were given a fair trial. Much has been made of the fact that one of the judges was a close friend of the slain governor and the other's son had been murdered by the rebels. The foreman of the grand jury was the slain governor's brother and one of the jurors a relative of the slain sheriff. Actually, the nature of the closely-knit community made it virtually impossible to exclude friends or relatives from such proceedings. Although some of the judicial proceedings might be considered unfair today, when one takes into account the charged atmosphere that existed at that time and the fact that such a trial was even held, a valuable precedent for the New Mexicans' introduction to the United States legal system was established. In all, some fifteen men were sentenced to death, one of them for high treason. The last case is the one that has brought most of the objections, on the basis that the man could not have been guilty of treason because citizenship had not yet been granted. However, Francis Preston Blair, the prosecuting attorney, believed that Kearny had granted citizenship and did not understand that such action was unacceptable in Washington until the treaty of peace had been signed.[31]

So it had been "the time of the gringo." From the first intrusion of Lieutenant Pike's tiny force through the onrush of American mountain men eagerly seeking the beaver to the traders bringing American manufactured goods to Santa Fe, the whole climaxed by the invasion associated with the Mexican War, the Americans had slowly but surely moved into New Mexico, the outpost which Spain, and later Mexico, had held for centuries. The expansive force of Manifest Destiny was not to be denied. New Mexico was now in the United States, but as one observer noted, it was to be a long time before New Mexico was to be of the United States.

[31] Garrard, *Wah-to-yah and the Taos Trail* is the standard authority for the trial of the conspirators.

VIII - New Mexico and the Sectional Controversy

THE TERRITORY ACQUIRED as a result of the war with Mexico brought into the open the long-smoldering dispute over slavery. Since New Mexico was a part of the area involved, it was inevitable that she would be influenced by the controversy between North and South from its very beginning. When New Mexico made its bid to enter the Union along with California in 1848, it went on record in a memorial as being opposed to the institution of slavery. In addition, it had banned slavery in the constitution drafted in 1850 but never allowed to go into effect. Naturally, this earned the territory the enmity of the proslavery faction in Congress and thus hurt its chances for statehood.[1]

The proponents of the Compromise of 1850, a measure which it was hoped would end the controversy over slavery, were reasonably well informed about the climatic conditions of New Mexico. Led by Webster, they convinced many of those with abolitionist sentiments in the North that Mother Nature had erected a more effective barrier against slavery and cotton culture than any law that could be drafted, and any attempt to ban the institution from the territory would needlessly alienate the sensitive Southerners.[2] Therefore, New Mexico was admitted as a territory under the terms of the Compromise of 1850 with no mention of whether it would be a slaveholding or a free territory.

[1] For more complete discussion see Chapter XII.
[2] The basic source for this section is Loomis Morton Ganaway, *New Mexico and the Sectional Controversy, 1846–1861*.

⌇⌇⌇ *The Texas Boundary Controversy* ⌇⌇⌇

It was not slavery but rather the dispute over the boundary between the territory and Texas that made New Mexico a pawn on the national political scene. The question of where New Mexico's eastern boundary lay was similar to countless other disputes that have plagued Spanish-American history. In colonial times, it was not necessary to set exact limits. In fact, it was advantageous not to do so, as this might prejudice claims to territories found to be valuable.[3]

The claim of Texas westward to the Río Grande was even more tenuous within New Mexico than it was southward to the Nueces River. Acceptance of the Texas claim would have meant the inclusion of Santa Fe within Texas. As this was the capital of the province under the Spanish-colonial governors long before Texas was settled by anything but scorpions and Indians, the claim seemed the more preposterous. The effective governmental control of the Spaniards went as far east as the hostile Indians would permit and varied accordingly. Only infrequently did the claim extend into the eastern plains region. But it most certainly included the various small settlements scattered along the Canadian River and, in some instances, the tributaries of the Pecos. Although the president of the Texas Republic stated that the western boundary should follow the Río Grande to its source and thence north to the 42d degree north latitude, he indicated that it might be necessary to accept a line halfway between the Nueces and the Río Grande, running toward the mouth of the Pecos and northwesterly along that river and the mountains to the source of the Arkansas River. However, this more reasonable claim was rejected by the Texas Congress, who demanded the line of the Río Grande.[4] Some Texans, with even more grandiose ideas, made the exaggerated claim that their jurisdiction should extend westward to include the Bay of San Francisco.[5]

[3] The involved controversy concerning the exact limits of the Louisiana Purchase is one example of this problem.

[4] Victor Truman Lewis, "Texas and the Nation, 1845–1860" (M.A. thesis, East Texas Teacher's College, 1940), 47.

[5] William C. Binkley, "The Question of Texan Jurisdiction in New Mexico under the United States, 1848–1850," *Southwestern Historical Quarterly*, Vol. XXIV (July, 1920), 1.

Neither during the Mexican period nor during its own brief existence as a republic was Texas to effect any kind of control over the disputed region, and hence on a basis of *uti possidetus* the claim did not have validity. Nor did the futile effort of the Texans to extend their authority to Santa Fe in 1841 lend credence to later claims.

Once General Kearny and the United States Army had accomplished what the Texans were unable to do—that is, conquer New Mexico—the Lone Star State was only too eager to press its claim westward to the Río Grande. In this, it had the active support of the Polk administration. The military authorities at Santa Fe were warned that the national government did not contest the claim of Texas to the territory east of the Río Grande. They were instructed that any civil authority which Texas had established or might attempt to establish should be respected and was to be assisted. Of course, the military was simply carrying out President Polk's declaration expressed in his message to Congress in which he had endorsed that claim of Texas.[6] Although Congress assumed that the Texas boundary did extend to the Río Grande, Polk was inconsistent in one of his messages, for he declared that the Texas which was admitted to the Union was the same Texas provided for in the boundary act of 1836; and in the same message he stated that the Mexican province of New Mexico with Santa Fe as its capital was under the control of the American military. Polk had also stressed that the question of boundary was not one for the executive but rather for the legislative branch of the government to settle.

A change in attitude on the part of Washington was reflected in the new administration of President Taylor. Shortly after military authorities had received instructions to co-operate with the Texas officials who would try to assert their claims, they also had to treat with a confidential presidential agent who was trying to carry out Taylor's policy of getting New Mexico into the Union as a state as quickly as possible. Perhaps one of the reasons for President Taylor's sponsorship of statehood was to make it possible for the boundary question with Texas to be turned over to the judiciary and thus head off what might become a nasty dispute.[7]

[6] *Ibid.*, 14.
[7] *Ibid.*, 17.

Texas had strongly asserted her claim during the course of the Mexican War, but had awaited final disposition pending the peace treaty. As the war ended, the government at Austin prepared to act on what they interpreted as Polk's promise to turn the disputed area over to them.

As early as March, 1848, the Texas governor had warned that the state had best act to enforce its authority in the region claimed, lest Texas rights be usurped. Hence, the Texas legislature passed a series of laws creating a county organization, providing for the control of the militia in the Santa Fe district, granting one representative in the Texas House of Representatives, and establishing a new judicial district of the state.[8] One Spruce M. Baird was sent to Santa Fe to serve as judge and supervise the organization of the newly created county.

In November, 1848, Baird received a cool reception from the people of Santa Fe. In spite of President Polk's endorsement of the Texas claim, the military authorities sided with the New Mexicans. The Santa Fe newspaper, controlled by the military, declared, "There is not a citizen, either American or Mexican, that will ever acknowledge themselves as citizens of Texas. . . . New Mexico does not belong, nor has Texas ever had a right to claim her as a part of Texas. . . . Texas should show some little sense, and drop this question."[9]

With the New Mexicans far more interested in statehood than in submitting to the magnificent rule of Texas, the government at Austin became alarmed. When Colonel Monroe issued his proclamation, in the spring of 1850, calling for a constitutional convention, the current Texas delegate to the claimed territory, R. S. Neighbors, withdrew from Santa Fe. Upon his report to Austin, the Texans were in a rage. Considering the calling of this constitutional convention "an outrage beyond which it was not possible to go," they felt that matters had now reached a point where their claims should be enforced by military power. Some believed that when Texas was admitted, all of her territorial claims had been sanctioned, and if they were now to be violated, then annexation should be rescinded and Texas should leave the Union. Newspaper comment within the state

[8] *Ibid.*, 7; Lewis, "Texas and the Nation," 58.
[9] Quoted in Lewis, "Texas and the Nation," 39. See also Holman Hamilton, *Zachary Taylor: Soldier in the White House*, 180–81.

as well as several mass meetings indicated that force could have been used by the governor if he so desired. Meanwhile, the Texas delegation in Congress was advised of the situation, and formal protests were made to President Taylor.

The letter from the Texas governor did not reach Washington until after Taylor's death, and was therefore acted upon by his successor, Millard Fillmore. Both Secretary of State Webster and the new President proceeded to answer the Texan's objections. Webster pointed out that Colonel Monroe was within his authority in calling such a convention and that the people of New Mexico always had the right to petition for statehood. The Secretary of State stressed that Texas had little authority to interfere in the boundary questions and that it was a matter for Congress ultimately to decide.

President Fillmore was less judicious in his approach than his Secretary of State had been. The President flatly denied that Texas had any claim to New Mexico whatsoever. Fillmore then began questioning the right of Texas to call a special session of the legislature so as to inflict her jurisdiction over a region under the control of the United States military. The President warned that his constitutional duty obligated him to act: "If Texas militia, therefore, march into any one of the other states, or into any territory of the United States, to execute or enforce any law of Texas, they . . . are to be regarded merely as intruders; and if, within such state or territory they obstruct any law of the United States, either by power or arms, or mere power of numbers, or constitute such a combination as is too powerful to be suppressed by the civil authority, the President of the United States has no option left to him, but that of using force in carrying out the acts of Congress."[10] As further warning to Texas, 750 additional troops were sent into New Mexico.

Alexander H. Stevens, of Georgia, declared in the House that "the first federal gun that shall be fired against the people of Texas without the authority of the law will be a signal for the free man from the Delaware to the Rio Grande to rally to the rescue."[11] Such an

[10] James D. Richardson, *Messages and Papers of the Presidents*, IV, 2605.

[11] Quoted in Binkley, "The Question of Texan Jurisdiction in New Mexico Under the United States, 1848–50," *Southwestern Historical Quarterly*, Vol. XXIV (July, 1920), 37.

attitude on both sides could easily have rent the Union asunder a decade earlier than it was to be. In spite of the fact that most senators agreed with Clay that "Texas has not a good title to any portion of what is called New Mexico,"[12] the situation was so serious that a compromise was needed. In order to effect a settlement, Senator Pearce of Maryland proposed the boundaries of New Mexico and suggested that Texas be given a compensation of $10,000,000 if she would be willing to relinquish her claims. This proposal was accepted and thus ended a controversy which was easily the most difficult part of the compromise of 1850.[13] Such a monetary adjustment was sufficient to salve the honor of Texas, and, besides, it was approximately the right amount to pay that state's outstanding indebtedness.

Although the settlement established the boundary at the 103d meridian, unfortunately, many years were to elapse before the eastern limits to New Mexico were established. In the subsequent laying out of the exact boundary, surveys were made both from the northern tip of the state and the southern. This left a gap of 130 miles between the two surveys. When the survey was completed, it was found that the two lines did not meet, and, since much time had elapsed since the previous surveying, it was not possible to make adjustments, for many people were already located either in Texas or in New Mexico. Hence a diagonal line was simply drawn arbitrarily to establish the state boundary. Worst of all from the New Mexican point of view, it was found that the line drawn was not on the 103d meridian. It lay about one-half mile west of it. As this line had been approved by Congress in 1891 and as Texas had already sold land in the disputed area, the Texas claim to it was honored. Despite the fact that the New Mexico constitution of 1911 claimed the region, President Taft granted it to Texas because the Texans were already in possession of it. Thus, the Texans were able to deprive New Mexico of approximately one-half million acres of land that was rightfully hers.[14]

[12] Ganaway, *New Mexico and the Sectional Controversy*, 29.

[13] *Ibid.*, 31.

[14] J. Evetts Haley, *The XIT Ranch of Texas and the Early Days of the Llano Estacado*, 61–70; Mary Lee Robinson, "History of Roosevelt County, New Mexico" (M.A. thesis, University of Texas, 1947), 57–62.

$\sim$ Union or Confederacy? $\sim$

Once the Compromise of 1850 was passed, New Mexico tended to fade from the national view. The territory did not have an abundance of rich farmland to entice the northern settler looking for free land, nor had its mines yet revealed the high hopes they did in the postwar period. There was nothing there to interest the North, and the twenty or so slaves in the territory, most of them servants of military personnel, hardly made it southern territory.

Nevertheless, during the 1850's there was a gradual shift in attitude from the pro-Northern proclivities evident in the quest for statehood from 1848 to 1850 to a more pro-Southern point of view. Although some historians have mistakenly claimed that "conspiracy in the very bosom of the national administration at Washington" existed for the purpose of advancing the interests of the South in New Mexico, careful investigation shows that the change was more the result of the natural influence of Democratic officeholders than the result of intrigue.[15] As evidence of this southern influence in the territory, a law was passed in 1856 which seriously curtailed the rights of free Negroes and, by implication, encouraged them to leave.[16]

Southern influences were more greatly increased as a result of the activities of Miguel Antonio Otero, who was the delegate in Congress in the late 1850's. Otero married a southern belle and aligned himself with the South while serving in Washington. Indicative of his influence was the passage of the slave code of 1859 by the territorial legislature. The primary motive for Otero's sponsoring this measure was to win favor with southern congressmen and thus influence legislation favorable to New Mexico.

In a letter to the territorial secretary, Otero pointed out that the laws of the United States, as well as the Dred Scott decision, established slavery beyond a question in all of the territories and that it would be in New Mexico's best interest to recognize this fact with

[15] Ganaway, *New Mexico and the Sectional Controversy*, 84. For an exposition of the southern "plot" see Robert Louis Reiter, "History of Fort Union" (M.A. thesis, University of California, Berkley, 1953), 78.

[16] Ganaway, *New Mexico and the Sectional Controversy*, 59.

the passage of an appropriate law.[17] As passed, this New Mexican slave code of 1859 was similar in many respects to the national fugitive slave act. But in addition to providing for proper punishment for those aiding slaves to escape and making their return easier, it also spelled out the punishment and treatment of slaves. The measure was to apply only to those of the African race, but it was alleged that many of the native members of the territorial legislature were in favor of this code because they saw it as a means by which peonage within the territory would be endorsed.

Many travelers in New Mexico quickly noted the similarity between peonage and slavery, although they usually agreed that Negro slavery was far more humane than New Mexican–style peonage. This latter institution had originally developed as a result of the campaigns of the seventeenth century against the Indians. Under peonage the master had all of the advantage, because he was able to obtain the best years of work from the poor native without having any obligation for his later care. The peons were controlled by means of indebtedness, and as few of them were able to satisfy debts owed their masters, their status usually lasted their lifetime. In theory, the peons were not to be bought and sold as were the Negro slaves. In practice, however, one observer claimed that "peons are as much an article of trade as a horse or sheep."

In 1867 it was estimated that there were between 1,500 and 3,000 actual Indian slaves in New Mexico. It is more difficult to estimate the number of peons. There were about 500 to 700 wealthy native families, with the rest of the native population numbering between 50,000 and 70,000 individuals, most of them held in a nominal state of bondage through the peonage of debt.[18] So with Indian slavery already established and a more important system of peonage providing the necessary workers, there was no advantage to New Mexico to add Negro slaves. As a result, a number of the leading native families were not interested in the national controversy one way or another.

As the showdown in the North-South controversy neared in 1860, most observers felt that New Mexico would follow the lead of the

17 *Ibid.*, 68.
18 *Ibid.*, 9–12.

Southern states. During the debate in the winter of 1861 over the Crittenden Compromise, which would have extended slavery to the Pacific on the Missouri Compromise line, this belief was further heightened. New Mexico would have been placed within the zone of slavery extension, and her representative, Miguel Otero, indicated that this was acceptable to the territory. A proposal to grant immediate statehood in March of 1861 failed of passage because of vigorous opposition of northern abolitionist leaders.

When it came time finally to make a decision, Otero surprised many by proposing a confederacy of the Pacific states and indicating that he was prepared to ignore both North and South. His position was probably that of another New Mexican who answered the question of what the territory's status should be as war began: "What is the position of New Mexico? The answer is a short one. She desires to be let alone . . . no interference from one side or the other of the sections that are now waging war. She neither wants abolitionists or secessionists from abroad to mix in her affairs at present."[19] Though declaring that he was very much opposed to the Republicans, Otero denied that it was necessary to dissolve the Union merely because that party happens to elect a president. Bancroft is perhaps correct when he cites apathy as the primary attitude of New Mexico towards the sectional conflict.[20]

With the exception of a few prominent natives, most of the New Mexicans not only remained loyal to the Union cause, but many of them performed ably as militia or scouts for the regular army. Undoubtedly affecting their loyalty was the fact that to them the Confederacy was identified with Texas, their ancient enemy.[21] The only defection to the South occurred in the southern part of the state near Mesilla. Most of the inhabitants of this area were Texans, many of whom had been granted land when that state had claimed the territory. The territory obtained from Mexico by means of the Gadsden Purchase was added to New Mexico, thus giving the Texans more area in which to settle. Isolated as they were from the Santa Fe government, they had made many proposals to establish a separate territory during the 1850's, all of which were unsuccessful.

[19] Quoted in *ibid.*, 91.
[20] Bancroft, *Arizona and New Mexico*, 680.
[21] *Ibid.*, 684.

When they heard that Texas had seceded, they organized a convention in March, 1861, and announced themselves as the Arizona Territory, taking in all of the land below the 34th degree of latitude, extending to California. Organizing a government, they petitioned for admission to the Confederacy as a territory. No natives were permitted to participate in the new government, as was explained in the following words: "One good company of Texan cavalry can do more to insure their [Mexican] loyalty to the confederacy than all of the officers in the territory."[22] Gradually federal authority in the area waned, the judge for the Mesilla district refusing to hold court unless protected by the Union army.

The Civil War in New Mexico

New Mexico was not to be left alone during the Civil War. Although not as large in scope as the eastern campaigns, the engagements fought in this western territory were of some significance. In New Mexico, the Union was successful in preventing the Confederacy from realizing its western ambitions.

In the spring of 1861, Federal forces held a number of small forts in New Mexico, primarily as a means of defense against the ever present hostile Indians. Along the Río Grande were Fort Craig, Fort Fillmore, and Fort Bliss near El Paso. East of the Río Grande were Fort Union near Las Vegas, Fort Marcy at Santa Fe, and Fort Stanton in the Lincoln Mountains. In the west were Fort Defiance, near the present Arizona state line, and Fort Breckenridge and Fort Buchanan, near Tucson. These scattered forts were dependent upon supplies hauled all the way from Fort Leavenworth, even horses, as the New Mexico range animal was not fit for military use.[23] Obtaining supplies was to be a critical problem throughout the Civil War for the Union forces, but, worst of all, they were frequently without money as well.

[22] Ganaway, *New Mexico and the Sectional Controversy*, 102–103.

[23] Stevens T. Norvell, "New Mexico in the Civil War," in *War Papers: Military Order of the Loyal Legion of the United States* (January 7, 1903), 4. The Civil War in New Mexico is treated in Ray C. Colton, *The Civil War in the Western Terri-*

More important than the problem of supplies, however, was the problem of military morale. As their home states seceded, officer after officer had to decide where his loyalties lay. At Fort Union one officer observed, "Nothing but secession is talked of at this post; I have had to warn everyone that if there is any effort to seduce my regiment from its allegiance I would assume command myself and fight it out." Propositions were made to the junior-grade officers to raise their rank if they would only join the Confederates. Usually, the rank and file soldiers remained loyal.[24]

The most ambitious scheme to take Union troops into the Confederacy was that of Colonel George B. Crittenden of Kentucky. This officer planned to march the infantry under his command, organized to fight the Apaches, into Texas, and there turn them over to the Confederacy. Colonel B. S. Roberts, his second in command, went to Colonel Loring, the departmental commander at Santa Fe, to report the matter. Unfortunately for Roberts, he himself got into trouble because several other high-ranking officers, including Loring, were sympathetic to the Confederate cause.[25]

Major Henry H. Sibley, one of the many high-ranking officers to desert their commands, later wrote that he regretted "the sickly sentimentality" which had prevented him from taking the forces under him over to the southern cause. Sibley asked Loring to delay his defection until Texas troops could arrive at Fort Bliss and seize the stores and ammunition there.[26] With the widespread desertion by their officers, it is a wonder that the Union troops in New Mexico could have been as effective as they were. As one soldier complained, "We were deserted by our officers to a point where we practically became an army without officers."[27]

tories; Robert Lee Kerby, *The Confederate Invasion of New Mexico and Arizona 1861–1862;* W. H. Watford, "Confederate Western Amebitions," *Southwestern Historical Quarterly,* Vol. XLIV (October, 1940); William A. Keleher, *Turmoil in New Mexico 1846–1868;* Charles S. Walker, "Causes of the Confederate Invasion of New Mexico," *NMHR,* Vol. VIII (April, 1933), and William I. Woldrip, "New Mexico During the Civil War,"*NMHR,* Vol. XXVIII (July, 1953; October, 1953).

[24] Quoted in Keleher, *Turmoil in New Mexico,* 191.

[25] Watford, "Confederate Western Ambitions," *Southwestern Historical Quarterly,* Vol. XLIV (October, 1940), 162–63.

[26] Keleher, *Turmoil in New Mexico,* 146.

[27] Quoted in Kerby, *Confederate Invasion,* 29.

The immediate object of the Confederate invasion of New Mexico was to seize this territory and thus satisfy the earlier but thwarted demand of the Texans. But the barren, poverty-stricken, and Indian-infested territory was only a small part of the grandiose Confederate scheme. The taking of New Mexico was to be only a prelude to the ultimate conquest of California and then Colorado. It was also assumed that the Mormons, smarting under their recent chastisement by federal troops, would be interested in making common cause with the South. With Mexico in one of her chronic periods of anarchy, the Confederates also thought the time might be right to annex some of the northern states of that nation, and so intrigued with their governors. Confederates assumed that the native Mexicans and the Indians would be ready to assist the secessionist group in southern New Mexico, Arizona, and Southern California in carrying out their grand design.

If these aims had been attained, the gold and silver of the Southwest would have been brought into the Confederate treasury, thereby making it possible to purchase the necessary supplies abroad. The vast seacoast of California and parts of Mexico would have been at the disposal of the Confederate commerce destroyers, and would also have provided a place of entry for supplies from Europe. Most important of all, the easy conquest of such a vast territory was expected to enhance the prestige of the Confederates in Europe to a point where recognition for the government at Richmond would be forthcoming. As such recognition could have undoubtedly brought England and France into the war against the North, the Confederates assumed that it would win the struggle for them.[28] Such was the grandiose scheme of the Confederacy.

As the war came to New Mexico in the summer of 1861, it appeared that the Confederate plan for conquering the Southwest was not just a wild dream, but was capable of realization. On July 1, 1861, Captain John Robert Baylor, in command of 258 Texas cavalry, occupied Fort Bliss. It was obvious that Baylor's immediate objective would be the capture of Fort Fillmore. Commanding this fort was Major Isaac Lynde, only recently transferred from Fort

[28] Walker, "Causes of the Confederate Invasion," *NMHR*, Vol. VIII (April, 1933), 97; Augustus Allen Hayes, Jr., *New Colorado and the Santa Fe Trail*, 163–65.

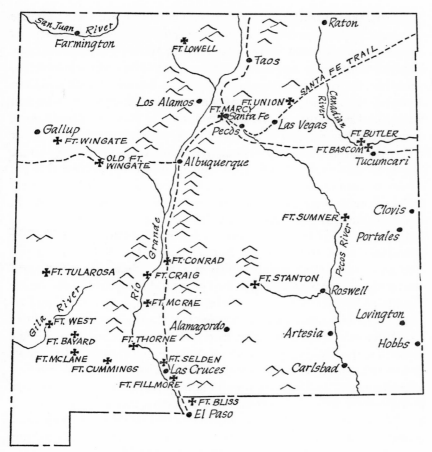

Old Forts and Trails in New Mexico

McLaine, which had been abandoned. The holding of Fort Fillmore was not important, except to make it possible for the Federal troops at Fort Buchanan and Fort Breckenridge to be evacuated. Lynde bitterly complained to Colonel Canby that Fort Fillmore was "located in a depression, commanded on three sides by the hills, within 6 pounder range, and that water for men and animals, had to be taken from the Rio Grande, a mile and a half away."[29] With Major Lynde convinced that the fort was not "worth the exertion to hold it," it is surprising that the fort was not surrendered earlier.[30] Fort Fillmore had been especially demoralized, and Lynde was not sure that his men would fight. Most of the officers deserting to the Confederacy from the west passed through Fort Fillmore en route to the South, and intrigue was the order of the day.

On July 23, 1861, Baylor moved his army northward from Fort Bliss and occupied Mesilla. At Fort Fillmore, Lynde had about 700 effective troops.[31] Canby had also sent him additional rations and ammunition, and assumed that the fort could easily hold out against Baylor's Texans, who totaled only 380 men. On the afternoon of July 25, Lynde moved his forces toward Mesilla and demanded the surrender of the Confederates. In the exchange of fire three Union soldiers were killed and six wounded. After this "battle" the Union forces returned to Fort Fillmore, where "Major Lynde took council with his fears."[32] The Union commander was certain that the fort could not be defended against the Confederate artillery and that it should be abandoned. He decided to flee to Fort Stanton, 154 miles to the northeast. Probably overcome with cowardice. Lynde did not consult his staff on the decision and ordered the abandonment of the fort immediately after the skirmish. The undisciplined soldiers, lack-

---

[29] Keleher, *Turmoil in New Mexico*, 148.

[30] Kerby, *Confederate Invasion*, 33.

[31] Keleher, *Turmoil in New Mexico*, 148. The estimates of effective troops vary widely. Many authorities set the figure as low as 400. Dr. McKee, who was present, claims that a force of 500 Union soldiers surrendered to some 300 Texans. James Cooper McKee, *Narrative of the Surrender at Fort Fillmore*, 2. Regardless of the actual number of troops available to defend the fort, one officer claimed that Fort Fillmore could have been held with 300 men against a force of 3,000. Colton, *Civil War in the Western Territories*, 15.

[32] *Ibid.*, 149.

ing proper supervision by their officers, were more concerned about the abandonment of good liquor than they were in properly planning for the retreat.

The following day, soldiers recovering from too much liquor, frequently with their canteens filled with that fluid instead of water, suffered in the open. Drunken stragglers were taken prisoner by the pursuing Confederates, and by afternoon Major Lynde had surrendered his entire command, which Baylor estimated at 700 men, the Confederates having only 200. Many Union officers protested that the soldiers surrendered without having been given an opportunity to defend themselves against an inferior force.[33]

After the debacle at Fort Fillmore, Colonel Canby, the departmental commander, took stock of his situation. He had only 2,466 men and was isolated and cut off without funds, provisions, horses, uniforms, or guns, and drastically short of officers; his position was desperate. In spite of these handicaps, Canby prepared to do the impossible. He issued a call for New Mexican volunteers and, exceeding his authority, requested the assistance of the governor of Colorado Territory. Recognizing that the Confederates must invade by one of two routes, either over the Santa Fe Trail or up the Río Grande, he prepared his defenses accordingly. Canby intended to protect the heart of New Mexico. To do this, he abandoned all of the forts except Fort Craig on the Río Grande, with which he could check the Confederates coming up the river, and Fort Union, which would block the entry from the east. Extensive fortifications were built at both places in preparation for attack.

While making these preparations, Canby was beset by insistent rumors of invading Confederate armies. Fortunately, one force led by Colonel Van Dorn was diverted for eastern service, and he gained more time in which to prepare. It was not long before the rumors were to be confirmed. Colonel Sibley, of previous army service in New Mexico, had been granted an independent command and the authority to raise an army in Texas for the purpose of capturing New Mexico. After journeying all the way to Richmond, Sibley had been

[33] McKee, *Narrative of the Surrender*, 22. Major Lynde was later dismissed from the army for cowardice.

able to convince President Jefferson Davis of the practicality of a Confederate conquest of the Southwest.

Sibley organized an army of approximately 3,700 men, consisting of many seasoned veterans and competent officers, and, unfortunately, too many irresponsible Texans who were interested in nothing but the possibilities of loot. The lack of discipline of Sibley's command was to plague him throughout the long march from San Antonio to Santa Fe and back. Sibley himself, though a popular commander, was not a good disciplinarian and drank too heavily, especially in critical moments.

Entering New Mexico in January, 1862, Sibley issued a grandiose proclamation to the New Mexicans and prepared to march up the Río Grande. He selected this route because it was easier for his army to forage, since supposedly there were rich quartermaster's stores at Fort Craig, Albuquerque, Santa Fe, and Fort Union.[34]

Reaching Fort Craig, Colonel Sibley, who was, incidentally, Colonel Canby's brother-in-law, tried to draw the Union forces into battle. For his part, Canby was intent upon keeping the Confederates away from the needed water supply, and also planned to prevent them from getting close enough to the heights overlooking the fort to mount artillery. Much of Canby's reluctance to fight stemmed from lack of confidence in his volunteers, but he felt that he had to prevent the Confederates from occupying the mesa overlooking the fort. Therefore, after some cavalry skirmishing, the Union armies left the safety of the fort, crossed the river, and prepared to meet the Confederates in the open field, as Sibley had hoped. At a key moment in the battle, one of the volunteer regiments mutinied, leaving the Union center exposed, and thus shifted the advantage in favor of Sibley's forces.

Canby was forced to flee across the Río Grande and to retreat within the confines of Fort Craig. The Union army suffered 306 casualties, which did not count New Mexicans, but, as Canby reported, "Their loss adds to rather than diminishes our strength." Confederate casualties were only 185. Because the way was cleared to Albuquerque, the Battle of Valverde must be considered a Confederate triumph. During the course of the conflict Sibley had lost a large

[34] Kerby, *Confederate Invasion*, 64.

number of wagons and mules, leaving only five days' rations on hand and precluding any thought of a siege of Fort Craig. Hence, it was decided to march to Albuquerque, leaving Canby in the rear. This setback convinced Canby that it was far more advisable to let the country defeat the Confederates than to risk open battle with them again.[35]

Sibley made his triumphant way up the Río Grande, forcing the Union quartermaster at Albuquerque to destroy what supplies he could not escape with. Reaching Santa Fe, the Confederates discovered that most of the supplies had been hauled to the safety of Fort Union. In addition, the territorial government had fled to the safety of the fort. For some unaccountable reason the Confederate commander fired what little in the way of supplies had been missed by the retreating Union army, in spite of the fact that his own troops were desperately short.

Wherever the Southerners went, they pillaged recklessly, seldom being concerned with whether or not the goods they were stealing belonged to a Confederate or a Yankee. This increased the already existing hostility of the native population. Although the invading army found it easy to overwhelm the native garrisons guarding the river towns and were in occupation of both Albuquerque and Santa Fe, they still had to attack and destroy Fort Union, the strongest of the North's defenses in New Mexico. In addition, they also had to worry about Colonel Canby's army, which they had left in their rear.

Meanwhile, news of the reversal at Valverde had prompted the Colorado troops to make a forced march and come to the aid of what they assumed would be the beleaguered garrison at Fort Union. Under the command of Colonel John P. Slough, a lawyer, some 1,300 regulars and volunteers marched 172 miles in five days. Resting briefly at Fort Union, they headed toward Santa Fe, in spite of the demands of Colonel Paul, in charge of the fort, that they remain there to protect the place. But the Colorado troops were eager to find the Confederates. On March 26, Major Chivington, in command of an advance guard of 418 men, stumbled into the Texans in Apache Canyon. Chivington, an elder of the Methodist church, was a natural leader of men who was inspired to great deeds by the pressures of

[35] Norvell, "New Mexico in the Civil War," 11.

155

wartime.[36] Although he knew little about the traditions and policies of military life, he commanded his forces so that they inflicted heavy damages upon the Confederates. The Colorado forces lost only five killed and fourteen wounded, while the Confederates lost thirty-two dead, forty-three wounded, and about fifty as prisoners.[37]

Two days later the main Union army under Colonel Slough met Colonel Scurry's Texan army in the Battle of Glorieta Pass. The Union troops were outnumbered, were forced on the defensive, and were compelled to retire after five hours of vicious fighting. The defeat of the Colorado forces was so great that some feared a mutiny on the part of the volunteer regiments. It was only later that it was realized that the Union forces had won the Civil War in New Mexico at the Battle of Glorieta Pass. Fate had taken a hand. Chivington led some 500 men, guided by Manuel Chávez, around to the Confederate's rear. Descending the mountain, they stumbled upon the entire supply train of the enemy. Some seventy-three wagons, containing the supplies, were destroyed, and six hundred mules and horses were bayoneted.[38]

While the raid was in progress, a Confederate courier rode up and, seeing what the Union forces were doing, hastened back to the front. By the time he had spread the alarm, the Texans mistakenly believed that it was Colonel Canby who had destroyed their supplies and was now between them and Santa Fe. Without supplies and deep in enemy territory, the demoralized invaders had to fall back.

Colonel Sibley, who had remained in Santa Fe, soon found himself in a precarious position. Canby had left his refuge at Fort Craig and was now laying siege to the Confederate garrison at Albuquerque. There was no choice open for the Southerners but to retreat. Except for a brief skirmish at Peralta, the fighting was to be over. The Union soldiers were not happy with Canby's tactics, some complaining that the fact that Sibley was his brother-in-law had kept him from trying to destroy the Texas forces. But the critics failed to understand Canby's strategy; he was more interested in driving the Confederates

[36] In spite of the later ill repute Chivington earned as a result of the Sand Creek Massacre, his earlier service should not be overlooked. See Reginald S. Craig, *The Fighting Parson: The Biography of Colonel John M. Chivington.*

[37] LeRoy R. Hafen, *History of Colorado*, III, 966–70.

[38] Kerby, *Confederate Invasion*, 113.

back to Texas than in taking them prisoners and then having to divide the half-rations available to the Union soldiers. His objective was to keep New Mexico safe, not to destroy the enemy army.[39] As a result, Sibley's original army of 3,700 troops staggered back to Texas in disorder with only 1,500 to 2,000 men left, depending upon the source of the figures.

If Sibley had known that the North had organized a 5,000 man division at Fort Leavenworth to march to the aid of New Mexico, he would have left earlier. Even if the Colorado forces had not been able to handle Sibley's army, General Carleton, in command of 1,500 Californians, was even then making his way over the difficult desert terrain and was to arrive in New Mexico shortly after Sibley had left.

So ended one phase of New Mexico's history. Had the Confederates won, the story might have been entirely different, and far more significance might have been attached to the New Mexico campaign. Many factors contributed to the failure of this invasion. First of all, Sibley's army of 3,700 men was not adequate; if he had simply remained in the territory until the summer of 1862, the Union would have had over 12,000 troops arrayed against him. Secondly, the poverty of New Mexico made it impossible for the Confederates to live off the land, and they lacked proper supplies. Their own carelessness in destroying stores they could have used added to their discomfiture. Third, the lack of discipline in the Texas army, partially attributable to Sibley's alcoholism and his failings as a commander, made success impossible. Finally, the Confederates were defeated because General Canby, despite the fact that he has never been given full credit, realized that his basic task was to hound the Confederate army out of New Mexico, and above all never to endanger his own army, and never to overextend himself, because of his supply shortage.[40] Hence, he concentrated his defense at two points and let the inhospitable geography of New Mexico weaken the invaders.

[39] *Ibid.*, 134; see also Ovando J. Hollister, *Boldly They Rode*, and William C. Whitford, *Colorado Volunteers in the Civil War.*

[40] See Max L. Heyman, "Prudent Soldier: A Biography of Major General E. R. S. Canby, 1817–1873," (Ph.D. dissertation, University of California at Los Angeles, 1952), chapter X, for a full treatment of Canby's handling of the Confederate invasion.

IX - The Quest for Law and Order

DURING THE PERIOD following the Civil War and lasting approximately until the turn of the century, New Mexico experienced a wave of rampant lawlessness unparalleled in the history of the United States. It was an era when stealing, killing, and lynching were so common as to be hardly worthy of mention in the press. At one bar in Cimarron eleven men were reputed to have been killed in the course of a single month.[1] A cemetery with forty-seven inhabitants could only number two as natural deaths. Every community had numerous gambling houses and the usual red light district. Other parts of the nation had experienced a breakdown in law and order, but in few areas had it lasted or been as complete as it was in the territory of New Mexico.

There are many explanations of why this anarchy should have occurred at this time. First of all, lawlessness is natural to a frontier community. As civilization moved westward from the Atlantic seaboard, many towns enjoyed a brief period of notoriety. Because of its very nature, the frontier attracted a particular breed of men. Here came men on the make, aggressive men who were out for the main chance, men eager to make their mark in the world, who, all too frequently, were not concerned about the legality of the methods used. Here came men who chafed under the restrictions of more civilized areas, men who were frequently misfits in their original environment, men who were seeking a new opportunity, freed of restraint.

[1] Reiter, "History of Fort Union," 123; Twitchell, *Leading Facts*, III, 80.

And as law and order came to the cattle towns of Kansas, the mining communities of Colorado, or even to Texas, the extreme rugged individualist who had a quarrel with the law-enforcement agencies moved to New Mexico. Even from Arizona, Utah, and California the human refuse found its way to New Mexico, the territory becoming "a sort of catch-basin" for a certain type of rough, lawless, and ruthless characters.[2] There, a variety of factors made the climate more conducive to their activity.

In many respects, the frontier in New Mexico was different from other frontiers in America. Here an American frontier society was superimposed upon a Mexican frontier society, and the combination made the situation of general lawlessness the more extreme. This is not to imply that the native element was alone responsible for the general acceptance of criminality. Early visitors to Santa Fe frequently commented upon the fact that serious crimes were conspicuous by their absence among the Spanish-speaking people. Petty thievery was very common, usually induced by the poverty of the people. In southern and western New Mexico, a more typically American frontier society developed, but lawlessness was as common there as in the more preponderantly Spanish-American communities. In fact, an examination of the "outstanding" gunmen or outlaws of this period indicates a definite lack of Hispanic names.

Such an extensive collapse of law and order must be attributed principally to the lack of a civil authority. Much of the blame for this state of affairs must rest with the federal government, for New Mexico was considered an orphan among the nation's territories. The general attitude in Washington was that the province was not worth defending, and many agreed with the remark credited to General Sherman that "we should have another war with old Mexico to make her take the territory back."[3] Military personnel and federal appointees resented being assigned to this most undesirable of all areas. As a general rule, appointments to the federal posts open in New Mexico were the last ones made in Washington and usually went to men who had been passed over for juicier political plums. In

[2] Miguel A. Otero, *My Life on the Frontier*, I, 181.
[3] Quoted in Lew Wallace, *An Autobiography*, II, 920.

one instance, however, Republican party chiefs, deeming the post of little importance, appointed General Lew Wallace as territorial governor, reasoning that President Hayes could not be accused of paying a political debt to the General.[4]

The political appointees in the territory, even including territorial judges, meted out justice on a political basis rather than on an impartial, legal one.[5] The local sheriffs, also, usually were guided more by politics than by justice. Many a man who surrendered to the "protection" of the law was either shot in the back by the sheriff or his posse or turned over to the vigilantes. The poverty of the area likewise made it difficult to get able men as agents of law enforcement. In 1872 an editorial in the Santa Fe *New Mexican* bitterly complained of the low rate of pay of the city policeman and demanded that something be done about it.[6] One observer pointed out that it was necessary to turn men out of jail because the counties lacked the money to feed them properly.[7]

With such a lack of normal law enforcement, it was inevitable that men should take the law into their own hands, too frequently with "Judge Colt" as their spokesman. Self-defense was the usual means of justifying murder, and perhaps in some cases it was a valid one. There were few arrests in such an atmosphere of disrespect for the law. And when there were arrests, it was difficult to get a conviction, partly because jurors feared reprisal at the hands of friends

[4] William A. Keleher, *Violence in Lincoln County 1869–1881*, 178.

[5] For an interesting discussion of some of the problems in trying to bring law and order to New Mexico see Arie W. Poldervaart, *Black-Robed Justice*. Governor Sheldon complained that when he arrived in New Mexico the desperadoes were virtually in control of the territory. He complained that "people were held up anywhere and everywhere, that stagecoaches were being robbed, and horses and cattle stolen." The governor complained that frequently the lawless element had the backing of the people, some newspapers, and even some law enforcement officials, and the bribing of witnesses and even judges were so common as to pass unnoticed. On different occasions Sheldon relates that he took military possession of Socorro, Santa Fe, Las Vegas, and Albuquerque when local law enforcement collapsed in these towns. From Hubert H. Bancroft Notes in Bancroft Library, University of California, Berkeley.

[6] Santa Fe *New Mexican*, September 8, 1872 in Oliver La Farge, *Santa Fe: The Autobiography of a Southwestern Town*, 81.

[7] John W. Caughey, "Early Federal Relations with New Mexico" (M.A. thesis, University of California, Berkeley, 1926), 77.

of the convicted. Even judges frequently had good cause to fear for their lives. Unscrupulous lawyers, accustomed to using tactics such as bribery and threats, likewise made difficult the proper operation of a legal system.

The very geography of New Mexico abetted the era of lawlessness. The task confronting even the most able and conscientious sheriff who sought to protect the citizenry of the territory before the advent of the telegraph or the railroad was awe inspiring. The vast open spaces, the mountainous terrain with its numerous hiding places, and the generally uninhabited areas, all combined to make it easy for the lawless elements to find a place of refuge after their misdeeds. Thus, it was inevitable that outlaws from other areas were to make their way toward New Mexico.

Texans had long been used to making their own laws relative to the handling of cattle. In earlier times when "mavericks" were virtually valueless, men simply took the livestock they needed, and questions were seldom asked since there was plenty of cattle for everyone. Many of the cattle herds of New Mexico had their origin in such means. Habits thus acquired were not easily broken, and rustling became an established custom on the frontier. Men who lost stock were not always careful about whose they obtained to replace it. As a result, conflicts arose between ranchers, who naturally distrusted each other.

Control of the open range in New Mexico usually was dependent upon force rather than upon law. Many a tenderfoot cattleman who tried to appeal his grievance to the courts was bankrupt before any action was taken. And even if the judgment was returned in his favor, there were few sheriffs with sufficient courage to back up the dictates of the court. When cattlemen found sheepmen grazing choice pasturelands, it was inevitable that they should simply attempt to drive them out, in spite of the fact that they may have been in the area long before the cattlemen made their appearance. As the sheepherders were normally Spanish-Americans, this gave the conflict a racial twist.

Although the Treaty of Guadalupe Hidalgo obligated the United States to give full faith and credit to the existing laws of Mexico, it was extremely difficult in practice to meet this obligation. A great deal of confusion arose over the authenticity of land titles, and disputes over title and possession were frequently settled by the gun instead of the courts.

In frontier New Mexico, life was cheap and killing was not considered a particularly heinous crime. Men hardened by the shedding of blood during the Civil War found it difficult to break the habit of fighting. Killing became an accepted means of settling disputes. The improvement in firearms greatly augmented the resort to a gun in time of need. No longer was there any fear about the reliability of a gun. Seldom did the six-shooter misfire.

For their own safety, men practiced their "draw" as well as their marksmanship. There were occasions when the whole town gathered to watch two gunmen shoot it out on Main Street, with victory going to whoever could draw the fastest. However, this open fighting was the exception rather than the rule. More often a killing was accomplished by the simple expedient of shooting a man in the back. There were far more instances of murder from ambush, where a man waited with a group of friends to attain revenge, than there were open gun duels. It was always easy to find someone who would swear that the other man drew first, and few coroners had the courage to question how this could be when the man had half a dozen bullet holes in the back.

Finally, adding to the general resort to firearms, were the twin factors of Indians and alcohol. In the long and bitter conflict between the white and the red men for the possession of New Mexico, bloodshed and atrocities were common and human life was cheap. In all frontier societies the consumption of alcohol was extremely common, and New Mexico was no exception. Cattlemen, long in the open and riding a dusty trail, miners used to hard work and dangers, as well as soldiers and others, all sought relief from the tedium of everyday life in the questionable joys of alcohol.[8] And men whose courage was buoyed up by liquor were readier to fight than they otherwise would have been.

---

[8] One governor was virtually run out of the territory for having preached prohibition. Keleher, *Violence in Lincoln County*, 6. One night in Las Vegas five men were slain as the result of a drunken spree.

~~~ *The Lincoln County War* ~~~

The Lincoln County War, 1876 to 1878, which demonstrates the laxity of government in Territorial New Mexico, involved all the elements of lawlessness in the territory. Lincoln County embraced about one-fifth of the territory, an area as large as Vermont and New Hampshire combined, and contained both desert and mountains.

With the re-establishment of Fort Stanton at the close of the Civil War, the area rapidly began to be settled by cattlemen and sheepmen, and also by farmers seeking to exploit the excellent farmland along the streams. Far removed from the more settled section of the territory, the area around Lincoln had its own law.[9] The Lincoln County War was a conflict between newcomers and residents of long standing who had the officers of the law on their side. This favoritism for the well-established constituted one of the primary problems of law enforcement.

Although Lawrence G. Murphy was one of the men principally responsible for the war, ill health forced him to retire to Santa Fe for medical treatment and he was absent during most of the action. Like many others, Murphy had come to New Mexico in the military service, and after he was mustered out remained to go into business. Establishing a merchandising center at Lincoln, he came to have other interests, such as cattle ranching and farming. An aggressive man, he soon controlled all business enterprises in the area, so that few men were able to obtain work, prove title to their land, or even remain in the territory if he disapproved. As he had the financial means and owned the only store around, the farmers and ranchers were forced to buy from him at exorbitant prices in order to obtain credit. Since he also controlled most of the wagon trains, he was able to force the farmers and ranchers to sell their goods to him. By such means he was able to dominate the economic life of the surrounding countryside to such an extent that he was accused of being a virtual dictator.[10]

---

[9] Edward B. Choate, "History of the Capitan Community 1890–1950" (M.A. thesis, Eastern New Mexico University, 1954), 6.

[10] Keleher, *Violence in Lincoln County*, 249. Murphy was accused of being de-

The sheriff was "his man," and assisting that officer was a choice selection of hired gunslingers, many of them refugees from the long arm of the Texas Rangers. The local district attorney, William L. Rynerson, backed him, as did Thomas B. Catron, the United States district attorney at Santa Fe. Even the territorial governor, Axtell, had borrowed money from him and hence was in his debt.

Murphy was alleged to have been behind the so-called Horrell War, which occurred in Lincoln County in 1873. This dispute showed that the area was accustomed to the ready shedding of blood. Members of a faction led by five brothers named Horrell (also spelled Harrold or Howell) had been run out of Texas because of a series of cold-blooded murders and had made a new start in Lincoln County in the spring of 1873. The night of December 1, 1873, they were engaged in the common pastime of shooting up Lincoln town when the constable tried to stop them. In the resulting fight the law officer was killed, along with one man of the Horrell party. One of the brothers and a friend were wounded and captured and thereupon shot in cold blood. One explanation for this act was that the Spanish-Americans were angry because some of them had been mistreated by the Texans. To avenge this deed, the remaining Horrell brothers attacked a group of Mexicans at a wedding on the night of December 20, 1873, murdering five of them. It is estimated that before the gunfire was over, fourteen people were killed. The Horrell brothers and their group finally decided that Texas might be better for them than New Mexico, so, after gathering as many horses and cattle as they could find, they left. Significantly enough, they left their ranch and property in the hands of Murphy. Later it was claimed that Murphy was behind the driving out of the Texans because they were a faction he could not control and because he wanted their possessions.[11]

Naturally, a man like Murphy had many enemies. Foremost of these was the great Texas cattleman John Chisum. The latter was convinced that the Murphy cattle holdings increased more rapidly

termined to rule the area or ruin it. He was reputed to have said, "You might as well try to stop the waves of the ocean with a fork as to try to oppose me."

[11] Philip J. Rasch, "The Horrell War," *NMHR.* Vol. XXX (July, 1956); Keleher, *Violence in Lincoln County*, 250.

than could be accounted for by the laws of nature. There was much contention between the two. Most of the people in the community were apparently likewise antagonistic towards Murphy. Indicative of this is the fact that the grand jury growing out of the Lincoln County War returned two hundred indictments, almost all of them being directed against the Murphy faction.

In 1875 Alexander McSween came to Lincoln, and in him the anti-Murphy faction was to find a man capable of leading them. McSween came from Kansas, but was probably originally from Canada. In all respects he was a unique man on the frontier. Though a lawyer, he had been trained for the Presbyterian ministry and did not touch alcohol, nor would he wear a gun. He was soon busy handling cases against Murphy, many of them for the cattleman Chisum.

Unfortunately, McSween was ambitious and aggressive, and was soon engaged in activities beyond the practice of law. He acquired an interest in a ranch, started a bank, and then built a store to challenge the trade monopoly Murphy had so long enjoyed. In this enterprise he probably had the financial backing of John Chisum.[12]

Aiding McSween in some of his business ventures was a young Englishman named John Henry Tunstall, a member of a wealthy family, who had become enamored with the American west and was eager to make a fortune in the cattle business. The extent of Tunstall's backing of McSween's projects has never been determined, but there is no question that the two were closely allied in business and that McSween frequently advised Tunstall. When, however, Tunstall bought the cattle of Robert Casey, who had been murdered, at higher prices than the Murphy faction was willing to pay for them, he earned their enmity on his own.[13] Because of ill health, Murphy took as partners two fellow Irishmen, James J. Dolan and John H. Riley, who were to figure prominently in the events of the Lincoln County War. Trouble was imminent: Murphy, a man who

---

[12] George Curry, *An Autobiography, 1861–1947*, ed. by H. B. Hening, 23. For a biased treatment of Chisum's role behind the scenes, see Harwood Perry Hinton, Jr., "John Simpson Chisum, 1877–88." (M.A. thesis, Columbia University, 1956). This author suggests that the trouble was started by McSween, with Chisum's support, in an effort by the cattlemen to drive out the settlers.

[13] Keleher, *Violence in Lincoln County*, 17.

had long dominated the community, was now confronted with Mc-Sween, an able man who had won the esteem of many and who, with the financial backing of Tunstall, was a very potent rival.

The conflict itself arose over the insurance money owed from the estate of one Emil Fritz, a former partner of Murphy who had died after returning to Germany. This policy, totaling $10,000, was turned over to McSween for collection, with the understanding that his fee would not exceed $2,500. There were some difficult legal questions involved in the collection of the policy, and the insurance company was reluctant to make payment. This made it necessary for the lawyer to go to New York and, as a result, to claim that he was forced to pay the $2,500 to lawyers in that city and also to spend $4,095 for his own expenses.

Believing McSween's charges to be excessive, the heirs of Emil Fritz took the problem to Murphy, who in turn retained Thomas B. Catron, for years one of the political powers of the territory, and W. L. Rynerson to recover the money. McSween was charged with embezzlement, and his property, worth $100,000, was attached for the amount due—$8,000. Bond was set at $16,000. In addition, Tunstall's property was attached on the grounds that McSween had an interest in his activity. There was no legal basis for this action whatsoever, as the partnership agreement between McSween and the Englishman was not to take effect until May 1878.[14] During the process of seizing Tunstall's property, valued at $50,000, the sheriff's posse met him on the road and, according to the best evidence, shot him down in cold blood.

It was later contended by the McSween faction that the Murphy-Riley-Dolan group had planned the Tunstall murder and also intended to murder McSween to eliminate them as business rivals. Circulars were distributed in Lincoln County accusing a group of distinguished people with having been in on such a "plot." Included in this group were Sheriff Brady; Thomas B. Catron, U. S. District attorney general; and Colonel William L. Rynerson, attorney of the

14 Frederick W. Nolan, "A Sidelight on the Tunstall Murder," *NMHR*, Vol. XXX (July, 1956), 206. This author throws interesting light on some of the international complications of the wanton murder of a British subject.

Third Judicial District, in addition to Riley and Dolan. To substantiate the claims, a letter, reputed to be a forgery, that Rynerson wrote to Riley and Dolan was found in which he said: "It must be made too hot for Tunstall and his friends, the hotter the better, shake that McSween outfit up till it shells out and squares up and then shake it out of Lincoln."[15]

The murder of Tunstall on February 18, 1878, opened the long-drawn-out conflict. More than likely, his death resulted from the desire of some of the choice scoundrels making up the sheriff's posse to get rid of this queer "foreigner," or else they simply wanted to avenge a grudge they had against him. Unfortunately for these murderers, one of the men who was with Tunstall at the time was one William Bonney. Another present was Richard M. Brewer, both close friends of the Englishman and indebted to him in many ways. Both were prepared to avenge his murder.

Knowing that justice was not to be had from Sheriff Brady, the McSween faction turned to Justice of the Peace Wilson, who issued warrants for the arrest of the men identified as the murderers. For daring to take the part of the McSween group, Governor Axtell removed Wilson as justice of the peace on a trumped-up charge. It was obvious that the legal authorities were not prepared to do anything about Tunstall's murder. Governor Axtell openly endorsed the celebrated letter written by William L. Rynerson. The Governor even excused Rynerson's prejudicial conduct in refusing to grant the McSween bond. (Later testimony showed that those who wanted to act impartially were warned from Santa Fe that their own activities would be open to scrutiny if they dared to offer assistance to any but the Murphy group.)[16]

An analysis of the various participants in the feud indicates that the McSween-Tunstall faction had men of more character and integrity than did the Murphy-Riley-Dolan group. A private investigator, Frank Warren Anchell, employed by the State Department

[15] Keleher, *Violence in Lincoln County*, 81.

[16] *Ibid.*, 91–95. There is little question that if Governor Axtell had enforced the law and made a real effort to avenge the slaying of Tunstall, there would have been no "Lincoln County War." For more on Axtell's failure to enforce the law see Philip J. Rasch, "Exit Axtell: Enter Wallace," *NMHR*, Vol. XXXI (July, 1957).

to gather evidence concerning the Tunstall murder because Tunstall was a British citizen, found that members of the McSween-Tunstall group were far more inclined to tell what they knew, and to sign affidavits, than those who had been identified with the other faction.

Finally despairing of ever getting the law to back them in the Tunstall murder, the Englishman's friends decided to take matters into their own hands. Richard Brewer had himself deputized as a constable by Justice of the Peace Wilson, and went after the guilty men. The McSween men captured two of the Murphy men and murdered them on the way back to Lincoln. They struck again on April 1, 1878, shooting down Sheriff Brady and his deputy, George Hindman.

The McSween faction were able to have one of their adherents, John S. Copeland, named to succeed Brady. However, Governor Axtell found an excuse to block this appointment and selected George Peppin instead. After a few more killings, the showdown came in the famous battle of Lincoln on July 16–19. McSween, a peace-loving man, was now the leader of his group and, gathering up his allies, took refuge in his home. Finally, on July 19 the house was fired, and in the shooting that ensued McSween and most of his followers, except William Bonney (Billy the Kid), were killed. Sheriff Peppin had the support of a detachment of troops from Fort Stanton who had previously stood by while the fight had raged, but had gone into action when a soldier was wounded. Colonel Dudley, their commander, was later to be charged with misconduct by Governor Lew Wallace and was to face a board of inquiry.

Large numbers of settlers left Lincoln County as rapidly as possible as the battle raged. So many left that it was feared that the county would soon be depopulated. Things had reached the point where something had to be done. In addition to the outrageous situation in Lincoln County, shootings in Colfax County at the same time were sufficient evidence that the Governor was unable to control the situation. Powerful foes within the territory besieged Washington with petitions requesting the removal of Axtell. The new governor was the celebrated Lew Wallace, famous as a Civil War leader, but of greater renown as the author of the novel *Ben Hur*.

Wallace had hoped for a better appointment than the one to New Mexico, as he was far more interested in his literary activities than he was in administrative duties. As one historian has said, "If the fame of Governor Wallace rested upon any of his official acts in New Mexico it would be far from secure."[17]

Arriving in Santa Fe in September of 1878, Wallace proceeded to handle the situation in Lincoln County by asking the President to declare martial law in the area and empower a military commission to act to punish offenders. Although the President was not prepared to go that far, he did authorize the use of troops to maintain law and order.

Perhaps the most important contribution Governor Wallace made to ending the conflict was his famous pronouncement of amnesty for all of those who would give testimony and desist from further disorders. This went a long way toward settling things. After an unaccountable delay, the Governor finally reached Lincoln on March 6, 1879. There he interviewed the various participants, including even Billy the Kid. But before his arrival the tragedy of the Lincoln County War had claimed another important victim. This time it was a lawyer by the name of Houston Chapman, who had come to Lincoln to aid in closing out the estate of McSween. The new sheriff, George Kimball, in an effort to end the feud and restore order in the county, had called a meeting of the leaders of the warring factions. After getting everyone to agree to bury the hatchet so deep that it could never again be dug up, he made the mistake of sealing the bargain with a few drinks. Leaving the saloon, Chapman is supposed to have made a disparaging remark to Jimmy Dolan, for which he was promptly killed by Jesse Evans, one of the more notorious Murphy-Dolan gunmen. Fortunately, this was to be the last fatality of the ill-fated Lincoln County War.[18]

There is some question whether General Lew Wallace can take credit for having ended hostilities, but he contributed by getting the various factions to present their sides, with the promise of amnesty making it easy for them to talk.

[17] Twitchell, *Leading Facts*, II, 425.
[18] Curry, *Autobiography*, 37.

The Colfax County War

Compared to the bloody struggle in Lincoln County, the conflict in Colfax County was relatively minor, despite the fact that the issues over which it was fought were far more valid. It resulted from the extended controversy over the legality of the Maxwell Land Grant.

As long as Lucien Maxwell was in control of the area, trouble had been averted, as he had, in general, been indulgent toward those who squatted on his lands. Usually content with a token payment or a share of the produce of the settlers, miners, or cattlemen, Maxwell was looked upon as more of a feudal overlord than a landlord. Then, early in the 1870's, the grant was sold to an English-Dutch combine who were interested in making money out of it, and the atmosphere quickly changed when the new owners attempted to run off the "squatters."

They had little difficulty winning suits in court against those who were occupying farms, ranches, or mines; carrying out the eviction notices, however, was an entirely different matter. Most of the people had settled with the belief that this was free country, and were not prepared to be embarrassed by an old land grant which had greatly increased in size, apparently through the manipulations of clever but dishonest attorneys. The people of the area therefore were divided into two factions—grant and anti-grant, with the agents of law enforcement on the grant side.

A Methodist preacher, the Reverend F. J. Tolby, was murdered in 1875, and it was rumored that the murder had been commissioned by the foreign company. Another Methodist clergyman, the Reverend Oscar P. McMains, thereupon became the crusader for the settlers, accusing the members of the foreign company of being murderers as well as robbers. McMains was to be on the scene for more than twenty years and was to defy every effort to remove his disruptive influence.

While there were frequent feuds between the two factions, sometimes resulting in bloodshed, the real flare-up occurred in 1885, influenced by the shift in national politics. Since the Republicans had long favored corporate interests controlling the grant, the owners

170

feared that the new Democratic officeholders might intervene on behalf of the settlers.

To prevent this and to insure that the law remained on their side, the pro-grant men convinced Governor Sheldon early in 1885 that they would need help to enforce the ejection decrees of the courts. (It had not been "healthy" for Colfax County officials to enforce the court decrees earlier.) Consequently, a militia force composed of about thirty-five men, under the leadership of James H. Masterson, a notorious gunman, was organized by the land company.[19] Most of the men were professional gunmen and gamblers. The settlers, alarmed that the company was able to get a band of hired killers to carry out its decrees, hurried to the Governor to protest. That official thereupon changed his mind and ordered the force disbanded, and the citizens of the area hastened to escort Masterson and his motley crew over the Colorado line with the request that they should never return.

Shortly afterwards several men were killed in a gun fight at Springer between the settlers and the grant faction. In spite of the hostility toward the land-grant people, the settlers eventually discovered that they had to accept the dictates of the court, and by 1893 most of the armed resistance had ceased.

General Lawlessness

The quest for law and order in New Mexico was a long and tedious one in virtually every community in the territory. Even the capital did not escape, three murders having been recorded as being committed near the plaza of Santa Fe in a single month. In many counties it was difficult to find men with sufficient courage to become sheriffs or deputies.[20] Even the United States Cavalry had its hands

[19] *Ibid.*, 49; see also William A. Keleher, *The Maxwell Land Grant: A New Mexico Item*, F. Stanley, *The Grant that Maxwell Bought*, and F. Stanley, "O. P. McMains, Champion of a Lost Cause," *NMHR*, XXIV (January, 1949).

[20] Rupert N. Richardson and Carl Coke Rister, *The Greater Southwest*, 401. Erna Fergusson, *Murder and Mystery in New Mexico*, Agnes Morley Cleaveland, *Satan's Paradise*, Dee Harkey, *Mean as Hell*, and F. Stanley, *Desperadoes of New Mexico*.

full fighting the desperadoes, whom they feared more than they did the Indians because they "combined savage cunning with intimate knowledge of the ways of the white man." Horse thieves stole extensively from the stock held at Fort Union, and on one occasion a detachment of troops was ambushed by common robbers. In 1870 an officer complained that the soldiers were spending more of their time chasing common thieves than they were fighting Indians.[21] Most communities had their legendary gunmen, such as Joe Fowler, Clay Allison, and "Blackjack" Ketchum. Some of these gunslingers even became folk heroes, rather than being remembered as the ruthless killers they were. In this category must be placed Elfego Baca, the most noted legendary figure of the day next to Billy the Kid.

Although he was born in Socorro, Baca lived in Kansas until he was fifteen years old and thus spoke English fluently. Back in New Mexico, as an adult, he resented the mistreatment of the Spanish-Americans by the incoming Texas cattlemen, who looked upon them with ill-disguised contempt and drove off the Mexican sheepherders, who were powerless before the Texans' six-shooters.

While campaigning for the Spanish candidate for sheriff, Elfego Baca pinned a badge upon his coat, and thus equipped, along with two six-shooters, went off to win votes. While he was electioneering in a small village known as Frisco, a Texas cowboy named McCarthy was busy shooting up the town and intimidating the natives. When the local Justice of the Peace refused to act out of fear, Baca saw an opportunity to distinguish himself as a champion of his people and thereby enhance his own political fortunes. Acting on his own authority, he arrested the Texan and announced that he was going to take him to Socorro for trial.

The cowboy's fellow Texans were immediately alarmed at this gross insult and doubtless magnified the affair into an uprising of New Mexicans against them. Gathering in force, they ordered Baca to surrender his prisoner. An exchange of shots occurred when Baca refused, and one cowboy was killed. This prompted the Texans to prepare for battle, accompanied by a local deputy sheriff.

McCarthy was tried in the local Justice of the Peace Court for dis-

[21] Reiter, "History of Fort Union," 117–20.

turbing the peace and fined five dollars, but the affair was not over. The mob that had gathered was spoiling for a fight, and when Elfego Baca fled to a small shed called a *jacal*, they decided to arrest him for the murder of the cowboy. In the subsequent "battle" Baca defended himself against eighty Texans, killing four of them and wounding eight without receiving so much as a scratch himself in the thirty-six-hour battle. It was claimed that over four thousand bullet holes were found in the shack after the fight and that a broom handle in the corner had nine holes in it. Baca finally surrendered when he was promised protection and a fair trial at Socorro. Although it is claimed that "his feat deserves to be remembered as one of the most heroic single-handed battles in all six-shooter history,"[22] there are those who feel that the facts have grown with the telling. Regardless of what actually did happen, what people believe has far more influence than the truth anyway, and not only did Baca get off scot-free, but the fame attendant upon his deed propelled him into public life and earned him a reputation that continues to be exploited.

Too frequently, lawlessness was not confined to six-shooter battles but found expression in common murder, sometimes even in political assassination. One notorious example was the slaying of John P. Slough, chief justice of the territorial Supreme Court. Slough, who had originally arrived in New Mexico with the Colorado volunteers during the Civil War, was shot down in La Fonda Hotel in Santa Fe in 1867 by William L. Rynerson on the pretext that the judge had reached for his derringer first.[23] Another, listed among the many unsolved crimes in New Mexican history, was the death of Albert J. Fountain and his son. Fountain disappeared while en route from Lincoln to his home in Las Cruces in February, 1896. Because he had been a judge, it has generally been assumed that he met death at the hands of political assassins. Indictments were returned, but no convictions were ever secured in the case.[24] There were many other murders with political connotations, and in some cases, leading state officials were accused of complicity or of tampering with evidence.

[22] H. Ferguson, *Rio Grande*, 266; Kyle Crichton, *Law and Order, Ltd.*

[23] Poldervaart, *Black-Robed Justice*, 71. This was the same Rynerson who played a prominent role in the Lincoln County War.

[24] LaFarge, *Santa Fe*, 159; Curry, *Autobiography*, 100–119 ff.

~~~ *The Land Grant Problem* ~~~

Far more prosaic than political assassination, range wars, or six-shooter duels was the controversy over the legality of Spanish and Mexican land grants. In terms of the future value and the amount of money spent on legal fees, these were perhaps more important than the more dramatic episodes.

The land grant problem had its origin in the Spanish practice of granting large areas of land to individuals or groups of men for meritorious service to the crown or for various other reasons. As New Mexico had been settled for about two and one-half centuries before the coming of the Anglo-Americans, it was inevitable that the best land along the streams should long since have been granted by the Spanish and Mexican governments. These grants were protected in the treaty of 1848. Unfortunately, there had been a great deal of careless informality regarding title papers, so that the boundaries of the grants were usually vague, and the grants themselves had become complicated by frequent transfers and subdivisions. In addition, the records of such grants were usually inaccurate and in many cases were even missing.[25] Bancroft contends that in 1886 there were 205 such grants, exclusive of the Indian claims.[26]

When the Anglo-American settlers began arriving and found title to the most desirable territorial land already taken, they demanded that the situation be clarified. A letter of appeal to President Cleveland contended that more than twenty-two billion acres of the best land, constituting about one-fourth of the state's acreage, was already covered by private claims, thereby making it impossible to encourage settlers and to conduct normal business relations.[27] The lack of clarity concerning title increased the existing confusion and created a situation in which the manufacturing of fraudulent private land-claim documents took place all too frequently.[28] The most notori-

[25] Poldervaart, *Black-Robed Justice*, 160.

[26] Bancroft, *Arizona and New Mexico*, 647.

[27] J. J. Fitzgerrell, "An Open Letter to President Cleveland," January 15, 1886, Las Vegas (broadside in Huntington Library, San Marino, California).

[28] Bancroft, *Arizona and New Mexico*, 756. There is much material on the land grant problem in the William Gillette Ritch Collection (Huntington Library, San Marino, California).

ous of these was the Peralta Reavis claim in Arizona that extended eastward into New Mexico. It presented a situation made to order for the clever attorney, and one of these, Thomas B. Catron, rose to power largely on his ability to defend the holders of these private claims in court.

Many a tenderfoot from the East, or even foreign investor, was defrauded by those who had sold land without having the proper title to it. The following example points up the problem which existed. A more cautious than ordinary purchaser of a mining lease was assured that there was no doubt of the validity of its title. Wary of such assertions, he submitted the documents and title papers in question to each of two established land-grant lawyers, neither of them knowing the other was involved. They reached their decisions, one concluding that the land was a pueblo grant, the other deciding that it was an individual grant.[29] "Experts in penmanship" were employed to manufacture proper documents to order.

Obviously, the really subtle swindler did not content himself with merely composing fictitious documents upon which to base a land claim. A recent historian asserts that many of the claims were deliberately drawn up carelessly or in conflict with known facts during the Mexican period in order to provide a basis for later court claims. Accusations of fraud in land titles were made as early as 1849 and were even commented upon by Governor James Calhoun.

The great Maxwell Grant, which ultimately embraced 1,700,000 acres and was approved in a United States Supreme Court decision, was drawn up with quite vague boundaries, since the original papers were contradictory and required surveys were not made. It was granted to Charles Beaubien and Guadalupe Miranda by Governor Armijo in the 1840's and apparently was intended to encourage Mexican colonization of northern New Mexico. Mexican settlers might come into the area if it were developed, and Beaubien and Miranda could tame it. These settlers would provide resistance to the influx of Anglo-Americans who might take over New Mexico, as they had Texas, if it were nearly empty.

---

[29] For an excellent discussion of the rackets that flourished in land grants, see Lena Paulus, "Problems of the Private Land Grants of New Mexico" (M.A. thesis, University of Pittsburgh, 1933).

The Maxwell Grant constituted the largest tract of land held by a single owner in the history of the United States. Lucien Maxwell came into possession of the property through marriage to the daughter of Charles Beaubien. He sold it in 1869 for $650,000 to an English syndicate, which in turn resold it almost at once. In 1872 it was taken over by a Dutch-English combine, which soon went broke. The owners of the grant were continually harassed by the influx of settlers in the 1870's and 1880's, who, used to taking whatever land lay open, were not prepared to accept the fact that any man or group of men could control almost two million acres of land. The resulting conflict began in the seventies and did not end until the nineties.[30]

Ultimately the costly litigation over the land claims was to draw to a close. In addition, the coming of law and order was to confirm many titles which were perhaps fraudulent but were able to stand up in court and, more important, stand the test of time.

[30] Twitchell, *Leading Facts*, II, 451–79, ff.

X - The Indian Menace

WHEN THE UNITED STATES acquired the Mexican Cession, they also acquired responsibility for controlling the Plains Indians. This was to prove far more difficult than anyone realized at the time, and was to result in almost forty years of bitter and costly struggle with much bloodshed on both sides. This long period of warfare grew out of the basic difference in the way of life of the primitive Indians and the frontiersmen who were trying to settle the land. In some respects, it was but a continuation of the age-old conflict between the nomad and the oasis farmer.

The Indians' way of life that had been evolved through the centuries was threatened by the encroachment of the frontiersmen. The Plains Indians usually lived as nomads, dependent upon the buffalo herds for most of the necessities of life. Some tribes also engaged in limited agriculture, the gathering of forest products, and trading with their neighbors. In times of adversity or when they considered their rights threatened, the Indians were prepared to make war upon those whom they considered their enemies. Raiding and plundering for gain were a significant part of such warfare. The influx of permanent white settlers destroyed the buffalo, as well as other game, and endangered the economic basis of the Indian's culture. It was inevitable that the red men would attack, raid, and plunder those whom they saw as their mortal adversaries.

As a real warrior, the Indian looked upon the white man's proffer of treaties as an indication of weakness. He assumed that his enemies were afraid of him and hence wanted peace by means of a piece of paper. Used to having their own way, the Navahos, Apaches, and Comanches believed themselves to be far superior to the white men with whom they came in contact; and when one considers the character of some of the white men, the savages could not be blamed for such an attitude. Like the Chinese of an earlier day who looked upon the Europeans as "foreign devils," the Indians could not comprehend the number of palefaces in the United States, and believed themselves to be more numerous. And, viewing the futile attempts of a handful of poorly mounted cavalry to punish them for their depredations, the Indians were convinced that neither the white man nor his treaties were to be taken seriously.

The savages, however, did not have a monopoly on misunderstanding. The American frontiersman has never been distinguished for his solicitude for the welfare of the Indians he met, and those who moved into New Mexico were certainly no exception. A man who has returned home to find his wife and children not only slain but brutally mutilated, could easily believe that "the only good Indian is a dead one," or as one man put it, "An Indian is a cross between a Gila monster and a coyote." The best of the frontiersmen looked upon the Indians as a necessary evil to be gotten out of the way as early as possible so that they could proceed with the proper exploitation of the farmland, the grazing land, the timber resources, or the mines. The worst of the frontiersmen frequently stole cattle, horses, or sheep from the Navahos, cheated the other Indians when they traded with them, sold them cheap firearms and cheaper firewater, and, in some instances, even amused themselves by shooting at the Indians they saw.[1]

The early Indian agents who were sent to New Mexico, beginning with James S. Calhoun, clearly saw the nature of the problem and recommended that a policy be carried out to chastise the nomadic Indians to a point where they would learn respect for the ways of the white man. Then they could be put on reservations and taught how to become sedentary Indians, with the government assisting them until they had made the adjustment. Calhoun stressed that it would cost a lot less to feed them than to exterminate them. Some

[1] Irving Telling, Jr., "New Mexican Frontiers: A Social History of the Gallup Area, 1881–1901" (Ph.D. dissertation, Harvard University, 1953), 123.

might dispute Calhoun's remedy of "compulsory enlightenment enforced at the point of a bayonet,"[2] but no one a century later could disagree with his observations that unless the government was prepared to spend a million dollars on a long-range program to aid the Indian to make the necessary adjustment to a new way of life, it would cost millions in the long run. Men familiar with the nomadic Indians were well aware that changing habits and customs established over centuries was not going to be easy. It is difficult to make a farmer or herdsman out of a warrior under the best conditions. But when one adds the fact that the government in Washington did not even recognize the problem that existed and was not prepared to spend enough money to handle the Indian militarily, let alone assist him to adjust to a new way of life, the task was all but impossible. Besides, authority over the Indians was divided between the agents of the Department of the Interior and the War Department, and these two agencies were usually at loggerheads. Even the custom of negotiating treaties with the Indians was foolish and short-sighted. The federal officials assumed that the Indian tribes had the responsibilities of nations, when in fact the chiefs of most tribes were powerless to enforce the provisions of the treaties upon their own members, even if they so desired.

The tragedy of the handling of the southwestern Indian problem was that nothing really was tried, officials in the field usually being forced to limp along under divided authority and without any kind of concrete policy from the government in Washington. This lack of a course of action complicated the already difficult problem of the troops in their efforts to contain the Indian menace, and was typical of Washington's attitude toward its stepchild, New Mexico.

General William T. Sherman, never a man to be cautious with his judgments, undoubtedly spoke for many in the national capital when he described the territory as "a damned ugly elephant we had on our hands, but as we were fools enough to buy New Mexico we must feed and maintain its mongrel population forever." To Sherman, "one county of Ohio will maintain a larger population than all of

[2] Quoted in Avery B. Bender, *The March of Empire*, 151. For Calhoun's basic recommendations on the Indians of New Mexico, see James S. Calhoun to William Medill, November 10, 1846 in Annie Heloise Abel, ed. *The Official Correspondence of James S. Calhoun*, 6–9.

New Mexico. . . . this territory has cost us over hundreds of millions of dollars already, and will always cost from three to five million a year, and never by any process can it ever contribute one cent to the national income. The population is a mixed band of Mexican, Indian and Negro, inferior to either race if pure. . . . we are spending annually more than all the country with its houses, land, cattle, sheep, and people would sell for." Sherman claimed that the New Mexicans could defend themselves if they would only try, but were interested in having federal troops in the territory so that the local people could profit from their presence. The distinguished General accused New Mexico of "nuzzling at the nearest treasury teat," and claimed that "the only profitable mines in New Mexico have their base in the United States Treasury in Washington."

With all of his antagonism toward the Southwest, Sherman outlined probably the closest to a policy the national government was ever to have for dealing with the Indians. He suggested that about all that could be done was to protect the settlers so as to keep them quiet "till time and events settle this, one of the most vexatious things I have ever had to deal with . . . time is helping us and killing the Indians fast, so that every year the task is less."[3]

The lack of a concrete policy regarding the Indians made the problem of the military more difficult. The troops used to fight the Indians were few in numbers, were not properly trained for such combat, and were usually poorly equipped. The Indians invariably were better mounted (in some instances infantry was used to chase the fleet ponies of the warriors) and had the additional advantage of knowing the terrain where most of the battles were fought. It is amazing that the troops, with such handicaps, were as successful as they were. The army was usually restricted to chasing individual Indians or groups of Indians who had committed a specific raid upon the white settlements or upon travelers through the territory. Seldom was a definite campaign planned. The only thing the savages feared was an attack upon their villages or retreats. Once the troops used such

[3] Robert G. Athearn, *William Tecumseh Sherman and the Settlement of the West*, 205–206. This crusty general's attitude toward the territory was well expressed when he said: "I would respectfully recommend, that the United States sell New Mexico, and all the region about, to Mexico for $15,000,000, and lend them the greenbacks to pay with!" Quoted in *ibid.*, 85.

attacks as their basic strategy, the hostile tribes were soon subdued.

Also handicapping the troops in their efforts to control the Indians were the humanitarian and even romantic concepts about Indian life prevalent in the East. To many people, these were the "noble red men" who had lived in idyllic happiness and contentment like simple children of nature until the rapacious frontiersmen put in their appearance and corrupted them. Whenever the troops chastised the Indians too vigorously, howls of protest arose from sentimental journalists, religious leaders who decried such brutal tactics, and other idealists (who had probably never been west of Philadelphia) who blamed the white man for all of the misconduct of the Indians. The activities of such people resulted in a policy which was contemptuously described as "feed 'em in the winter, fight 'em in the summer." The defenders of the Indians consistently charged that the army exaggerated the deeds of a few irresponsible savages in order to justify the military campaigns.[4]

To the "yellow leg" on duty the Indian was anything but a romantic being, and protecting the advance of the American frontier was a harsh and forbidding task. One of these soldiers, resenting the Easterners' smug attitude and the abuse heaped upon the troops, described matters from the lowly enlisted man's point of view: "Almost every dollar was spent for some luxury like goat's milk, butter $2.50 per pound, and seldom obtained, poor sardines at $1.50 a box, and the poorest kind of shirts and stockings at the sutlers. . . . in loneliness time dragged on, seldom if ever a letter or newspaper, everlasting wishing to know what was going on in the world and how it fared at home. . . . Oh, the loneliness of it, the darkness of the evenings, the silence of it, save the calls for drills, guard mount, retreat, and other drum and fife calls. When ammunition was almost gone, we saw a cruel fate of unpreparedness; all this made us bitterly regard the government which seemed to have deserted us. Now and then news came of this and that command, too few in number to stem the everlasting superiority, slaughtered and mutilated, every captive tortured to death by demonish redskins. Then would come what seemed the day of reckoning, and after terrible marches where men maddened with thirst opened their veins and drank their own

[4] See Andrews, "Indians of Arizona and New Mexico," 20–21.

blood, and after all sorts of gloriously brave exploits of our boys in blue, the murderous devilish Indians would be cornered for the whipping they needed."[5]

Before proceeding with a more detailed discussion of the Indian menace that confronted New Mexico from 1846 to 1886, there is an obvious question: Considering the neglect of Washington, the lack of adequate army forces, and the prowess of the warlike Indians, how were the whites ultimately able to win? General Sherman's suggestion that time was on the side of the white men is one answer, but there are others. Despite the fact that the army was outnumbered in almost every engagement with the Indians, as also were the frontiersmen who fought them, they still won most of the battles. The Indians were invariably better mounted than their adversaries, and the whites were not always better armed. The bow and arrow in the hands of a well-trained savage was a far more effective weapon than the six-shooter. A warrior could shoot fast enough to keep four or five arrows in the air, and it is recorded that one put eight into flight before the first touched the ground.[6] A good rifle was accurate at about one hundred yards compared to the seventy or so of a bow, but usually the Indian was able to obtain firearms that were the equal of the white's.

The primary explanation for the success of the white man was his better organization. The Indian's style of fighting was to strike, accomplish his aims, and then run. He was never able to adjust himself to the white's ability to remain cool under attack and withstand a prolonged siege. The warriors grew very excited during a conflict, and frequently even their best marksmen wasted their arrows in a flurry of shooting without a target. Largely because of superstitions they did not attack during the night, and thus were unable to keep up a prolonged attack. Like most primitive people, they would panic whenever something occurred which they did not understand. They believed, for example, that the white man's cannon was capable of

5 William Thornton Parker, *Annals at Old Fort Cummings*, 16–17. The soldiers at this fort were reported as "deserting every few days on account of being so lonesome." From Maria Christina Shrode, "Diary of a journey from Hopkins County, Texas to San Diego, California, May 11–December 25, 1870" (Huntington Library, San Marino, California).

6 Gregg, *Commerce of the Prairies*, 416.

shooting holes through the earth and killing on the far side of a mountain. The Indian fought for personal glory and for gain as a result of a battle. He was the epitome of the rugged individualist in battle. Hence, it was impossible to organize Indian armies. The Indian, with immediate gain his object, fought in a raiding party rather than in a formal engagement. When the fighting went against him, it was easy for him to run away and fight again another day. Thus, the ultimate success of the better-organized whites, with their foresight and planning, was well-nigh inevitable.

The Problem to the Civil War

Although General Kearny had received representatives of the Pueblos, Navahos, Utes, and Apaches who offered their submission in August, 1846, it was not to be long before there would be an outbreak of hostilities that would last indefinitely. The Utes were mainly a Colorado tribe, but frequently made their headquarters in the mountains of the northern part of New Mexico. They were allies of the Jicarilla Apaches. The brief flare-up of hostilities on the part of the Pueblo Indians was quickly handled, but the nomadic tribes were to continue their forays for some time. Long at war with the Spanish-speaking settlers, these warriors could not comprehend the American position that such raids would no longer be tolerated. Their acceptance of Kearny and his forces originally stemmed from the belief that he would co-operate with them in their attacks upon their traditional enemies. Their bitter hostility towards the Spanish-speaking peoples came from the centuries-old tradition of raids in which Indian children were seized and sold into slavery, a practice that was to continue even under the Americans: a healthy Indian commanded as much as three hundred dollars on the Santa Fe market.

The Navahos continued hostilities, but this group never was as destructive as some of the other tribes. They simply raided the settlements, taking a toll of livestock, but were careful not to destroy things, as they wanted the Pueblo Indians and the Spanish to continue raising crops for them to harvest. The Jicarilla and Mescalero Apaches, along with their Ute allies, were on the warpath most of the time. Fortunately, it was to be in the last years of the 1850's before the Comanches extended their forays westward. Compared to their later activities, the western Apaches were also relatively quiet. They contented themselves with attacking and murdering many of the goldseekers who flocked over the southern route from Texas to California. Beside the road, little mounds of stone, some marked by a rude cross and others with a wooden headboard, provided mute testimony to the activity of the feared Apaches. It was not until the white man moved into the Apache country in force that the fearful outrages of later years were committed.

To protect the settlers, and, perhaps of more importance, to keep open the avenues of transportation, New Mexico was organized into the Ninth Military Department. A large number of forts were established as bases of operation, with the headquarters of the department located at Fort Union, in 1851. Protecting the Santa Fe Trail and located near the retreat of the northern tribes, Fort Union was to be the center of defense. Other important forts were located just across the present Arizona state line in the Navaho country, at Fort Defiance, in 1851, and Fort Stanton in the Mescalero Apache country, in 1855. Other forts were established as the need arose and were located in the particular domain of the tribe that was currently causing trouble.

Unfortunately, the army had available only 1,400 to 1,800 men to garrison twelve to fifteen forts. This meant that frequently the troops would be doing very well if they protected themselves, let alone punishing the Indians or even overawing them by their strength.[7] It cost the government as much as three million dollars a year to maintain this force. It was estimated that the number of wild Indians in New Mexico at this time totaled about 17,000: 10,000 Navahos, 5,000 Apaches, and 2,000 Utes; these figures are probably too high.

Most of the trouble with the nomadic tribes before the Civil War involved the Navahos. Secure in their mountain fastness at Canyon de Chelly, which they believed to be impregnable, this tribe con-

7 Bancroft, *Arizona and New Mexico*, 655–56. On one occasion, Apaches raided Doña Ana and carried off two Mexican boys not a mile from the fort. By the time the pursuit could be organized, the savages were beyond capture. From Peter Stuyvesant Ten Broeck, "Letterbook" (Huntington Library, San Marino, California).

tinued its traditional pattern of attacking the settlements primarily to carry off livestock. With the Americans now curtailing the Pueblos and the Spanish from returning the raids, the Navahos grew increasingly bolder. Both Indian agents and the military joined hands in an effort to curb them, and countless treaties were signed, with the Indians clamoring for peace every time the whites made a show of force. Usually the Navahos had little intention of abiding by the treaties. Instead, they used the breathing spells afforded by treaties to check the effectiveness of an occasional expedition against them. The ink was seldom dry on one of the new treaties before the Navahoes were raiding again. Even when the soldiers were successful in tracking the Navahos to their home ground, the wily savages were usually able to drive their flocks and herds off before their arrival. When the troops destroyed their corn, the Indians were simply forced to increase the tempo of their raiding to prevent starvation.

The contempt of the Navahos for the white men grew as a result of what they regarded as weakness in submitting to the many treaties. Frequent changes of either Indian agents or military commanders made it difficult to maintain a sustained action against them, with the incoming official frequently calling off the campaign already launched by his predecessor and offering the Navahos another treaty instead of using force. Adding insult to injury, the Navahos, attacked Fort Defiance in force in the spring of 1860, the only time in the history of the wars that the Indians had the effrontery to attack a military garrison.[8] It was not until General Carleton arrived with the California Column during the Civil War that the Navahos were to meet their masters and be finally subdued.

One of the intermittent periods of peace was ended in 1852 with the White Massacre. The Jicarilla Apaches residing in northeastern New Mexico were generally considered to be lazy and cowardly, having been driven from the Plains by the more warlike Comanches. They intermarried extensively with the Utes, with whom they were usually allied. A group of them, having been fired on without provocation by some soldiers, took revenge on the first party coming west on the Santa Fe Trail. In this group was E. J. White of Philadelphia, who was en route to Fort Buchanan to take a civilian post. The angry

[8] *Ibid.*, 658.

Indians attacked the wagon train, killing Mr. White and ten others and taking his wife and child captive.

A rescue party later overtook the Indians, killing seven of them, but in the struggle Mrs. White was murdered by the Indian woman guarding her. The white settlers, as well as the soldiers, were outraged and sought immediate vengeance against the Jicarillas. The situation worsened in 1853 when William Carr Lane, the Indian agent, attempted to locate the Jicarillas on a reservation, promising them food if they would settle down. The treaty he negotiated was not honored by the federal government, and the infuriated Indians went on the warpath, killing and raiding the surrounding countryside. The military kept scouts in the field, and in February of 1854 thirty men under Lieutenant David Bell fought an engagement with an Indian war party, killing an Indian named White Wolf, who had led the White Massacre.

Near Taos, a Jicarilla-Ute war party composed of about 250 men attacked a cavalry unit of 60 on March 30, 1854. In the ensuing fight only 17 soldiers escaped, but they claimed to have killed over 200 of the attacking Indians. This prompted Colonel Philip St. George Cooke, the commander of Fort Union, to carry the war into the Indian country. The regular troops, augmented by a force of volunteers and Pueblo Indians from Taos led by the famed Kit Carson, chased the Indians into the rugged mountain country and inflicted a serious defeat on them.[9] Subsequent campaigns against these Indians were to result in a peace that lasted in northern New Mexico for some time. Only the Jicarillas and the Utes were to be classed as "Union Indians" during the Civil War, and their loyalty was partially due to the effectiveness of the chastisement given them.

At first, relations with the Mescalero Apaches were relatively peaceful, a treaty having been signed with their leader on the second of April, 1851. Despite the fact that some of the tribe doubtless were involved in the raids with the warlike western Apaches and some perhaps even with the Jicarillas, the leaders of the Mescaleros tried to remain on peaceful terms with the white men. In May, 1853, the

[9] The story of these campaigns is based upon the reports of Colonel Cooke and Major Carleton contained in the Ritch Collection. A worthwhile secondary account is in Reiter, "History of Fort Union," 57–62.

Mescalero chiefs came to Santa Fe to report that their people were doing well, their crops were good, and they hoped that the government would keep its promise to establish a fort in their area.

The tribal leaders, however, could not always control the younger braves, and some Mescaleros joined the western Apaches and the Jicarillas in the fighting of 1854. Thus identified with the warlike Apaches, the Mescaleros were attacked by the army and had no choice but to fight back.

In January, 1855, Captain Richard S. Ewell led a winter campaign into the Mescalero Apache country in an effort to subdue them. Despite the rugged terrain and frequent ambushes, the troops were able to destroy the Indian villages completely, driving the savages into the wilderness without food or shelter. Completely crushed and without food, the Mescaleros made sincere peace overtures at a time when the army was preparing another major blow against them. A fort was established to keep them in check and was named after Captain Stanton, who had given his life in the campaign against them. After this, the Mescaleros tended to settle down and till their fields, and if the whites had been able to feed them properly until they were able to get a start in their agricultural activities, there probably would have been no more trouble from them. Unfortunately, as was frequently the case, they were driven to raiding and stealing in order to keep from starving to death.[10]

In the spring of 1858 the Comanches attacked a white settlement on Red River, about 130 miles from Fort Union, looting and burning it. In the same year they began attacking the Overland Mail with monotonous regularity. It is not possible to estimate the number of lives lost in these forays, but it doubtless was large. More than likely, the Comanches were prompted in their deeds by a group of treacherous Spanish-Americans known as *Comancheros*, who moved with impunity through the hostile Indian country, furnishing the tribes with needed supplies as well as trading for stolen horses and cattle.[11]

The outbreak of the Civil War and the resulting Texan invasion of New Mexico led the Indians to believe that they were finally successful in driving out the hated palefaces. Fort after fort was aban-

10 This account is based upon Sonnichsen, *The Mescalero Apaches*, 74–88.
11 Bender, *The March of Empire*, 163.

doned, leaving the warriors in command and convincing them that it was they and their raids which had forced the abandonment.

Between 1847 and 1861, the government had spent an average of three million dollars a year in an effort to control the Indians of New Mexico. Unfortunately, little had been accomplished by this expenditure. If anything, the Indian was stronger than he had been before the Americans arrived. The basic weakness obviously was the policy of fighting the Indians with the saber in one hand while holding out the olive branch in the other. The Indians grasped the olive branch when it was to their advantage, only to fight as soon as the military force was moved elsewhere. And as Federal troops began leaving for active service in the East, it was a signal for the wild tribes to reassert their power.

The Navaho Problem

When James Henry Carleton led his California Column into New Mexico over the vast desert area of Arizona and California, his soldiers were disappointed to discover that the Confederates had already left. But there was to be enough fighting available to satisfy their appetites, as the Indians were virtually in control of New Mexico. Carleton, one of the ablest military commanders in the history of the Indian wars, had had previous service in New Mexico and was thoroughly familiar with the problem he confronted.[12] Furthermore, his campaigning against the Indians had convinced him that stern measures would provide the only solution to the problem, and he had sufficient courage to take what he believed were the necessary steps.

While Carleton and his army turned their attention at first to the Apache problem, the Navahos continued to raid the settlements along the Río Grande from Santa Fe south to Socorro with reckless abandon, terrorizing the inhabitants and driving off all the livestock they could find. They even stole sixteen hundred sheep grazing near Fort Craig. But the days of their forays were numbered, and the end

[12] Clarence C. Clendenen, "General James Henry Carleton," *NMHR*, Vol. XXX (January, 1955).

of the Navaho menace was at hand.[13] The tribe was to pay dearly
for the transgressions of the past.

Advising his officers to slay all of the Indian men whenever and
wherever they could be found and to take the women and children
prisoners, Carleton was not ready to make peace with them until
their ability to make war was completely destroyed. He believed
that his measures would in the long run be the most humane; some
solution had to be found to the periodic raiding of the Indians, and
he was confident that it lay in teaching them to respect the laws of
the white man and forcing them to adopt his ways.[14]

The expedition against the Navahos was under the command of
Colonel Kit Carson, whose force was largely composed of New
Mexican volunteers, along with some Ute Indians, traditional enemies
of the Navahos. Carson attacked the Navahos where they were most
vulnerable by destroying their food supply and capturing their
sheep. By the fall of 1863 this task had been accomplished, and Carson's army then invaded Canyon de Chelly, long thought to be impregnable. The result was inevitable: the Navahos were ultimately
overwhelmed.

General Carleton believed that the long-range solution to the In-

---

[13] A memorial of the territorial legislature to President Lincoln and Secretary
of War Stanton claimed that Indian raids had recently cost the area $340,405.15.
January 26, 1863, Ritch Collection, RI 1193. A report of Indian depredations dated
January 4, 1864, claimed that in the preceding year 80 lives had been lost and 38
people wounded in the chronic struggle for survival. In addition, 748 horses, 3,626
head of cattle, 42,044 sheep, 254 mules, 2,075 goats, 78 burros and 2,103 other animals
were reported stolen. Ritch Collection, RI 1549.

[14] This attitude was well expressed in the famous instructions: "The Indian men
. . . are to be killed whenever and wherever you can find them: the women and
children will not be harmed, but you will take them prisoners. . . . If the Indians
send in a flag and desire to treat for peace, say to the bearer; [they have broken]
their treaty of peace, and murdered innocent people and run off their stock: that
now we are going to punish them for their crimes, and that you are there to kill
them wherever they can be found. We have no faith in their broken promises and
we intend to kill enough of their men to teach them a lesson.

"I trust that this severity in the long run will be the most humane course that
could be pursued toward these Indians." James H. Carleton to Christopher Carson,
October 12, 1862, in William McCleave, "Papers and Memoirs as Officer, 1st Cavalry,
California Volunteers." (Bancroft Library, Berkeley).

dian problem lay in establishing a large reservation where both the
Navahos and the Apaches could be forced to farm under the watch-
ful eye of the army. Unfortunately, the site Carleton selected was at
Bosque Redondo, near the present city of Fort Sumner. The General
was convinced that this place would be an excellent "reformatory
for Indians," as it was a vast area of vacant land which he believed
could be used for grazing sheep and cattle, as well as raising crops.
The nearby Pecos River would provide adequate water for both
drinking and irrigation. The great expanse would make it easier to
control the Navahos, who would not be able to retreat into their old
haunts in the mountains where they were difficult to find.[15]

It was to this area that the defeated Navahos were now escorted.
Gradually their numbers grew until more than eight thousand of
them were gathered. At first hopes were high for success, and the
fact that the twentieth century has seen this particular area develop
into a fertile irrigated farming area indicates that Carleton had far
better judgment than he has usually been given credit for. But in
the end the noble experiment was to prove a dismal and heartbreak-
ing failure. The reasons for the debacle rest upon the fact that the
government of the United States in the nineteenth century did not
realize the scope of the undertaking at hand and was not prepared
to give it enough financial support to put it on a firm basis from the
very beginning. Adequate planning with proper construction of
some kind of dwellings, assistance and proper supervision of the
Navaho farming methods, and adequate provision for food, along
with efforts at irrigation, might have insured the success of the
venture.

The project was dogged with ill luck from the very beginning.
First of all, it was fatal to have included both the Navahos and the
Mescalero Apaches, for they could not get along together and were
constantly fighting. An unseasonable drought led to a series of crop
failures and made even drinking water difficult to procure. The
ravages of worms, hail, and floods were exceptionally severe. Disease
took a frightening toll of the Indians as they were swept by epi-
demics of smallpox, chicken pox, whooping cough, and pneumonia.

[15] Keleher, *Turmoil in New Mexico*, 309–10.

But, according to an army surgeon, the most prevalent disease was syphilis, the Navaho women having proved attractive to the large number of soldiers around.[16]

Far from their home grounds, the Navahos seemed to suffer psychologically from being away from their beloved mountains and virtually refused to work in the fields. The Mescalero Apaches fled Bosque Redondo on November 3, 1865, foreshadowing the ultimate failure of the effort. The campaign of the Navahos to return to their home grounds in the northwestern part of the territory was aided by the frontiersmen who coveted the land on which they had been settled. Hence, "New Mexico politicians, expert in the Machiavellistic art of accomplishing the removal of officials," plotted so effectively that Carleton was ousted in 1866.[17] In 1868, General Sherman negotiated a treaty with the Navahos which provided for their return to the abode of their forefathers, where the Navaho reservation exists to the present time. After years of hardship, the Navahos are increasing in numbers and are prospering. Had General Carleton planned the containment of this tribe on their native ground, his experiment might have been a success.

The Apaches

The Mescaleros were the first to feel the sting of Carleton's methods in his dealings with the Apaches. When Fort Stanton had been abandoned at the beginning of the Civil War, they had taken to the warpath again, profiting from the confused situation and general lack of protection to raid the frontier settlements. Their depredations were so extensive that in the month of August, 1862, alone they killed forty men and six children.

Again, it was Colonel Kit Carson who was placed in charge of the troops, with orders to kill all of the male members of the tribe if they resisted and to make captives of the women and children. Carson reoccupied Fort Stanton, and his campaigning against the Mescaleros

---

16 Sonnichsen, *The Mescalero Apaches*, 105.
17 Keleher, *Turmoil in New Mexico*, 454-55.

was so successful that in March, 1863, the remnants of the tribe surrendered, throwing themselves on the mercy of the whites, begging only that it be remembered that "we are men and braves." With few rifles, little or no ammunition, and desperately little food, the tribesmen were in no condition to resist the superior forces brought to bear against them.

Within a short period of time Carson's men had rounded up between four and five hundred Mescaleros and taken them off to Bosque Redondo. At first, the Mescaleros tried to adjust to their new life, but the conflict with the Navahos was too much, and on November 3, 1865, they simply walked away. Using the old Apache trick of scattering in order to elude pursuers, fragments of the tribe returned to their old stamping grounds in the Sacramento Mountains, while others made their way eastward onto the trackless waste of the *Llano Estacado* and many joined their cousins west of the Río Grande.

It was not until 1873 that the Mescalero Reservation was formally established, but before that the members of the tribe had slowly returned to their own land. Through the years the Mescaleros have prospered and have shown surprising ability to adjust to the ways of the white man. Their reservation has made money by the sale of timber, the grazing of sheep and cattle, and catering to the tourist trade.[18]

It was the western Apache tribes who were to terrorize southwestern New Mexico, Arizona, and the northern states of Mexico. They included the Mimbreños, Mogollones, and the Chiricahuas, probably totaling in numbers 1,500 to 1,800 in 1864.[19] These were the tribes that were to strike terror into everyone's heart, the name Apache being used to frighten small children. Superb warriors and intelligent people, they were extremely difficult to bring under control.

The inevitable clash with the Americans was precipitated as soon as travelers began making their way to California through the southwestern part of the territory. Open hostilities began when Lieutenant George Bascom tricked Cochise, the chief of the Chiricahuas, into surrendering. Cochise escaped, but his family were executed as

---

[18] Sonnichsen, *The Mescalero Apaches*; Tate, "History of the Mescalero Reservation"; McCord, "Economic History of the Mescalero."

[19] Bancroft, *Arizona and New Mexico*, 744.

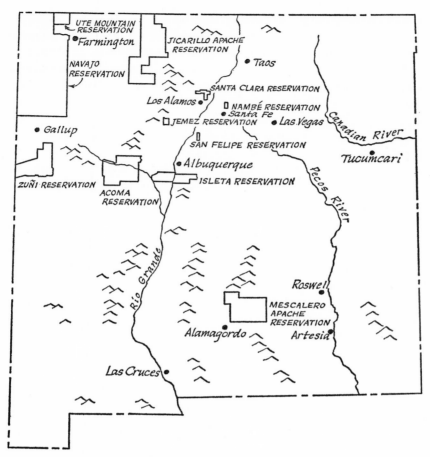

Indian Reservations in New Mexico

hostages, thus prompting the destructive raids that were to last for many years.[20] Finally having the excuse that they had been long waiting for, the Apaches assaulted mines, ranch houses, and small settlements and made it virtually impossible for travelers to get through without protection. The outbreak of the Civil War and the consequent abandonment of many forts prompted the Apaches to become increasingly daring in their outrages.

In the summer of 1862 the Apaches killed two messengers whom General Carleton had sent to General Canby in New Mexico. The first detail of the California Column was met by a group of Apaches who killed and mutilated two soldiers who ventured away from their comrades while a peace parley was in session. A supply detachment under Captain Roberts, composed of only 126 men, was attacked in Apache Pass by forces under Cochise and Mangas Coloradas, estimated to have been in excess of 2,000. The soldiers won the battle by utilizing howitzers, which frightened the savages unused to "having wagons shoot at them." The army lost only two men killed and three wounded, while the Indians had sixty-six killed. So began the first formal encounter between the army and the Apaches, initiating a war that was to last for over a quarter of a century.

Much of the story of this conflict is more correctly a part of the history of Arizona rather than of New Mexico, but the battle raged from Las Cruces westward to the territorial line. It was a conflict in which the white man was at a definite disadvantage, as the Apache was capable of striking and then disappearing into the wild terrain, where the soldiers and frontiersmen were usually powerless to follow. It was a conflict in which the civilized white man discovered that his only hope of success lay in becoming just as much a savage as his adversary. In fact, as the war progressed, it was sometimes difficult to be sure which was the savage.

Once the Civil War was over, the problem was intensified by the movement of miners into the mountain country of what later became Grant County. The Apaches preyed on one and all without discrimination, causing the settlers to demand assistance from the government, which was not easy to obtain. Angered by what they considered neglect by the authorities, a group in Arizona wantonly at-

20 Lockwood, *The Apaches*, 103–105.

tacked the Indians assembled at Camp Grant, killing more than one hundred of them, most of whom were women and children.

The Camp Grant Massacre received national attention, and many groups in the East, safe from the raids of the Apaches, complained bitterly of such brutality. This led many persons, especially a Quaker named Vincent Colyer, to the conviction that if the Indian was treated fairly, the white man would have no problem in dealing with him. Hardened frontiersmen, having seen many times the bodies of women and children mutilated by the Apaches, were naturally cynical about such an attitude.

Vincent Colyer, however, had the backing of the government, and he proceeded to establish an Apache reservation near Tularosa, selecting this site because it was remote from the white settlements and was surrounded by mountains with plenty of arable land, water, wood, and wild game. The Apaches were not any more enthusiastic about leaving their home ground than the Navahos had been several years earlier. Only a few of them went to Tularosa, and those who did go did not remain long.

Far more effective in controlling the Apaches than the efforts of the Quaker Colyer was to be the policy of General George Crook. An able soldier, Crook knew his Indians well. He knew that force was necessary to treat with people who had lived by the sword so long. He also knew that there were good Indians and bad Indians, just as there were good and bad men in all races. Crook recognized that unless the Apaches were given a decent economy, all peaceful overtures would be a hopeless failure. The policy followed elsewhere of aiding the Indians to get started in a white man's world had to be applied.

Forced into temporary inaction while the olive branch was being extended to the Apaches, Crook carefully laid his plans for what he knew to be a necessary military campaign against them. A more effective peace emissary than Colyer was General Oliver O. Howard, whose long and distinguished military career had included heading the famous Freedmen's Bureau. The highest ranking officer in the Southwest, Howard was assured of the co-operation of the military, something that other peacemakers would not be apt to get. With tremendous courage, Howard went into the mountains without an escort, met Cochise, and convinced him that reservation life was the only course in the future.[21]

Unfortunately, not all of the Apaches followed their famous chief to the reservation, and many who did began to use it as a base of operations for murderous forays. Crook organized his military forces in such a way that they pursued and harassed these Apaches until they would send a messenger with a white flag pleading to return to the reservation. General Crook would allow them to return only if they would bring in the leaders who had persuaded them to leave. If they refused to do this, he said, he would hunt them down and kill them all. Such a policy quickly convinced the Apaches that once they agreed to accept reservation life, they had better not again venture on the warpath. Needless to say, this course of action brought down upon Crook's head the violent criticism of those who did not understand how to deal with the Apaches. Despite his harshness, Crook earned a reputation among the Indians as a just man whose word could be accepted.[22]

Despite Crook's efforts, however, Apaches still left the reservation to return to their warlike ways. But the story was always the same; they were ultimately hunted down and captured. Geronimo, the most infamous of these bandits, was not finally apprehended until 1886, thus closing the book on the Apache outrages.

The Comanches

The Comanches, strictly speaking, belonged more to the entire region of the Southern Great Plains than to New Mexico alone. They were the epitome of the Plains Indians, whose culture was built around the horse, the buffalo, and the easily moved tipi. With their allies, usually the Kiowas, the Comanches had raided the New Mexico settlements since the early part of the eighteenth century.

21 See *ibid.*, chapter VII, for a discussion of these events.

22 General Crook first warned the natives: "Send out runners to all the renegades . . . telling them they had better come in and take their one month in the guard house, than to be all killed in the mountains." George Crook to Walter Scribner Schuyler, June 23, 1874; August 17, 1874, in Schuyler Papers (Huntington Library, San Marino, California).

Taking advantage of the preoccupation of the soldiers with the campaign against the Navahos in the summer of 1864, the Comanches began attacking wagon trains on the Santa Fe Trail, taking a fearful toll in lives and plunder. Hence General Carleton had to divert his attention to handle the new threat.

Again it was Kit Carson who was placed in charge of the expedition intended to chastise the raiders. As would be expected, General Carleton gave him orders to let the Plains Indians know that if they did not molest the white men, they in turn would be left alone; but if, on the other hand, they continued to rob and commit brutal murders, they would be held accountable. Carson's force of 335 soldiers was augmented by 75 Ute and Jicarilla Apaches. Near Adobe Walls, an abandoned fort located on the Canadian River in the Texas Panhandle, Carson was surprised by a large force of about 1,000 Indians. Carson himself admitted that if it had not been for two howitzers that effectively frightened the savages, there probably wouldn't have been anyone to write the story of the battle.[23] The fight did some good, as in January, 1865, Comanche representatives showed up at Fort Bascom asking for a peace treaty, and for a time an uneasy truce was in effect.

However, Fort Bascom, which was located near the present city of Tucumcari, was kept busy, its soldiers charged with defending the Navahos penned up at Bosque Redondo against the raiding Comanches. The Plains Indians appreciated this conveniently located concentration of livestock, which made easier their regular forays.

As Fort Bascom had originally been established expressly to deal with the Comanche menace, its personnel were alert to anything that complicated their problem. They resented the *Comanchero* trading which had been going on since the beginning of the century. The *Comancheros* were native New Mexicans who knew the country well, and who were accustomed to dealing with the Comanches. These traders made their way down from Santa Fe, Las Vegas, or other towns, laden with merchandise for the Indians. Especially in demand were firewater and firearms. Ultimately trade in stolen cattle and horses came to dominate this unique business. It was even claimed

[23] James M. Foster, Jr., "History of Fort Bascom 1863–1870" (M.A. thesis, Eastern New Mexico University, 1955), 39–43.

that when no cattle or horses were available for trade to the New Mexicans, the traders would lend the Indians their guns and horses and wait at the Comanche camps until the Indians had had a chance to go to a Texas settlement to get the necessary stock.

The enmity toward the *Comancheros* was increased when Carson reported that some of the guns used by the Indians at Adobe Walls had only recently been furnished them. Carson also complained that *Comancheros* going through Fort Bascom, after learning of the contemplated military movement, had proceeded to warn the Indians as well as to furnish them with guns and ammunition, thereby making possible their surprise attack upon Carson's force.

Orders were issued prohibiting all traders from dealing with the Indians unless they had a license and posted a bond. Army pickets guarded the trails leading into Comanche country and dealt harshly with guilty parties. Unfortunately, whenever the traders were tried in the courts of Las Vegas or Santa Fe, their countrymen promptly freed them. One army officer contended that "all these traders are scoundrels who succeed too frequently in smuggling contraband goods through to the Indians and in bringing back stolen cattle in return."[24]

The peace policy embarked on by the government in 1867 failed, and the raids flared up again throughout the Southwest, especially in eastern New Mexico, during the springs of 1867 and 1868. As a result, the decision was made that another winter campaign similar to that waged by Carson in 1864 was necessary before the Comanches and their Plains allies would be ready to accept peace. Selected to lead the troops this time was General Phil Sheridan, the famous Civil War cavalry leader. Under Sheridan was an officer named Custer. In command of the troops in New Mexico was another experienced officer, a Colonel Evans. Again, the Comanches were dealt a staggering blow.

It was obvious that their days of freedom were numbered. No longer was there a place for them to hide, even in the dead of winter. The military campaigns of 1874 were carried out by several large

---

[24] *Ibid.*, 95–100; J. Evetts Haley, "The Comanchero Trade," *Southwestern Historical Quarterly*. Vol. XXXVIII (January, 1935), 164–65.

units which converged on the *Llano Estacado* from all directions, catching the Indians within the jaws of a gigantic trap.

This campaign effectively ended the threat of the Indian on the high plains.[25] Periodically, there were to be individuals who left the reservation and hid out in the open country, but by 1880 the Indian menace to the settlement of New Mexico was over. It was now possible for ranchers and others to settle in the open without fear of the marauding savage. An important phase of New Mexican history had drawn to a close.

[25] *Ibid.*, 87–91.

XI - The Spanish Heritage

THE MANY AMERICANS who made their way into New Mexico during the nineteenth century wrote extensively about what they saw in what was to them a strange land. As changes within the province took place very slowly, their impressions of what life was like at this time can be accepted as a fair interpretation of what colonial life during Spanish times must have been. Most Americans were sufficiently taken with the differences to write about them, but they were uniformly antagonistic in their evaluation. What these observers failed to grasp was that in New Mexico had been preserved a little of the Middle Ages. It was a land where time had almost stood still.

Within nineteenth-century New Mexico much that was common to sixteenth-century Spain still existed. The position of the *ricos* in society was comparable to that of the feudal nobles of prior centuries, and the practice of peonage made the lower classes virtual serfs. The role of the church was not unlike its role in Medieval Europe. Some observers suggested that the agricultural implements could be traced back to biblical times. Even the house furnishings may have originated among the Moors.

Santa Fe, the metropolis of the province, was described as having the appearance of an extensive brickyard or of looking like a group of flatboats clustered together at a river wharf. Taos, the other important town, likewise failed to impress visiting Americans. It was depicted as a collection of mud houses around a miserable square with a few alleys down which Mexicans drove their jackasses.

The governor's palace, the most important building in the province, was seen as only a mud building supported by rough pine pillars. The homes of the people were built for utilitarian reasons and were not intended to impress outsiders. The building style which evolved was based upon designs already inherited from the Spaniards but modified by the limitations of building material and by immediate needs. The Spaniards found the Indians using "puddled" adobe, but soon taught them how to make adobe bricks, which were more adaptable. Such walls were well-nigh impregnable, as even the American artillery was unable to breach them. The rooms were grouped around an inner courtyard that was entered by means of a single large gate. This design was strictly in the interest of safety. Usually there were no windows or doors on the outside walls, only portholes. Only the homes of the early wealthy had glass, plates of mica being used in its place. Floors were of earth treated with a protective surface. Some of the better homes had stone slab floors. Heat was provided by means of a fireplace located in the corner of most rooms. Because iron was at a premium, andirons were unknown and wood was turned upright. The roofs of the houses were flat, and the width of the building was usually determined by the size of the beam available. To the discomfort of the dwellers, the roofs usually let rain in. The interior walls were treated with a limelike substance similar to whitewash, and although it added to the appearance of the building, it usually came off on the clothing of anyone who touched it.

The same style for houses was followed throughout the territory. Naturally, as one went down in the social scale, the houses became less pretentious, with those of the lowest classes frequently being one-room huts. Even the homes of the *ricos* were practically barren of furniture. New Mexico lacked the artisans to make it, and the high cost of shipping it in made it too expensive. There were a few hand-hewn cupboards, tables, and stools, and most homes had a chest for valuables. Bedsteads were almost completely unknown. Instead, mattresses and bedding were made up into a roll in the daytime and utilized as a sort of sofa, to be spread out on the floor at night. Upon the floor there was usually some kind of rug, sometimes woven with designs of Navaho origin. Storage was provided by rawhide trunks. Even in the poorest homes walls were decorated with statues of Christ or one of the saints. Kitchen utensils were usually copper or

201

earthenware, although some of the *ricos* did have silver. Within the courtyard or in front of a house in town was a mud oven, shaped like a cupping glass, that was used for baking.[1]

If the incoming Americans looked with disdain upon the houses and towns of the New Mexicans, they were usually unanimous in approving their food. The basic staple was mutton, which was prepared in various ways so that it did not become tiresome. Beef, poultry, and game were the other meats, the amount served depending upon social status. The Indian foods, now familiar throughout the Southwest, such as *tamales, tortillas, tacos, enchiladas,* and *chile con carne* were all favorites. When wheat was available, white bread was baked in the outdoor ovens, and, judging from the laudatory comments, it must have been of uniformly high quality. The basic beverage was cocoa, New Mexicans using it as coffee is used today. Supplementing this diet were fruits and vegetables in season.

Another object in New Mexico that was universally approved by the Anglos, at least by the men, was the ladies. One observer described them as "certainly far more beautiful than those of the same rank in America; their jetty black eyes, slender and delicate frame, with unusually small ankles and feet, together with their gay winning address, make you at once easy and happy in their company."[2] Even Garrard, who commented that when it came to selecting a wife he would prefer one from his own country, was charmed by the friendliness of the *señoritas,* and even decided, though shocked, that the way in which they handled their *cigarillos* enhanced their already flattering appearance.[3]

The *rebozo,* a basic article of feminine apparel, was worn by all classes. Actually, it was little more than a long scarf, up to six feet in length and varying from one to two yards in width. Thrown over the shoulders so that the ends dangled below the waist, it served at the same time as a bonnet, shawl, apron, veil, and bodice. Above the waist the ladies wore a chemise, usually fitted, with short sleeves. This garment displayed to advantage their fair shoulders and charming necks. Their skirts were somewhat shorter than those worn in the

[1] Garrard, *Wah-to-yah and the Taos Trail,* 242.
[2] Clipping from *Niles Register* in Ritch Scrapbook.
[3] Garrard, *Wah-to-yah and the Taos Trail,* 238.

States at the same time, and Susan Magoffin was dutifully shocked when women wading in the creek pulled their dresses above their knees.[4] Indian-style moccasins were the usual type of footwear. On festive occasions, "the ladies and girls were dressed in silks, satins, ginghams, and lawns, embroidered crape shawls, fine rebozos—and decked with various showy ornaments, such as huge necklaces, countless rings, combs, bows, ribbands, red and other coloured handkerchiefs, and other fine fancy articles."[5]

Needless to say, the apparel of New Mexican men never attracted the attention accorded the women's clothing. Normally they wore close-fitting sleeved jackets, knee-length pantaloons open on the outside seam, which, as they were lined with buttons, could be fastened to the pleasure of the wearer. Buckskin leggings, woolen stockings, and moccasins completed the outside attire. Underneath, the men wore white drawers, a fancy colored shirt and vest, and usually a brightly colored belt, often with a colored scarf over it. On festive occasions, men as well as women wore a vest called a *bolero*. It was usually very fancy, frequently made of either velvet or leather, and was sometimes worn in place of a jacket. One of the most distinctive pieces of male apparel was the *sombrero*, its quality frequently designating the social standing of the wearer. The crown was either high or low, but the low crown was predominant. The brim, quite wide, was held in place by a chin band. These hats were frequently heavily decorated with silver. The *serape* was an all-purpose garment for men, much as the *rebozo* was for the women. Usually slung over the shoulder, it could serve as overcoat, raincoat, or even blanket. Normally, it contained an opening through which a man could thrust his head to wear the *serape* over his shoulders. When it was used in this way, it was called a *poncho*. The *serape* was normally bright in color. Most Spanish men carried a knife just as the Anglo frontiersmen carried a six-shooter.[6]

Life may have been hard in frontier New Mexico, but it was not

[4] Magoffin, *Down the Santa Fe Trail*, 238.

[5] *Ibid.*, 124. At home, the standard feminine apparel was a loose-fitting chemise and shirt and no shoes. The women's hair was "long and plaited in two long plaits and hangs down the back." From Maria Christina Shrode, "Diary of a Journey from Hopkins County, Texas to San Diego."

[6] Hallenbeck, *Land of the Conquistadores*, 348; Twitchell, *Old Santa Fe*, 225.

without its diversions. Like people everywhere, the New Mexicans had their own particular forms of amusement. Most important of these was the dance. There were various types of dances, and they are mentioned so often that apparently there was a dance every night of the year. Some of the dance steps could be performed in the living rooms of homes, and doubtless were. Some kinds of dances were more formal, such as the *baile*. The most common dance was the *fandango*, actually a public dance. The usual accompaniment was violin and guitar. James Ohio Pattie describes his participation: "All that chose to dance stood up on the floor, and at the striking up of a certain note of the music, they all commenced clapping their hands. The ladies then advanced, one by one, and stood facing their partners. The dance then changed to a waltz, each man taking his lady rather unceremoniously, and they began to whirl around, keeping true, however, to the music, and increasing the swiftness of their whirling. Many of the movements and figures seemed very easy, though we found they required practice, for we must certainly have made a most laughable appearance in their eyes, in attempting to practice it."[7]

Dances of some kind were held in connection with the frequent *fiestas*. These could be associated with a wedding, one of the frequent saint's days or other church holidays, or a large variety of other occasions, the New Mexicans finding many excuses to hold a dance. At dances there was usually very little drinking, wine and a mild brandy being the primary intoxicants. This was one deficiency which the Anglos hastened to remedy.

Second only to dancing as a diversion was gambling. The New Mexicans would bet on anything. Horse racing was common, with purses ranging up to ten thousand dollars for a single race.[8] Cock fighting was likewise common. During the nineteenth century the

[7] *Personal Narrative*, 168. Following is another description of a Spanish dance: "We had a fandango given us at night and here, for the first time, I had the opportunity of seeing the Spanish dance in the true Spanish style and witnessing that remarkable grace and beauty of carriage remarked by so many travellers. Some of the young señoritas were very pretty and the dancing was beautiful. They use the violin and the guitar and accompany the music of these instruments with the voice." From Lt. David Sloane Stanley, "Diary of an Expedition . . . from Fort Smith, Arkansas . . . to San Diego (1853–1854)" (Huntington Library, San Marino, California).

[8] Louis H. Warner, *Archbishop Lamy* (Santa Fe, 1936), 186.

natural interest of the Spanish-Americans in gambling was augmented by the Anglo frontiersmen, who were always eager for excitement. At one time, Santa Fe had sixty licensed gambling places to take care of those who had money to lose.[9]

As might be anticipated in the quasi-medieval society existing in New Mexico until the nineteenth century, most of the forms of artistic expression were concerned with religion. Although the church buildings as a general rule were humble structures, many of them contained art work in the form of statues, frescoes, or wood carvings that would have been a credit to many European craftsmen. The making of *santos* flourished for a time so that every household could have its own figurine of Christ, the Virgin, or a favorite saint. As related elsewhere, most of the metal work was of Indian origin, but the Mexican silversmiths showed unusual talents in decorating saddles.

Among predominantly illiterate people the drama has always been a basic form of expression. Medieval-type morality plays, perhaps originally written by missionaries to instruct the Indian converts, were performed in connection with religious holidays. Most communities had their favorite play, some stressing the Christmas story, while others, especially in the Penitente communities, paid more attention to the tragedy inherent in the passion season. Other plays presented famous scenes in Spanish history, such as *Los Moros* or *Los Cristianos*, and others relating important incidents in the early history of New Mexico.

Music was one of the most significant forms of artistic expression in New Mexico. The Spanish missionaries to the Indians early discovered that music was one means by which the Indians could be more quickly attracted to the Holy Faith. Both vocal and instrumental music were used effectively, and it is probable that music was taught more extensively to the savages than any other subject.

[9] *Ibid.*, 257. During Spanish-Mexican times women from the better classes were regular visitors at the gambling houses. With the coming of the Americans, however, such women gradually abandoned the gambling salons leaving only the lowest classes there. The reason for this change was that the Americans misunderstood their presence. The most notorious of all Mexican women gamblers was Gertrudes Barcelo, more familiarly known as La Tules. For an interesting but fictional account of this women's life, see Ruth Laughlin, *The Wind Leaves No Shadow*.

The first European music teacher in the area of the present United States was a Franciscan, Percival de Quinanes, who came to Mexico between 1598 and 1604. This father brought an organ with him and soon taught the Indians to sing at church services. Church bells were probably just as important as organs in impressing the Indians, but the cost was so great that many of the churches could not afford them.[10] The violin and the guitar were also used as a part of the worship service.[11]

In addition, there was much secular music. Impromptu songs were sung in the manner of the medieval troubadour as a means of folk expression, to explain an accident or some valorous deed of battle or hunt. Such folk music was similar to that heard among the Spanish Gauchos of the Pampas. Many of these troubadours, with a guitar slung over their shoulders, more than likely improvised on medieval ballads that had been handed down for generations, frequently changing the wording to suit the current situation.[12]

 *Education*

In many parts of the territory, education lagged because of what could be described as a tri-lingual situation; the Spanish, the Anglos, and the Indians were each divided from the others by the barrier of language. It is difficult enough for a teacher to communicate with pupils when they all speak the same tongue. Pity the poor instructor trying to impart knowledge in the presence of three tongues! The insistence of the Spanish-speaking people upon the retention of their status and the resulting guarantees which they wrote into the state constitution have unquestionably retarded education in New Mexico—so much so, in fact, that one observer wryly remarked, "This is the only state where the students are illiterate in two languages."

Consistently unfavorable to the cause of learning in nineteenth-century New Mexico were political and social conditions. With the

[10] Lota M. Spell, "Music Teaching in New Mexico in the 17th Century," *NMHR*, Vol. II (January, 1927), 27.

[11] Magoffin, *Down the Stanta Fe Trail*, 138.

[12] For a more complete treatment see Charles F. Lummis, *The Land of Poco Tiempo*, 217–50.

heritage of the Spanish-Mexican social stratification in which the *ricos* kept the bulk of the people in a state of quasi-servitude, thereby exercising political as well as economic power, there was little real incentive toward mass public education. Many of the leading citizens questioned their being taxed in order to send someone else's children to school. Perhaps they foresaw that educating the lower classes would endanger their own position at the apex of the social pyramid. In general, the upper classes sent their sons and daughters to church schools in Mexico or, later, at St. Louis. Primary schools were opened, but Bancroft notes that in 1834 "there was no school at Santa Fe, and probably none elsewhere."[13] In 1832, Barreiro found schools well provided for financially, but did not see much result of the primary instruction. This unfortunate circumstance was attributed "to the neglect, laziness and ignorance of many schoolmasters, and due likewise to the lack of zeal on the part of the authorities."[14]

A number of factors contributed to the sad plight of education in New Mexico, a condition that was not to be alleviated until well into the twentieth century. First of all, the extreme poverty of the area, which led Spain to neglect schooling there, continued throughout the nineteenth century. In most parts of the territory there were simply not sufficient funds available for the purposes of education. And most people had such a difficult time wresting a living from the inhospitable soil that children were needed for many tasks and could not be spared to the schoolroom, even if the parents did have the meager fees for tuition and books. The very vastness of New Mexico complicated the problems of education. Before the advent of motorized vehicles, it was almost impossible to get children from isolated areas to the schoolrooms. In many communities the hazards presented by hostile Indians, which lasted until the 1880's made impossible the maintenance of schools in the outlying districts.[15]

Under such a social structure, it was inevitable that most people were apathetic towards education. The Spanish-speaking simply did not look upon "book learning" with the same reverence that the

[13] *Ibid.*, 341.

[14] Barreiro, *Ojeada Sobre Nuevo-México*, 29.

[15] Leland W. Corbin, "The Educational Activities of the Evangelical United Brethren Church in New Mexico" (M.A. thesis, University of New Mexico, 1950), 19.

English frontiersmen did. Even after school attendance became compulsory in the 1890's there was little enforcement. In many communities the local *patrón* saw that such regulations were not too harshly enforced in order to preserve his own position more effectively.[16] When one considers the fact that in 1889 a law was passed that required school teachers and officials to be able to read and write either English or Spanish, one shudders to think of what conditions actually were in the schools of that day. Then, too, the public school system was considered an integral part of the state patronage, and in many communities teachers, officials, and even janitors were selected for their party affiliations rather than for their qualifications.

In addition to the desire of the Spanish-speaking to preserve their native tongue, another force retarding public education was the opposition of the Roman Catholic church. In the latter half of the nineteenth century, the church was engaged in a vigorous controversy in Italy, France, and Germany in an effort to retain its historical position. In some respects, this dispute was transferred to New Mexico, as many of the leading church teachers and leaders fled from the restrictive measures in the European countries.

The church leaders accurately saw that in public schools the time would come when "even the name of God shall not be mentioned . . . there shall not be made in [these schools] even a short prayer invoking the light of the divine Spirit, that in them there shall not be taught a single word nor be seen a single sign of religion; in one word, that there shall be no more question of religion in educating our youth than in educating a mule." The church contended that because New Mexico was predominantly Roman Catholic, public funds should be used to teach the Catholic Dogma to children of communicants, and that if the Protestants and Jews wished, they could do likewise. A church spokesman denied, with much justification, that the sad plight of education within New Mexico could be attributed to religious instruction alone, but was the result of a variety of factors.[17]

---

[16] A worthwhile study of how the local *patrón* seeks to retain control is contained in the novel by Robert Bright, *The Life and Death of Little Joe*.

[17] Statement of J. A. Truchard, Vicar General in *Revista Catolica*, February 8, 1879 as quoted in *The Era Southwestern*, April 29, 1880. From the Ritch Scrapbook.

Unfortunately, many of the Catholic educational leaders were Italian Jesuits, only recently expelled from their homeland. These men, like Father Finotti and Father Gasparri, were dynamic and competent exponents of their point of view and vigorously assailed the advocates of public schools in the harshest language. The vigor of their attack upon public education as practiced in the rest of the United States attracted widespread attention in the national press and undoubtedly had much to do with the opposition to New Mexico's attempts to attain statehood.[18]

Naturally, the Protestant advocates of public schools replied with equal vigor, and in some cases even greater intemperance. The Jesuits were denounced as adventurers and refugees, and the entire opposition to public education was depicted as a popish plot. Needless to say, the intemperate utterances of both factions appear foolish a century later.

One of the earliest effective schools was that conducted by Padre Martínez at Taos. Although the school was established primarily for the purpose of training boys for the priesthood, many of the students went on to attain recognition in other fields. The textbooks used were printed on the Padre's own printing press, and the school building was merely one of the rooms of his house.[19]

During the first twenty-five years of the American occupation very little was accomplished regarding schools. In 1856 a public education bill was defeated 5,016 to 37, indicating that there was little support for public schools. The 1859–60 territorial legislature provided for a school in each settlement, to be supported by a tax of half a dollar for each child. Attendance was to be required from November till April, but few schools were in operation under this system. Other laws were passed, but in 1874 a town like Santa Fe did not have a single public school. In that same year there were only

[18] This story is largely taken from material in Ritch Scrapbook and correspondence in the Ritch Collection. Ritch was a bitter foe of the Jesuits and collected all of the material to substantiate his cause he could find. A worthwhile secondary account based upon the same sources appears in Frederick G. Bohme, "A History of Italians in New Mexico" (Ph.D. dissertation, University of New Mexico, 1958).

[19] An extensive account of the general nature of education in the Taos area and perhaps applicable to all of early New Mexico is in Enos E. Garcia, "History of Education in Taos County" (M.A. thesis, University of New Mexico, 1951).

128 public schools in the entire territory, with an enrollment of 5,420 pupils served by 143 teachers. Not until 1891 were compulsory attendance laws passed, when some real progress was made in the field of public education. The coming of the railroads in the 1880's had brought an influx of Anglos, who were far more interested in public education and greatly advanced the progress of learning.[20]

As soon as the Anglo settlers were situated, they turned their thoughts towards the establishment of public schools. In Silver City, a typical mining community, a memorial was drafted and signed by several citizens in 1872 requesting the territorial legislature to pass a special law authorizing the county in which it was situated to assess a tax for the purpose of public education. This marked the first attempt by the electorate of any county to establish schools based upon taxation.[21] Pending the enactment of a law, the citizens of the community took matters into their own hands, raising the funds by public subscription and building their own schoolhouse. Dissatisfaction with the ultimate law prompted the citizens of Grant County to petition Congress to be annexed to Arizona on the grounds that the government at Santa Fe was not interested in public schools. Similar efforts to establish public schools were made at E'Town and other mining communities.

As would be expected in a predominantly Roman Catholic state, parochial schools have played a vital role in the educational history of New Mexico. Upon his arrival at Santa Fe in 1851, Bishop Lamy decided that the over-all position of the Catholic church could best be served by a vigorous and progressive educational program. At his urging, in 1852 the Sisters of Loretta founded in Santa Fe a girls' academy that is still in existence. In 1859, the Brothers of the Christian Schools established St. Michael's High School and College, also at Santa Fe. Other Catholic organizations established parochial primary schools and academies in various parts of the state, and by re-

[20] See *ibid.;* Corbin, "Educational Activities of the Evangelical Brethren"; Louis Avant, "The History of Catholic Education in New Mexico Since the American Occupation" (M.A. thesis, University of New Mexico, 1940); Clyde R. Hardesty, "The History of Public Secondary Education in New Mexico" (M.A. thesis, University of New Mexico, 1949).

[21] Conrad K. Naegle, "The History of Silver City, New Mexico 1870–1886" (M.A. thesis, University of New Mexico, 1943), Chapter IV.

cruiting from their church abroad were able to staff schools with dedicated and qualified personnel. A Jesuit college established at Las Vegas was later moved to Denver and still exists as Regis College. In spite of the heroic work of Bishop Lamy and others, however, the level of education in New Mexico did not greatly increase, and, as Bancroft noted in 1880, learning was still in a backward state.[22]

Once public education became a reality, the church accepted it and in many instances was able to control the academic programs of public schools, even to having priests on the school board. An important contribution was made by the various Catholic orders whose members taught in the public schools. This practice was accepted in New Mexico because of the predominantly Catholic population. Usually, the members of such orders—men and women—were better qualified as teachers than available laymen, and they would also teach for a smaller stipend. In spite of Protestant dissent, members of the religious orders continued teaching in the public schools into the middle of the twentieth century.[23]

Various Protestant denominations were likewise to establish parochial schools within the territory of New Mexico. The first such school was begun by the Baptists at Santa Fe in 1849, but lasted only a year. In 1866, the Presbyterians started a school at Laguna Pueblo and later were to be the leading Protestant group in the educational field. The United Brethren church, the Methodists, and the Mormons likewise carried on extensive church school programs. Most Protestant leaders charged that their work was seriously handicapped by the antagonism of Catholic priests.[24] It is contended that Presby-

[22] Bancroft, *Arizona and New Mexico*, 775. The attempts of the Roman Catholic church to improve the educational lot of New Mexico is fairly treated in Frederick M. Bacon, "Contributions of Catholic Religious Orders to Public Education in New Mexico Since the American Occupation" (M.A. thesis, University of New Mexico, 1947); Sister Blandina Segale, *At the End of the Santa Fe Trail;* and J. B. Salpointe, *Soldiers of the Cross.*

[23] See Bacon, "Contributions of Catholic Religious Orders," for a full treatment of this topic.

[24] The story of Protestant parochial education is told in Corbin, "Educational Activities of the Evangelical United Brethren"; Lucius Edman Buck, "An Inquiry into the History of Presbyterian Educational Missions in New Mexico" (M.A. thesis, University of Southern California, 1949); John C. De Corne, *Navaho and Zuñi for Christ;* and Thomas Harwood, *History of New Mexico Missions.*

211

terian mission schools acted as precursors of the public school system in many communities. As soon as the public was prepared to support the schools that the church had established, control would be surrendered to the local school board and the church would establish schools in other areas.

During most of the nineteenth century there was little higher education in New Mexico. Not until 1889 was there a publicly supported college or even high school. In spite of its excellent academic standards, St. Michael's College at Santa Fe has never truly prospered, and the Jesuit College at Las Vegas was early transferred to Denver. In 1889 a bill passed the territorial legislature establishing a university at Albuquerque, a school of mines at Socorro, and an agricultural college at Las Cruces. In 1891 a private military academy was established at Roswell, and was later taken over by the state as the New Mexico Military Institute.[25] But it was not until the midtwentieth century that higher education in New Mexico reached a respectable status.

The Church in New Mexico

Soon after New Mexico was ceded to the United States, the American Catholic leaders meeting at Baltimore in 1848 petitioned the Holy See to let its ecclesiastical administration come under their jurisdiction. Doubtless influencing their request were the many reports by visitors to New Mexico of the sad state of the clergy there. Lieutenant Zebulon Pike described a New Mexican priest he met as "strutting about with a dirk in his boot, a cane in his hand, whispering to one girl, chucking another under the chin, going out with the third, etc."[26]

Barreiro, a far more sympathetic observer than most American Protestants, likewise was sorely concerned with the sad state of spiritual affairs. He lamented that it was common for people to die without

[25] J. R. Kelly, *A History of New Mexico Military Institute 1891–1941*.

[26] Coues, ed., *The Expedition of Zebulon Pike*, II, 605–606. Another American traveler was dutifully shocked by the ready acceptance of the mistress and children of the priests. From John W. Gunnison to Martha A. Gunnison, August 21, 1853, Gunnison Papers (Huntington Library, San Marino, California).

confession and extreme unction, corpses had to remain unburied for days, and infants were baptized only at a tremendous risk to the parents. Most Sundays went without mass being heard at all, and even church buildings were in a condition of decay, some being "surely unworthy of being called temples of God." This sorry state of affairs was ascribed to an absolute lack of priests.

Barreiro attributed the obvious deficiencies of the clergymen in New Mexico to the corrosive effects of the difficult frontier environment. The clergymen were forced to subsist on very scanty funds, were placed in isolated corners of the land, and were separated from cultural intercourse with other people. The privations these men endured undoubtedly lessened their ability to perform their duties.[27]

After Mexico attained its independence, the clerical situation grew worse, because the flurry of nationalism had prompted that nation to expel all Spanish clerics, most of whom were administering the outlying territories. This action virtually stripped New Mexico of its clergy, there being only fourteen priests in the territory when Bishop Lamy arrived. Of the Franciscans, only two who were willing to take the oath of allegiance to the new government remained to administer the missions. Most of the diocesan priests served the towns, virtually causing the disappearance of the once flourishing Indian missions, the natives quickly lapsing into the primitive state from which they had earlier been rescued. Even in Santa Fe, supposedly the center of spiritual life in the province, Bishop Zubiria, upon his visit in 1833, found things in a sad state. The parish church was so badly neglected that it lacked the necessary vestments for the celebration of mass. Among the few clergymen who remained, there seemed little inclination to discharge their priestly duties.[28] Responsibility for church affairs during the Mexican period rested with the Bishop of Durango, and although he did make a visit to Santa Fe,

[27] Barreiro, *Ojeada Sobre Nuevo-México*, 41–42. When Fray Martínez of Taos resigned, he stressed that he had always upheld the principle of voluntary giving instead of the forced exactions demanded by the new bishop, but that his congregation had been so niggardly in their gifts to the work of the church that he was unable to maintain himself on them. From message of Fray Martínez to his congregation May 4, 1856 in Ritch Collection.

[28] Rodríguez, "New Mexico in Transition," *NMHR,* Vol. XXIV (July, October, 1949), 288.

economic poverty and distance made it impossible for him to oversee the territory adequately.

The opportunity to reinvigorate the Catholic church in New Mexico was presented to a French clergyman, Jean Baptiste Lamy, who had already had much experience in America as a priest in Ohio. Lamy was appointed Vicar Apostolic for the former Mexican territories east of California, and arrived in Santa Fe on August 8, 1851, accompanied by Father Joseph Machebeuf. Within New Mexico, Lamy found conditions equally as bad as the American travelers had described, some priests preaching to their congregation only once a year, and then only under the condition that they be paid a specified sum for doing so. Exorbitant prices were charged for the administration of the sacraments, with most of the priests bitterly resenting any outside interference in the way in which they had been conducting their affairs. Above all, they were prepared to challenge the authority of a foreigner like Lamy.

Jean Baptiste Lamy, consecrated as a bishop in 1853, possessed an abundance of the usual traits associated with a man in his position, being a humble, devoted, and conscientious servant of the church. In addition, he possessed an unflagging store of energy that made it possible for him to impart to his diocesan duties a zeal which insured success. When he found it necessary to obtain adequate evidence of his authority from the Bishop of Durango to convince the native clergy who did not welcome him, Lamy made the trip southward on horseback. Later, he traveled extensively through the wilds of Arizona and New Mexico, acting more as a missionary than as a bishop overseeing the duties of others. An able administrator, Lamy saw that education was the key to the future of the church in New Mexico and, as has been said, took steps to remedy the educational deficiency. In addition to handling the many duties associated with his clerical office, Bishop Lamy found time to bring to New Mexico many flowers and plants from the other parts of the world, soon making his garden in Santa Fe famous for its fine collection of fruits, vegetables, and flowers.[29]

The work of Bishop Lamy in re-establishing the Catholic church

[29] Warner, *Archbishop Lamy*, 151. *Death Comes for the Archbishop*, by Willa Cather, is based on Lamy's experience in New Mexico.

in New Mexico was so outstanding and his over-all contribution as a civilizing force in the territory was so great that he earned the respect of men of all faiths. In fact, he has become almost a legend, so that it is difficult for the historian adequately to evaluate his contribution. By 1866 he was able to increase the number of priests in the territory to forty-eight and had established 135 mission churches with one or more schools attached to each mission. The more populous centers had schools and convents. And by the end of his more than thirty-five years of service in New Mexico, the church was to command respect from all.

The contributions of Bishop Lamy were not all on the positive side. Although Lamy worked zealously to be a part of the new land, there is some question that he ever fully understood New Mexico. The great bishop had the outlook of a cultured Frenchman, that apparently had not been modified by his residence in Ohio, and simply did not grasp the rather crude frontier character of the land. From the beginning he preferred to surround himself with foreign-born clergy who thought and acted as he did, and he had little respect for the native priests. The latter in turn looked upon Lamy as a foreign usurper who was out to destroy their position. Had Lamy more fully understood the hostility of the isolated frontiersman toward the outsider and treated the problem with greater care, much unpleasantness might have been avoided.

Long free of supervision, the native priests had adopted habits that needed correcting. Early in 1852, Bishop Lamy was forced to suspend the master of San Miguel when he got drunk and fell from his horse, breaking a leg. That the Bishop wanted to handle others the same way is implied in the following words: "There are several other cases in which I might use the same severity but still, as they have not been caught in the act, I must wait with patience and try at least to keep them under fear." Lamy complained that it was necessary to go slow with the local clergy because they "not only have great influence but they have been the rulers of the people."[30] He hoped that most of them would soon leave.

In all, five native clergymen were excommunicated. One of these was Manuel José Gallegos of Albuquerque. In his case the reasons

[30] Francis, "Padre Martinez," *NMHR*, Vol. XXXI (October, 1956), 271–72.

for disciplinary action were drinking, gambling, dancing, and causing a public scandal. The priest was so bitter over the Bishop's action that at first he refused to abide by it and tried to incite a local following to back him in refusing to obey the order. Gallegos even went so far as to openly challenge the Bishop from the pulpit. As evidence of Gallegos' following, he was elected New Mexico's territorial delegate to Congress in 1853, in spite of the open opposition to Bishop Lamy. Bancroft describes this selection as a struggle "between two factions of the Catholic Church, one headed by Bishop Lamy—of French origin and his new clergy, and the other by the Mexican priest, who regarded the newcomers as intruders."[31]

In a quarrel of this nature, there was no question as to who would ultimately succeed. In 1854, the first group of French priests arrived in Santa Fe, thereby strengthening the Bishop's position. Lamy now prepared to end the resistance of the native clergy to his authority.[32]

The most powerful of the native clergy was Father Antonio José Martínez of Taos, and it was he who caused Bishop Lamy the most trouble. Fortunately, recent research has laid to rest most of the folklore associated with this legendary figure and has brought Padre Martínez into proper perspective. The quarrel between Martínez and Lamy was largely a clash between two strong personalities, one of whom was defending what he believed to be the established position of the native church in contrast to the new approach of the foreign intruder. Lamy himself commented that the Mexican priests objected that he did not "observe the rules prescribed by Canon Law in inflicting these censures. The truth is that if I would comply with all the formalities they want, I could never stop the abuses."[33]

The primary objection of Father Martínez to Bishop Lamy's tactics lay in the manner in which he disregarded established precedent in trying to enforce the collection of church levies. Lamy insisted upon the collection of the customary tithes and first fruits, even going into the *alcalde's* court to secure collection. On January 14, 1854, the Bishop announced that all priests were to exclude from the sacraments those heads of households who had not paid their tithes and

---

31 Bancroft, *Arizona and New Mexico*, 650.
32 Francis, "Padre Martinez," *NMHR*, Vol. XXXI (October, 1956), 275.
33 Quoted in *ibid.*, 274.

to insist upon triple fees for baptisms from other members of such families.[34] Lamy has been accused of squeezing money out of the poor people by such tactics. As one writer put it, "Bishop Lamy *would* build his cathedral,"[35] and for this, money was necessary. Like most clergymen, Bishop Lamy was convinced that he could not be rated as a great servant of the Lord without a proper edifice built in His honor, and the French-style cathedral in Santa Fe was to be the result.

As Martínez had vigorously fought the collection of tithes and had established a precedent that the faithful should make church contributions voluntarily rather than by any system of compulsion, it was natural that he would oppose the Bishop in this matter. Finally, Martínez was excommunicated after a clash that does not enhance the otherwise great stature of Bishop Lamy. In many respects the struggle between the new clerical order and the old native clergy is one that New Mexico has experienced many times. The area has been called upon to adjust to the demands of various waves of invaders from Spanish times until the coming of the Anglos in the twentieth century. The stronger or more dynamic force has always won, and in the process of winning has destroyed much of what has been unique to New Mexico.

It is only natural that the historian pay greater attention to the Catholic heritage than to the Protestant minority during the nineteenth century, because Catholicism was practically the only religion in the territory. Not until the coming of the railroads brought the Anglo settlers in numbers were the Protestant clergy to make their efforts, usually following members of their own churches and setting up parishes in the larger population centers. In some instances, however, the Protestants did attempt to establish mission stations among the Indians. The Baptists were first in this area, beginning their work in July, 1849, when the Reverend Henry W. Read arrived at Santa Fe. Their lead was followed by the Presbyterians, and that denomination has always been strong in the territory. The Methodists were also early in the field, but it was not until the coming of the Reverend Thomas Harwood in 1871 that their efforts were put

[34] Ritch Collection.
[35] Grant, *When Old Trails Were New*, 112.

on a firm and lasting basis. Most of the other Protestant denominations likewise made their way to New Mexico, and all of them complained that the Catholic church hampered their efforts.

Another kind of missionary invasion of the territory was that of the Mormons. Interest in New Mexico and even northern Mexico as mission grounds was undoubtedly a result of the information received through the service of the Mormon Battalion during the Mexican War. Many members of the battalion were in the vanguard of the Mormon missions who were seeking to expand their faith in the West. They established the mission stations at Kirtland, Fruitland, Ramah, Blue Water, Luna, and Virden, all located in the western portion of the state. Because of their system of communal living and their understanding of the control of water supply in an arid land, the Mormons made a lasting contribution to the development of the frontier territory.[36]

The Penitentes

One of the most unusual results of the Spanish heritage in New Mexico is the Penitente Order, a religious organization among the Spanish-Americans of the state. Their practice of flagellation and their actual dramatization of the passion story during the Lenten season have attracted much attention. Because of the secret nature of the association much misunderstanding of its role and the extent of its influence has occurred, so that the historian, in evaluating its over-all impact upon nineteenth-century New Mexico, must be exceedingly wary. At the height of its strength, it probably included virtually all of the total Spanish-American population, and, in addition to its obvious religious function, it performed a vital political, social, legal, and cultural role during the period, 1850 to 1890.

Many writers have mistakenly attributed the origin of the Penitentes to Indian practices, the flagellants of the Middle Ages, or, more commonly, the Third Order of St. Francis. Modern scholarship has effectively dispelled these myths and has correctly attributed the

[36] H. Mannis Foster, "History of Mormon Settlements in Mexico and New Mexico." (M.A. thesis, University of New Mexico, 1937).

origin of the Penitentes to the natural environment of Spain. Those who would find the Penitentes inspired by the Indians were merely engaged in wishful thinking. Aside from the fact that the Penitentes and the Third Order both existed in New Mexico, there was little real similarity between the two groups. Finally, there is no evidence that the medieval flagellants were ever directly established within Spain.[37]

The Penitentes traced their origin to the confraternities established in Spain for the purpose of providing for needy members, assisting at funerals, caring for widows and orphans, and undertaking other charitable activities. Some members marched through the streets barefoot and engaged in processions during Holy Week, doing public penance by carrying candles and whipping themselves. Such organizations found their way into Mexico and from there were carried by the Spaniards northward into New Mexico.

As Villagrá notes, Oñate and the other leaders of the expedition took part in the customary self-torture associated with the passion celebration. During the long and torturous period of the colonial occupation, the confraternity helped to preserve the Spaniard's concept of his relationship to God. To the Spaniards, religion is intensely personal. And as they tried to find oneness with God, an important part of their spiritual outlet was through vicariously experiencing Christ's suffering by means of flagellation, thereby bringing them closer to their Lord. As Professor Woodward so ably puts it, "It is devotion to a realistic, individualistic faith, a faith that approved the crusader's sword, supported the inquisitors of fanaticism, believed in the Spanish mystics, and successfully accomplished the counter reformation. This is the belief of a country that knew no schism in her national church, and where the reformation did not penetrate."[38]

It has been this faith which the Penitentes, though often fanatical and often misled, have been able to preserve in New Mexico. Isolated

[37] Dorothy Woodward, "The Penitentes of New Mexico" (Ph.D. dissertation, Yale University, 1935).

[38] *Ibid.*, 144. A competent scholar in New Mexico church history maintains that the Penitentes were founded between 1777 and 1833, denying that their roots could be traced back to Spain. Fray Angelico Chavez, "The Penitentes of New Mexico," *NMHR*. XXIX, (April, 1954), 108.

from their homeland, the Spaniards in New Mexico sought to preserve the traditions of their native Spain by a nostalgic clinging to the ways of their fatherland. So the essentials of the Penitentes in all their characteristics of sixteenth-century Spain were preserved in New Mexico into the twentieth century.

Beginning with the ousting of Spain in 1821, the territory went through a long period of transition wherein the simple social mores of the natives were constantly challenged. First, their priests were largely driven out by the Mexicans, creating a spiritual vacuum which the Penitente order attempted to fill. Officials of the group soon performed many of the functions of priests. Frequently, the *hermano mayor* was also the local *alcalde*, or leader of the town. And as the old way of life was consistently threatened with change, the Penitentes became "an organization of the common man against his masters—a brotherhood with temporal benefits and a pure solidarity and a secretiveness so relentless that it punishes betrayals of its laws and business with burial alive."[39] Although its religious basis remained predominant, the absence of qualified clerical supervision led to a perversion in its teachings, which the Catholic church was later to have much difficulty in controlling. In fact, when Bishop Lamy arrived, much of the support of the native priests was furnished by their Penitente followers.

Early travelers to New Mexico found that the Penitente processions and worship services were held openly and could be observed by anyone. But with the influx of the curious Protestants, who tried to make a festive occasion out of what was a most serious affair, the Penitentes began to go underground and to shun publicity. The attempts of the church to control them led to additional secrecy. Until the twentieth century it was common for the order to identify its membership with tattooed insignia, usually the cross. It has even been reported that young men inducted into the army during World War II could be identified by such markings as members of the order.

Each community has its own organization of Penitentes which may or may not have had contact with neighboring groups. Over each chapter is a president or *hermano mayor*, who is normally elected every year or, in some cases, is even selected for life. Assisting

[39] Fergusson, *Rio Grande*, 118.

220

him is a group of other officers, each of whom has a particular duty to perform in much the same manner as in many modern fraternal organizations. These officers and older brothers make up the Brothers of Light. They do not participate in the public ceremonies, but are there mainly to supervise the rites.

A *morada* is the meeting place of the order, and one was found in most Mexican communities. It is a small one-story building, without windows, and with only one door, and can be identified by the crude wooden cross that stands outside in front of it. Originally, *moradas* were located in the villages, but they were later moved to isolated locations to get away from the curious. These chapter houses are used as chapels, and as such usually have crude altars, draped in black, sometimes decorated with skulls cut out of white cloth. Human skulls, candles and crucifixes, cheap statues of the saints, of the Holy Mother, and the Christus are likewise in evidence.

The monumental religious expression of the Penitentes is concerned with the Lenten season. The ceremonies usually begin on Wednesday of Holy Week when the members gather at the *morada*, usually staying there until Sunday. Although rites vary, one is an enactment of the entire passion story, the betrayal of Judas, Pilate's role, and the procession to Golgotha, climaxed by the crucifixion of Christ. The role of Christ is the most important, and selection is usually made by drawing lots.

Originally, the ceremonies were held Wednesday and Thursday evenings in the *moradas*. Naturally, a high point in the processional was the crucifixion. The men in the procession wore black caps and white trousers, with their backs bare. As they marched they whipped themselves until the blood flowed, and when they were no longer able to continue whipping themselves, friends assisted them in their self-torture. As the men marched, they made a fearful noise, which was heightened by the wail of the flute player, blowing into bottles, and the rattling of chains and tin cans. In the processional was a crude wagon which carried a skeleton representing death. Struggling to carry a huge cross, perhaps weighing a hundred pounds, came the Christ. Originally, the crucifixion took place at the *morada*, but in more recent times it has been done in isolated places. The man bound to the cross was formerly held in place with nails; more recently

221

he has been bound tightly to the cross and remained there for perhaps an hour. Trouble with the authorities over frequent deaths has prompted the Penitentes to be very careful to prevent trouble in modern times. Earlier, if the man enacting the role of Christ lived, it was assumed that he was cleansed of sin, and if he died, his family was greatly honored at the contribution they had made.

Such is, in general, the nature of the religious rites of the penitentes. They have been so drastically altered in recent years that it is difficult to obtain an accurate picture of what goes on. In order to meet the problem of curious Anglos, the Penitentes have reportedly engaged in fake ceremonies, charging admission, and then, after the curious have departed, gone ahead with their regular ceremony. But the religious role was not the only one performed by the Penitentes, their activities cutting across the entire framework of New Mexico in the nineteenth century.

Membership in the Penitentes is open to all practicing Catholics. Some Protestants, especially if they are friends of the community or politicians, have been given honorary membership, and, more recently, many have joined for strictly political purposes. Women were at one time members but were not permitted to participate in the public ceremonies, although they probably did private penance. As most of the Spanish-Americans at one time belonged to the society, it is obvious that its potential political power was tremendous. Perhaps the most apt comparison, for purposes of understanding its political role, is with the Ku Klux Klan in the South in the post–Civil War period.

The word of the head brother is law, and if he instructs members of the order to vote Republican, they do so. It was thus inevitable that politicians of both parties should vigorously court the Penitentes, or at least not do anything to antagonize them. Although it cannot be proved, it is more than likely that the virtually solid Republican support by the Spanish-Americans was delivered through the backing of the penitentes. It is alleged that at one time no one could be elected to public office in New Mexico without the blessing of the society.

The political strength of the early Penitentes is usually associated with the Taos uprising in 1847. The fact that the participants in this revolt went to their death without revealing the possible complicity of Padre Martínez would indicate that their lips were sealed by the vows of the society. Later, the political prowess of the Penitentes was displayed in the election of the former priest, Gallegos, to several terms as New Mexico's territorial delegate to Congress, in spite of vigorous opposition. The selection of Padre Martínez as president of the council of the first territorial legislature in 1850 is further evidence of their power.

Though again adequate proof is lacking, it is generally believed within New Mexico that the political power of the Penitentes has lasted well into the twentieth century. For obvious reasons the extent of that power in 1960 is not known. Archbishop Salpointe was closer to the truth than he knew when he commented that the Penitente Society "has degenerated so that it is nothing today but an anomalous body of simple credulous men, under the guidance of unscrupulous politicians. Their leaders encouraged them, despite the admonitions of the church, in the practice of their unbecoming so-called devotions in order to secure their votes for the times of political elections."[40] In some communities there were both Republican and Democratic *moradas,* and the activities of the society were interwoven with politics.

At one time the political power of the society was so great that it virtually administered justice itself. In Spanish-American counties it was almost certain that a member of the society would appear on a jury. And when one considers that the Penitentes are sworn to assist and protect one another, even to the extent of perjury in the courts, it is obvious that it would be difficult if not impossible to administer justice involving them. Instances abound in which the sheriff, the local judge, or other leading officials were Penitentes, and thus would not press a case against a member. Even in the twentieth century there is a record of an attempt of the Penitentes to intimidate a federal court.[41]

This is not to suggest that culprits go unpunished. During the virtual absence of law enforcement in Mexican times, the Penitentes developed their own system of punishment, and have preferred to use it rather than surrender their members to what they consider

[40] Salpointe, *Soldiers of the Cross,* 161–62.
[41] James, *New Mexico,* 299.

foreign courts. First of all, since they believe that a man can atone for his sins by doing penance, backsliding brothers apply the whip to their naked backs the more vigorously. The Penitentes even have their own courts where they hear criminal cases. Some are expelled from the order and their right hip cut three times with a flint so that everyone will know that their offense was great. It is alleged that the punishment for infidelity was burial alive.[42]

The fraternal and benevolent role of the society remained in most communities. Members would co-operate in time of need to assist those who were sick or who had suffered some disaster or another. Frequently, they arranged for the burial of the dead when priests were not available. They took care of widows and orphans or aided a disabled member to till his fields or tend his flocks. Visitors have seen *moradas* that were well stocked with supplies held in a common storehouse to be used only in time of communal need.

During the nineteenth century the Penitente Society was the center of social activity of the community. What little relaxation there was from the toil of everyday life was furnished by members of the society. And thus they have unwittingly preserved the cultural heritage of the Spain that is no more, for many of the plays given by the society have their roots in sixteenth-century Spain. These plays, based upon biblical texts, have been handed down from one generation to another and are still produced in isolated villages, the parts being learned from memory, for most of the actors cannot read. There are also many poems that are preserved in the same manner.

The hymns sung by the Penitentes come from many sources. Some are undoubtedly of early Spanish origin, some have been recently taken from Catholic services, and others have been either improvised or composed by the Penitentes. In the *santo*, a crudely carved figure, the New Mexican has preserved some of the traditions of the religious art of the sixteenth century originally brought in by the conquerors.

The Penitente Order is fast going the way of most of old New Mexico. The notoriety attached to some of its activities caused influential Spanish-Americans to be reluctant to be associated with it. But the greatest factor leading to its decline is the same as that which is destroying most of the original culture of the state, the consistent

[42] Woodward, "Penitentes of New Mexico," 97.

deterioration of the small Spanish communities. People once content to eke out a living in isolated mountain valleys are finding their way into the towns and cities, where they now work in factories, mines, or oil fields. The end of the isolation of the people has likewise ended efforts to retain their distinctive culture. The coming of all-weather roads has reduced the economic significance of the small village, and the local country store (the storekeeper exercising a role not unlike that of the *patrón* of the past) now stands empty. The pressure of military service in two world wars and the continuation of the draft have effectively Anglicized the young men of the Spanish communities. The jobs available in the big city, along with other inducements, have stripped the rural country-side of its population. Thus, it is safe to predict that the Penitente Order will soon disappear. Perhaps an enterprising chamber of commerce will soon stage the Penitente processions and ceremonies as a tourist attraction.

XII - *The Forty-seventh Star*

JUST AS THE HISTORY of New Mexico has been unique in many other respects, so also was its quest for statehood unparalleled. No other state has fought so vigorously to be admitted to the Union nor had as many setbacks as New Mexico when it was on the threshold of success. Scarcely a Congressional session between 1849 and 1910 was without a bill providing for statehood; in all, some fifty acts were introduced during the sixty-year struggle.

Virtually all of the forces influencing national politics between 1850 and 1910 were to play a role in the statehood battle. To begin with, statehood was originally denied because of the opening of the slavery issue in 1850. After the Civil War the many bills for New Mexico's statehood were blocked because of the bitter antagonism over Reconstruction, the intense rivalry between the two major parties, and the East's fear of Western domination in the Senate. Unfortunately, more potent forces working against statehood were religious bigotry, racial discrimination, and general ignorance concerning conditions in the Southwest. Even the free-silver issue and the Populist crusade were factors.

But not all of the blame for the failure of New Mexico to be admitted as a state rested upon Washington. Much of the responsibility for the monotonous succession of failures must be attributed to conditions within New Mexico itself. From the very inception of the battle for statehood, many were opposed to it, preferring territorial status instead. Usually, the mining interests, the large merchants, the railroads, and some of the bigger landowners were opposed to state-

226

hood because it would mean higher taxes. And as territorial politics were usually influenced by these groups, they provided potent opposition. The stories that found their way into the eastern and middle-western newspapers about widespread corruption in politics and the very common practice of ballot-box stuffing did not win respect for the territory. Finally, the politicians were either for or against statehood depending upon whether they were in or out of office. Fearing that statehood would come when the opposition was in control and thereby give them a strong initial advantage, the "outs" usually fought statehood with all of the resources at their command.

Shortly after the United States conquest, New Mexico was to make a determined bid for statehood and barely miss success; perhaps the attempt was thwarted only by the untimely death of President Zachary Taylor.[1] Had Southerners been in control at Santa Fe, it is more than likely that admission would have been granted, as New Mexico's population in 1850 was over sixty thousand, more than enough to qualify for statehood.

While Congress was busily debating the question of the Texas claim to the Río Grande and, more important, the issue of slavery extension,[2] a faction in New Mexico began stirring itself in spite of President Polk's admonition that the adherents of statehood should remain passive until Congress had provided a civil government for them. Acting upon Senator Thomas Benton's suggestion that they form their own government, they drew up a memorial to Congress which requested a territorial form of governnment and protection from the greedy Texans and, contained, unfortunately for the cause of statehood, a demand that they be protected from the introduction of slavery.[3]

[1] Bancroft comments upon these efforts to attain statehood in the following words: "It must be understood that the whole matter was manipulated by a few men at Santa Fe . . . the various conventions and petitions and plans in no sense emanated from the New Mexicans, being the work of a few Americans who acted for their own personal interest or that of their party or section in the states, and aroused popular enthusiasm only slightly by their false appeals to native fears—notably that of Texan encroachment. A few of these politicians thought they saw an opportunity . . . to serve themselves by putting the state government into immediate operation." Bancroft, *History of Arizona and New Mexico*, 451.

[2] See pages 140 ff. for a more complete treatment of these events.

[3] Bancroft, *Arizona and New Mexico*, 443–44.

The reading of this memorial in Congress stirred the wrath of many Southern senators, who proceeded to assail New Mexico violently. Naturally, such Southern attacks brought antislavery groups of the North to the defense of New Mexico and resulted in a veritable flood of petitions to Congress on behalf of the banning of slavery.[4] Thus, the status of government in New Mexico became intermingled with the paramount national political issue, the extension of slavery.

In the fall of 1849 another "convention" was held in Santa Fe and attended by nineteen delegates. Meeting for only two days, this group drafted a plan of territorial government and elected one Hugh N. Smith as a delegate to Congress to present their proposal at the national capitol. But in July, 1850, by a vote of ninety-two to eighty-six, the House declined to admit Smith as the territorial delegate.[5]

In a message to Congress, President Zachary Taylor expressed the hope that New Mexico would soon be admitted to the Union as a state.[6] The national administration believed that statehood would help ease the perplexing problem of the Texas claim to the Río Grande as well as fulfill the treaty guarantees to Mexico. To aid in making his hope reality, the President had sent James S. Calhoun as an Indian agent in the spring of 1849. Actually, Calhoun had unofficial authorization from the President to promote agitation for a state government.[7] He was soon joined by Colonel George A. McCall, who came to command his regiment in New Mexico. McCall likewise was an unofficial agent of the administration with instructions from the Secretary of War to promote statehood. Upon his insistence that a territorial form of government would not be granted, opponents at that time acquiesced, and a constitutional convention was called.

Meeting in the spring of 1850, this convention drafted a consti-

[4] Ganaway, *New Mexico and the Sectional Controversy*, 22–24.

[5] Twitchell, *Leading Facts*, II, 269–70. This setback was ascribed to the intrigues of the Southerners.

[6] James Richardson, *Messages and Papers of the Presidents*, IV, 2,557.

[7] Twitchell, *Leading Facts*, II, 270. President Taylor's efforts to bring both New Mexico and California into the Union as states in an attempt to head off the slavery controversy is treated in Holman Hamilton, *Zachary Taylor: Soldier in the White House*, 180–82.

tution which was largely copied from some of the newer middle-western states. Perhaps the most significant provision was the banning of slavery. Without waiting for approval from Washington, a group attempted to put the state government into immediate operation. Perhaps it was assumed that such approval would be forthcoming, and it probably would have been if it had not been for the untimely death of President Taylor.

State elections were held, with the various officials being chosen along with two United States senators. Unfortunately, the conduct of this election and the notoriety growing out of it convinced many that the territory was not ready for statehood.[8]

The succession of President Fillmore and the course of national politics were to spell doom for the infant state government. The Compromise of 1850 settled the Texas boundary dispute and organized New Mexico as a territory without any mention of slavery.[9] Indian Agent James S. Calhoun was inaugurated as the first territorial governor on the third of March, 1851, thus ending the first bid for statehood. The "state" government of New Mexico "so soon was done for that it wondered what it was begun for."[10]

In spite of several efforts, it was 1875 before the next serious move to attain statehood was made, and this time it was to be lost as a result of the historic "Elkins Handshake." Stephen B. Elkins, territorial delegate to Congress, was the law partner of Thomas B. Catron, long one of the powerful influences in territorial politics. Elkins, a charming and grandiloquent orator, delivered a speech on the floor of the House carefully extolling the virtues of New Mexico and winning many adherents to the cause of statehood. More important,

[8] *Ibid.*, II, 275.

[9] Ganaway, *New Mexico and the Sectional Controversy*, 27–28. Senator Daniel Webster had been convinced by territorial delegate Hugh Smith that New Mexico was unfit for slavery for geographic reasons. Hence, the Massachusetts lawmaker supported this provision of the Compromise on the basis that it would be pointless to alienate the Southerners over it.

[10] Twitchell, *Leading Facts*, II, 277. Indicative of the dominance of the quest for statehood by recent newcomers into the area is the fact that the two senators, the governor, and the lieutenant governor were all Anglos with the exception of Manuel Alvarez, who was from Spain. Yet, 90 per cent of the constitutional convention of 1850 was composed of Spanish-Americans. They probably did the bidding of the "carpetbaggers."

as a Republican he was able to gain the support of many party members for the measure. In addition, his father-in-law, Henry G. Davis, was a Democratic senator from West Virginia who was able to win his party to the support of the bill.[11]

When the New Mexican statehood bill passed the House by a vote of 160 to 54 and the Senate by the decisive majority of 32 to 11, it appeared that statehood was all but accomplished. It was necessary to return the bill to the House to act upon minor Senate amendments, and here fate played a hand.

As the session was drawing to a close, it was necessary to get a two-thirds vote to act on the measure or it would simply die. At this time, reconstruction measures for the South were being bitterly disputed. During the consideration of the Force Bill, Representative Julius Caesar Burroughs of Michigan made an impassioned speech, waving "the bloody shirt" and rehashing all the Southern crimes of secession and the Civil War in behalf of the bill. During this speech, Elkins had been in the lobby and only re-entered the House chambers when a group of Northern supporters crowded around Burroughs to congratulate him. Knowing nothing about the contents of the speech and seeking to be cordial, Elkins joined them and likewise complimented the Michigan congressman. Southern members, already embittered over what they justly believed to be a vicious tirade, observed the New Mexican delegate's action and assumed that he endorsed Burroughs' stand. In spite of Elkins' later attempts to placate the angry Southerners, enough congressmen from Georgia and Alabama changed their position so that New Mexico failed to get the necessary two-thirds vote.[12] That Elkins' famous handshake was the decisive factor was indicated when the same congressmen voted for Colorado statehood.

The drama attached to the defeat of statehood as a result of a handshake prompted many newspapers to pay considerable attention to New Mexico's qualifications as a state, especially since Elkins was able to get another bill through the next session of the Senate. The following are typical reactions:

11 *New York Sun*, March 16, 1876, in Ritch Scrapbook.
12 Twitchell, *Leading Facts*, II, 404–406.

From the *Milwaukee Sentinel*: "If any geographical division of this country were to be selected for the final jumping off place for the American citizen, it would surely be New Mexico. A man could pass into the mysteries and doubts of his future existence in that region with perfect equanimity. The change could hardly be for the worse. It comprises the tag end of all that is objectionable in an imperfect civilization. The scum and dregs of the American, Spanish, Mexican, and Indian people are there concentrated. . . . In making this assertion we do not mean to include those exceptions which prove the rule. There are doubtless a limited number of respectable people in New Mexico, but the number is so small comparatively that it could no more control the politics of the proposed state than a rowboat could sink the *Great Eastern*. The mass of the inhabitants—half-breeds, 'greasers,' 'outlaws,' etc.—are no more fit to support a proper state government than they are to turn missionaries." The question was raised as to whether or not it would be fair to place "the mixed and half-civilized people of New Mexico on a par with the people of Massachusetts and Wisconsin."[13]

Another journal asserted that the "Romish priesthood" would so completely dominate the state as to make successful government impossible.[14] Much was made of the bilingualism of the people as well as the general lawlessness that existed. Misinformation was handed out concerning the geography of the state. The *Chicago Tribune* observed that "New Mexico has but a few oases amid its volcanic deserts." The area was depicted "as the Siberia of America," and it was alleged that it would never support a population adequate to maintain a state government. Although knowledge of the geography of the state was to become more extensive, the national press continued to oppose statehood because of antagonism toward the Roman Catholic church and resentment toward the Spanish-speaking populace, "who haven't troubled to learn English."[15]

Colorado's admission to the Union and its Republican vote in 1876 cost the Democrats the presidential election. As a result, leaders of

[13] *Milwaukee Sentinel*, April 6. 1876 in Ritch Scrapbook.

[14] *New York Observer*, March 9, 1876 in Ritch Scrapbook.

[15] Quoted in *Rocky Mountain News* (Denver) February 18, 1875, in Ritch Scrapbook.

both parties were wary of admitting any more states.[16] After the election of 1888, the lame-duck Congress considered an "Omnibus Bill" providing for the admission of the territories of New Mexico, Dakota, Montana, and Washington. North and South Dakota, Montana, and Washington were promptly admitted. In 1889, Idaho and Wyoming were also admitted. Despite the fact that New Mexico had a larger population than most of these states, its petition was again rejected. As one authority said, "The Republican majorities in Congress were not interested in creating potentially Democratic states."[17] Besides, the citizens of these states largely spoke English and were predominantly Protestant.

With the hope that Congress would finally grant statehood, a constitutional convention was called in the fall of 1889. The constitution drafted was submitted to the voters in October, 1890, who promptly rejected it with a resounding majority.[18] Apparently the reasons for rejection had nothing to do with the merits of statehood. The Democrats were angry because the apportionment to the convention was unjust to their party, and, with a few exceptions, they vigorously opposed the constitution. Many people felt that the drafters had cleverly written a document which would throw the weight of taxation upon the shoulders of those least able to pay. The Roman Catholic church vigorously opposed the constitution because it provided for the establishment of non-sectarian public schools, which they had fought ever since the beginning of territorial status. Although many deny that the role of the Roman Catholics in the election was decisive, there was no question that their interference in political activity gave the state much adverse publicity throughout the nation.[19] Finally, fear on the part of the Anglo element that they

[16] Marion Dargan, "New Mexico's Fight for Statehood," *NMHR*, Vol. XVIII (January, 1943), 66.

[17] John D. Hicks, *The American Nation*, 214. Perhaps New Mexico could have been admitted at any time between 1883 and 1888 if the Democrats had been more astute politicians. They could have bargained the admission of New Mexico and Arizona against the admission of the Dakotas as long as they held control in the House. After the election of 1888 and the Republican success, they had nothing to offer in return for potentially Democratic states. Dargan, "New Mexico's Fight for Statehood," *NMHR*, Vol. XIV, 8.

[18] Santa Fe *New Mexican*, October 8, 1890, in La Farge, *Santa Fe*, 144–45.

[19] Dargan, "New Mexico's Fight for Statehood," *NMHR*, Vol. XV, 186.

would be overwhelmed by the native "Mexicans" was a factor in the rejection of the constitution.[20]

In the period between December, 1891, and June, 1903, some twenty odd bills to admit New Mexico to the Union were introduced in Congress. Only three of these passed the House and were considered by the Senate committee. All of the territorial delegates, regardless of party, worked zealously in an effort to attain success, so as to gain credit for statehood for their party.[21] Unfortunately, the existing objections to statehood by the rest of the nation remained, and Populism and the silver issue were added to further complicate matters. Easterners feared that the admission of New Mexico might augment the strength of the pro-silver men in the Senate. The *New York Evening Post* declared, "We don't want any more states until we can civilize Kansas."[22]

Indirectly, the Spanish-American War increased the chances for statehood. More of Theodore Roosevelt's Rough Riders came from Arizona and New Mexico than from any other area, a fact which many hoped would have a direct influence upon the fight for statehood. After the Spanish-American War, Roosevelt continued on close terms with his Rough Riders, many of whom turned to him for jobs or other kinds of assistance.[23] The first reunion of the Rough Riders was held at Las Vegas, New Mexico, in June, 1899. While there, Roosevelt pledged himself for statehood, saying: "All I shall say is if New Mexico wants to be a state, you can count me in, and I will go back to Washington to speak for you or do anything you wish."[24]

When President McKinley had stopped in Deming, New Mexico, in May, 1901, while en route to the West Coast, he had been careful not to commit himself on the statehood issue; but after an assassin's bullet made the irrepressible leader of the Rough Riders President of the United States, New Mexicans prepared to celebrate statehood. Unfortunately, they failed to realize that Roosevelt the Rough Rider

20 *Ibid.*, 187.
21 *Ibid.*, XVI, 70.
22 Quoted in *ibid.*, XIV, 7.
23 Henry F. Pringle, *Theodore Roosevelt* (New York, 1931), 198.
24 Quoted in Charles E. Maddox, "The Statehood Policy of Albert J. Beveridge: 1901–1911" (M.A. thesis, University of New Mexico, 1938), 25–26.

and Roosevelt the politician who became President were not always in agreement.

From 1902 until 1910, when statehood was finally granted, New Mexico stood on the brink of success. In May, 1902, a bill to admit Arizona, New Mexico, and Oklahoma passed the House. Within the territory itself most of the sentiment against statehood had steadily declined, or opponents had found it more discreet to remain silent. Many people may still have been concerned about the increased rate of taxation and the problems of corruption in government, but they were nevertheless prepared to risk statehood. In general, the newspapers of the territory, many of which had remained indifferent to the long-drawn-out campaign, now found it wise to become advocates of statehood. Most people agreed with Charles F. Lummis that territories had a right to self-government, regardless of whether it proved to be good, bad, or indifferent.[25]

But the House bill of 1902 was not to become law. Standing as a stone wall between New Mexico and statehood was the personage of Senator Albert J. Beveridge of Indiana. The silver-tongued Progressive senator, famed for his eloquent orations on the floor of the Senate and on the public platform, was obsessed with a desire to keep New Mexico out of the Union and made a veritable crusade of it. Although the Hoosier senator did occasionally make reference to the fact that the people of New Mexico were of different racial and linguistic backgrounds from the rest of the country, he was not a religious bigot, nor was he opposed to statehood on racial grounds. Hence, it was an injustice to accuse Beveridge of inconsistency because he objected to New Mexican statehood while approving of territorial status for the Philippines, where there were more than ten million people who could not speak English.[26]

It would be more accurate to stress that Beveridge, in his opposition to statehood, was wrong for all the right reasons. First of all, "Beveridge was motivated primarily by the conviction that the creation of a state concerns the nation and not alone the territory involved."[27] In the past many states, with less population than a single

[25] Edwin R. Bingham, *Charles F. Lummis—Editor of the Southwest.*
[26] *Ibid.,* 85.
[27] Claude G. Bowers, *Beveridge and the Progressive Era,* 196.

Congressional district in Indiana contained, had been hurried into the Union solely for the purpose of adding another representative and two more senators to the ranks of the party in power. Beveridge referred to these as "rotten borough" states and deplored such shoddy tactics in order to remain in office. He felt that it was not fair to the people to ask them to support a state government under such circumstances, and that it was also not fair to the nation as a whole to give the small western areas the status of statehood before they were prepared for it. However, the primary source of Beveridge's opposition to New Mexico statehood was his belief that it was all a diabolical plot on the part of special interests. Thus, in his mind, his fight against it became just one more of his many encounters with "the malefactors of great wealth." He was especially intrigued by the eagerness with which powerful corporations and outstanding public men were demanding immediate action on statehood. Subsequent events were to confirm Beveridge's suspicions. He learned that three members of the House who had made a junket trip into Arizona and New Mexico had stock in Arizona mines; indeed, Beveridge himself was offered such stock. He wrote to a friend, "When I was down there I quite accidentally—met an Indianan who also accidentally owned a mine, and when I got back he accidentally sent me a block of stock in the mine. Well, I just accidentally returned it to him—damn him."[28]

The activities of W. H. Andrews, New Mexico's delegate to Congress, further confirmed Beveridge's suspicions. Andrews, originally from Pennsylvania, was on friendly terms with Senators Quay and Penrose of his home state. Pennsylvania capital had aided in the building of a railroad in which Andrews had an interest, and this connection further strengthened the Indiana senator's belief in a "plot" by large corporate interests. The assumption that Andrews would be one of the senators from New Mexico made it appear that the admission of the territory was a means by which the Pennsylvania senators could help an old friend join them.

In order to block a vote in the Senate, Beveridge decided on an on-the-spot trip to the Southwest to conduct his own investigation. The Indianan and his senatorial colleagues shunned all attempts to

[28] Quoted in *ibid.*, 216.

be influenced by the more important people in the territory and refused to participate in the various receptions and entertainments that had been planned. It has been said that "in each community postmasters, ministers, businessmen, and lawyers were invited to testify on commercial, agricultural, mercantile, mining, and industrial conditions. No possible detail was overlooked . . . thus Arizona, New Mexico, Oklahoma, and Indian territory were thoroughly combed for essential facts."[29]

The evidence, however, indicates that the junketing senators were more interested in cementing their preconceived opinions than they were in objectively gathering the facts. The territorial governor, Miguel Otero, described the behavior of L. G. Rothschild, a member of the senator's group, in the following manner: "He would sneak around in the slum districts and meet impossible people in order to make an adverse report of conditions as found by him. Absolutely not the slightest attention was paid to the favorable side of the territory, and no inquiry was made covering education, industry, manufacturing, banking, stock-raising, mining, or farming. The sole attention seemed to be to gather the unfavorable side." Photographs were taken of all of the lower classes of humanity and later used to convince the East of the degraded state of New Mexico.[30] Through interpreters, the Spanish-speaking were examined on their knowledge of United States history and were usually found to be deficient. One story the committee brought back which circulated in the national capital was of the county superintendent of schools who expressed amazement when told that Christopher Columbus was dead. Naturally, New Mexicans were alienated by the unfair tactics of the investigators.

Even before leaving on this trip, Beveridge had been busily gathering information and seeking people who would confirm his belief that most of the Southwest was useless. These facts were to be made available to leading magazine editors so that "the conservative thought of the country will be with us."[31]

In the next session of Congress, Beveridge continued to play for

---

[29] *Ibid.*, 194.
[30] Miguel Antonio Otero, *My Nine Years As Governor*, 212.
[31] Quoted in Bowers, *Beveridge and the Progressive Era*, 194.

time, realizing that public opinion was on his side. It was not easy to dispel the decades of misinformation that had been spread about New Mexico. The eastern tourist, used to the green pastures, woodlands, and lakes of the Middle West or the East, came to the territory and went away skeptical of its value. News stories of outlaws and crimes committed, in combination with the unique character of the Spanish and Indian heritage, convinced many that this was an area that should never be granted statehood.

In the Senate from December, 1902, through February of 1903, Senator Quay and other backers of New Mexico statehood had the votes necessary for success; however, Senator Beveridge, as chairman of the Committee on Territories, was able to block all efforts to bring the matter to a vote by astute and at times unscrupulous parliamentary maneuvers. He later described his efforts during this period as "the hardest and most notable fight perhaps seen in the Senate for many a year."[32]

Bottling up the bill for New Mexico statehood in a committee was one thing; solving the problem of statehood was something else again. Beveridge was too able a politician to believe that such tactics could succeed indefinitely. He therefore accepted the idea of jointure and in 1905 proposed that Oklahoma and the Indian Territory come in as one state, with New Mexico and Arizona coming in as another. Combining Arizona with New Mexico as a single state had been recommended by the *Chicago Tribune* as far back as March 17, 1876,[33] and since they had once been joined as territories, the tradition was already established. This would solve the vexing problem, redeem Republican campaign pledges, and at the same time not give too many votes to the West in the Senate. President Roosevelt expressed the sentiment favoring this action when he said, "The only reason I want them in as one state now is that I fear the alternative is having them as two states three or four years hence."[34]

With all the eloquence at his command, Beveridge endorsed admitting the two territories as one state and made a speech titled "Ari-

---

[32] Quoted in *ibid.*, 201.

[33] *Chicago Tribune*, March 17, 1876, in Ritch Scrapbook.

[34] Quoted in Donald D. Leopard, "Joint Statehood: 1906" (M.A. thesis, University of New Mexico, 1958), 4–5.

zona the Great," delivered in the Senate on February 5, 1905. Stressing that the two territories would become a single economic unit, thereby minimizing the problem of supporting the state government, the Indiana senator belittled the objections to physical size by pointing out that the proposed new state would still be much smaller in area than Texas.[35] The bill combining Arizona and New Mexico into a single state passed Congress and was signed by the President. Jointure was accepted by Oklahoma Territory and Indian Territory, and it was assumed that Arizona and New Mexico would follow suit. This doubtless would have happened if it had not been for the foresight of Senator Joseph Foraker of Ohio. Correctly foreseeing that if Arizona and New Mexico voted as a single unit, the larger population of New Mexico would dominate, he insisted upon an amendment whereby joint admission would be effective only if it were ratified by a majority of the voters of each territory.[36]

Most people in New Mexico prepared to accept this measure as necessary in order to get into the Union at all. While preferring single statehood and objecting to the fact that the combined state would be known as Arizona, they felt that any kind of self-government would be desirable. The Santa Fe *New Mexican* spoke for most newspapers in the state when it called upon citizens to back joint statehood in spite of the fact that it meant surrendering the long-existing territorial name.[37] Only a few New Mexicans, led by Governor Otero, opposed joint statehood. In fact, Otero had campaigned vigorously against it when it had been proposed as early as 1903.[38]

New Mexico accepted the measure by an overwhelming margin. In Arizona the story was different. Preferring to wait for single statehood rather than joining the dominant Spanish-speaking element of New Mexico, that territory voted just as overwhelmingly against the bill and thus defeated it for both territories.[39]

When success was finally attained, victory was assured when Presi-

[35] Congressional Record, 58 Cong., 3 sess., Vol. 39, Pt. 2, p. 1,924.

[36] Maddox, "Statehood Policy of Beveridge," 63; Leopard, "Joint Statehood: 1906," 4.

[37] Santa Fe *New Mexican*, June 15, 1906, in La Farge, *Santa Fe*, 188.

[38] Otero, *My Nine Years as Governor*, 215.

[39] Arthur S. Wylls, *A History of Arizona*, 300.

dent Roosevelt deserted Senator Beveridge and went "over to the enemy, bag and baggage."[40] Always the practicing politician, Roosevelt had no liking for bucking public sentiment, and, as he told Beveridge, it is "mere folly to kick longer against the pricks." To the President the fight had been fought and lost. "I do feel very strongly that no good whatever comes with any further delay," he wrote the Indiana senator. "You will have to take them both in. You cannot take them both in together and by keeping them out for a short time, which is all you can do, you merely irritate the people there against the Republican party."[41] In its national platform of 1908, the Republican party concurred and unqualifiedly endorsed statehood for Arizona and New Mexico.

That statehood was finally granted in 1910 should perhaps be credited to the efforts of Albert B. Fall, one of New Mexico's ablest political leaders. President Taft visited New Mexico during the first year of his administration, stopping at Albuquerque, where he was feted by the dignitaries of the state. No expense was spared in an effort to impress the President; "even bluepoint oysters from the Atlantic Coast graced the plates of the sixty-five specially chosen guests." Many speakers of both parties advised the President of the cultural, economic, political, and social attainments of New Mexico, hinting as they spoke that these would be greatly advanced by statehood. Governor George Curry had selected Fall to give the key address of the evening and assumed that it would be more eulogy of the state and compliments to the President.

Instead, Fall reviewed the long history of past broken promises of statehood and stressed "that the territory had a right to statehood and that Presidents had a habit of making promises while touring the country, only to forget them later on." To the consternation of the gathering, Fall sarcastically commented that Taft, their distinguished guest, was no exception.

Though not scheduled to speak, the President extemporaneously defended himself. He told a story about a judge who, after hearing a verbose argument by a young lawyer, replied that he agreed with

[40] Bowers, *Beveridge and the Progressive Era,* 268.
[41] Quoted in *ibid.,* 301.

him on the law and was with him "in spite of the reasons the young lawyer advanced." The President concluded, "Judge Fall, I have heard your argument and am for your cause in spite of it."[42]

Although many tried to excuse Fall's discourtesy to the President on the grounds of ill health, he later told friends that he had planned the speech deliberately in order to get the President on record publicly in favor of statehood. The President's commitment and the resulting publicity undoubtedly aided statehood far more than it harmed it.

In January, 1910, the House passed the Hamilton Bill, the enabling act for statehood for Arizona and New Mexico. In the Senate it was referred to the Committee on Territories, over which Senator Beveridge presided. But New Mexico's old nemesis had a change of heart. Resigned to the inevitable, the Indiana senator was now concerned only with writing a statehood bill that would be in the public interest. Working with experts from the Reclamation Service, the Department of the Interior, and the Department of Justice, Beveridge added several progressive amendments. He wrote the bill in its final form, making sure that the President approved of it. Because of some of the protective features of Beveridge's bill eastern senators vigorously opposed it, and the Senator found himself fighting for statehood with the same tenacity that he had once opposed it. But in the end, "his was the triumph." The House accepted the revisions by a unanimous vote, and on the twentieth of June, 1910, President Taft signed the bill, afterward turning to Senator Beveridge to congratulate him for his work on it. The citizens of Arizona invited the Indiana senator to visit them and receive their applause, but New Mexico did not have a similar warm spot in its heart for Senator Beveridge.[43]

The news of statehood flashed to Santa Fe and "a large crowd assembled and cheered itself hoarse over the victory for which New Mexico had been fighting for three score years."[44]

After constitutional conventions in Arizona and New Mexico

---

[42] Curry, *Autobiography*, 245–46; David H. Stratton, "Albert B. Fall and the Teapot Dome Affair" (Ph.D. dissertation, University of Colorado, 1955), 35–37.

[43] Bowers, *Beveridge and the Progressive Era*, 379–80.

[44] Santa Fe *New Mexican*, June 20, 1910, in La Farge, *Santa Fe*, 199.

drew up acceptable constitutions, Congress passed the Flood State-hood resolution, which provided for statehood for the two territories, on August 18, 1911, and President Taft formally announced New Mexican statehood on January 6, 1912. The long struggle was over, and New Mexico was in the Union.

XIII - Mining in New Mexico

IN THE SECOND HALF of the twentieth century it has become obvious that the original Spanish faith in the mineral potential of New Mexico has been realized, although in a fashion vastly different from that anticipated. The value of mineral production first exceeded that of agricultural pursuits in 1937, and mining continues to rank in first place in value of production among industries of the state. Its importance is reflected in the fact that in 1958 mining accounted for 6 per cent of all wage employment, 9 per cent of total wages, and 24 per cent of the gross state product.[1]

The original motive for Spanish exploration and conquest of New Mexico was the search for precious metals. In fact, the very name was derived from the hope that this province far to the north might have treasures equal to or even greater than those found in the Aztec Empire. Cabeza de Vaca, who was probably the first white man to set foot within the state, helped build these high hopes when he reported "many signs of gold, antimony, iron, copper, and other metals."[2] The appetite for precious metals which had been whetted by Vaca's report was further excited when Friar Marcos returned from a preliminary exploration with his fanciful tales. The imaginative Friar reported that this was "a land rich in gold, silver, and other wealth." The people were so rich that "the women even wore belts of gold."

[1] Ralph L. Edgel, "Mining in New Mexico," reprinted from *New Mexico Business,* Vol. XII (August, 1958), 1.

[2] Bolton, *Coronado,* 14. A detailed account of early mining in the state is in Stuart A. Northrop, *Minerals of New Mexico.*

Such reports provided the incentive for Coronado's exploratory expedition. Throughout the hardships encountered by the explorer and his men, there always lingered the expectation that it would all be worth the trouble when they found the proverbial pot of gold at the end of the rainbow. The stories the Indians told them about other peoples who had plenty of gold may have been mere fabrications to encourage the Spaniards to move on. Early learning how rapacious were the white men who readily plundered their meager supplies, made off with their choice women, and frequently left their brothers with not even their lives, the resourceful natives grasped the fact that the promise of gold would prompt the Spaniards to leave in search of it. Hence, the Indians always "knew" where gold could be found at some distant point. The stories that the Turk told of Quivira, where "there was so much gold there they could load not only horses with it but wagons," was perhaps the most fanciful tale of them all.

Despite the ill fortune that befell Coronado's expedition and the rather conclusive proof that the streets of the Indian villages were not glistening with gold pavement, there were still Spaniards who believed that precious metals could be found in New Mexico. Although other factors may have been important, the expedition of Espejo was partially influenced by the search for gold. There is a good possibility that knowledge of Coronado's trek was not available in Mexico in the 1580's. This explorer reported that the area abounded in great mineral wealth. The fact that Don Juan de Oñate, the leader of the group that first successfully colonized New Mexico, was himself a wealthy mine owner is sufficient proof of the continuing hope that mineral wealth would yet be found in New Mexico.

Many stories exist about the extent of mining in colonial times. There is an unfounded claim that the brutality of the Spaniards toward the Indians who worked in the mines was one of the causes of the Pueblo Revolt of 1680. As a matter of fact, the first mining claim of which there is a record was filed in 1685. There was doubtless considerable mining during the eighteenth century, but the information concerning it is sketchy. The first mining activity of lasting importance began about 1804 in the copper deposits of Santa Rita in the southwestern part of the state.

Crudely made mining tools, which were probably relics of early Spanish mining, have been found in recent years. The terrain gives evidence of having been dug up in a manner that would indicate attempts at mining. It is believed that the Spaniards abandoned these holdings in the northern part of the state because of the extreme isolation of the diggings from the population centers, inability to get the Indians to work in the mines, depredations by hostile savages, and lack of sufficient capital to develop them properly.[3]

The real cradle of New Mexico's modern era of mining was located at Santa Rita. Here was a mountain from which Indians had been digging copper to fashion into crude utensils for countless numbers of years. Beginning in 1804, mining on a large scale was begun, with about four million pounds of copper being taken out annually. It was crudely smelted into ingots weighing about 150 pounds each, which were then carried by muleback to Mexico City.

It was this mine which the father of James Pattie had leased and which he operated successfully until a rascally Spaniard bilked him out of most of his working capital.[4] Zebulon Pike, as well as other travelers, reported that this mine was in operation during the early nineteenth century. A Frenchman named Coursier worked the mine for seven years and reportedly cleared one million dollars in its operation. However, he, like his successors, was forced to abandon it as a result of Apache hostility. Not until the Indian menace was finally removed in the 1870's did the Americans take over Santa Rita and did it again flourish. The coming of the railroads in the 1880's obviously improved the position of the mine, and it has remained the center of copper mining in New Mexico.[5]

―――――――――――――――――――――――

~~~ *Gold* ~~~

―――――――――――――――――――――――

In 1828, gold was discovered in the Ortiz Mountains between Albuquerque and Santa Fe. This is probably the oldest gold-mining

[3] Jim Berry Pearson, "A New Mexico Gold Story—The Elizabethtown–Red River Area" (Ph.D. dissertation, University of Texas, 1955), 8.

[4] Pattie, *Personal Narrative*, 171–78.

[5] Margaret Meaders, "Copper Chronicle: The Story of New Mexico 'Red Gold,'" reprinted from *New Mexico Business*, Vol. XII (May and June, 1958), 2.

district in the present United States. Between the years 1832 and 1835 gold valued at from sixty to eighty thousand dollars a year was extracted from this area. By the time the Americans occupied New Mexico, the output was valued at about three million dollars.[6] As a general rule, mines were worked by Indians who had but little knowledge of mining work and considered themselves fortunate if they made expenses. A law was passed prohibiting foreigners from engaging in mining activity. This measure kept the necessary capital and energy from developing the mines fully. When the Americans took over in 1848, Spanish-American natives were washing gold in the streams around Taos. Information about the extent of such mining work and the amount of precious metals obtained is not available. Considerable gold must have been found in the area, because in 1852 newspaper editors urged the citizens around Taos and other parts of northern New Mexico to wash gold. Their motive lay in the hope that this evidence of New Mexico's wealth would bring an influx of settlers and perhaps even create a favorable atmosphere that would lead to the building of the Pacific Railroad, the projected transcontinental road then under consideration, along the 35th parallel.[7]

The Indian troubles of the 1850's and the uncertainty within the territory during the Civil War curtailed mining operations. In 1861, a group of Anglos took over mining at the old Ortiz Grant, but were unable to operate it effectively because of the lack of water, a deficiency which has continually plagued exploitations of New Mexico's Mineral resources.

The post–Civil War era was truly to see the birth of gold mining in the territory. In most cases the discovery of gold was pure accident, although there were exceptions. Colonel William Craig had heard stories of an old Spanish mine near Taos while he was stationed in that area before the war. Returning in 1869, he located the site of the mine which was to open a field in the Arroyo Hondo.[8] Another story is told of an Indian found dying, who was taken to Fort Union to recover and later brought a "pretty rock" to the fort as

[6] Twitchell, *The Leading Facts of New Mexican History*, II, 180. There is an interesting and worthwhile presentation of the manner in which the natives carried on gold mining in this area in Ruth Laughlin, *The Wind Leaves No Shadow*, 88–111.
[7] Pearson, "A New Mexican Gold Story," 175.
[8] *Ibid.*, 182.

a gift. Investigation revealed that it contained gold, and in 1867 a gold rush was on in the area.[9]

After one means of discovery or another, within a short period of time gold was to be mined in twenty-three of the state's thirty-two counties. The most important concentrations were in the Elizabethtown–Red River area lying northeast of Taos, in the southwestern corner of the state, and in the area northeast of Santa Fe.

The story of gold mining in New Mexico is comparable to that in most of the western states. There was the same flurry of excitement at the discovery of a new field, the mad stampede, the hasty building of a tent city, the erection of more durable buildings, and the influx of a large number of people. In most cases, high hopes were soon dashed, and people left to seek greener pastures elsewhere. In fact, a pattern seemed to exist wherein as soon as disillusionment had set in at one mining site, there was another to attract the optimistic prospector. Today, the vast mountain regions of the state are dotted with ghost towns in various stages of disintegration, mute testimony to man's continual search for wealth. The fact that gold was found in most sections of the state was enough to kindle the fires of enthusiasm in the breasts of the prospectors. But, as one of them later ruefully remarked, "If we had only known how deep the ore veins were we would not have made the venture."[10] Unfortunately, the geology of the state was little understood in this early period. Geological problems have made impossible profitable gold mining in New Mexico.

Miners were constantly frustrated when they ran across rich fingers of gold and expected them to lead to the "mother lode." The lodes and tributary veins had originally been formed in bedrock layers by the solidification of eruptive magma masses. These bedrock layers, which were rich in gold, had then been broken up by various stages of uplifts, faulting, and subsequent weathering action, so that the veins intersected the brittle slate and metamorphic limestone and sandstone. An enthusiastic miner, finding a finger of gold ore, would believe he had finally struck it rich; but he would usually end up by working out the finger or coming up against a rock formation that cut off further digging. Today, only deposits relatively close to the

[9] *Ibid.*, 16.
[10] Quoted in Winifred Oldham Hamilton, *Wagon Days in Red River*, 7.

surface have been uncovered. The expense of lode mining was so great in terms of the return that it was never really profitable.

On the other hand, placer gold deposits are formed by disintegration and the forces of erosion on gold-bearing rocks. Over a long period of time the gold is separated from the lighter materials by the action of running water in the stream beds. Such gold is recovered by washing the earth and gravel along the streams. In New Mexico lack of water made the mining problem most formidable. A large quantity of water was needed, and that the state has never had. Countless efforts were made to solve the water problem by diverting streams, building canals, and digging wells. In spite of the expenditure of millions of dollars, however, sufficient water was never available for profitable mining.[11] The successful exploitation of New Mexico's placer gold awaits the perfection of a dry extraction method. Even Thomas Edison lost two million dollars in a vain effort to obtain New Mexico gold by dry methods.[12]

The extreme isolation of the state also made mining difficult. When a piece of machinery broke down, it was usually necessary to dispatch a man with it all the way to Kansas City to have a duplicate part made. Ultimately, the large mining companies imported their own blacksmiths and even maintained their own foundries. The coming of the railroad to New Mexico between 1879 and 1882 helped spur mining activity. However, the prohibitive cost of building railroads over the mountains left many a mining community still isolated, despite the entreaties to the railroads that it would be financially worth their while to enter such regions.

Statistics for gold mining before 1905 are inadequate. There is no question but that some individual miners made large sums of money. For example, more than one million dollars in gold was claimed to have been produced at the Aztec Mine in a three-year period. Some enthusiastic observers claim that millions of dollars in gold were taken out of the Elizabethtown area in the space of a few years.[13] One suspects, however, that many of these claims were in-

[11] W. L. Emerick, "Geology of the Golden Area, Santa Fe County, New Mexico" (M.A. thesis, University of New Mexico, 1950), 62.

[12] Erna Fergusson, *New Mexico: A Pageant of Three Peoples*, 303.

[13] Hamilton, *Wagon Days in Red River*, 33.

tended for the benefit of eastern investors and were little founded in fact. Since 1905 the United States Bureau of Mines has been keeping records, and it is recorded that in 1915 gold from New Mexico was valued at $1,461,000, a figure which has never again been equaled. The value continued to decline until in 1958 only $118,000 worth of gold was extracted.

On the national mining scene, New Mexico was, then, never important in gold production. However, gold mining had a value far in excess of statistics in the industry of the state in the seventies and eighties. It acted as a powerful magnet to bring the Anglos in. Once there, and having failed to find their pot of gold, many of them lacked the means to return to their home states. Settling down as farmers and, more frequently, as ranchers, they provided a powerful stimulus to the economic activity of the territory. Thus, families of the old miners are scattered throughout New Mexico, and many of them have become leaders in their communities. Even the unscrupulous swindler who went about "salting" mines provided a service. Countless fake gold mines, as well as silver and even diamond mines, enticed eastern and even foreign capital to invest in the future of New Mexico. In a number of instances, these outside investors had enough capital left to engage in farming, ranching, or legitimate mining activities.

Silver

Like gold, silver was never to be important in New Mexico by comparison with other western states. But it, too, served its purpose. In some ways silver mining had more of a civilizing influence than gold mining because a greater labor force was required to process the ore. With this labor also went expensive smelters and the necessity for railroad transportation. Magdalena and Socorro were the initial centers of silver mining beginning in 1863, but it was Silver City that was to become the leader in such mining activity, though silver was ultimately mined throughout the southwestern part of the state. The peak of silver production was reached in 1916 when ore valued at $1,162,208 was processed. In 1958 the value of silver produced was $144,000. The decline of about one-half of the previous year's production reflects the fact that most of the silver is obtained as a by-product of copper production and that decline in the output of the latter reduced silver production also. The year 1905 proved to be pivotal in the history of New Mexico mining. Prior to this date gold and silver were the leading minerals in value, but afterwards the value of the baser metals far exceeded that of the precious metals. Of these, copper has consistently been the leader.

Copper

As previously mentioned, most of the early copper mining was at Santa Rita in the southwestern part of the state, and perhaps this mining activity was the earliest production of copper in the United States. Although in 1936 there were thirty copper mines being worked in the state in ten different counties, 90 per cent of the total production remained within Grant County. As early as 1905 the value of the copper mined was almost double that of gold and silver, and the proportion has grown ever since. In 1956, a peak year, the value of copper was $63,193,000, and accounted for 39.6 per cent of the value of all metallic minerals. Unfortunately for the state's economy, there is little processing of copper in addition to the immediate milling done in the mining area. It is shipped elsewhere for the necessary finishing.

Lead and Zinc

Usually found in the same areas as copper, but of less economic significance, are lead and zinc. The total value of these metals in 1905 was slightly more than that of copper, but they have failed to keep pace with copper in growth of value. Their peak year was reached in 1952 when total production was valued at $19,185,000. Among the other metallic minerals found in the state are manganese, molybdenum, and vanadium, in the order of their relative importance. There doubtless are greater deposits of these minerals which may be exploited more extensively at some time in the future. Naturally, the mining of sand, gravel, clays, and similar materials used in the building of roads, bridges, and buildings represents a substantial part of the dollar volume of the state's mining industry.

Coal

Coal mining in New Mexico may be every bit as old as copper mining, but the lack of records and of knowledge of the use to which coal was put limits the historian's knowledge of such details. For some time coal was second only to copper in value, and in a state where wood has usually been at a premium it was invaluable as a fuel.

There is no way of determining how long people have used coal for home consumption in New Mexico, but there are records to show that during the Civil War period it was hauled into the army camps for fuel. Even ranches in Texas found it necessary to haul in wagonloads of coal to provide their winter heat.[14] The coming of the railroads between 1879 and 1882 put coal production on a firm footing. The first area opened was that in Colfax County near Raton, and this district has traditionally led the state in production. In 1882 the railroad reached the Gallup area, and existing mines in the neighborhood were promptly put into production to supply most of the coal for the railroad between Albuquerque and California.[15] Until very recently, coal mining was the primary economic concern of the Gallup region.

The Raton and Gallup fields accounted for about 90 per cent of the total coal output, although mines were worked in Lincoln County which employed three hundred men to produce over 120,000 tons in 1902.[16] At one time the most valuable mineral deposit in the San Juan Basin was not gas and oil, but coal.[17] Mines near Santa Fe and Socorro have also been worked.

[14] Haley, *The XIT Ranch*, 167.
[15] Telling, "New Mexican Frontiers," 45.
[16] Choate, "History of the Capitan Community," 52.
[17] Duke, "History of San Juan County," 5.

At its peak the coal industry in New Mexico produced more than 4,000,000 tons of coal from some sixty-one mines and employed nearly five thousand workers. But the conversion of the railroads to diesel power and the wide use of natural gas and oil for heating and commercial purposes have prompted a steady decline of the coal mines in the state. In 1958 coal production continued to decline, totaling only 117,000 tons, with a value of $719,000.

Most of the coal mined has been subbituminous, although there has been some anthracite produced near Madrid. Should there be an increase in steel production in the West, it is hoped that New Mexico can find a use for its coal mines.

Potash

The production of potash in New Mexico is of comparatively recent origin and is a growing mining activity instead of a declining one. About 85 per cent of the nation's production comes from a small area near Carlsbad.

Potash is used mainly for commercial fertilizers, but has some use in silk manufacturing and the chemical industry. Until World War I, the American supply of that mineral came from Germany. Because of the wartime shortage, the United States Geological Survey searched for a supply within the country, and in 1925 an oil geologist accidentally found the potash deposits near Carlsbad.[18] Mining was begun in 1931 and has continued ever since. Since potash has a low value per unit weight, shipping costs are a major expense in the industry, and the rail charges on it are so high that foreign producers can ship it into the eastern ports for much less than the cost of extracting the New Mexico product. Hence, the state's Congressional delegation consistently keeps an eye out for any relaxation of the tariff barriers that would spell disaster for this important part of New Mexico's economy.

[18] William J. Cunningham, "The Control of Mineral Resources in New Mexico" (M.A. thesis, University of New Mexico, 1950), 27. Louis H. Kurrelmeyer, "Recent Developments in the Economics of the Potash Industry, With Particular Reference to Carlsbad, New Mexico" (M.A. thesis, University of New Mexico, 1950), 27. See also Louis H. Kurrelmeyer, "The Potash Industry."

251

The New Mexico deposits lie in horizontal beds 4 to 10 feet thick at a depth below the surface varying from 500 to 3,800 feet. As the potash lies in seams, it is mined in much the same way as coal. The production of potash has shown a steady, and at times a phenomenal, rate of growth. By 1957 the value of the total production was $73,-243,000. The figure slumped slightly in 1958 to $69,106,000. The value of potash to the Carlsbad area was demonstrated in a recent strike, when retail sales declined approximately 25 per cent before the miners went back to work.

~~~ *Uranium* ~~~

The newest addition to the New Mexico family of minerals is, of course, uranium. Its value unknown but a short time ago, it has achieved a position of great importance in less than a decade, and some predict that in New Mexico it may some day be second only to petroleum in value. The success story associated with the rise to prominence of uranium sounds very much like the gold booms of a century ago. Even its accidental discovery by a Navaho in the spring of 1950 was as romantic as anything associated with gold discoveries; the difference is that the boom in uranium apparently is much more stable.

Thus far most of the uranium has been mined in the area around Grants, with some mining being carried on near Gallup and in the San Juan Basin. It is claimed that Grants has 72 per cent of the known uranium-ore reserves and 52 per cent of the total milling capacity in the United States. Because of the mushroom nature of the industry, reliable statistics are difficult to find. In 1958, New Mexico led the nation in production with 3,210,281 tons,[19] up some 61 per cent from the previous year.

Unlike some of the other extractive industries of New Mexico, uranium mining and processing entails a great deal of labor. The necessity for such processing has led to a sizable investment in the facilities for mining and milling and a large influx of people from

[19] *The Denver Post*, January 1, 1959.

outside the state. Such an enormous investment will undoubtedly help put uranium mining on a lasting basis and will encourage the development of a peacetime use for it once there is a reduction in military demands. Needless to say, the confidence in the future of New Mexico's uranium mining is boundless.

⤳ *Natural Gas* ⤳

Of more immediate value to New Mexico is natural gas. Second only to petroleum, extraction and processing of this resource, which was once thought to be worthless because of the lack of marketing facilities, has now become a leading industry. The first extensive use of gas was in the 1920's.[20] It was discovered in the exploration for petroleum.

Natural gas production in the state is concentrated in two distinct areas, one in the southeastern corner and the other in the northwestern. That in the southeastern, the Permian Basin, extracts gas as a by-product of the petroleum industry. In the northwestern part of the state, the San Juan Basin has distinct gas wells producing dry gas. As late as 1957, Lea County within the Permian Basin accounted for about two-thirds of the natural gas production of New Mexico. However, since that date the San Juan Basin has shown a marked spurt in production. The rapid increase in the value of natural gas has largely taken place since the end of World War II and is directly associated with the rapid increase in population along the Pacific Coast and in the Rocky Mountain Area. For example, California can produce only about 10 per cent of its needs, and the resultant building of pipe lines has provided a market for the natural gas from both corners of New Mexico. The total value of this product in 1957 was $97,020,000 but had increased to $111,900,000 in 1958.

[20] Helpful in the recent story of oil and gas in New Mexico is Arthur A. Blumenfeld, "Oil and Gas, Three-Letter Words for Progress in New Mexico's San Juan Basin" *New Mexico Business* Vol. X (September, 1957), 9. Vicente Ximenes, *Natural Gas in New Mexico.* Also *Minerals Yearbook,* various years.

Petroleum

The real giant of the New Mexico mineral industry is petroleum. From modest beginnings in 1924, the production of oil rose until it was valued at $293,783,000 in 1958 and accounted for a little less than 53 per cent of the total value of New Mexico's mineral production. As in the case of natural gas, the bulk of the state's production is located either in the Permian Basin in the southeastern part uof the state or in the San Juan Basin in the northwest.

This oil boom has primarily accounted for the large increase in population in the Farmington area and on the east side. It has also led to changes in the social and political character of the region, bringing in as it does the influence of oilmen, mainly from Texas.

It is ironical that the naïve faith of the early Spanish settlers that New Mexico possessed great mineral potential should be realized in the second half of the twentieth century. Although the once great promise held for the development of gold and silver has not been realized, oil, natural gas, uranium, and potash have made the state a leading mineral producer. Unfortunately, mining is an extractive industry, and it is easy to predict the inevitable end of what has become the leading economic activity of New Mexico. But such predictions are unsafe in this age of science, as new technology can easily prolong current mining activity or even open new and at present unheard-of fields of mineral exploitation. In any event, it will doubtless be many years before the state faces a day of reckoning so far as mining is concerned.

XIV - Sheep, Cattle, and Farming

THE ECONOMIC HISTORY of New Mexico has been mainly a story of the raising of sheep and cattle and of farming. The Indians were tilling the soil for untold centuries before the white man put in his appearance, and the early Spanish colonists were forced to become farmers and stock raisers if they wanted to survive in the new land. This early importance of agriculture in New Mexico was to remain into the mid twentieth century. As recently as 1950 the prosperity of the New Mexicans depended largely upon weather conditions and the prices of sheep, wool, cattle, cotton, and the grain sorghums. The amount of rainfall received was usually the prime determinant of whether or not the people of the state were going to be prosperous. Since 1950, however, the relative importance of agriculture to New Mexico has been rapidly declining.

Sheep

Until the influx of the Anglo cattlemen after the Civil War, sheep absolutely dominated the agricultural economy of New Mexico. The first permanent settlers who came in with Oñate in 1598 discovered that sheep were completely at home in the new area. Because the semi-arid climate was similar to that of Spain, their sheep were able to find enough grazing in the dry pastureland. Mutton became the basic food and woolen garments the most common apparel. The

Indians quickly accepted the sheep, and many of them learned to weave blankets, which became a significant article of trade in colonial times.

The Spanish system of granting large tracts of land to men who were in favor with the king or his authorities in America made sheep raising a large enterprise. The *patrón*, having control of most of the land, incorporated a sort of share-cropping system wherein those who tended the flocks received a percentage of the wool and mutton. Tradition has it that one of the Spanish governors owned as many as two million head of sheep, and others as many as one million. These figures are doubtless exaggerated, but it is known that many families in the 1880's had flocks of 250,000 each. The usual practice was for flocks of sheep to be about 2,000 in size with two men to care for them. The Indians, patient and accustomed to desert life, were especially well adapted to this work.[1] The shepherds grazed the sheep in dry areas, since the animals could exist without a source of water, and the men had to carry their own water supply.

Sheep were the staple commodity of the isolated economy of New Mexico. Josiah Gregg asserts that as many as 500,000 were exported in one year, and it was not uncommon for 200,000 to be driven to market to the mining areas of Mexico.[2] The gold rush in California provided another important market for meat. In 1849 ten thousand head were driven westward, and after that large numbers were to follow annually, with some drives even being made eastward to Missouri.

In 1859, purebred Merino sheep were brought to New Mexico from Kentucky in an effort to improve the quality of the flocks. In spite of these efforts, the market for mutton declined, principally because the Anglos refused to eat it. The army never succeeded in feeding mutton to its troops stationed in the West, as they preferred beef. This antipathy to mutton brought about a change in the importance of the marketable item from meat to wool.

The wool clip rose from 32,000 pounds in 1850 to 493,000 pounds

[1] Edward Norris Wentworth, *America's Sheep Trails*, 113–14; Curry, *Autobiography*, 17.

[2] Gregg, *Commerce of the Prairies*, 134.

in 1860, 685,000 pounds in 1870, and 4,000,000 pounds in 1880.[3] These gains doubtless reflect the improvement in sheep breeding, the fact that the raising of sheep became more extensive as the army brought the hostile Indians under control and permitted the extension of the sheep grazing lands, and, finally, the fact that a market was now available. Huge wagonloads of wool made their way eastward over the Santa Fe Trail until the coming of the railroads.

To facilitate the handling of such large quantities of wood, there emerged a group of merchants who were virtually storekeepers for the sheep business. In an area where there were no banks, these storekeepers advanced the sheepmen the necessary supplies until wool was sheared or lambs were shipped. Of necessity, these men became more than storekeepers, usually being bankers as well as wool brokers along with their regular mercantile activity. Firms such as the Bond Brothers of Española and Charles Ilfeld of Las Vegas, as well as many others, frequently came to dominate the economic, political, and social activity of New Mexico because of the nature of their operations.

The end of the open range in the early twentieth century and the accompanying battle with the cattlemen have changed the status of sheep in New Mexico. Sheep raising continues to be most important in the western part of the state, particularly among the Indians. Some sheep are also raised in the mountain area and in the southeast portion of the state.

In the twentieth century, the sheep raiser has long since lost his position of economic dominance in New Mexico to the cattlemen. An examination of the records of livestock down through the years indicates that the number of sheep and lambs on the farms of New Mexico has shown almost a consistent decline, so that by 1957 the total was only 1,166,000. By that year the percentage of income from sheep, lambs, and wool of New Mexico's farm marketing was only seven per cent.[4] So, even if the raising of sheep has local impor-

[3] Frank H. Grubbs, "Frank Bond: Gentleman Sheepherder of Northern New Mexico 1883–1915" (M.A. thesis, University of New Mexico, 1958), 3–4; Coan, *History of New Mexico*, I, 389.

[4] Frederick C. Irion (ed.), *Natural Resources of New Mexico, 1900–2000*, 62.

tance in parts of the state, the heyday of the sheepman has long since passed.

Cattle

With approximately 98 per cent of New Mexico's land unfit for crop production, it was inevitable that grazing would be the principal use of the land. But it was by raising cattle, and not sheep, that the state was to become most noted. Cattle had been first introduced along with sheep by Oñate in 1598, but they never assumed a significant commercial role until after the Civil War. The production of sheep was much better suited to the needs of those who lived in New Mexico.

The hated Texans brought the cattle industry to New Mexico, and in this case their invasion of the state was successful. In some respects this influx of the Texans and their herds of cattle was just another phase of the periodic Anglo invasion of the state.

When the Civil War was over, the Texans found themselves with about five million head of cattle roaming the downstate area. High beef prices during the war had depleted cattle in the North. Therefore, the great cattle drives to the Kansas railheads were on. One Texan, Charles Goodnight, decided to drive his herds in a different direction, believing "the whole of Texas would start north for market" along the same trail and that greater opportunities existed to the west.[5] Gold mining was just beginning in northern New Mexico, and Goodnight was sure that the miners would not only have money but would be prepared to spend it for beef. In the event he could not sell his herds, he believed that the open country would provide an excellent range where he could hold them. Combining his herd with that of Oliver Loving, later his partner, Goodnight left from a point west of Fort Worth in June of 1866.

The trail which they blazed led from Fort Belknap on the Brazos

[5] J. Evetts Haley, *Charles Goodnight: Cowman and Plainsman*, 121. Clara M. Love, "History of the Cattle Industry in the Southwest" *Southwestern Historical Quarterly*, Vol. XIX, (April, 1916) and Vol. XX, (July, 1916); see also Ernest S. Osgood, *Day of the Cattleman*, and Edward E. Dale, *The Range Cattle Industry*.

River southwestward until they reached the Pecos at Horsehead Crossing. They followed the Pecos northward, entering New Mexico at Hope's Crossing. At first the terminus was near Fort Sumner. Later the trail branched off, with one part going through Las Vegas, then through Raton, and on to Denver. Another branch swung east of Las Vegas, passing near Fort Bascom, and crossed into Colorado at the Trinchera Pass in order to evade Dick Wootton's toll, which was extremely high.

Goodnight and Loving succeeded beyond their wildest dreams. Not only were the miners eager to purchase all of the cattle that they had available, but they also discovered a tremendous market at the numerous forts scattered throughout New Mexico where soldiers were trying to hold the Indians in check. In addition to the needs of the soldiers, the government had to feed some 8,500 Indians at Bosque Redondo who were penned up on the reservation near Fort Sumner. Despite the antagonism existing toward Texans, their former enemies, the Union soldiers welcomed the herds of cattle. The venture was so successful that Goodnight hurried back to bring another herd northward that same season. Countless others were to follow the trail laid out in 1866. Then, as competition increased, Goodnight sent his herds ever farther northward. Discovering the needs of ranchers in Colorado and Wyoming, he drove his cattle in that direction. Most of his herds were sold to the great Colorado ranchman, John Wesley Iliff. It is estimated that in three years' time Goodnight delivered about thirty thousand head of cattle to this distant market.[6] The Texas cattle were used to populate the Plains area as well as to feed the miners and railroad-building crews.

Although it lasted only from 1866 to 1880, a period of fourteen years, the story of the Texas cattle drives has become one of the most dramatic of frontier America. "To those who took part, accustomed as they became to all the possible incidents of the drive, near as they were with the solitudes over which they passed, each drive was a new adventure and its successful completion always brought to the most experienced something of the thrill of achievement. . . . to all those who saw that long line of Texas cattle come up over a rise in the prairies, nostrils wide for the smell of water,

[6] Haley, *Charles Goodnight*, 206.

dust caked and gaunt, so ready to break from the nervous control of the riders strung out along the flanks of the herd, there came the feeling that in this spectacle there was something elemental, something resistless, something perfectly in keeping about the unconquered land about them."[7] And the Texas cattle drive was as much a part of the history of New Mexico as it was of the remainder of the West.

Gradually, Texas cattlemen brought their herds into New Mexico and prepared to stay. With ample grassland and water, cattle, unlike sheep, could be turned loose unattended. All that the prospective rancher needed was a log cabin or even a dugout for his headquarters. With the proceeds resulting from the sale of the natural increase of his stock, he was later able to build a ranch house and erect corrals for his horses. Usually, a rancher claimed all the land from one bank of a stream back to the highland area. As others moved in, it was frequently necessary to back this claim by force. The annual spring roundup enabled the ranchers to identify their own particular stock by branding them.

Perhaps the greatest of the early New Mexican cattlemen was John Chisum. For a time Chisum had driven his herds northward for delivery to Goodnight and others. According to some accounts Chisum got his start by driving other Texans' cattle northward and then forgetting to pay the owners. Others insist that he was one of the greatest rustlers in history. At the height of his power Chisum raised the largest herd in the Southwest. His range extended 150 miles up and down the Pecos from approximately the Texas border to Fort Sumner. From the river it extended "as far as a long-legged cow could graze."[8] At one time Chisum is estimated to have had 60,000 head of cattle carrying his brand. In one year alone he sold 30,000 head to a commission house in Kansas City, and then claimed that rustlers made off with an additional 10,000. His headquarters near the present site of Roswell placed him within driving distance of Tucson and Prescott in the Arizona mining country, as well as being convenient to the markets to the north. In many respects,

[7] Osgood, *Day of the Cattleman*, 26.

[8] Haley, *Goodnight*, 233; The most complete story of this cattle baron is found in Hinton, "John Simpson Chisum 1877–1884."

Chisum resembled a feudal monarch of the Middle Ages. There was no question that his hired hands were as lawless as any of the knights of old. And if they did not carry broadswords and lances, it was because their six-shooters were far more effective.[9]

All of the early cattlemen of New Mexico faced countless problems. At first the most important of these were the attacks by the Indians who were more often after horses than cattle. What cattle the Indians did steal were usually for trading purposes rather than for consumption. Wherever there have been cattle grazed, rustlers have hovered about to exact their toll. Since many of the new migrants into New Mexico had left home to evade legal prosecution, it was inevitable that cattle thievery should be carried out on an extensive scale. Then, too, the native populace was not morally opposed to rustling, especially if the owners were Texans. On many occasions stolen cattle could be traced to the corrals of New Mexicans, but getting them back through the local courts was virtually impossible for the outsider; hence, the Texans usually took the law into their own hands, dealing out frontier justice to cattle thieves. This use of force increased the already existing enmity toward them.

Even without the hazards of preying Indians and rustlers, the early cattlemen had to contest with the elements. Years of drought-shriveled grass and dried-up waterholes caused many a rancher to go bankrupt. Fire was one of the worst hazards in the early days. Sometimes grass fires burned for weeks on end. Undue cold and heavy snows likewise took their toll during the winter.

By the end of the nineteenth century, cattle raising was to be found in almost every part of the state. Great ranches totaling perhaps thirty or forty square miles dotted the eastern side, extending northward to the Colorado line, and were also to be found in the northwestern part of the state, as well as in the currently existing cattle country around Magdalena. The invention of barbed wire, the invasion of the nesters, and the introduction of blooded stock gradually sounded the death knell of the open range, although in parts of New Mexico it still remains as a romantic reminder of a hectic past.

By judicious control of water holes, some men held huge ranges through possession of grazing rights on state and federal land. One

[9] William MacLeod Raine, *Cattle, Cowboys, and Rangers,* 160.

261

great cattle baron, Senator Albert B. Fall, amassed approximately 750,000 acres of grazing land. The Fall ranch included some forty different small ranch units, each with its separate houses, windmills, pumping stations, and similar facilities.[10] But this ranch is an exception; most of New Mexico's ranches are now relatively small, usually numbering only a few thousand acres, although some do run as high as the hundred-thousand-acre mark. Gone are the picturesque cowboys, who today are usually found at rodeos for an occasional appearance of the sheriff's posse. Modern cattlemen ride their range in a jeep or even an airplane. The emphasis is upon quality beef production rather than quantity. One rancher sold six hundred cattle in 1950 for much more than two thousand head would have brought in 1900.[11] The modern New Mexico cattleman is more a businessman than a romantic adventurer. In fact, many of the state's ranches are owned by outsiders who are interested in them both as places of refuge and as business investments.

In general, New Mexican cattle are produced to be sold to cattle feeders. They are bred and raised in the open in New Mexico where the business can be managed cheaply. The stock is then shipped to middle western states to be fattened for market. New Mexico does not raise enough corn for fattening purposes, and it costs too much to ship it in.[12]

Unlike sheep raising, which has been continuously declining in New Mexico, the cattle industry has retained its earlier importance.

In 1890 there were about 1,340,000 head of cattle in the state, and this figure has been largely maintained through the years, except for the fluctuations during drought years and the depression. In fact, this was very close to the figure during the 1950's. However, the value of cattle marketed has continued to increase, so that in 1957 the total valuation was $88,993,000. This figure accounted for 45 per cent of the total cash receipts from farm marketing, a fact indicative of the continued importance of cattle raising.[13] Although

10 Stratton, "Albert B. Fall and the Teapot Dome Affair," 111.

11 E. Fergusson, *New Mexico*, 325.

12 Edward Moulton, *New Mexico's Future: An Economic and Employment Appraisal*, 91–92.

13 Irion (ed.), *Natural Resources of New Mexico*, 62.

this return is small compared to that received from mining or as a result of federal defense activities, the cattle industry, partially because of its historical traditions, still exerts a great deal of influence within the state. The New Mexican Cattle Growers' Association has long been a potent political factor and will doubtless continue to be important.[14]

⮞ *Agriculture* ⮜

For untold centuries before the coming of white men, the Indians had tilled the soil of New Mexico. Raising mainly cotton and corn in some areas, they practiced a crude form of irrigation. More frequently, with the aid of the rain gods, they depended upon the rather meager supply of rainfall. Abandonment of the many sites of ancient civilization may have resulted from periodic drought more than from any other cause.

Outside of bringing in many new crops, the Spaniards probably added little to the Indians' agricultural knowledge. The staple crops were corn, wheat, and pinto beans. The techniques of irrigation brought in by the Spaniards were those that they had learned centuries before from their Moorish overlords. One New Mexican commented in 1832, "Agriculture is utterly neglected, for the inhabitants of this country do not sow any amount, as they might do to great profit without any doubt. They sow barely what they consider necessary for their maintenance for part of the year, and for the rest of the year they are exposed to a thousand miseries."[15]

Several factors account for the agricultural backwardness of the Spanish settlers. First of all, the Hispanic attitude toward hired labor in the field restricted manpower to the Indian slaves or to the peons. No gentleman would condescend to such work; therefore, there was little interest in improving the agricultural techniques. Secondly, the Spanish methods of agriculture were obsolete, such practices as crop rotation, common even to medieval Europe, being unheard of.

[14] Jesse R. Hagy, "The New Mexico Cattle Growers' Association" (M.A. thesis, University of New Mexico, 1951), 103.

[15] Barreiro, *Ojeada Sobre Nuevo-México*, 23.

Farming implements were crude and ill adapted to extensive use. One observer suggests that the New Mexican cart, plow, and yoke should be preserved for posterity; otherwise, no one would believe such things existed. "The plow takes you back at once to Biblical simplicity. In looking at its heavy beam, some 16 feet long with a small fork piece of wood attached, you wonder, first, how it could ever be moved, and, secondly, what earthly . . . good it could ever effect."[16] Third, as the cultivated land was not closed with fences, for cultural reasons as well as the fact that fencing material was seldom available, growing crops were subject to frequent devastation by the flocks of roaming sheep owned by one of the *patrones*, who had little respect for such farming efforts. Fourth, during most of colonial times, outlying districts were subject to periodic Indian raids. Too often what the Spaniards sowed, the Indians reaped. Livestock could be driven away in the event of such raids, but the cornfield must be left to be destroyed or harvested by the Indians.[17] Fifth, the lack of markets discouraged hard work in the fields. People were simply content to raise what they could get by with. When the trading caravans began making their way to Santa Fe, the settlers around Las Vegas began raising apples, apricots, and other small fruits as well as beans, peas, squash, and melons to be sold to the wealthy Americans who could afford such luxuries. Fresh milk and cheese, along with fresh fruits and vegetables, were welcomed after the long, weary journey across the Plains.[18]

In some respects the coming of the Americans made the position of the New Mexican farmer more difficult, because the Americans quickly acquired riparian rights along the principal streams, ignoring the traditions of Hispanic law so far as irrigation was concerned. In other respects, however, the Americans made a very considerable contribution to agriculture, besides providing a market. They brought with them new methods and implements of farming as well as new crops. Although the New Mexicans were slow to use the iron plows and other tools brought in by the Anglos, they gradually did so. More important, the Anglos brought with them a new atti-

---

[16] James F. Meline, *Two Thousand Miles on Horseback*, 122–23.
[17] Rodríguez, "New Mexico in Transition," *NMHR*, Vol. XXIV (1949), 204.
[18] F. Stanley, *Fort Union*, 25.

tude toward farming. To them, it was one of the most honorable economic activities, instead of work reserved for slaves or those who could do nothing else. This attitude helped to break down slowly the traditional Hispanic resentment toward such manual labor as degrading.[19]

An interesting early agricultural activity of both Indians and the Spaniards which has continued down to the present time was the gathering of piñon nuts. Gathered from the trees on nearby hills, they were sold in the town markets, roasted at home, or even sold to the traders, who shipped them particularly to the New York City area. Although never profitable, the piñon industry has continued down to the present time and still occupies the attention of large numbers of New Mexicans.[20]

The real invasion of New Mexico by "the man with the hoe" waited upon the coming of the railroads between 1879 and 1882. As fast as the bands of steel found their way across the state, the nesters followed them. Homesteading land and bringing in their equipment, they tried to farm as they had back home. Long, clear stretches of excellent land, unmarred by rocks or stumps, fascinated the early settlers. As one of them put it, "I could start a plow point into the soil and turn a furrow two or three hundred miles long without a break."[21]

Whole counties were settled, frequently within a year or two, with the home land claims office being swamped with eager applicants. Every train from Iowa, Missouri, and Arkansas came laden with those who were seeking farms on this, the last frontier. Lacking building materials, these early settlers were frequently forced to return to the caves of their ancestors or build sod houses. Small towns, churches, schoolhouses, and the inevitable windmill soon dotted the plains of eastern New Mexico and were also to be found in the High Plains area of the western part of the state. By 1900, more than five million acres were under cultivation.

At first the cattlemen tried to keep out the nesters by fencing in

[19] Rodríguez, "New Mexico in Transition," *NMHR*, Vol. XXIV (1949), 204.
[20] Arthur L. Campo, "Piñon as an Economic and Social Factor," *New Mexico Business Review*, Vol. II (October, 1932).
[21] Quoted in Haley, *The XIT Ranch*, 204.

the water and using force to frighten them off. With money, and hence the law, the cattle barons only postponed the inevitable, however. Some cattlemen tried to reason with the newcomers, pointing out that while 160 acres might be enough land to support a family in the Middle West, it would not do in the semiarid area of New Mexico, and that for the settlers' own good it would not be wise for them to try.[22]

Mother Nature was to succeed where the cattlemen failed. As often as not, the early settlers would enjoy a few years of average or above average rainfall which enabled them to raise corn and crops similar to those of the Middle West. Unfortunately, those who came to New Mexico did not profit from knowledge of the disaster that had previously hit western Kansas and parts of the Texas Panhandle. In those regions drought in the 1890's had driven out most of the settlers.

What happened in Roosevelt County has been repeated in much of the state. In 1900 the county had about 350 people, but by 1904 this number was in excess of 3,000, and by 1910 more than 12,000. Scarcely a quarter-section was to be found that did not have a shanty or a dugout as evidence of its being claimed. But the inevitable happened; another dry period came. Beginning in 1909 and lasting until 1912, the lack of rainfall drove approximately three-fourths of the nesters out. By 1912, a quarter-section of land, which had sold as high as $1,000 in 1906, could be bought for around $200, if one could find a purchaser.[23] Foundations of homes, or even the remnants of entire communities, remained as mute testimony of man's failure to cope with the problems of nature.

Much of the abandoned land returned to range, and cattle again grazed it. However, many farmers who remained mastered the techniques of dry farming and raised crops suited to the arid conditions. Crops such as millet, sorghum grains, and kafir corn were introduced. Dry farmers also began raising cattle as a buffer when rainfall was scarce. Dry farming has remained important, producing wheat as well as the sorghum grains. Roosevelt County specializes in the production of broom corn, for example. But even in the middle

22 Agnes Morley Cleaveland, *No Life For A Lady*.
23 Robinson, "History of Roosevelt County," 91–93.

of the twentieth century the dry farmer who had lasted for decades was finding the going difficult. Some who had survived the drought of the 1930's and who had become wealthy through the war years were bankrupted by the drought of the 1950's. Many farms continued to be abandoned, further evidence of the prediction that New Mexico should remain a grazing land.

An interesting trend has occurred in New Mexico's agriculture, as the following data show. The total number of farms in 1910 was 35,676, averaging in size 316 acres. By 1954 the number of farms had been reduced to 21,070, but the average value per acre had likewise increased from $9.92 to $20.38, largely as a result of the introduction of irrigation. As was previously pointed out,[24] irrigation, by surface means as well as by ground water, has become the determining factor in New Mexico's agriculture. In 1958, the total harvested acreage in the state was greater than one million acres, with one-half of that being in hay and sorghum crops. Since the area of the state is just under seventy-eight million acres, one can readily see that agriculture is not the leading industry of New Mexico.

Of the total cropland of 1,135,000 acres, some 650,000 acres are irrigated. The early settlers who recognized the importance of irrigation frequently attempted it by private means, but the raising of private capital to build the necessary dams and reservoirs was not feasible, and an extensive campaign was launched to win governmental support. The building of the dams along the Pecos and Elephant Butte on the Río Grande helped supplement already existing irrigation systems. Similar attempts were made to produce irrigated crops with ground water. Although these attempts were frequently successful, the problem of markets for the produce was not easily solved. The raising of garden truck and fruits was not practical because of the remoteness from the large cities. Improved pumping techniques after World War II, along with the crop subsidy program, has made possible the profitable production of irrigated crops, especially cotton.

Cotton remains New Mexico's most important cash crop. In 1958 it accounted for 58 per cent of the total value of all crops, being second only to cattle in terms of farm marketing receipts. With the

[24] Irion, ed., *Natural Resources of New Mexico*, 61.

growth of urban centers, truck crops have shown an increase and account for about 4 per cent of the total. Hay, wheat, and peanuts are the other significant crops.

The future of New Mexico's agriculture will depend largely upon how fast the ground water is depleted and the success of surface-water irrigation plans. The influx of people will insure a ready market for many crops. Staples such as cotton will remain important regardless of government programs, for New Mexico could probably raise cotton in direct competition with the deep South in a free market. Despite the past role of agriculture, however, it will continue to be of lesser importance in New Mexico than many other activities. Indicative of its decline is the fact that in 1958 New Mexico led all of the other states in the amount of land placed in the soil bank, most of this being in dry-farming counties along the east side. And the fact remains that personal income from the farm in recent years has usually been around 6 per cent of the total personal income of New Mexico, hardly enough to make agriculture significant.

XV - Industry, Labor, and Transportation

INDUSTRY HAS HAD LITTLE IMPORTANCE in the history of New Mexico. The little manufacturing that has been done was dictated by sheer necessity. Isolated from the centers of economic life from colonial times until the coming of the railroad, the people were compelled to make their own articles for household and farm use. Until very recently, the state's manufacturing was confined to the production of domestic goods, handicrafts, the processing of agricultural produce, or the finishing of wood products.

The preparation of hides and furs for home use and the weaving of woolen goods were common types of early manufacturing. Wood was in common use for many purposes. Objects such as hoes, spades, and other tools were made from it as well as most of the furniture and the doors of the adobe houses. The *carretas*, those indispensable vehicles of early transportation, were usually also of solid wood. As sawmills were not introduced until the American occupation, the wood was usually hewn to shape by hand with a clumsy hatchet.[1]

As would be expected in such a frontier environment, the items produced were crude and intended more for utilitarian purposes than for show. However, in some areas, the early New Mexican did excel as an artisan, especially in the making of jewelry. The bridles and saddles of the wealthy were richly trimmed with silver, and, as Gregg comments, "It would no doubt puzzle the 'cutest' yankee to fashion" the beautiful bridle-bits or spurs made by the average workman in New Mexico.[2]

[1] Twitchell, *Leading Facts*, II, 174.   [2] Gregg, *Commerce of the Prairies*, 144.

269

An interesting and unique home industry of the nineteenth century in New Mexico was the making of *santos*. The use of religious pictures and statues was an important part of the private devotions of the deeply religious people. In a land where priest and physician were lacking, the *santos* gave the people a feeling of security and were usually the only decorations in the poorer homes. A group of artisans known as *santeros* arose to fill this need. During the winter, the craftsman would make his statues and paintings, usually assisted by his family. When spring came, he traveled about selling his wares.[3] The arrival of the French missionaries sounded the death knell of the *santeros*. Because the clergy brought in with Bishop Lamy were interested in molding the church to conform to current European standards, they looked with disfavor upon this native expression of religious feeling.

The coming of the Americans with the Santa Fe trade made consumer goods available at prices that led to wider distribution, and the advent of the railroads (1879–82) further reduced the necessity of producing consumer goods, although many New Mexican communities remained self-sufficient until the advent of the motor car. Instead of manufacturing firms, large mercantile companies such as Seligman Brothers or the Bonds, who brought in needed finished articles and shipped out the state's raw materials, were a feature of New Mexico's economic life.

By 1899 the state had only 174 manufacturing establishments employing 2,490 workers. In the depression year of 1933 there were only 160 such establishments with 2,996 employees. The only manufacturing activity of any importance before World War II was the processing of forest products. Other activities were printing, the preparation of foods, and similar fields. It has only been since 1940 that industry has begun to be important in New Mexico.

Indicative of the growing importance of manufacturing to the state's economy is the fact that in 1939 manufacturing accounted for 7 per cent of non-agricultural hourly employment, while in 1955 it was about 10 per cent. In 1939 manufacturing provided 17 per cent of the total cash receipts from marketing, but by 1955 this fraction

[3] Rodríguez, "New Mexico in Transition," *NMHR*, Vol. XXIV (1949), 209-11.

had increased to 68 per cent.[4] The fact that agricultural earnings constituted 2.7 per cent of all earnings in 1956, whereas manufacturing wages and salaries amounted to 11.2 per cent, is further indication of the recent economic revolution in New Mexico. In 1958 manufacturing employed more than fifteen thousand workers and added $134,700,000 to cash receipts from sales.[5]

Much of the recent growth of manufacturing has been a direct result of the population influx into the state and the need to satisfy the increased consumer demands of the local market. Hence, the processors of foods and beverages and related industries have shown large gains in recent years. Of more lasting economic significance, however, have been the gains of industries which depend on the national or even the world market. These have been largely concentrated in the chemical industry, which has been closely related to the rise of mining and petroleum extraction.

Like New Mexico's transition from a predominantly rural to an urban state, the increase in manufacturing has been prompted by defense spending. The state's most important industry is ordnance work. (Of course, statistics in this area are not available for publication.) In addition to the actual ordnance work, there are countless parasitic industries, such as precision machine shops, electronics firms, factories for the manufacture of scientific and professional instruments, and others which supplement primary establishments.

The fact that ordnance accounts for the largest number of workers in the state's manufacturing points up the fact that New Mexico's largest industry is serving the federal government. In 1956 the government was the single largest source of personal income in New Mexico, accounting for 21.6 per cent of the total. Included were wages paid to military personnel and the civil employees at Los Alamos, White Sands, Sandia, and similar establishments.[6] Clovis reported that of its income of twenty-seven million dollars in 1957,

[4] Ralph L. Edgel, "Manufacturing Gains in New Mexico," Reprint from *New Mexico Business* (November, 1956).

[5] "Prosperity During Recession," Reprint from *New Mexico Business* (February, 1958), 25.

[6] Vicente T. Ximenes, "Where the Money Comes From," Reprint from *New Mexico Business* (August, 1957), 5.

nine million, or one-third, was furnished by nearby Cannon Air Force Base. The recent population growth of many cities has occurred as a result of an increased federal payroll.

Another important industry in New Mexico is catering to tourists. Some suggest that it could well be the single most significant economic activity of the state. Unfortunately, statistics either to prove or disprove this point are not available.

The natural scenic beauty of the mountains, the invigorating climate, and the glamour associated with the state's distinctive past and the combination of cultures have long attracted visitors to New Mexico. The modern tourist era began when the Santa Fe Railroad built its fabulous Montezuma Hotel near Las Vegas in 1881 as a resort for wealthy vacationers from the East. Excellent highways have recently made it possible for the nation's vacationing motorist to view the monuments of the state's past whether they are the relics of centuries-old Indian civilizations or the ruins of Civil War days. Cities like Santa Fe and Taos have preserved their distinctive characteristics in order more effectively to lure the tourist.

In addition to the interesting aspects of the man-made past, New Mexico's geological heritage has generously endowed it with unique features for the sight-seer. Rock formations resembling cities or battleships and other distinctive shapes abound, along with famous holes in the ground like Ice Cave and Carlsbad Caverns. The latter, a national monument, regularly attracts almost half a million visitors a year. Hunting and fishing provide attractions for those not interested in sight-seeing. Then, too, the location of the state makes it necessary for tourists to pass through it en route from the East to Southern California. The rows of motels, eating places, and filling stations along the highways testify to the economic importance of such visitors to New Mexico.

The Indians squatting outside the historic Governor's Palace in Santa Fe symbolize the role of the curio trade made possible by the visiting tourist. For the Indians, this market has provided an economic outlet for their ancient handicrafts. They sell hand-fashioned silver jewelry which frequently is enhanced by fine stones of turquoise or petrified wood. Hand-woven Navaho blankets, rugs, and jackets are also produced for the tourist. Unfortunately, many of

272

the Indians have gone to work for the city souvenir shops with a resulting decline in the beauty and originality of their work.

Labor in New Mexico

As would be expected in a predominantly agrarian society, organized labor has played an insignficant role in the economic history of New Mexico. Politically, labor has not been a factor at all, and New Mexico has been almost completely spared the disorders and turbulence that have marked the history of other Rocky Mountain states.

The lack of unionization can be attributed to several factors. First of all, the nature of the industries of the state has been such that they were not readily adaptable to labor organization. Usually employing only a few workmen and seldom relying upon skilled help, these industries have been very difficult to organize. Of more importance has been the role of the Spanish-American. The heritage of peonage, which was an ill-disguised form of slavery, made a lasting impression on the native worker. Used to oppression, these people were not susceptible to the arguments of labor leaders. As they were naturally individualistic, organization into unions did not appeal to them. And the extreme poverty of the natives made it easy to use them for strike-breaking purposes, as they were ready to work for a pittance. Their partial dependence on a plot of land made it possible for them to live on a lower cash income than the Anglo.

Also retarding the state's union movement has been its geographical location. With plenty of cheap labor available from Mexico, the employer has found it relatively easy to use Mexicans as "scabs" and has consistently encouraged their migration into the state, at times even illegally. The state's position as a haven for health seekers has also affected the union movement. Workers forced to live in the dry arid climate have usually been content with whatever employment they could get and have not been prepared to risk it by challenging the authority of their employers.

The typical rural frontier distrust of organized labor has remained strong in New Mexico. The deeply ingrained images of rugged individualism and free enterprise which have had such a strong appeal to the West have made a labor movement most unpopular. In fact, politicians are reluctant to boast that they have the support of organized labor, for such backing is usually a political kiss of death. Only Governor Arthur Hannett, of Gallup, who was elected in 1924 for a single term, has had the backing of organized labor.

Organized labor has been strongest in the mining regions of the state, and it has been in these areas where most of New Mexico's labor unrest has occurred. Gallup has been the scene of many futile efforts to organize an effective union capable of speaking for the workers. Raton, another coal-mining center, has likewise had a turbulent history. There, fear of the Industrial Workers of the World (I.W.W.) prompted the calling out of the National Guard in 1928. The United Mine Workers has made its greatest strides in the copper-mining districts of the southwestern part of the state.

Organized labor has made most of its gains in New Mexico since the advent of the New Deal, as in the rest of the nation. But the real establishment of organized labor in New Mexico has come since 1947, as a direct result of the growth of manufacturing. Since that date the number of workers employed in non-agricultural activities has increased 78.6 per cent. And as this increase has been largely in industries amenable to unionization, it can be anticipated that the role of organized labor within the state will be vastly more important in the future than it is now.

New Mexico has established various agencies and has passed many laws dealing with the protection of labor. A state labor commissioner performs the tasks normally associated with that office, but has never been provided with enough funds to carry out his duties properly. The state's unemployment compensation act is in conformity with the Federal Social Security Act of 1935 and is similar to that law. A workmen's compensation law was passed in 1929, and was then improved in the passage in 1945 of an occupational disease disablement act. Laws regulating the employment of women and children have also been enacted, but the statutes dealing with male employees have been inadequate. No minimum wage law had been passed at the time this book was written.

That organized labor has been treated as fairly as it has been in New Mexico has been largely due to the role of the Catholic church.

274

For example, there has not been a "right to work law," as in neighboring states. When one was proposed in 1948, the Archbishop of Santa Fe vigorously denounced it on the grounds that it would deal unionism a death blow and would interfere with the individual dignity of man and would be contrary to the spirit of the Constitution.[7] The position of the Roman Catholic church on labor is doubtless determined by the fact that most of its constituency are workmen. Hence, although New Mexico has not profited from pro-labor legislation, neither has it been unduly hampered by anti-labor legislation.

Transportation

The significant factor impeding industry and commerce in New Mexico has been lack of transportation. The great distances between the settlements and the absence of navigable rivers have made overland transportation necessary, and until the coming of the railroads, it was extremely expensive and slow. The Indians carried their own burdens or perhaps used dogs for such purposes. It was not until the coming of the Spaniards that improvements were made in the transport system of the area.

The first method used by the white man to carry goods in New Mexico, and one which lasted well into the nineteenth century, was the use of pack animals, usually mules. These sure-footed little beasts could carry loads up to four hundred pounds and were able to negotiate trails too precipitous for wagons or even horses. Their efficiency and endurance under all travel conditions was such as to make them almost legendary heroes in the history of the Southwest. It was customary for them to travel about fifteen miles without a halt, because once they would lie down, it was difficult for them to rise again with their heavy loads.

During the nineteenth century, travelers from the outside world were amazed at the efficiency of this method of transporting goods and have left many descriptions of it. In preparing for the day's journey two men handled each mule, first blindfolding the animal so as

[7] Frederick C. Irion, "Politics in New Mexico," 44. Nathaniel Wollman, *An Appraisal of New Mexico Labor Legislation.*

not to frighten it. After a soft piece of raw sheepskin had been thrown over its back, a woolen blanket was added, and then the packsaddle. The last was a large leather pouch padded with straw to prevent the packing cases from rubbing the animal's back. After the packsaddle had been securely fastened with a belt under the mule's belly, the load was added. If the load happened to be a single package, it was laid across the mule's back, but if it was composed of two items, they were placed lengthwise, side by side, and then were bound tightly with rawhide.[8] Six men usually were required to handle from forty to fifty mules. Such a system sufficed where the roads were difficult or where wagons were not available.

During the Spanish period, pack mules were used far more commonly than wagons, though the latter did make their appearance. The *carreta* became more common during the Mexican era. It was a clumsy vehicle constructed almost entirely of wood, there being little iron or steel available. The wheels were thick blocks of wood sawed from the same tree, with a hole in the middle through which the axle was passed. Seldom round, such wheels must have given a very rough ride. The axles were made of pine, and as there was no grease available, horrible sounds were emitted, and the mortality rate on axles was so high that at times it was necessary to half fill the cart with them. The bed and body of the cart was a rectangular block about four feet long and two and one-half feet wide. The wagon tongue was attached to the body with rawhide, and four posts were embedded in the corners of the body to hold the load. Oxen were attached by means of a yoke of timber placed directly on the heads of the oxen, behind the horns, and fastened with rawhide. Thus the cattle pushed, rather than pulled, heavy loads with their heads. These clumsy carts were the main means of transportation until the coming of the Americans.[9]

Once independence had been obtained from Spain, American-made wagons made their appearance, along with other types of goods.

---

[8] Gregg, *Commerce of the Prairies*, 128. For a complete treatment of early transportation see Max L. Moorhead, "Spanish Transportation in the Southwest 1540–1846," *NMHR*, Vol. XXXII (April, 1957).

[9] Meline, *Two Thousand Miles on Horseback*, 159; Moorhead, "Spanish Transportation in the Southwest," *NMHR*, Vol. XXXII (April, 1957), 111.

Gas fractionating plant near Gallup

Testing a rocket sled at Holloman A. F. B.

El Paso Natural Gas

Uranium mine near Grants

East Side ranch

Gila River Valley ranch

Clinton P. Anderson   Dennis Chavez

Four New Mexican Senators

Albert B. Fall   Bronson Cutting

Museum of New Mexico   *Library of Congre*

Albuquerque Chamber of Commerce

Modern Albuquerque

The Santa Fe Opera
Photograph by Tyler Dingee

The Santa Fe Opera

White Sands

Carlsbad Caverns

Elephant Butte Reservoir

They were of the Conestoga or Murphy types described below. Since the Americans returned with less bulky loads than they had brought, it became common practice for them to sell some of their wagons at Santa Fe or even at Chihuahua. Thus the primitive carts of the Mexicans were slowly replaced by the majestic prairie schooners.

The entry of the American heralded by General Kearny's invasion produced a change in the transportation system of New Mexico, for it led to the occupation of the area by federal troops, and supplying and equipping them provided a powerful incentive to commercial entrepreneurs. The scattered military stations found it impossible to obtain many of their supplies within New Mexico and so had to import them. These frontier garrisons required four types of material: ordnance supplies, military clothing and equipment, medical and hospital supplies, and subsistence stores. In the process of meeting these needs an elaborate supply system was built up, and frequently the trading posts at the government forts became supply centers for the civilian population as well as the military.[10]

The influx of people into California was to play a vital role in helping end the remoteness of New Mexico from the rest of the country. Once statehood had been attained and a sizeable population built up, it was obvious that some better means of transportation and communication with this remote outpost of the country would have to be established. In the early 1850's debates began on a possible railroad route, but as the construction of such a facility would take a long time, it was obvious that something of an intermediate nature was necessary. New Mexico added its pleas to those of California for some kind of federal assistance. Unfortunately, the efforts to establish improved mail and passenger transportation became enmeshed in the growing sectional controversy.

Bills were introduced into Congress favoring either a northern or southern route. In order to get some kind of action, western representatives decided to avoid the sectional issue. Therefore, a bill was written which authorized the postmaster-general to let the contract without specifying the route. When they were thus able to avoid a north-south controversy, the bill was passed authorizing gov-

[10] Averam B. Bender, "Military Transportation in the Southwest, 1848–1860," *NMHR*, Vol. XXXII (April, 1957).

ernment assistance in March, 1857, with only the jealous easterners opposing the measure.[11]

Out of the many bidders, Postmaster-General Brown selected the group headed by John Butterfield of Utica, New York. His company had the advantage of substantial financial backing as well as extensive experience in stagecoach operation. In addition, the fact that they were from New York would minimize the sectional issue. Then, too, the Butterfield syndicate acquiesced to Postmaster Brown's insistence that the route of the overland mail should go through St. Louis and Memphis to Fort Smith, Arkansas, then westward through El Paso and Fort Yuma to Los Angeles before swinging northward to San Francisco. For the government subsidy of $600,000 a year the company guaranteed semiweekly service, with a maximum distance of 2,795 miles being covered in twenty-five days or less.

Acceptance of the southern route created a storm of protest in the North. The *Chicago Tribune* spoke for many when it claimed this was "one of the greatest swindles perpetrated upon the country by the slaveholders."[12] In spite of the opposition and numerous threats to rescind the contract, John Butterfield went ahead with vigorous preparations to fulfill the contract terms. His Overland Mail Company, with a capital stock of $2,000,000, had enough money to meet contract obligations within the twelve-month time limit. The primary vehicle used was the Concord coach, 250 of them being purchased initially. In extensive use in the East and costing $1,400 each, they carried nine passengers as well as mail and some freight. Men to tend the way stations and to supervise operations were hired with considerable care. The drivers were selected with similar care, with the admonition to "remember, boys, nothing on God's earth must stop the United States mail!"[13]

The success of the Overland Mail Route went far toward eliminating the remoteness of New Mexico, the average travel time from Missouri to San Francisco being only twenty-one days. But the sec-

[11] Oscar Osburn Winther, "The Southern Overland Mail and Stagecoach Line 1857–1861," *NMHR*, Vol. XXXII (April, 1957).

[12] Quoted in Ray Allen Billington, *Westward Expansion*, 279.

[13] Quoted in *ibid.*, 281.

tional controversy was to cause the abandonment of Butterfield's enterprise when the Civil War began, and the line was transferred northward via Salt Lake City. Again New Mexico was cut off from the outside world.

Persons desiring to go to Santa Fe at first made their way with some trader willing to carry them. Then in 1849 a monthly coach traveled the Santa Fe Trail, the fare being $250 per passenger. Later the coaches were regularly established with monthly and weekly service, but again regular service was the goal rather than the fact, and service was more often than not interrupted. It took thirteen days of constant traveling to make the difficult run, and such a ride sorely tested the endurance of the traveler. As in the case of the Overland Mail, service was discontinued during the Civil War.[14]

After the war, travel was maintained with some degree of regularity. Even after the coming of the railroad in 1879 the stagecoach retained its importance in the territory. Stagecoaches were indispensable as feeder lines, and in 1882 there were still thirty-eight separate stagecoach lines, mainly serving the various mining centers.[15] Some of these stagecoach lines continued to carry passengers into the twentieth century, ceasing operations only when the motor car put them out of business. Many parts of the territory lacked established stagecoach lines and remained completely isolated, especially on the east side. In some areas it was necessary for a person to travel a great distance on horseback before finding a stage line that would take him to the railroad. It was also necessary to use heavy wagons to haul freight to supply the ranches or the small communities. Provisions were hauled usually with six mule teams drawing two wagons, though oxen were more commonly used to freight the heavier loads of lumber so badly needed in parts of the territory. Wool and other products were hauled to the railroad centers by similar means.

The chances of New Mexico being crossed by the first transcontinental railroad were lost as a result of the Civil War, the defeat of the South sounding the death knell of a proposed route through the

[14] Twitchell, *Leading Facts*, II, 139.
[15] William S. Wallace, "Stagecoaching in Territorial New Mexico," *NMHR*, Vol. XXXII (April, 1957).

southern part of the territory.[16] The first railroad to enter New Mexico was the Atchison, Topeka and Santa Fe, the road which ultimately came to dominate the state's traffic. Following approximately the route of the old Santa Fe Trail, the railroad built down through Raton Pass by means of a 200-foot tunnel. It narrowly missed losing this important entrance to New Mexico to the Denver and Rio Grande Western Railroad, which attempted to challenge the Santa Fe but was unsuccessful in its efforts. Hence, in 1879 New Mexico finally became a part of the rest of the United States.

A railroad town was established at Raton to provide the necessary repair shops and mine the needed coal. Building was continued southwestward, but by-passed the city of Santa Fe itself. Instead, a new railroad center was built near Albuquerque.

The Santa Fe had planned to use the southern route westward to California, and construction south from Albuquerque to Deming was continued. However, the Southern Pacific had reached El Paso in 1881 and did not take kindly to the efforts of the Santa Fe to parallel its route. To forestall ruinous competition, a temporary compromise was arranged between the two railroads.

The Santa Fe arranged with an affiliated road, The Atlantic and Pacific, to build westward from Albuquerque. Again, the road suffered vigorous competition, some of it unfair, from Huntington's Southern Pacifice line. In 1897, the Santa Fe completely took over the bankrupt Atlantic and Pacific and made a trade of part of its route with the Southern Pacific that settled the long-standing feud.

Perhaps a more serious competitor for New Mexico traffic than the Southern Pacific was the Denver and Rio Grande Railroad. This narrow-gauge line planned to build from Denver to Mexico City and immediately to divert traffic from the Santa Fe Trail through Denver. It built southward to Pueblo in 1872, but was handicapped by the panic of 1873 and failed to obtain the necessary right of way through Raton Pass. Thereupon, the road built westward to the mining areas of Colorado, considering them more attractive than the Mexican route. It ultimately extended its operations southward into

[16] William S. Greever, "Railway Development in the Southwest," *NMHR*, Vol. XXXII (April, 1957).

the northwestern part of New Mexico, however, even running a line to Santa Fe.

While the larger railroads were spanning western New Mexico, the eastern portion of the state was virtually isolated, as it was thought that there was not enough traffic there to make a railroad profitable. Those who believed in the irrigation potentiality of the southeastern corner of the state planned and built their own railroad under the leadership of James Hagerman. It was correctly forecast that such a line would bring in settlers, provide a market for agricultural produce, and, more important, allow the shipment of cattle to Kansas City instead of driving them overland. The first part of the Pecos Valley line was built from Eddy (Carlsbad) to Pecos, Texas, where it joined the Texas and Pacific Line.[17] Later it was extended northward to Roswell. But until the line could make the connection northward so that the cattle could be shipped to Kansas City, the Pecos Valley Railroad could not pay for itself. Construction of the extension from Roswell to Amarillo, Texas, was handicapped during the 1890's by the panic of 1893. This important segment of the railroad was only completed in 1899 through the assistance of the Santa Fe, which in 1901 acquired control of the Pecos Valley road.

With this acquisition the next step was to run a road westward to connect with the transcontinental line at Isleta. Such an extension, soon to be known as the Belen cutoff, would eliminate the long and hazardous journey through Raton Pass for the transcontinental trains and would constitute an obvious link in the system.

It was at first assumed that the division point would be Portales, but the greed of certain citizens of that town allegedly prompted the Santa Fe to change its mind and create some nineteen miles to the north the new town of Clovis, which was to be an important railway center.[18] The line was open to through trains in 1908 and soon was hauling the great bulk of the Santa Fe transcontinental traffic. In 1914, the Santa Fe built the last segment of its road be-

[17] Richard H. Gravel, "The Pecos Valley Railroad, 1889–1906" (M.A. thesis, Eastern New Mexico University, 1954).

[18] *Ibid.*, 64; Robinson, "History of Roosevelt County," 88; Eugene V. Sofford, "History of the Farwell, Texas Community" (M.A. thesis, Eastern New Mexico University, 1955), 14.

tween Galveston and Clovis, thereby linking New Mexico with the Gulf. Projected lines from Raton to Clovis were never constructed. Countless other feeder lines were built either to mines or to get timber to market, but none of them were significant and most of them were soon abandoned. Many of these roads were purchased by the Santa Fe. The Southern Pacific line from El Paso northward to Carrizozo, Vaughn, and Tucumcari has remained. At the latter point it has linked up with the Rock Island Road, which built into New Mexico in 1898.

Without the coming of the railroads, the subsequent development and influx of Anglos into New Mexico would have been impossible. They made possible settlement of many parts of the state which would otherwise have remained empty, and provided assurance that minerals, livestock, and crops could be shipped to market. The railroads effectively ended the centuries of isolation that had plagued New Mexico since the white man first came and made it a part of the world community.

282

XVI - The Urban Age

ACCORDING TO THE 1960 United States census, New Mexico had a population of 951,023, representing a growth of 39.6 per cent from the 681,187 of 1950. During the entire period from 1920 to the present the rate of growth has far exceeded that of the nation as a whole.[1] Despite the fact that the state usually leads the country in birth rate, the recent large growth must be attributed to migration into New Mexico. This influx has lessened the relative importance of the Spanish and the Indian populations, the distinct ethnic groups within the state. In 1940 persons having Spanish surnames made up about half of the population; by 1950 this figure had been reduced to 36.5 per cent. By 1960 the Spanish represented only 25 per cent of the state's total. The Indian population was 34,510 in 1940; 41,901 in 1950; and 56,255 in 1960, constituting a little more than 5 per cent of the total. There were 17,063 Negroes in New Mexico in 1960, more than twice the 1950 figure of 8,408.

New Mexico has traditionally been a predominantly rural state. But since World War II the situation has rapidly changed. In 1890 the state's population was 93.8 per cent rural, and as late as 1920 the figure was 82 per cent. Partly as a result of the depression, by 1940 the preponderance of those living on the farm had shrunk to 66.8 and by 1950 to only 49.8. In 1960 only 34.1 per cent were rural dwellers. And there is every indication that New Mexico will follow the nation in the trend toward urbanization.[2]

[1] Ralph L. Edgel, "New Mexico Population: Its Sizes and Its Changing Distribution," Reprint from *New Mexico Business*, Vol. XII (October, 1958).

[2] *Ibid.*, 14.

Indicative of this growing importance of the cities is the fact that in 1957 it was estimated that the state's farm income was only 5.8 per cent of the total. The days when New Mexico's prosperity rested mainly on weather conditions and the prices of sheep, wool, and cattle have passed. Now government defense spending and market conditions for oil and gas, for uranium, for copper, and for potash have more meaning in relation to the state's economy than the amount of rainfall.[3]

Of the 1960 population of 951,023, some 510,454 persons reside in seventeen metropolitan centers of more than 8,000 each. In fact, 27 per cent of the total (262,199) reside in a single county, Bernalillo (Albuquerque). Between 1950 and 1960 urban centers gained 284,590 in population, while the rural areas lost 3,705. This loss reflects the decline, in part, of farming and ranching in New Mexico. It also reflects the increased mechanization of the farm, which requires an ever smaller proportion of the population for agricultural work. In many instances farmers and ranchers have taken up residence in the city and commute to their land. This kind of movement is reflected in the substantial growth of a county seat while the county itself is actually losing population.

A number of factors have accounted for New Mexico's increase in population, as well as the pattern of urbanization. First of all, the federal projects during World War II required large tracts of inexpensive land, with which the state has been amply endowed. Since the war, the mining of uranium, the increase in oil and gas production, and the expansion of atomic research and special weapons programs, plus the retention of wartime military installations, have created greater economic opportunity, with a resulting influx of people. Besides, private industry has moved into New Mexico at an increasing rate.

The recent acceptance of air travel places the state close to either coast, ending its previous isolation. Much of modern manufacturing is in defense weapons, precision mechanisms, or electronic instruments; these items have a high value per unit of weight and can stand shipping costs. The clamor to decentralize industry in the event

[3] Ximenes, "Where the Money Comes From," *New Mexico Business*, Vol. XI (August, 1957), 2.

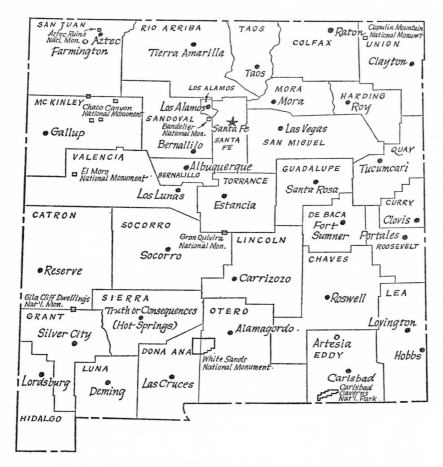

Modern New Mexico showing counties, principal cities,
national monuments, etc.

of a nuclear attack has aided New Mexico. Last, and surely not least, the immigration into the state can be partly attributed to the desirability of New Mexico as a place to live. To many, the vast area of the state, with its superb hunting and fishing, gives New Mexico the glamour of the frontier and makes it a place where one can "get away from it all." To others, the dry, invigorating climate, with its abundant sunshine, is the main attraction.

The rise of the cities to importance in New Mexico has been accompanied by the same problems which have occurred elsewhere. But just as the state is so different in other respects, it is also different in respect to its cities. The New Mexican has been famous for his ability to let time solve his problems for him. This is the "Land of Poco Tiempo." In a slow-moving rural environment, temporizing may be possible, but the problems of the modern city—sanitation, health, police and fire protection, utilities, planning and zoning—do not solve themselves. One observer claims that "most of New Mexico's cities at present are not doing outstanding jobs in providing the necessary facilities."[4]

The newcomers to New Mexico's cities, many of whom have come from the more advanced cities of the East and Middle West, expect the services they were used to "back home." The older citizens of the state, who have become accustomed to lower levels of service and lower payments in support of local government, do not want any changes that are going to cost them money. As a result, a basic conflict has developed between the inhabitants of the sprawling new housing developments and people living in more settled areas who resent the demands of these newcomers. Although it is difficult to analyze, this conflict is frequently between the Spanish and the Anglos. The former have seen their position in the state decline, and would not be human if they did not resent the individuals who are so rapidly changing "their" state. More frequently, though, the conflict is simply between the older New Mexican resident who, having no standard of comparison, is not aware that his current city government is unequal to the tasks brought by growth and the new arrival who expects some degree of efficiency. The full impact of

[4] Arthur A. Blumenfeld, "Some Aspects of Municipal Finance in New Mexico," reprint from *New Mexico Business*, Vol. XII (January, 1959), 2.

urbanization upon the Spanish-speaking citizens has doubtless been great, but it will take time for them to understand it fully.

Unfortunately, providing adequate city services requires money, lots of it. And money is what New Mexico's cities lack. The municipal sources of revenue are supplied by property taxes, gasoline taxes, city sales taxes, franchise taxes, and various special taxes. In addition, there are other miscellaneous sources of revenue for the hard-pressed cities, but these returns are not adequate to meet the increased needs. One authority says, "It is fairly clear that most New Mexican municipalities are financially unable to provide the services expected of modern cities, that the over-all problem of city financing has never been attacked, that the structure of revenues and expenditures is a make-shift arrangement which has been built on expediency, and that a complete overhauling is urgently needed to prevent civil decay and provide a sound basis for economic development."[5] Unlike the problems of the growing urban areas of other sections of the United States, the problems of the cities of New Mexico are new to the state and their solution will take time.

A study of the leading cities of New Mexico reveals much concerning the economic, political, and social changes of recent years. Among the urban centers with populations in excess of 8,000 are some historic places which trace their origins back to Spanish times. There are also others which are so young that many of the first settlers still survive—some of whom are not yet advanced in years.

Santa Fe, established in 1610, is not only the oldest city in the state, but also the oldest capital in the country. To many, Santa Fe is New Mexico. Located in a valley surrounded by snow-capped mountain peaks, its attractive natural setting is enhanced by the glamour of its history. The flags of Spain, Mexico, the Confederacy, and the United States have all flown over the city. Its ancient winding streets, its distinctive architecture, its Indians selling their wares, and its unique atmosphere have made Santa Fe a mecca for tourists. Today the major industry is the tourist trade.

In 1960 the population of Santa Fe was 34,676.[6] Second only to catering to the needs of the vacationer is the business of government.

[5] *Ibid.*, 13.
[6] The basic source for population statistics is the 1960 United States census.

As the state capital, the city is the nerve center of New Mexico. In addition to the actual employees of the state, whose numbers have grown in recent years, Santa Fe is also the residence of those individuals and firms which hope to do business with the state. What little manufacturing there is, is largely associated with the production of items for the tourist trade.

In 1960 the metropolitan area of Albuquerque had a population of 262,199, more than one-fourth of the state's total. Between 1920 and 1958 the rate of increase was 700 per cent,[7] while between 1950 and 1960 it was 80 per cent.

Founded in 1706, the "Duke City" was the center of trade, religion, and culture during Spanish days. Its use as a military post during the Mexican and early American periods insured its continuing importance. The coming of the railroad in 1881 made its central location more valuable. Albuquerque soon became the trade center for the prosperous irrigated valley farms, for the thriving wool industry, and, to some extent, for all of New Mexico. But perhaps its most important industry during the late territorial and early statehood years has been caring for the health-seekers. The city's excellent year-round climate has been a boon to persons suffering from pulmonary ailments. Much money was invested in private and public hospitals, and Albuquerque's reputation as a health resort has had a tremendous influence on the business and social structure.

Within the environs of the city can be found all of the nostalgia associated with the Spanish past. "Old Town" is the principal tourist magnet, though there are other small Spanish-type communities absorbed by the metropolitan area. The tourist, however, is not as conspicuous as in Santa Fe. The hustle and bustle of modern Albuquerque hide its heritage.

Although the city has doubtless grown simply as a result of the state's growth, "one particular activity has supplied the most persuasive prod to the economy since 1940—the expansion of federal spending."[8] This spending has taken place in the form of growing air bases and the establishment of facilities for atomic research and

[7] Edgel, "New Mexico Population," *New Mexico Business*, Vol. XII (October, 1958), 4.
[8] *Ibid.*, 9.

production. These activities have served as a magnet for related private industry. In addition, the presence of the University of New Mexico has helped Albuquerque retain its position as cultural leader.

Compared to Santa Fe and Albuquerque, Las Cruces is a virtual newcomer as a city, having been founded in 1848. In 1960, the city had a population of 29,367. Its original importance rested upon its location in the midst of a fertile irrigated plain along the Río Grande. Cotton has always been an important staple crop and attracted early settlers from Texas, who made the town a center of Confederate activity during the Civil War. In spite of its relative youth, the Spanish influence is evident in its architecture.

The recent growth in population of Las Cruces can be largely attributed to the growth of the government installations at White Sands Proving Ground and Holloman Field. Many residents are employed at these facilities and commute. In addition, the consistent prosperity of the surrounding irrigated lands has aided the city's growth. New Mexico State University, as the second institution of higher learning in the state, has likewise influenced growth. Finally, Las Cruces has become the commercial center of southwestern New Mexico and has thereby profited from the growth of the area.

Many of the urban centers of New Mexico in 1959 either did not exist twenty years ago or were merely sleepy ranch towns. World War II and its aftermath have wrought many changes. The most unique example is Los Alamos, a city with a population of 12,584 in 1960. Up until 1942 it was the site of a ranch school for boys. Then, because of its remote location and the ease with which it could be guarded, it became the center for nuclear research.[9]

In many respects Los Alamos is an extreme example of the influence of federal spending upon the recent development of New Mexico's cities. Here only the rugged countryside is evidence that one is even in the Southwest. The Spanish-Indian heritage is almost completely gone. The population is about what one would expect to find in such a community: very young, well-educated people, only recently arrived, without any permanent roots in New Mexico. Although Los Alamos, as a federally owned company town, may be

[9] "Los Alamos—Boom Town Under Control," *New Mexico Business*, Vol. VI (May, 1953).

an extreme example, most new housing areas of the state's mush-rooming cities are similar. And therein rests the basis for the cleav-age between the old and the new in the state.

Alamogordo was founded in 1898 as a railroad division point. Its proximity to the lumber areas and to marble provided the town with its main economic activities. In addition, the state school for the blind was located there. The attraction of nearby White Sands also made the tourist trade important.

Between 1950 and 1960 the population increased 220.3 per cent. By 1960 Alamogordo had a population of 21,723. This phenomenal increase has resulted from the recent emphasis upon missile research and development. The acceleration of this program has been concentrated at the White Sands Proving Grounds and the Air Force Missile Development Center at Holloman Air Force Base. The future of Alamogordo if such research were to be halted is problematical.

In 1960, Farmington had a population of 23,786. Its metropolitan area (San Juan County) had a population of 53,306. The rate of growth since 1950 was 191.4 per cent. Located where the Animas and La Plata rivers join the San Juan, the town was first settled by whites in 1875. The fertile soil of the river valleys and the avail-ability of water for irrigation led to the introduction of the fruit industry. This, along with sheep and cattle ranching, remained the primary economic activity of the area until recently.

Farmington's recent phenomenal growth (which will undoubtedly soon make it the second city in the state) has been made possible by the development of the oil and gas resources of the San Juan Basin. Although it was known as early as 1882 that there was oil in the region, improved technology following World War II has helped end the isolation of the area and make possible the exploitation of its resources. In addition to oil and gas, Farmington has also been the center of much uranium mining and processing.

Gallup was incorporated in 1891.[10] Located in the midst of coal fields, the city was an important mining center until the middle of the twentieth century. However, the dieselization of the railroads and increased use of oil and natural gas have dealt the coal mines a

---

[10] The early history of the Gallup area is ably presented in Telling, "New Mexican Frontiers; Gallup Area, 1881–1901."

near fatal blow. Unlike other coal mining regions in New Mexico, Gallup has been saved a decline, and instead has prospered, because of the discovery of uranium deposits near the city. The subsequent mining and milling of the uranium ores have more than offset the decline in coal mining. By 1960 the city's population was 14,089, and McKinley County had 37,209 inhabitants.

In the center of the Navaho country, Gallup has always been an important wool center. Of perhaps more economic importance than wool, however, is the tourist industry. The festivities of the Intertribal Indian Ceremonial in August attract thousands of tourists to the city and have earned Gallup repute as the "Indian Capital of America."

In 1940, Grants had a population of 814; in 1960, 10,274. The reason for this phenomenal growth is uranium. Originally a coaling station for the Santa Fe Railroad, Grants also was the trading center for the irrigation farmers of the area. In 1959 some 74 per cent of the city's workers were employed in mining or construction. The only other economic activity of importance is the tourist trade. Having as attractions the great lava flows, the perpetual Ice Cave, Acoma and Laguna pueblos, and Inscription Rock, Grants will always find the tourist trade economically important.

Among the most rapidly growing portions of New Mexico has been the southeastern corner. Within a relatively small area of the state seven significant urban centers have emerged. They are Roswell, Hobbs, Carlsbad, Clovis, Artesia, Lovington, and Portales. Looked on with ill-concealed contempt by the citizens of Albuquerque and Santa Fe, this region will doubtless play an increasingly important role in state affairs. The area is aptly nicknamed "Little Texas," and the residents there have little in common with the rest of New Mexico. Most of them are recent arrivals from Texas and bring with them the prejudices, the religion, and the outlook of Texas.[11] The Baptists rather than the Roman Catholics predominate, and in most of the above cities the Spanish are a minority huddled

---

[11] One author contends that the social, economic, and political domination of New Mexico's east side by former Texans has made the state a satellite of the Lone Star State. See David Hamilton, "Imperial Texas and its Satellite States," *Frontier* (August, 1959).

291

on "the other side of the tracks." The rapid population growth of the cities of the "East Side" can be attributed to the development of the oil and gas industry, the increase in federal spending for defense purposes, and the increase in irrigation through the exploitation of ground water.

Roswell, with a population of 39,593, was the second largest city in New Mexico, and its growth has been caused by all three of the factors listed above. Nearby Walker Air Force Base has brought considerable federal money and many migrants into Roswell. Recent exploitation of oil in the surrounding region has made the city a significant petroleum center. But agriculture, Roswell's original basis, has remained important. Because the city is located in a large artesian basin, irrigation has been carried on from both ground water and some surface water from the Pecos River.

Roswell was originally a watering point for cattlemen who drove their cattle northward to Fort Sumner. In 1869 a professional gambler, Van C. Smith, built a store at the site and named it for his father, Roswell Smith.[12] The attraction of water in the midst of such barren land soon made Roswell an important trading center. The discovery of an artesian water source in 1890 brought in farmers and fixed the early character of the community. Roswell was incorporated as a village in 1891, the same year that saw the beginning of what was to be the New Mexico Military Institute, the city's most outstanding educational institution.[13]

The population of Hobbs in 1960 was 26,275. The 1930 census showed it to be 598. In terms of percentages, Hobbs has easily been New Mexico's fastest-growing city. Within twenty years the sleepy trading village for cattle and sheep ranchers became an oil metropolis. The importance of oil to Hobbs is everywhere in evidence. Derricks and pumping apparatus abound, and several refineries and associated enterprises add to the city's payrolls. Some 90 per cent of New Mexico's oil production is in Lea County.

Deposits of potash located a few miles west of Hobbs provide a new industry. Accompanying the oil boom has been an agricultural

[12] James A. Hense, "The History of Roswell, New Mexico—1885–1908" (M.A. thesis, Eastern New Mexico University, 1955), 7.
[13] J. R. Kelly, *A History of New Mexico Military Institute.*

boom. Located among the oil wells are numerous water wells which pump the shallow underground water to the surface. The main crop of the area is cotton.

Another city of Lea County that has enjoyed a development similar to that of Hobbs is Lovington, the county seat. The 1950 census showed a population of 3,134, but in 1960 this had increased to 9,660. Again, the primary reason has been oil. Prior to 1940 there was only one small oil field located in northern Lea County. In 1950 the Denton pool northeast of Lovington was hit and in a short time had ninety-six flowing wells. Subsequent exploratory work has continued to extend the oil fields in the area. Lovington, like Hobbs, has a number of refineries, and there are other evidences of the importance of oil to its economy.

From its establishment in 1908, Lovington was primarily the center of a ranching community. Wool warehouses, cattle and sheep pens, and auction centers are still in use. The city annually ships 600,000 pounds of wool, 36,000 sheep, and 40,000 head of cattle. But the primary agricultural activity has become irrigated farming, with cotton the leading cash crop. Most of the exploitation of the ground water has occurred since the end of World War II.

The growth of Carlsbad has not been as spectacular as that of Hobbs and Lovington, having reached 25,541 in 1960. Potash is the primary explanation for the slow but steady increase in the city's size. New Mexico leads the nation in the production of potash, and most of it is mined near Carlsbad. The nearby location of Carlsbad Caverns makes the tourist trade important.[14] Irrigation agriculture has been significant in the area since the founding of Carlsbad in 1893. The lands cultivated as a result of the Carlsbad Reclamation Project have been increased by the recent utilization of ground water. Cotton is the most important single crop.

Artesia has also been influenced by the increase of potash mining, but its population increase has been mainly caused by oil. The city of 12,000 has thirty-eight oil fields within a radius of forty miles, with new discoveries constantly being made.

The name of the city comes from the vast artesian basin which

---

[14] The full story of how Carlsbad Caverns were developed as a tourist attraction is told in Ruth Caiar, *One Man's Dream: The Story of Jim White.*

underlies the area. Hundreds of artesian wells are used for irrigation. In addition to the usual raising of alfalfa and cotton in the area, Artesia serves as the commercial center for cattle and sheep ranchers.

Clovis was established in 1907 as a division point of the Santa Fe Railroad. It is the service center of a dry-farming area producing wheat, grain sorghums, and broomcorn. There is also some deep-well irrigation carried on. The city has several packing plants and is also an important center for trading in livestock that is to be shipped eastward for fattening.

The 1960 population of 23,713 has been the result of the establishment of Cannon Air Force Base nearby. In terms of payroll in the Clovis area, the air base is easily the leader. The only other significant economic activity is contributed by the Santa Fe Railroad.

Some of the prosperity brought to Clovis by the presence of Cannon Air Force Base has rubbed off on Portales, an adjacent city of 9,695. Many airmen choose to live in the latter city, since it is less crowded than Clovis. Even a little of the oil prosperity of Lea County has spilled over into Roosevelt County and aided Portales.

But the real reason for the existence of Portales has been its location within a saucer-like depression beneath which lies shallow ground water.[15] Since 1909 wells have been pumping this water to irrigate fields of cotton, peanuts, sweet potatoes, and alfalfa. Within the Portales Valley are 35,000 acres under cultivation, many having been added since 1945. Dry farming is carried on as in the Clovis area, but it is continuing to decline in importance. In addition to acting as the trade center and processor for the agricultural community, Portales is the home of the Eastern New Mexico University.

Las Vegas City (7,790) and Las Vegas Town (6,028), with a combined population of 13,818 in 1960, is one of the older cities of New Mexico that has not participated in the recent growth experienced in other parts of the state. Lacking federal expenditures, new mines, or agricultural improvements, it is the center of an area that has lost in population. Established in 1833, Las Vegas figured prominently in the nineteenth-century history of New Mexico.[16] After

[15] Portales has been described as having "the appearance of an oasis of a desert," Browne, "The Llano Estacado," 184.

[16] F. Stanley, *The Las Vegas Story.*

the coming of the railroad in 1879 the city shipped out in one year ten million dollars' worth of hides, wool, and pelts. The Montezuma Hotel at adjacent Hot Springs was built by the Santa Fe Railroad as the first of its lush mountain resorts in 1882. Today, the hotel is a Catholic seminary. About 1900, Las Vegas began to lose its commercial prestige, a process of decline which has continued. The city is the home of the New Mexico Highlands University and the New Mexico State Hospital.

Raton, with a 1960 population of 8,146, has suffered a fate similar to that of Las Vegas. Colfax County as a whole suffered a 17.6 per cent population loss between 1950 and 1960. This loss has resulted mainly from the decline in coal production in the area caused by the conversion of the railroads to diesel power. Raton is the trade and service center for the surrounding ranches and farms. Its location at the foot of Raton Pass and at the entry to the vacation spots of northern New Mexico has insured the importance of the tourist trade. Like Las Vegas, Raton is a community where the Spanish influence still predominates.

The foregoing summary of the leading cities of New Mexico should give some idea of the impact recent urbanization has had upon the state. There is no question that the move to the city will continue, and the small isolated villages which have been losing population will soon cease to exist; and with their passing and the decline of the ranch and farm, the distinctive character that is New Mexico's can easily be lost in the new cities.

295

XVII - Things Political

To UNDERSTAND PROPERLY THE POLITICS of New Mexico it is necessary to remember that the state "may be in the United States but
is not of the United States," for the political history of New Mexico
is unlike that of any other of the fifty states.

New Mexico is one of the last frontiers in politics, just as it is in
many other areas. Here, politics are conducted in the vigorous manner of the Jacksonian era. Competition for office on all levels is keen,
and the electoral battles are bitterly fought. There is not the kind
of indifference to politics on the part of the average citizen that is
found in other states. If anything, the problem has been how to keep
the politically enthusiastic New Mexican from voting several times
in the same election.

Several factors have contributed to the distinct political problem
of the state. First of all, the principle that "to the victors belong the
spoils" is very much in operation. To the winning faction goes the
right to hand out political patronage from top-level jobs to the distribution of license plates. As late as 1959 the business of state government almost came to a standstill when a new administration took
over.[1] Many attempts to establish a state merit system have been
made, but the patronage is too attractive for such an innovation. Of
course, there are never enough "political plums" for all of the party
faithful, and dissatisfaction over the spoils of office has spelled disaster for many a state administration. The Spanish-American, with
his close-knit family structure, has found especially attractive a

[1] Irion, "Politics in New Mexico," 51.

patronage system which can get his whole family on the state pay-roll. Then, too, as this group has been kept from realizing its fullest potential in the economic or social realms, they have found in politics an opportunity denied them elsewhere.

Until recently, the population of New Mexico was very sparse; hence a single vote counted a great deal.[2] Election to office came, not through the ability to deliver statesmanlike addresses, but rather through the ability to meet the voter face to face. The votes went to the man the New Mexican personally liked and to the man he felt would do the most for him. International affairs, or even na-tional affairs, for that matter, have failed to interest the New Mexi-can. The local issues, rather, have influenced him and have deter-mined his vote.

But the most significant factor molding the political pattern of New Mexico has been the Spanish-American.[3] He has given to the state's politics a distinct Latin-American flavor, without the armed revolutions.

The Spanish-American has been captivated by the great game of politics. Unlike the Anglo, who views politics as something repulsive and outside his interest, he turns eagerly to it. One observer even likens his interest to that of a religion: "Politics is a religion above the family. It streams into the *niño* from his mother's breasts; it is patted into the *tortilla*, and ladled with the *frijole*, masticated with every mouthful of chili, washed down with every glass of beer. Sacred, ingrained, ritualistic, mysterious, it is its race, color, creed— politics."[4]

Unfortunately, the enthusiasm of the Spanish-American for poli-tics has not always been matched with an understanding of demo-cratic practices. Just as the immigrants in the larger cities were once the prey of political bosses, so also have been the so-called "natives" of New Mexico. As the people were used to tyranny under the rule

[2] Thomas C. Donnelly, ed., *Rocky Mountain Politics*, 249.

[3] The role of the Spanish-speaking in New Mexico politics is ably treated in the following dissertations: Ernest Barksdale Fincher "The Spanish-American As a Political Factor in New Mexico, 1912–1950" (Ph.D. dissertation, New York Uni-versity, 1950); Walter, "A Study of Isolation and Social Change in Three Spanish Speaking Villages in New Mexico"; Russell, "State Regionalism in New Mexico."

[4] F. Stanley, *Socorro: the Oasis*, 121.

297

of Spain and Mexico, the trappings of democracy brought in by the Americans were not readily understood.

During territorial days the system of *patrón*-peon continued. The *patrón* was used to dominating the life of the peon, and he simply continued after the Americans came. In each county a few wealthy and influential Spanish families co-operated with the handful of Anglos to control the elections and handle governmental affairs. The illiterate peon voted for whom he was told to vote[5] and found little time to concern himself with politics as long as his *patrón* or the *hermano mayor* of the Penitentes looked after him.

Since the governor of the state has about five thousand jobs at his disposal, this office has always been the most significant in the state.[6] Candidates are measured in terms of their ability to deliver a choice appointment to the voter or to his family. Registration laws were nonexistent for most of the territorial period, and since being enacted, they have been lightly observed in New Mexico. Many stories have been told of how the large landholders used to vote their sheep when an election was in doubt. The open purchase of votes has continued to exist, with the price continuing to rise from one dollar to as much as ten dollars a vote more recently.

On one occasion the southwestern corner of the state, an Anglo mining community, so despaired of ever obtaining a decent administration at Santa Fe that its citizens petitioned Congress to let them secede and join Arizona.[7] Despite this obvious lack of confidence in the territorial government of New Mexico and the lack of amenities when it came to balloting, politics were probably little better or little worse than in other parts of the West.

During territorial days New Mexico was Republican. The reason for this preference was that the national administration was usually

[5] Thomas C. Donnelly, *The Government of New Mexico*, 15; Fincher, "Spanish-Americans as a Political Factor," 105.

[6] As the better positions in the economic areas have been closed to the Spanish-speaking in the past, they have sought an outlet for their talents in politics and government jobs. Hence, the candidate who can provide jobs gets the votes. Party loyalties have traditionally been extremely elastic, with politicians and voters shifting easily from one party to another. Walter, "A Study of Isolation and Social Change," 72–73.

[7] Naegle, "History of Silver City," 45.

in the hands of the Republicans, and with the President appointing the governor and the other territorial officials, patronage was also usually in Republican hands. Hence, an effective alliance came into being between the Anglo politicians and the leaders of the Spanish-Americans.

This political "wedding" made possible the concessions to the Spanish-Americans at the state constitutional convention which have enabled the native New Mexican to retain his unique position. Of the seventy-one Republican delegates at the convention, thirty-eight were Anglo and thirty-three were Spanish American. All of the twenty-nine Democrats were Anglos.

It is usual for minority groups to clamor to protect their interests, and the Spanish-Americans sought to preserve their heritage at the constitutional convention. They protected themselves by inserting into the constitution provisions to make the Spanish language equal to English. This has made necessary the printing of ballots, statutes, and other legal notices in both languages. It has also caused an interpreter system in the courts. Provision was made that education was to be provided in both languages and a normal school for Spanish teachers established. The net effect of these provisions has been to slow down the assimilation of the Spanish-speaking into Anglo society. Legislation which might attempt to break down racial lines is carefully avoided by both political parties.[8]

If the Spanish-Americans had been scattered through the state, they would have lost their political importance long ago. But they were settled in a relatively small area in the Upper Río Grande Valley, and the area which they dominate has been, until recently, the most important region of the state politically.[9] Adding to their domination of a specific area that makes them politically powerful is the fact that the Spanish-Americans are a distinct racial group. As such they are quite conscious of their historical and traditional background,[10] and the consciousness of their heritage has kept them to-

[8] One author contends that the parochialism of state politics was ensured by the special provisions written into the constitution. Russell, "State Regionalism in New Mexico."

[9] Donnelly, *Rocky Mountain Politics*, 232.

[10] Russell, "State Regionalism in New Mexico," 46.

gether in a vain effort to avoid being engulfed by the dynamic culture of the Anglo.

To prevent the racial issue from being raised at election time, rival candidates usually consist of Anglo running against Anglo and Spanish-American against one of his own race. Octaviano Larrazola is credited with working out this compromise as well as reserving certain state offices on a racial basis. In addition, the Anglo realizes that to the Spanish-American the game of politics is what counts, so traditionally the native New Mexican has been left in political control at the lower levels. However, only two of their race have been governor, and in general they have been discriminated against, the Anglos winning a disproportionate share of elective offices, as well as holding the lion's share of appointive jobs.[11]

Party Politics

Between 1912, when New Mexico became a state, and 1930, each of the major parties won four of the races for governor. Actually, however, politics were not that evenly divided. The first five legislatures, 1913 through 1921, were Republican. In 1923 and again in 1925 the Senate was Republican and the House was Democratic. From 1927 through 1931 both houses were Republican, indicating a very definite preference for the G.O.P. despite the gubernatorial contests. From 1932 to the present both houses have been Democratic, with one exception when the House went Republican by one vote. The presidential vote in New Mexico has always been cast for the winning candidate.

The source of Republican strength in the early days of statehood came from the support of the Spanish-Americans and the talents of several colorful leaders whose control of the G.O.P. was virtually undisputed.

Typical of those early Republican politicians were Thomas B. Catron and Albert B. Fall, who became New Mexico's first United States senators. Catron had arrived in the state in 1866, and until 1896 was virtually a dictator of his party. He "formed its policies,

[11] Fincher, "Spanish-Americans as a Political Factor," 267–68.

wrote its platforms, controlled its conventions, represented the party in national conventions, and was a member of the Republican National Committee."[12] With the appointment of Miguel Otero as territorial governor in 1897, Catron's absolute power began to wane, but he remained a force within party ranks until his death in 1921.

An able attorney, Catron recognized the confusion existing because of the loose wording of the old Spanish and Mexican land grants. Specializing in this type of legal work, he earned an enviable reputation as an expert on land grants, and also made himself one of the largest landowners in New Mexico. Frequently accused of unprofessional conduct as a lawyer, of corruption as a politician, and of intimidation and threats as a political boss, he made almost as many bitter enemies as he had close friends. Reflecting the methods Catron used to gain his ends was a letter he wrote to Bronson Cutting's uncle in which he threatened to have the legality of New Mexican bonds held by the Cutting family questioned unless the political attacks on him ceased.[13]

Despite Catron's unscrupulous tactics and domineering methods,[14] he had a deep affection for his adopted state. At considerable personal expense he collected material dealing with the early history of New Mexico and the Southwest. He purchased part of the library of Father Augustine Fischer, who was once the private secretary to the Emperor Maximilian. Fischer had spent some forty years gathering the material, especially on Mexican literature.[15]

Of more national renown, or, rather, ill repute, was Albert B. Fall. A Kentuckian, Fall arrived in Las Cruces in 1888, where his natural talents soon made him outstanding in the frontier community. Admitted to the bar soon after his arrival, he was appointed a judge of the territorial Supreme Court by President Cleveland in 1893. (He was originally a Democrat.) His personal popularity was so great

[12] Twitchell, *Leading Facts*, II, 520.

[13] Quoted in Patricia Cadigan Armstrong, *A Portrait of Bronson Cutting Through His Papers, 1910–1927*, 5.

[14] Governor Otero said of him: "Mr. Catron never remained friendly toward anyone whom he could not boss." Otero, *My Nine Years as Governor*, 145.

[15] Violle Heffernan, "Thomas Benton Catron" (M.A. thesis, University of New Mexico, 1940), 39; Mary Elizabeth Sluga, "The Political Life of Thomas Benton Catron, 1896–1921" (M.A. thesis, University of New Mexico, 1941), 4.

that local Republican leaders schemed to obtain a captain's commission for him when the Spanish-American War began, if Fall would only agree to leave the state permanently.[16]

Converted to Republicanism, Fall was one of the key men at the state constitutional convention in 1910. There he was depicted as an "astute, cool, suave defender of the special privileged interests."[17] His first election to the United States Senate took place amidst charges that bribery and intimidation had been used in the state legislature.[18] The New Mexican's friendship with Senator Harding was to result in a cabinet appointment, when the new Secretary of the Interior promptly "sold" the navy oil leases for $409,000, which he pocketed. The result was the Teapot Dome scandal, which brought New Mexican politics into the national limelight.[19]

Despite the fact that Fall had transferred his political talents from the state to the national level, he still retained a strong following in New Mexico. Wearing a large black hat and a string tie, "with a long drooping mustache, he looked like a stage sheriff of the Far West in the movies."[20] In addition to catering to his home state's preference for western attire, Fall had a winning personality well suited to the personal political contact of New Mexico. Friendships on the frontier were not easily come by nor were they easily broken. When Secret Service agents were investigating Fall, one of them was told in Alamogordo that "Albert Fall is a pretty big man around here. He's always taken care of us, and we aim to take care of him."[21] Along with being refused information, one agent had his briefcase stolen and was threatened with mob violence if he didn't leave the state immediately.

It was not easy for Senator Fall's New Mexico friends to believe that a man of his intelligence and record of service to the state would betray the public trust as he did. The full story will perhaps never be known, but recent scholarship, which is fairer to Fall than has been the case previously, throws additional light on the Teapot

[16] Otero, *My Nine Years as Governor*, 47–48.
[17] Quoted in Donnelly, *Government of New Mexico*, 41.
[18] Armstrong, *Bronson Cutting*, 13–14.
[19] M. R. Werner and John Starr, *Teapot Dome*, 29.
[20] *Ibid.*, 6.
[21] Quoted in *ibid.*, 170.

Dome scandal. David H. Stratton contends that Fall had the typical attitude of the western rugged individualist and that he would have leased the oil lands to Doheny and Sinclair without a monetary consideration. The New Mexican is depicted as a victim of circumstances who was taken in by his old friend, Doheny, and what started out as a loan became construed as a bribe when the oilman tore up the note Fall gave him for the initial $100,000. Once Fall found himself in that deep, he simply went the rest of the way, and then lied to protect Doheny when the matter came into the open.[22]

That the control of men like Thomas B. Catron, Albert B. Fall, and other G.O.P. leaders such as Solomon Luna, Holm Bursum, and Charles Springer was vastly reduced after statehood was more the result of factionalism in the Republican ranks than of the vigor of the Democratic opposition; and much of the resistance to the control of the "old guard" was furnished by Bronson Cutting, a Progressive in the Teddy Roosevelt mold.

Cutting, a member of an old-line eastern family, came to New Mexico in 1910 for reasons of health. Throwing his great talents and, of more importance, his great wealth into state politics, his leadership of the liberal reformist element among the Republicans kept the party in turmoil until his death in 1935. His own party would have liked to be rid of him, and although he flirted with the Democrats, he remained a Republican.

If Cutting had had a choice, he would undoubtedly have preferred a third party. His newspaper, the Santa Fe *New Mexican*, with its emphasis upon reform and exposure, was a thorn in the flesh of both parties and was a frequent target for libel suits. The role played by the Progressive Republicans doubtless helped elect a Democrat in the state's first gubernatorial contest. Difficult to evaluate, but still significant was the ground swell of Anglo resentment against the Republicans for what was considered a complete surrender to the Spanish-Americans at the constitutional convention. The victor, William C. McDonald, won by a margin of 3,017 votes. Hampered by a Republican legislature, his administration was uneventful. When the Republicans in 1916 nominated a member of the old guard, Holm Bursum, for governor, Cutting again led the Progressives into the

[22] Stratton, "Albert B. Fall and the Teapot Dome Affair," 294–96.

Democratic camp. To accomplish this, he was forced to break politically and personally with his good friend Theodore Roosevelt, who had supported the full state Republican ticket.

The Democrat, Ezequiel Cabeza de Baca, was the winner, and has remained the only Spanish-American native of New Mexico to be so honored. Unfortunately, De Baca died in February, 1917, just as his term was beginning. During the campaign the Democrats were accused of trying to perpetuate the McDonald administration by nominating the incumbent governor as lieutenant-governor and then selecting a Spanish-American who was known to be in ill health to make the race for governor. He would attract the Spanish-American vote and, if, as expected, De Baca was unable to complete his term, McDonald would succeed him. The accusations associated with this maneuver played a role in the election of a Republican lieutenant-governor.

Washington E. Lindsey, the lieutenant governor who succeeded De Baca, had been a Roosevelt Progressive, even being described as "the most progressive of the progressives."[23] At the constitutional convention he had advocated such liberal measures as the initiative, referendum, and recall, women's suffrage, the direct primary, and similar electoral reforms vigorously opposed by old guard Republicans. As would be expected, the effectiveness of his administration was reduced by the bitter factionalism that developed between the two wings of the party, particularly when Lindsey pressed for the enactment of a corrupt practices law, the Australian ballot, and other liberal legislation. However, the intra-party strife was perhaps overshadowed by the problems associated with the entry of the country into World War I.

Lindsey's failure to win renomination typified the bitterness of party rivalries and patronage problems faced by New Mexico's governors. As a progressive, Lindsey was unacceptable to the regular Republicans. In addition, the Governor's advocacy of the direct primary, the initiative, the referendum, the recall, and women's suffrage earned him the distrust of the Spanish-Americans and the large com-

[23] The definitive study of Lindsey is Ira C. Ihde, "Washington Ellsworth Lindsey, Third Governor of New Mexico" (Ph.D. dissertation, University of New Mexico, 1950).

mercial interests that were supporting the Republicans. Finally, Senator Fall, in order to insure his own re-election, dictated the selection of Octavian A. Larrazolo, an outstanding Spanish-American leader.

Though born in Old Mexico, Larrazolo was educated at St. Michael's College, in his adopted state. Originally destined for the priesthood, he turned to the study of law, opening an office in Las Vegas in 1895. A gifted speaker, he emerged as one of the most able leaders of the Spanish element.[24] Once a candidate for the territorial governorship on the Democratic ticket, the new governor had become a Republican in 1911 because he was convinced that his defeats for office were the result of Anglo opposition to a member of his race and that the Republican party would be more sympathetic and co-operative. While Solomon Luna, the great sheep baron, and other Spanish-American Republicans played down the racial issue, Larrazolo used it at every opportunity for political purposes. He recognized that ethnic considerations were far more important to the natives than party, and by using race he could insure election. More than likely the support of Republican Larrazolo had elected the Democrat De Baca in 1916, such cutting across party lines being common in New Mexican politics.

Larrazolo proved to be as difficult for the old guard as Lindsey had been. He had imbibed too freely of the heady wine of Wilsonian idealism, and his goals were not those of Republicans seeking "normalcy." The liberal program espoused by the Governor was similar to that of his predecessor except that he stressed improvement in bilingual instruction, free textbooks, and other measures that would aid the Spanish-Americans. Larrazolo's fervent defense of his race had always worried the Republican leaders, and many resented his preference for the Spanish-speaking when he dispensed state offices. Some party chieftains feared that a too earnest espousal of the racial issue would disrupt the party. The old guard found the excuse they had been seeking to get rid of the Governor when he vetoed a bill to repeal the state income tax that had been dictated by the mining interests of the state. Larrazolo was offered the nomination for Con-

[24] Alfred G. Cordova, "Octaviano Ambrosio Larrazolo, The Prophet of Transition in New Mexico; An Analysis of his Political Life" (M.A. thesis, University of New Mexico, 1950), 2.

gress instead—this would get him out of state politics—but he refused. Although his party later nominated him for the state Supreme Court in 1924 and elected him to the United States Senate in 1928, Larrazolo always felt that they had surrendered to the Anglo interests on the racial question.[25]

Judge Merritt C. Mechem was the choice of the party chieftains and won in the Republican year of 1920, despite much defection from party ranks led by Bronson Cutting. The new governor was virtually a political neophyte, but brought to the office a capacity for making friends even in the ranks of the opposition. Those who attacked Mechem did so on the grounds that he was the unwitting tool of the party bosses, which he doubtless was. Naturally, such a man was expected to heal the wounds created by the ousting of Larrazolo, and that was probably his principal attainment as governor.[26]

In 1922, James Hinkle of Roswell, a rancher and banker, won an easy victory over Dr. Charles L. Hill of Las Cruces, the Republican nominee. The newly elected Democrat had campaigned on a liberal platform which included a promise of a $2,000 property-tax exemption for veterans. The measure was passed, but the Hinkle administration brought much discord among the Democrats. Bronson Cutting, now a Democrat, and his powerful newspaper, the Santa Fe *New Mexican*, led the opposition. The main source of difficulty arose over the accusation that the Spanish-Americans had been discriminated against when the choice patronage plums were handed out. As one observer commented, "In New Mexico racial antagonism is the sword of Damocles ever hanging by a horse hair over the head of the politician."[27] With the sword falling on Hinkle, he was replaced as the Democratic nominee by Arthur T. Hannett of Gallup.

The campaign of 1924 was bitterly contested, and personal abuse and wild accusations on both sides reached extremes, even by New Mexico's standards. Hannett, a former mayor of Gallup, was accused of being the protector of brothel-keepers and others of like nature. Of more importance, Hannett was depicted as a wild-eyed

25 Fincher, "Spanish-Americans as a Political Factor," 216–17.

26 John Paul Seman, "The Administration of Governor Merritt Cramer Mechem (1921–1923)," (M.A. thesis, University of New Mexico, 1953), 97.

27 Robert Thompson and Charles Judah, *Arthur T. Hannett: Governor of New Mexico*, 5.

radical only a few steps removed from Moscow. (After all, he had been attorney for the New Mexico Federation of Labor.)

The Republican gubernatorial candidate was Manuel B. Otero, a very competent man. Hence, the Democrats concentrated their attack on the senatorial candidate, Holm Bursum. Although the incumbent Bursum was one of the old-style G.O.P. bosses, his activities had never been on a high plain. Then, too, Bursum suffered from having been an intimate and a colleague of Albert Fall, whose notoriety as secretary of the interior was being publicized in 1924. Hannett accused Fall of having brought so much disrepute that "New Mexico will be a hundred years living down the disgrace which he brought to the state."[28]

Victor by a scant margin of 199 votes, Hannett was hampered by the post-election contest of the results and the Republican control of the state senate. Nevertheless, his program was the most liberal of any New Mexico governor, and, although much of it failed of immediate passage, most of the measures he advocated were ultimately enacted into law. Hannett was not completely successful, because of the realities of New Mexico politics more than any other single factor.

Patronage, the Achilles' heel of many New Mexican governors, was likewise to rear its ugly head during the Hannett administration. Actually, the conflict that arose was more a fight between the Governor and Bronson Cutting for control of the Democratic party than an immediate squabble for the spoils of office.

Cutting, a man who spent his public career tilting at windmills, was incapable of compromise or of following any political leadership other than his own. At his best opposing something or somebody, he was by nature a radical and usually found himself the nucleus of a splinter group around which the disaffected could rally. Larrazolo was the last Republican acceptable to Cutting, so he marked time while he built up his own political following. Taking a keen interest in the American Legion within the state, he built that body up until it became the core of his support. And most of the Legion strength rested upon the Spanish-Americans. Early recognizing their role in New Mexico politics, Cutting identified himself with the Spanish-

[28] Quoted in *ibid.*, 9.

speaking, fought their battles, and was one of the few Anglos to be completely accepted by them. In many respects, Cutting, or "El Don," as he was affectionately dubbed by these supporters, was a typical old-line political boss such as was found in America's larger cities. He lent money generously to the Spanish-Americans, got them out of trouble with the law, obtained jobs for them, and attended their social functions with the same enthusiasm with which Boss Curley of Boston would attend an Irish wake. His enemies accuse him of cynically manipulating his constituents in order to influence them in the direction of his own selfish interests. His friends contend that Cutting was sincerely interested in the welfare of the Spanish-Americans and would have aided them even if he had not been in politics.

Nominally a Republican, Cutting had thrown his support to Hannett and doubtless helped provide the winning margin. After the election he realized that the Democratic governor was an astute politician who was using patronage to build up an administrative and political organization manned by his own loyal supporters. Such a political machine might some day be strong enough to win without the aid of the renegade Republicans. Thus the balance of power, which was the key to Cutting's political success, would be destroyed.[29] These fears were, of course, justified, as the roster of Hannett's supporters reads like a who's who of later New Mexico politics. Clinton Anderson, Dennis Chavez, Sam Bratton, and John Miles were included in this group.

The initial break between Hannett and Cutting came when the Governor refused to create a state labor commission and a veteran's bureau, which would have been subject to Cutting's control. The request was denied on the basis of economy, but Hannett really feared helping to augment the already formidable Cutting following. Other squabbles over appointments quickly followed, but the real fight came over the election code.

In his inaugural address Hannett had called attention to the need for reform of the state's election laws. He had appointed a bipartisan committee to study the problem and make the necessary recommendations. The need for such a measure arose from the fact that it

[29] Thompson and Judah, *Arthur T. Hannett*, 17.

had been permissible for an election judge to mark the ballot for a voter or to assist him to do so. Furthermore, the registration laws were most inadequate. The possibilities for manipulating the vote of a large segment of the populace were tremendous, and such skulduggery was, in fact, widely practiced. The Hannett Election Code provided for a system of registration, voting for office instead of a straight party ticket, the use of pen and ink to mark the ballot instead of pencil, and a prohibition against anyone except the voter marking the ballot or entering the voting booth.

As necessary as these measures were, they threatened the Republican control of the Spanish-American vote. Hence, the G.O.P. vigorously opposed the code. Cutting, who had always posed as the champion of all that was right, was in the same position as the Republicans regarding his Spanish following. One observer contended that "Cutting always managed to be on the side of God, even when he arrived there by purely Machiavellian means."[30] Therefore, he returned to the political fold from which he had so recently departed.

The attack on the Hannett Election Code was bigoted, sordid, and irresponsible. The racial issue was raised, the basic charge being that the Democrats were out to disenfranchise the natives. Fearful of innovation and naturally distrustful of the Anglos, the Spanish-speaking believed their friend Bronson Cutting when he told them that this was a plot against them. Larrazolo worked zealously with Cutting in these efforts. The fact that a bipartisan commission of leading citizens had made the recommendations and that the changes advocated were common laws in other states was ignored. Unfortunately, the racial issue in New Mexico is like the segregation issue in the South: it can be conveniently used to defeat much needed legislation, and it has been so used by both parties.

With Cutting back on their side, the Republicans had to find a gubernatorial candidate acceptable to all factions. In Richard C. Dillon they had such a man. From a humble beginning, Dillon had become a respected business manager. Usually associated with sheep and mercantile interests, he had built up many contacts in the state. Blessed with a capacity for winning friends and influencing people, he was a natural Republican candidate. As a businessman he was

[30] Quoted in Fincher, "Spanish-Americans as a Political Factor," 144.

"safe," he was not tainted by long association with the party bosses, and, of vital importance, he had not been in politics long enough to have run afoul of Bronson Cutting.

Whereas Hannett defended the election code, Dillon confined his campaign to "promising a business administration and praising virtue in the guise of prohibition, Calvin Coolidge, and New Mexico's sunshine."[31] Dillon was in favor of a Republican election code, but he failed to spell out what it would cover. Although Dillon won by a count of 56,294 to 52,543, the results were close when one considers the enmity stirred up by the election code and the return of Bronson Cutting and the Spanish-Americans to the Republicans.

Governor Dillon's indebtedness to Cutting was taken care of when death necessitated an interim appointment to the United States Senate. The maverick Republican, who had never before held office, was appointed because Dillon considered him a loyal friend and the best man for the job. Besides, his residence in Washington might confine his activities to the national scene and lessen his influence in state politics.[32]

As governor, Dillon had a clear and honorable, albeit empty, record. Being a businessman, he believed "that government governs best which governs least." Normally, the business of state government was turned over to subordinates on the business team. Only when the safety of the state was threatened did Governor Dillon act decisively. Fearing a deluge of Industrial Workers of the World from the North, he declared a state of insurrection along the Colorado–New Mexico border and called out the militia in January, 1928, to provide for the common defense. Later, it was proved that the danger was more imaginary than real, and even public opinion at the time found little justification for the action.[33]

The first man to be elected to a second term, Governor Dillon in 1928 was to preside at the liquidation of the Republican party in New Mexico. On the surface the issue that spelled disaster was innocuous enough. Beneath the surface was the old factional fight between the

[31] Thompson and Judah, *Arthur T. Hannett*, 31–32.

[32] Charles B. Judah, *Governor Richard C. Dillon: A Study in New Mexico Politics*, 26.

[33] Charles J. Bayard, "The Southern Colorado Coal Strike of 1927–1928 and New Mexico's Preventative Measures" (M.A. thesis, University of New Mexico, 1949).

Cutting progressives and the old guard for party control, with racial overtones.

The Republican platform had promised the creation of a state labor commissioner. Because Cutting had previously advocated such a post while Hannett was in the statehouse, the Republicans feared his motives. Apostasy has never been looked on with favor by any political party, least of all by the Republicans. Still distrustful of Cutting, the party chieftains decided to renege on their campaign promise.

When opposed, Cutting was a vigorous fighter, and this fight was the equal of that over the Hannett Election Code, although the issue was trivial by comparison. The duties of the labor commissioner consisted mainly of "furthering noble ends through good intentions and wishful thinking."[34] Had the bill been passed, Cutting would have been deprived of an issue over which to fight his party; however, the breach was destined to come, as Cutting had to have full control in any party to which he belonged.

The party split thus begun was completed in 1930, when again Cutting threw his support to the Democrats and insured the election of their candidate, Arthur Seligman. The Hannett Election Code returned to haunt the Republicans as their gubernatorial candidate, Judge G. H. Botts of the Supreme Court, had been a member of the bipartisan election committee that had made the original recommendations. This role damned him in the eyes of the Spanish-Americans, and the Democrats were not above exploiting it for their own ends.

The year 1930 was a pivotal one in New Mexico politics. Conspicuous has been the decline of Republican strength since. Edwin L. Mechem has been the only man of that party able to win in the race for governor (1950, 1952, 1956), and he failed to carry his ticket to power with him. The decline of the Republican party in New Mexico has been so complete that one party leader ruefully remarked, "It looks like we have become part of the Solid South."[35]

The loss of the support of the Spanish-speaking started the Republican decline. Cutting's hold upon the Spanish-Americans was so extensive that he probably took many of them into Democratic

[34] Judah, *Richard C. Dillon*, 30.
[35] Quoted in Donnelly, *Rocky Mountain Politics*, 243.

ranks. The rise of Senator Dennis Chavez to a position of power also helped pull them from their former allegiance. Of more importance has been the fact that the Democrats have had control of patronage. A poor state to begin with, New Mexico found its economy virtually paralyzed by the depression. At its height, the relief load in January, 1935, was 135,670 persons, or about one-third of the state's population. There was no question but that control of the relief administration was effectively used by the Democratic leaders as a political weapon.[36] Here was more patronage to dispense as the spoils of office than had ever existed before.

The population shifts since 1930 have also aided the decline of the Republican party. Most of the new migrants into the oil fields of the East Side were from Texas and were, naturally, Democrats. Those coming from other states usually were also members of the opposition in accordance with the national trend. Since 1945 the influx has been one of scientists, technicians, professional people, and skilled workmen who have been moving into the cities. It is possible that in the future this group will provide New Mexican Republicans with much-needed support. In any event, the deluge of the Anglos has led to a decline in importance of the Spanish-Americans in state politics. In fact, it is reasonable to assume that their status as a distinct political group will some day disappear.

The shift of the Spanish-speaking to the Democratic ranks since 1930 has helped that party take on some of the attributes of the earlier Republican party. The same tendency towards bitter factionalism exists. The same cries of "bossism" and accusations of corruption in state government have been raised, not always without foundation. Just as the Republicans once were more interested in holding office than in governing properly, so also have been the Democrats since 1930. Few occupants of the statehouse at Santa Fe have been men of real stature. There have been fewer real issues brought up than in earlier years. The problems before the state have simply been ignored.

Twenty years of uninterrupted tenure in the statehouse by the Democrats came to an end in 1950 when Edwin L. Mechem was elected by the Republicans. Re-elected in 1952 and again in 1956,

[36] *Ibid.*, 244.

Mechem has been a symbol of voter dissatisfaction with the too heavily entrenched Democrats. Since he has been the only member of his party in New Mexico to be elected to high office since 1930, his victories have been personal triumphs which have not benefited the party as a whole.[37] And with the Democrats in control of the state legislature and in other state offices, his accomplishment has been limited.

Fortunately, while politics in Santa Fe have been lack-luster since 1930, New Mexico's representatives in Washington have made worthwhile contributions on the national scene. Bronson Cutting was the only Republican from the state in either the House of Representatives or the Senate during this period. But, as in the past, his Republicanism was of his own brand. Cutting supported Franklin D. Roosevelt in 1932 and, in many respects, was more radical than the New Dealers.[38] Such tactics completed his estrangement from the New Mexican Republicans, and, since his death in an airplane accident in 1935, Cutting's followers have largely drifted into Democratic ranks. Thus far, no leader of his stature has appeared to lead the Republicans out of the New Mexican wilderness.

Carl Hatch, U. S. senator from 1933 to 1948, has been aptly described as "a lone wolf in New Mexico politics."[39] Remaining aloof from the intense factionalism of the Democrats, Hatch tended to ignore state politics and concentrated on his duties in Washington. He was a consistent New Deal liberal, and his most notable accomplishment was the Hatch Act, which limits the partisan political activity of federal employees. Accepting a federal judgeship in 1948, Hatch seemed eager to retire from the turmoil of political office.

Like so many others, Clinton P. Anderson came to New Mexico for reasons of health. A native of South Dakota, Anderson earned an enviable reputation as an Albuquerque newspaperman. A story is told that Albert B. Fall stormed into the offices of the *Albuquerque Journal* after a series of articles dealing with his activities as secre-

[37] Thomas A. Donnelly, "The 1950 Gubernatorial Campaign in New Mexico as Interpreted Through the State Press" (M.A. thesis, University of New Mexico, 1952).

[38] Billy G. Reid, "The Voice of New Mexico in the Seventy-third Congress" (M.A. thesis, Eastern New Mexico University, 1956), 20–22.

[39] Donnelly, *Rocky Mountain Politics*, 246.

313

tary of the interior had appeared, shouting, "Where's the son-of-a-bitch that's been printing all the lies about me?"

Anderson rose from his desk to confront the irate Fall and mildly answered him, saying, "I'm the man, and I don't print lies."

As congressman from 1941 to 1945, as secretary of agriculture from 1945 to 1948, and as a senator since 1948, Clinton Anderson has emerged as one of the nation's outstanding statesmen. Particularly important for his work on the Atomic Energy Commission, Anderson has been frequently mentioned as possible vice-presidential timber. With his growth in national stature, Senator Anderson has taken an increasingly less active role in state politics.

The dominant figure in New Mexico politics for many years has been Dennis Chavez. After a long career in state politics, Chavez was elected New Mexico's lone congressman in 1930. Re-elected to the House in 1932, he challenged Cutting for the Senate in 1934 and lost in a close race. Chavez challenged "El Don" because he wanted to succeed him as the political leader of the Spanish-Americans of the state. Upon Cutting's death he was appointed his successor and has served since 1935. Dennis Chavez is the last great champion of the rights of his people, though his control over them may not be as complete as that which Cutting enjoyed. He has defended the Spanish-speaking in every conceivable manner, and although he has regularly denounced racial intolerance, he has not been above using it to his own ends by raising the issue of race against others, as in the 1948 campaign. He has frequently been accused of supporting Republicans who were Spanish-Americans, although this was done behind the scenes. Chavez has consistently tried to get a Spanish-American into the governorship, even backing his brother in 1950, but to no avail. Much of the propaganda he hands out to his constituency is in Spanish. The fervent manner in which he backs the Spanish-speaking has antagonized many Anglos against Senator Chavez. This doubtless contributed to the narrow victory the Senator scored over Patrick Jay Hurley in the disputed election of 1952.

Early in his political career John Garner gave Chavez the following advice: "The men who are most successful as Congressmen are the ones who don't talk much. Good Congressmen are just errand boys for the people who elected them."[40] Judging by his senatorial career, Chavez has undoubtedly followed this admonition. For he has been most interested in being a good "errand boy" for New Mexico. In fact, the extensiveness of federal installations in the state has been generally credited to the efforts of Senator Chavez in Washington. A Republican businessman once remarked to this writer: "New Mexico's advancement during the war and after have been the result of the work of one man—Senator Chavez. Much as I dislike Democrats, I'm voting for him. This state needs him." Whenever the Air Force has contemplated abandoning, or even reducing, the size of one of its installations, Senator Chavez has acted promptly to apply the necessary political pressure. In a similar way he has labored tirelessly on behalf of the mining, farming, and ranching interests of New Mexico.

It is ironical that the talents of Senator Chavez as an "errand boy" have led to so many changes in the state's economy, for the new business enterprises and the federal installations have resulted in the huge influx of Anglos, and they in turn have lessened the political importance of the Spanish-Americans of New Mexico. Because of this decline in relative strength, Senator Chavez could very well be the last of his race to hold a Senate seat. But no matter what the future of New Mexican politics might be, a safe prediction is that they will continue to be interesting.

[40] Quoted in Reid, "The Voice of New Mexico," 137.

XVIII - Things Cultural

To A LARGE EXTENT this entire work has been a presentation of the culture of New Mexico. The original Indian civilization was blended with that of the Hispanic, but the Spaniards were in turn deeply influenced by the Indians with whom they came in contact. This distinctive civilization was, in its turn, modified by the impact of the Anglos during the nineteenth century. But just as the Spaniards were influenced by the Indians, so also have the Anglos been greatly affected by the culture they found in New Mexico. Many writers like to depict the modern culture of New Mexico as being a synthesis of the Indian, Spanish, and Anglo heritage.[1] Others have stressed the results of a conflict of culture as the concepts of one civilization have been challenged by those of another. In any event, the cultural heritage of modern New Mexico is unique among the fifty states.

In the middle of the twentieth century the culture of New Mexico presents a bewildering array of contrasts. In many respects, the frontier environment still exists. Many isolated areas remain; indeed, some of the most desirable recreation spots can be reached only on horse- or mule-back. In the shadow of the great metropolitan area of Albuquerque, Indians maintain a civilization unaffected by the twentieth century, in the 1950's, New Mexico was one of the nation's fastest-growing states, and its new wealth was largely associated with mining, the defense community, and the service trades. In many other states the Indian and Spanish heritage has been largely destroyed, but in New Mexico modern businessmen have helped preserve as

[1] Fergusson, *New Mexico: A Pageant of Three Peoples.*

316

much of the old as possible. Picturesque Spanish centers are maintained for the benefit of the tourists, and some Indians perform what were once serious tribal dances or ply their native crafts for the Easterners on their way through to California. The Spanish language, like the French in eastern Canada, has not only persisted, but promises to do so for a very long time to come, enriching the idiom and the civilization in ways which every observer can at least partially evaluate. The cowboy, who is vanishing like much else within the state, attempts to preserve his traditions in rodeos.

Nowhere is the contrast between the old and the new more evident than in the changes which are taking place among the Indians. It is not unusual to find beside a pueblo that is two centuries old a new vehicle that has recently arrived from Detroit. The Indian woman who emerges from her dwelling wearing the garb of her ancestors sees nothing incongruous about the television aerial that hooks heavenward from her roof.

Writing about the contemporary cultural scene in New Mexico presents a serious problem. It is a state in which three distinct cultures have existed for generations; but in a brief history it is impossible to treat all definitively. Yet to neglect a particular phase of modern, Indian, Spanish, or Anglo culture places one in the position of being open to criticism for his omission. Neither is it possible to discuss all of the individuals who have enriched the aesthetic life of the state. Trying to discuss only the few who have made lasting contributions and neglecting the work of lesser-known luminaries likewise leaves one open to attack. Further complications are encountered because New Mexico's climate has attracted many artists from the rest of the world. Some of these have been influenced by brief periods of residence within the state, while others do not reflect their sojourn in New Mexico at all.

The writers and artists of New Mexico have been influenced by the Indian heritage, the Spanish heritage, and the Anglo impact on these two ancient civilizations, with its introduction of cowboys and miners, and by the colorful conflicts of the nineteenth century. Of perhaps as much importance in New Mexican artistic themes has been the landscape itself. The state has been a Shangri-La for artists from other places. Many have come under the spell of the "Land

317

of Enchantment," seeking refuge from the world in its vastness and isolation. No other area of the United States presents such a variety of scenery or so many modes of life side by side. Writers have found themselves far better able to work in hidden mountain valleys than in the crowded cities of the East. Some of the authors influenced by New Mexico who later attained international distinction are D. H. Lawrence, Maxwell Anderson, and Willa Cather.

Literature

The literature of New Mexico can be divided into several categories. The archaeologists and ethnologists are joined by the students of Indian affairs and deserve to be grouped together. In a second category are those who write of the old New Mexico, who are enthralled with the Spanish way of life and are concerned with depicting the conflict of cultures that occurred when the Anglo entered. The literature dealing with the cowboy is the most extensive and, frequently, most useless. Finally, there are the historians, who are few in number when compared to the popular writers, but who have sought to tell the story of New Mexico objectively.

The first to till the rich archaeological soil of New Mexico was Adolph Bandelier. Born in Switzerland in 1848 and reared in Highland, Illinois, this remarkable man had little formal training for his life's work; in fact, he started life as a businessman. Convinced that writers of the nineteenth century had inaccurately portrayed the aboriginal society of North and South America and desiring to show the essential unity of all Indian civilizations, Bandelier came to New Mexico with a great deal of enthusiasm. His zeal was to go a long way toward making up for his lack of formal training, but was also to lead to a lack of thoroughness in his explorations. Historians have described him as an archaeologist, and archaeologists have called him a historian. Actually, Bandelier was an able propagandist in behalf of the natives of the Western Hemisphere.[2]

[2] Edgar F. Goad, "A Study of the Life of Adolph Francis Bandelier, With an Appraisal of His Contributions to American Anthropology and Related Sciences" (Ph.D. dissertation, University of Southern California, 1939); Lester Raines, *Writers and Writings of New Mexico*, 18.

A prolific writer, Bandelier published both books and articles. Although some of his studies have not stood the test of modern scholarship, they remain interesting. In his only novel, *The Delight Makers*, Bandelier sought to explain ancient life in the Rito de los Frijoles. It is an engaging romance which attributes the abandonment of the pueblo to feuds at home and attacks from without. This novel was a financial failure at the time it was published, but has since enjoyed considerable success.[3] If nothing else, Bandelier achieved lasting fame as a precursor of modern Indian archaeology. He provided an incentive for countless disciples, most of them better trained than he, who continued the work he had begun.

Of equal importance in charting unknown trails was the contemporary and frequent colleague of Bandelier, Charles F. Lummis.[4] Born in New England and receiving some education at Harvard, Lummis was primarily a journalist before being stricken with paralysis. Going to New Mexico to recuperate, he lived for five years in the Indian pueblo of Isleta, where he learned the Indian language and customs. Later, he traveled throughout the Indian country of the Southwest, Mexico, Central America, and South America. Like Bandelier, Lummis resists classification. He has been dubbed a journalist, historian, promoter, ethnologist, writer, archaeologist, poet, scholar, and folklorist. Perhaps all these titles are applicable to him. Not a journalistic writer in the modern sense, he nevertheless had an aptitude for picturesque phrasing, as when he described New Mexico as "the land of sun, silence, and adobe."[5] Among his works Lummis counted *A New Mexico David*, *The Land of Poco Tiempo*, and *Pueblo Indian Folktales*. In addition, he wrote many other books dealing with the Southwest and a number of articles.

Inclined to a greater degree of care in his research was Frank Hamilton Cushing, who first entered New Mexico in 1879 at the age of twenty-two with the Powell Archaeological Expedition. Remaining behind at Zuñi for six years, he made a careful study of that pueblo, and his accounts of Zuñi creation myths and folktales remain classics in the treasury of American mythology.

[3] *Ibid.*, 144.
[4] Edwin R. Bingham, *Charles F. Lummis—Editor of the Southwest*.
[5] *Ibid.*, 155.

Another early student of Indian civilization was Edgar Lee Hewett who conducted extensive archaeological exploration and excavation. Hewett was for many years director of the School of American Research in the Museum of New Mexico. He was the author of more than two hundred articles and reports, along with several books, the most significant of which are *Ancient Life in the American Southwest* and *Indians of the Río Grande Valley*. Hewett was a sympathetic interpreter of Indian life and attempted in his writings to make that life understandable to modern man.[6]

Much of the literature of New Mexico concerns the Indians, a great deal of it sympathetic and even sentimental, whether fictional or journalistic. Prominent among the writers who portrayed the Indians sympathetically is Mary Austin, who originally became famous as a champion of the Indians in California. Moving to Santa Fe in 1918, Miss Austin began a vigorous campaign to present the Indians in what she believed to be their proper perspective. Carefully studying their tribal organization, economy, and culture, she obtained an over-all knowledge of the Indians which gave her an insight into their character that enabled her to interpret them quite competently despite her obvious lack of objectivity.[7]

Among the followers of Mary Austin were Dane and Mary Roberts Coolidge, who both wrote extensively on western problems. Together they wrote *The Navaho Indian*, gathering most of the material directly from the natives themselves and recording Navaho legends and history, life and customs, arts and crafts, mythology and ceremonies.[8] In her *Dancing Gods*, Erna Fergusson has portrayed the ceremonials of Indians in Arizona and New Mexico. She analyzes the various dances, paying special attention to the purposes of the dances.[9] Oliver La Farge, in *Laughing Boy* and *Enemy Gods* and other works, depicts cultures in conflict, with the Indian looking back nostalgically to the time before the white man. Frank Waters, in *The Man Who Killed the Deer*, wrestled with the same problem

[6] *Ibid.*, 64; Mabel Major, Rebecca W. Smith, and T. M. Pearce, eds., *Southwest Heritage: A Literary History*, 74.

[7] T. M. Pearce, "Mary Austin and the Pattern of New Mexico," in T. M. Pearce and A. P. Thomason, eds., *Southwesterners Write*, 234.

[8] Lester Raines, *More New Mexico Writers and Writing*, 17.

[9] *Ibid.*, 47.

of the ability of the Indian to adjust himself to a world not of his own making.

Second only to the Indian way of life as a theme for New Mexico's writers has been the impact upon the Spanish heritage of the coming of the Anglo. The world of Spain's domination in New Mexico is often idealized. According to one author, *"Los pobres* of New Mexico are the luckiest poor people in America, if not in the world."[10] But, alas, this world in which everyone was happy was to be despoiled by the Anglo-American. Writers portray the confusion of the Spanish-American as his world fell down around his shoulders much the same way the South collapsed after the Civil War.

Perhaps the most highly acclaimed work of fiction with a New Mexico setting is Willa Cather's *Death Comes for the Archbishop.* Although primarily concerned with the problems of Bishop Lamy and his French clergy as they seek to bring about reforms within the church, it also contains much information about early customs and local traditions of New Mexico. The influence of her sojourn in New Mexico is also illustrated in Miss Cather's *The Professor's House.* A crucial episode in the life of the hero of this novel occurs with the discovery in a dream of a cliff-dweller village in a New Mexico canyon. Here is depicted a beautiful civilization that has been preserved when all other values are fading.[11]

Another national literary figure who was to select a New Mexico setting was Maxwell Anderson in his play *Night over Taos*. It presents the conflict between the old feudal system of the Spanish world and the new ideas of the Americans, during the Taos uprising in 1847.

Ruth Laughlin Barker's *Caballeros* romanticizes the quasi-feudal civilization of Spain and Mexico in the extreme. A more recent work by the same author, *The Wind Leaves No Shadow*, is a fictionalized biography of Doña Tules, the renowned madam and gambling house proprietor of Santa Fe. It is the result of careful research and gives an authentic picture of the habits and customs of the lower classes from which Doña Tules came. It also relates the story of Governor Armijo's alleged selling out to the Americans. A novel by Elliott Arnold, *The Time of the Gringo*, is based on the life of this same

[10] Ruth Laughlin Barker, *Caballeros*, 300.
[11] E. K. Brown, *Willa Cather, A Critical Biography*, 241.

governor. Arnold has his hero stress the futility of resistance to the Americans, claiming that the people have already been corrupted by the goods brought in by the Santa Fe traders and that it would be impossible to stop the soldiers. If we are successful once, Arnold's Armijo says, it will be to no avail, for it is "the time of the gringo."

The decline of the Spanish-American ethic as a result of contact with the Anglo is ably presented in Harvey Fergusson's *Blood of the Conquerors,* one of the earlier novels dealing with Spanish-American life. Though educated in the East and for a time a journalist in Washington, Mr. Fergusson returned to his native Albuquerque for the setting of most of his writings, In addition to eight novels, he has written books of nonfiction. In his *Rio Grande,* Fergusson describes a lost and isolated fragment of a past religious world as it comes into conflict with the dynamic Anglo civilization. Handicraft as well as the machine has some place in life in the Río Grande Valley; the primitive persists besides the civilized; and changeless mountains offer refuge to the three sons of change. *Home in the West* is an autobiography which also gives much information on New Mexico. *People and Power—A Study of Political Behavior* is in many respects an intellectual autobiography, analyzing the role of Mr. Fergusson in New Mexico politics and his tenure as a member of Congress. Harvey Fergusson justly deserves the designation of "first and foremost novelist native to New Mexico."

Erna Fergusson is the author of many non-fiction works dealing with New Mexico. These vary from a study of Albuquerque and an account of the fiestas of the state to a review of its unsolved murders and are climaxed by the author's general history of New Mexico. In all of her works, Miss Fergusson's devotion to the Indian-Spanish culture and her resentment at its corruption by the Anglos is evident.

In *The Life and Death of Little Joe* Robert Bright fictionally presents the problems of a small Spanish village, its ignorance and superstition, the power of the local storekeeper who has succeeded the *patrón,* and the final collapse of isolation when better roads and World War II comes. Another novel, *People of the Valley,* by Frank Waters, depicts the struggle between the Spanish and the Americans for the control of land in a small and isolated mountain valley and the impact of this struggle upon the individuals involved.

322

The most prolific and best known of recent New Mexico authors has been Paul Horgan. Horgan first won attention as a writer with a novel about upstate New York musicians, doubtless based upon some of his own experience in opera production. Then he returned to the New Mexico scene and wrote a very effective satire on the wealthy Anglos who were seeking culture in New Mexico. More and more he has become concerned with the impact of the changeless New Mexico scene upon people, and he has used this theme in a number of novels. Horgan's deep interest in the state is reflected in the gradual transition to the writing of popular history as he views it through the eyes of individuals. This technique is exemplified in *The Centuries of Santa Fe*. His greatest work to date is *Great River*, a fine example of a literary and literate popular history.

One of the most enduring themes of American fiction has been the exaltation of the cowboy, in which New Mexican fiction writers have shared. Most works dealing with life on the cattle range have presented an overdrawn, romantic, glamorous picture of the fate of the cowboy. The literary value of such works is limited because of the stereotyped style, unconvincing characters, and exaggerated plots. Fortunately, two outstanding writers of cowboy fiction picked New Mexico for their setting.

While practicing law in White Oaks, New Mexico, Emerson Hough became familiar with the frontier environment, and obviously must have had close contact with cowboys to have been able to relate intimate experiences so vividly. His two best known works are *Heart's Desire* and *North of Thirty-Six*, both of which have enjoyed enduring popularity.

One of the ablest and most widely read western writers influenced by New Mexico was Eugene Manlove Rhodes.[12] As a young man Rhodes rode the range in New Mexico, spending some twenty-five years in the cattle country, and he writes of cowboys and cattle with a realism that few have been able to equal. In fact, his fiction was so realistic that he didn't dare show his face in New Mexico because "certain characters have threatened to shoot him on sight." Knowing the West, he avoided over-drawn love attachments and glam-

[12] See W. H. Hutchinson, *A Bar Cross Man: The Life and Personal Writings of Eugene Manlove Rhodes*.

323

orous villains, for he knew these elements were not to be found. Rhodes' best known story is *Paso Por Aquí*. Another New Mexico resident who used cowboy themes was Lynn Riggs, a native Oklahoman who wrote the drama *Green Grow the Lilacs* which provided the basis for the famous musical *Oklahoma*.

There is a notable and unfortunate lack of recent first-rate historical accounts of New Mexico. This is well illustrated by the fact that the best history of the state is still that of Hubert Howe Bancroft, *A History of Arizona and New Mexico*, originally published in 1889. Other early general histories of New Mexico were contributed by L. Bradford Prince, Benjamin Read, Charles Coan, George F. Anderson, and Helen Haines. Although all suffer from certain deficiencies in basic research, the authors have stressed the phases of New Mexican history with which they were most familiar, and thus all have value. More a compiler than a historian was Ralph Emerson Twitchell. *The Leading Facts of New Mexico* (five volumes), *The Spanish Archives in New Mexico* (two volumes), and *Old Santa Fe Trail* all contain copies of documentary material as well as biographical sketches. Fortunately, the first half of the twentieth century has seen many sound monographs dealing with a variety of phases of New Mexico history. Based upon documentary material instead of secondary works or travel accounts, this body of worthwhile writing is fast filling the void that had existed in the story of New Mexico, thereby making possible general histories. Doctoral dissertations and master's theses have been written at universities throughout the country, and articles based upon a number of the latter have been published in the *New Mexico Historical Review* and other historical journals.

The story of Coronado's explorations has been definitively told in Herbert E. Bolton's *Coronado, Knight of the Pueblos and Plains*. The story of the actual founding of the first Spanish colonies is well handled by George P. Hammond in *Don Juan de Oñate and the Founding of New Mexico*. The involved history of the colonies during the seventeenth century is presented in a picturesque but still authentic fashion by France V. Scholes in a series of monographs. The story of the Indian uprising at the end of the century is presented by Charles Wilson Hackett in *The Revolt of the Pueblo Indians of New Mexico*.

Two studies relate the work of Don Diego de Vargas and the reconquest. They are J. Manuel Espinoza, *Crusaders of the Río Grande* and Jesse Bailey Bromilow, *Diego de Vargas and the Reconquest of New Mexico*. Though several brief studies exist, much of the story of the eighteenth century has yet to be written, the most significant work on the century being Alfred B. Thomas' *Forgotten Frontiers*, which evaluates the Indian policy of Don Juan Bautista de Anza, who was governor from 1777 to 1787.

Most of the material available on the first half of the nineteenth century consists of reports of travelers. The first of these was by Lieutenant Zebulon Pike, who wrote *A Tour Through the Interior Parts of New Spain* as a result of his forced stay in New Mexico between 1805 and 1807. After 1821 the inroads of the Americans led to an increase in travel literature. Books by James Ohio Pattie, Lewis H. Garrard, George Frederick Ruxton, and countless others yield valuable information about New Mexico. The finest book of all is Josiah Gregg's *Commerce of the Prairies*. First published in 1844, it not only covers the story of the traders as they made their way to Santa Fe, but is a worthwhile portrayal of much of the life of the area as the author saw it.

One of the earliest books after the American occupation was *El Gringo, or New Mexico and Her People*, published in 1854 by W. W. H. Davis. The accounts of native life that it contains have never been surpassed, and the book has remained a favorite. Many other works by Americans entering New Mexico were published, among them being works by Philip St. George Cooke, F. S. Edwards, J. T. Hughes, and perhaps the best of them all, Susan Shelby Magoffin's *Down the Santa Fe Trail*.

The period after 1846 is well covered by the accounts of several able historians. William A. Keleher has performed a service in many respects similar to that of Ralph Emerson Twitchell in that he is an able compiler of documentary material. His works include *Turmoil in New Mexico: 1846–1860, Violence in Lincoln County: 1869–1881*, and *Fabulous Frontier*, which is mainly a group of biographies of nineteenth-century political leaders. Loomis Morton Ganaway handles New Mexico's role in the Civil War in his *Sectional Controversy in New Mexico*.

Frank D. Reeves of the University of New Mexico is an able student of nineteenth-century Indian affairs. In addition to writing about the federal government's relations with Indians, Reeves has served as the editor of the *New Mexico Historical Review* and has thus made possible the publication of many accounts of New Mexico history. Although not a historian, Fray Angelico Chavez has contributed many studies dealing with religious folklore and a number of other matters.

The twentieth century has seen a large number of theses and dissertations dealing with political figures, specific aspects of recent history, economics, and the problems of conflicting cultures. A few of these have appeared in journals, but most remain unpublished. Accounts of recent economic and political events have been made available through the publications of the Division of Government Research and the Bureau of Business Affairs of the University of New Mexico.

The University of New Mexico Press is comparatively new in the book-publishing field, and it is difficult for a contemporary to assess the scope of its influence upon writing in New Mexico. Undoubtedly, however, since the publication of its first titles in 1933, it has stimulated interest in scholarly writing within the state and has prompted the publication of documentary materials related to the area.

Approximately half of its titles have dealt with historical, literary, and scientific aspects of the Southwest, but it has not limited itself to regional themes, and continues to publish books without regard for regional boundaries. Although nearly half of its authors have been drawn from the University of New Mexico, others have come from many parts of America and from foreign countries. Besides the American Southwest, its major fields of interest have been history, anthropology, biology, geology, and literature. Through the *New Mexico Quarterly*, it has been enabled to work with creative materials in the foreground of contemporary literature, especially in poetry and the short story. And through the University of New Mexico

Publications Series, it continues to make contributions to specialized scholarship.

Among the distinguished books published by the Press are the Coronado Historical Series, ten volumes of which have been released, including Herbert E. Bolton's *Coronado on the Turquoise Trail*, Hammond and Rey's *Oñate, Colonizer of New Mexico*, and Pfefferkorn's *Description of Sonora*. Another ambitious undertaking was Domínguez's *The Missions of New Mexico*, translated and annotated by Eleanor B. Adams and Fray Angelico Chavez. Books contributing to an understanding of Southwestern culture have included Frank McNitt's *Richard Wetherill: Anasazi*, Harold S. Colton's *Hopi Kachina Dolls*, Dorothy L. Pillsbury's *Roots in Adobe*, Olga Wright Smith's *Gold on the Desert*, and Douglas D. Martin's *Tombstone's Epitaph*.

First established in 1930 as the printing plant of the University with only occasional book publication, the University of New Mexico Press grew to full book-publishing stature under the directorship of Fred E. Harvey from 1933 to 1949. The present director, Roland Dickey, assumed the position following reorganization in 1956 and is himself the author of one of the Press's most distinguished titles, *New Mexico Village Arts*. Under Mr. Dickey's direction, the Press took over publication of the *New Mexico Quarterly*, established in 1931 as a general interest magazine, and of the scholarly monograph series, both of which had been separate departments. As the oldest and largest publishing house between Oklahoma and the West Coast, the University of New Mexico Press is in a singular position to publish and distribute books of regional and national interest.

The Arts in New Mexico

Painting is the only art outside of literature, in which New Mexico has attracted attention. The state has produced few outstanding painters in its own right. This has been true in spite of the fact that there are more resident artists per capita in New Mexico than in any other state in the Union.[13] The outsiders brought with them pre-

13 Fergusson, *New Mexico: A Pageant of Three Peoples*, 378.

conceived ideas of art, and many of them continued to paint street scenes of eastern cities or European villas long after they arrived. Gradually, artists began turning to New Mexico themes for inspiration. However, in spite of its large number of artists with national recognition, New Mexico has never developed a distinctive art tradition or even a school of artists.

The first painters to "discover" the attraction of New Mexico for artists were Burt Phillips and Ernest L. Blumenschein. While driving a camp wagon from Denver to Mexico City in order to paint landscape scenes, they stopped at Taos in the fall of 1898 and remained there. Fascinated by the grandeur of the mountaintops, the pines and aspen, and the open stretches of country, they saw endless opportunity for the landscape artist. The presence of Taos Pueblo with its primitive mode of life was an additional attraction. Phillips and Blumenschein publicized Taos, and it was not long before other artists made their way to this isolated village. About Taos there was material everywhere for the artist; mountains, plains, canyons, pueblos, and distinctive flora and fauna, as well as color and tradition. Soon a Taos Art Society was formed, and the fame of the Taos artists spread through the world.

Although Taos has remained a significant art center in New Mexico, with many artists residing there with studios to sell their wares to the tourists, it was inevitable that Santa Fe should succeed Taos. Since it was more readily accessible and not quite as primitive, many painters preferred to live there. But it was just as inevitable that Albuquerque should ultimately become the art center of the state, having the advantage of the Art Department of the University of New Mexico. Individual artists are scattered throughout the state, many still preferring relative isolation to the comforts of life in the city. Then, too, many other cities have earned respect as art centers. Roswell has an excellent museum as well as many resident artists, and museums are also to be found in many other cities.

The motives which have prompted artists to seek out New Mexico since 1898 are varied. Some doubtless preferred it because at one time the cost of living in some parts of the state was lower than in the metropolitan centers of the East. Others were health seekers. Perhaps the largest group could be defined as exploiters of the uniqueness of New Mexico. This group quickly learned that there was a ready market for paintings that depicted New Mexico scenes. The result was that many paintings of New Mexico scenes became stereotypes. The usual paintings were landscapes at different seasons of the year showing snow-capped mountain peaks, small streams, and man and his dwellings dwarfed by nature. Adobe houses, scenes in Spanish villages, or paintings of the distinctive dress of the Spanish-Americans became standard productions. Indians were painted in countless poses: painted warriors, Indian matrons grinding corn, the dances, the terraced lines of the pueblo, and the unique appearance of a hogan. The cowboy was treated in a similarly complete fashion. Finally, the history of New Mexico was depicted in countless scenes from the time of Coronado to the present.

The productions of these painters coincided very well with the literature of the day, which sought to romanticize the life of the Indian and the Spanish heritage. Readers of books with Indian themes were excellent prospects for the purchase of pictures showing the Indian with his deep-lined face and picturesque garb. The Santa Fe Railroad early discovered the importance of art as a means of selling prospective tourists train rides to New Mexico. Fred Harvey was likewise to be an early patron of New Mexican art. Valuable patronage was also provided by other business interests which saw the advantage of having the state depicted in a romantic light. Such commercialization led to a greater appreciation of all forms of Indian art and was instrumental in the creation of the flourishing business of selling native items to tourists. Indian pottery, blankets, baskets, and jewelry were soon purchased and sold to the tourist. In fact, it is impossible to overstate the influence of tourists on the culture of the Southwest, and of New Mexico in particular.[14]

Not all of the painters who came to New Mexico produced "calendar art." Many were recognized masters before they ever saw the state, and their work in depicting both native and landscape scenes greatly enriched the culture of the state. These serious artists knew life and sought to present it as they saw it in New Mexico.

Of all the painters associated with New Mexico who have attained national recognition, the greatest is a native son, Peter Hurd. He has

[14] Alice Marriott, *María: The Potter of San Ildefonso*, xix.

painted almost every scene one would expect of a native artist, perhaps reaching his greatest perfection in his landscape work. As is so frequently typical of artists in the arid regions, Peter Hurd has always given water a vital role in his work. A master craftsman, he studied many of the Renaissance masters to obtain better tools with which to work. The technique of tempera on yeso which Hurd has effectively used for many frescoes has been regarded as perhaps his most distinctive characteristic.[15]

As previously noted, the artistic renaissance in New Mexico led to an appreciation of and market for Indian art. Like primitive man everywhere, the New Mexican Indians found an outlet for the mysteries of life in their artistic portrayals; the designs and decorative symbols often reflect their deep religious feelings. Most of the symbols used in art decoration stress a desire for rain and a unity of life. However, geometric designs are placed on wares for sale while the sacred symbols are reserved for objects used in ceremonies.[16]

Without the potter's wheel and using only a primitive kiln, the Indians of New Mexico produced pottery of high quality and authentic beauty. Each village is distinguished by its own particular design. Most famous of the innovations in pottery was the work of María Martínez who, in 1921, discovered a means of etching dull black designs on a polished black background.[17] Similar to the work in pottery is the making of baskets. They, too, were originally only a utilitarian household item but have become symbols of the Indian artistic expression and are used in different ceremonies.

At one time most of the pueblos of New Mexico may have practiced weaving, but only the Navahos have preserved the art to any extent. It is assumed that the nomadic Navahos learned to weave from pueblo captives. However, the student soon outstripped the teacher, and the blankets of the Navaho became so famous that they were a much sought after item of trade during the nineteenth cen-

[15] *New Mexico Artist Series* No. 3 is a collection of essays on ten of the state's leading artists. George Wharton James, *Land of the Delight Makers*, has an interesting chapter, "Influence of New Mexico on Art." The origins of the Taos colony are treated in Grant, *When Old Trails Were New*.

[16] Coolidge, *The Rain-makers*, 112.

[17] The life of this remarkable woman is told in Marriott, *María: The Potter of San Ildefonso*.

tury. In order to encourage the commercial production of these blankets, "symbolic stories and designs were conceived by the traders, colors were dictated, and Navaho weaving was wholly directed into the tourist channel."[18] As a result of this forced evolution many present-day blankets lack both the quality and the authenticity of the early period.

Silversmithing is another distinctive art form associated with the Indians of New Mexico. Spanish silversmiths taught the Navahos how to work in metal, and they have distinguished themselves in this area. Today, the Indian makes buttons, beads, pins, rings, necklaces, earrings, belts, and ash trays. Before the advent of the workshop and production for the tourist, each piece was distinctive in shape and design. Some of the same type of design found in pottery, basketweaving, or in the weaving of blankets is worked into the pieces until they truly emerge as works of art.[19] Turquoise, the ancient precious stone of the southwestern Indian, has been used to embellish the silver work.

Unfortunately, the movement of the Indian silversmiths to the workshops has resulted in a loss of originality and has led to a standardization of the items produced. Fred Kabotie, a Hopi, has made exquisite jewelry and table silver, and thus has been able to resist the trend toward standardization. The United States Indian Arts and Crafts Board has also tried to preserve the authenticity of Indian jewelry by establishing standards in hand-worked silver.

Painting among the Indians of New Mexico had its origins in the dry sand paintings of the Navahos and Hopis. Such artistic portrayals were up to twelve feet in diameter and were used on altars and in the decoration of the kivas. Painting in water colors is a product of the twentieth century, and although it is new to them, Indians have already distinguished themselves in this form of artistic expression.

Music

Music completely envelopes the cultural expression of the American Indian. It played a part in every personal experience and was essen-

---

[18] *New Mexico: A Guide to the Colorful State*, 158.
[19] Catherine Oglesby, *Modern Primitive Arts*, 90.

tial to the expression of religious feeling.[20] There was a song and dance for every occasion among the New Mexican Indians. There were songs to accompany the grinding of corn, to the rain gods, in preparation for the hunt or the warpath, and for countless ceremonies. The songs varied from one tribe to another in the same way that European folk music differs among nations.

Civilized man has had difficulty in understanding Indian music because it is quite different from that of Europe. D. H. Lawrence suggests that to white men's ears "the Indian song sometimes sounds like a rather disagreeable howling around the drum."[21] The concept of harmony is foreign to the Indian mind, and he likewise has no conception of scales, modes, or tonality as such. The Indian's melodies tend to be similar to certain basic tonal patterns found among primitive peoples throughout the world.[22]

Fortunately, the rich ceremonial music of the Pueblos and the Navahos has been preserved by scholars, who have made recordings of them. Even the fact that the Indian ceremonials have become important tourist attractions has also helped to preserve native music as well as the native dance.

Spanish music of the seventeenth century has been preserved in New Mexico Spanish-American folk songs. The *alabado,* a religious ballad which was an outgrowth of the Gregorian chant, was brought to the New World and is still used by the Penitentes and sung at wakes. Other Spanish song forms have disappeared or have been merged in the contemporary *canciones populares,* literally, popular songs.[23] First to use Spanish songs was J. Donald Robb, of the University of New Mexico, who composed the opera *Little Joe.* Based upon the novel by Robert Bright, *The Life and Death of Little Joe,* it used twenty-five Spanish themes. The opera portrays the simplicity, suffering, and joys of a Penitente village. It is significant as the first opera with a New Mexico setting.[24] As is true of Indian music, recordings and transcriptions have been made in order to preserve the Spanish-American folk music that might otherwise disappear.

[20] Gilbert Chase, *America's Music: From the Pilgrims to the Present,* 403.
[21] *New Mexico Guide,* 141.
[22] Chase, *America's Music,* 407.
[23] *New Mexico Guide,* 144.
[24] Fergusson, *New Mexico: A Pageant of Three Peoples,* 380.

The Anglo music of the state has mainly been concentrated in the folk songs of the cowboy. The men who came to the range country of the Southwest brought with them the folk tunes of English and Scottish ballads, Irish reels, Negro spirituals, and the sentimental songs of the day. To these were added words which portrayed the loneliness, life, and death, in the cow country. The singing of this type of song helped relieve the monotony of the night watch and provided an important source of entertainment in a grim and cheerless world. Among the more important cowboy songs of New Mexico were "Little Joe the Wrangler," "When the Work's All Done This Fall," "Santa Fe Trail," and "Billy the Kid." Cowboy songs and similar folk music were used by Aaron Copland in the writing of the ballet score for "Billy the Kid."

In spite of the rich heritage of folk music in the state, New Mexico has been slow to develop music as a fine art. Most important in the recent advances in this respect has been the improvement of music education in the state. Departments of music in the state's institutions of higher learning, including a very active one at the University of New Mexico and a new one at New Mexico State University, have trained a large number of competent teachers, who in turn have raised the standards of both vocal and instrumental music. Today, many cities have bands, orchestras, and choral groups of quality.

The success of the Santa Fe Opera Association, which enters its sixth season in 1962, reflects the advancement of musical tastes in the state. The Santa Fe Opera brings some of the leading artists of the world to its open-air performances and has already made a foreign tour under State Department auspices, with Igor Stravinsky as guest conductor. In 1959 and 1960, Stravinsky also conducted soloists, chorus, and orchestra of the Santa Fe Opera in two programs of his own religious compositions held in the Cathedral of St. Francis in Santa Fe, under the patronage of the Most Rev. Edwin V. Byrne, Archbishop of Santa Fe.

The Albuquerque Symphony Orchestra, the Río Grande Symphony Orchestra at Santa Fe, and the Santa Fe Sinfonetta are three notable symphonies in New Mexico. There are chamber music seasons at Los Poblanos in Albuquerque, under the patronage of Albert G. Simms, and at the Museum of New Mexico, under the patronage of the Santa Fe Chamber Music Society. As in other states, annual concert series in all the leading cities of New Mexico are of great importance in bringing music to large numbers of people.

⟳ *Education* ⟳

Most of the problems which plagued education in New Mexico in an earlier period have largely been eliminated by the second half of the twentieth century.[25] The impact of geography which isolated students and made school attendance difficult, and in some instances impossible, has been lessened by the movement of population from the rural areas and small towns into the urban centers. Improved roads have made it easier to transport isolated school children.

The complications resulting from bilingual instruction in the public schools have also been reduced. Military service, employment in the cities, and other contacts with the Anglo world have reduced the number of children who are unable to use English. Those students who come from Spanish-speaking homes are normally kept in the first grade for two years, where they are taught enough English to proceed with their schooling in that tongue. Spanish is seldom taught in the elementary grades. English is the medium of instruction required by the Constitution, and the children are expected to adapt themselves to it. Whether forcing the Spanish-speaking children to accept the Anglo world in this manner is wise has been the subject of much controversy.

In spite of the large number of Roman Catholics in the state, the percentage of children in the parochial schools is surprisingly small. In 1959–60 there were 253,419 students in all the elementary and secondary schools, while only 20,948 were in Roman Catholic schools.[26]

In 1940 one observer indicted the state's schools when he commented, "The educational policy followed in New Mexico is startling in its ineptitude."[27] New Mexican education has been backward,

[25] See Chapter XI.
[26] S. H. Steinberg, ed., *The Statesman's Year-Book 1961–1962*, 732.
[27] Sanchez, *Forgotten People*, 33.

compared to that in older and wealthier states. But just as the state has changed in other ways, so also has its educational program been altered for the better since 1945. The increase in wealth has made available more money for educational purposes. The recent influx of population has brought the educational standards of other regions of the country to the state. As a result, New Mexican education compares favorably with the other states. For example, New Mexico expended $342 per pupil in average daily attendance in 1958 compared to a national average of $341.[28] The average salary paid elementary and secondary teachers in New Mexico for the same year was $5,039 in contrast to the national average of $4,703.[29] Unfortunately, such figures do not tell the full story. Most of the improvement has been in the urban centers, and there remain many rural and small-town school systems that are substandard.

New Mexico has eight state institutions of higher learning and two private colleges. The University of New Mexico at Albuquerque is the most important. With some 7,595 students, it has a complete educational program. New Mexico State University, at Las Cruces, was originally established as an agriculture and mechanical arts school, but now offers work in most fields. In 1961 it had an enrollment of 3,696 on campus and also sponsored community colleges in Alamogordo, Carlsbad, and Farmington. Located at Portales, Eastern New Mexico University is the youngest of the state schools, having been established in 1934, but is third in size with an enrollment of 2,080. Highlands University at Las Vegas was originally established as a normal school and in 1960 had an enrollment of 1,188. New Mexico Western University at Silver City was also begun for the training of teachers, and in 1960 had an enrollment of 705. New Mexico Institute of Technology at Socorro has 305 students and stresses work in mining and geological engineering. New Mexico Military Institute at Roswell is an academy and junior college. Originally founded as a teacher-training institution for the Spanish-Americans, Northern New Mexico College at El Rito is also an academy and junior college. All of the institutions of higher learning are under the budgetary con-

[28] *Statistical Abstract of the United States 1961*, 104.
[29] *Ibid.*, 120.

trol of the Board of Educational Finance.[30] The College of St. Joseph on the Río Grande at Albuquerque and St. Michaels College at Santa Fe are the only two private colleges in the state. Both stress the humanities and a liberal arts program. St. Michael's College had an enrollment of 576 in 1961 while that of the College of St. Joseph was 456.

Most of the faculty members in the colleges and universities either have come to New Mexico from other parts of the country or have received their academic training elsewhere. There has thus been a stimulating cultural interchange between New Mexico and the rest of the nation. The colleges have been a significant force in reducing the once prevalent provincialism of New Mexico and in making this western state culturally comparable to older and wealthier sections of the United States.

[30] Edward M. Goldberg, "The New Mexico Board of Educational Finance: A Study of State Supported Higher Education" (M.A. thesis, University of New Mexico, 1956).

Bibliography

 I. *Unpublished Materials*

1. DIARIES, LETTERS, ETC.

At the Bancroft Library, University of California, Berkeley:
Bancroft, Hubert Howe. Notes.
McCleave, William. "Papers and Memoirs as Officer, 1st Cavalry, California Volunteers." Civil War manuscript.

Huntington Library, San Marino, California:
Andrews, Ferdinand. "The Indians of Arizona and New Mexico." Manuscript.
Gunnison, John W. Papers.
Pease, C. T. "Report on Floods and Drainage, San Marcial, New Mexico, Elephant Butte Reservoir." Manuscript, October, 1925.
Ritch, William Gillette. Papers and scrapbook.
Schuyler, Walter Scribner. Papers.
Shrode, Maria Christina. "Diary of a Journey from Hopkins County, Texas, to San Diego, California, May 11–December 25, 1870." Manuscript.
Stanley, Lt. David Sloane. "Diary of an Expedition . . . . from Fort Smith, Arkansas . . . to San Diego (1853–1854)." Manuscript.
Ten Broeck, Peter Stuyvesant. Letterbook, February 10, 1850.

Irion, Frederick C. "Politics in New Mexico." Manuscript by the chairman of the Department of Government, University of New Mexico, 1959.

337

2. Doctoral Dissertations

Bingham, Edwin R. "Charles F. Lummis and His Magazine." University of California, Los Angeles, 1950. Also published under a different title.

Bohme, Frederick G. "A History of Italians in New Mexico." University of New Mexico, 1958.

Bromilow, Jessie E. "Don Diego de Vargas and the Reconquest of New Mexico, 1692–1704." University of Southern California, 1936. Also published under a different title: see Jessie Bromilow Bailey.

Browne, Walter Anderson. "The Llano Estacado: A Geographic Interpretation." George Peabody College, 1935.

Carroll, H. Bailey. "The Route of the Texan–Santa Fe Expedition." University of Texas, 1935.

Espinosa, José M. "Diego de Vargas and the Reconquest of New Mexico, 1691–1704." University of California, Berkeley, 1935. Also published under a different title.

Fincher, Ernest Barksdale. "The Spanish-Americans As a Political Factor in New Mexico, 1912–1950." New York University, 1950.

Ganaway, Loomis Morton. "New Mexico and the Sectional Controversy." Vanderbilt University, 1941. Also published under a different title.

Goad, Edgar F. "A Study of the Life of Adolph Francis Bandelier, With an Appraisal of His Contributions to American Anthropology and Related Sciences." University of Southern California, 1939.

Heyman, Max L. "Prudent Soldier: A Biography of Major General E. R. S. Canby, 1817–1873." University of California at Los Angeles, 1952.

Hughes, Willis B. "The Army and Stephen Watts Kearny in the West, 1819–1846." University of Minnesota, 1955.

Ihde, Ira C. "Washington Ellsworth Lindsey, Third Governor of New Mexico." University of New Mexico, 1950.

Moke, Irene A. "Santa Fe, New Mexico: A Study in Urban Geography." University of Nebraska, 1935.

Pearson, Jim Berry. "A New Mexico Gold Story—The Elizabethtown–Red River Area." University of Texas, 1955.

Russell, John C. "State Regionalism in New Mexico." Stanford University, 1938.

Scholes, France V. "Church and State in New Mexico in the Seventeenth Century." Harvard University, 1943.

Stratton, David H. "Albert B. Fall and the Teapot Dome Affair." University of Colorado, 1955.

Telling, Irving, Jr. "New Mexican Frontiers: A Social History of the Gallup Area, 1881–1901." Harvard University, 1953.

Walter, Paul A. F. "A Study of Isolation and Social Change in Three Spanish Speaking Villages of New Mexico." Stanford University, 1938.

Walz, Vina E. "A History of the El Paso Area, 1680–1692." University of New Mexico, 1951.

Woodward, Dorothy. "The Penitentes of New Mexico." Yale University, 1935.

3. MASTER'S THESES

Avant, Louis. "The History of Catholic Education in New Mexico Since the American Occupation." University of New Mexico, 1940.

Bacon, Frederick M. "Contributions of Catholic Religious Orders to Public Education in New Mexico Since the American Occupation." University of New Mexico, 1947.

Bayard, Charles J. "The Southern Colorado Coal Strike of 1927–1928 and New Mexico's Preventative Measures." University of New Mexico, 1949.

Bode, Gilbert R. "The Life and Times of George Wilkins Kendall." University of Texas, 1932.

Buchanan, John V. "Education in New Mexico During the Territorial Period, 1850–1912." University of Kentucky, 1933.

Buck, Lucius Edman. "An Inquiry into the History of Presbyterian Educational Missions in New Mexico." University of Southern California, 1949.

Carter, Rufus H., Jr. "A Historical Study of Floods Prior to 1892 in the Rio Grande Watershed, New Mexico." University of New Mexico, 1953.

Cason, Ina Wilson. "The Bent Brothers on the Frontier." University of New Mexico, 1939.

Caughey, John W. "Early Federal Relations with New Mexico." University of California, Berkeley, 1926.

Choate, Edward B. "History of the Capitan Community, 1890–1950." Eastern New Mexico University, 1954.

Corbin, Leland W. "The Educational Activities of the Evangelical United Brethren Church in New Mexico." University of New Mexico, 1949.

Cordova, Alfred G. "Octaviano Ambrosio Larrazolo, The Prophet of Transition in New Mexico: An Analysis of his Political Life." University of New Mexico, 1950.

Cornish, Beatrice Quijada. "The Preliminaries to the Oñate Expedition Into New Mexico." University of California, Berkeley, 1915.

Cunningham, William J. "The Control of Mineral Resources in New Mexico." University of New Mexico, 1950.

Dalager, Rudolph L. "The Espejo Expedition into New Mexico, 1582–1583." University of Southern California, 1929.

Donnelly, Thomas A. "The 1950 Gubernatorial Campaign in New Mexico as Interpreted Through the State Press." University of New Mexico, 1952.

Duke, Robert W. "Political History of San Juan County, New Mexico, 1876–1926." University of New Mexico, 1947.

Emerick, W. L. "Geology of the Golden Area, Santa Fe County, New Mexico." University of New Mexico, 1950.

Folmer, Henri. "French Expansion Toward New Mexico in the Eighteenth Century." University of Denver, 1939.

Foster, H. Mannis, "History of Mormon Settlements in Mexico and New Mexico." University of New Mexico, 1937.

Foster, James Monroe, Jr. "History of Fort Bascom, 1863–1870." Eastern New Mexico University, 1955.

Garcia, Enos E. "History of Education in Taos County." University of New Mexico, 1951.

Goldberg, Edward M. "The New Mexico Board of Educational Finance: A Study of State Supported Higher Education." University of New Mexico, 1956.

Gravel, Richard H. "The Pecos Valley Railroad, 1889–1906." Eastern New Mexico University, 1954.

Grubbs, Frank H. "Frank Bond: Gentleman Sheepherder of Northern New Mexico, 1883–1915." University of New Mexico, 1958.

Hagy, Jesse R. "The New Mexico Cattle Growers' Association, 1914–1934." University of New Mexico, 1951.

Hardisty, Clyde R. "The History of Public Secondary Education in New Mexico." University of New Mexico, 1949.

Healey, Ettie Miriam. "The New Mexico Missions in the Middle Eighteenth Century." University of California, Berkeley, 1922.

Heffernan, Violle. "Thomas Benton Catron." University of New Mexico, 1940.

Hense, James Albert. "The History of Roswell, New Mexico—1885–1908." Eastern New Mexico University, 1955.

Hinton, Harwood Perry, Jr. "John Simpson Chisum, 1877–1884." Columbia University, 1956.

Kahl, George Garry. "The Apaches in New Mexico: 1846–1861." University of California, Berkeley, 1928.

Kearney, Lelia. "French Intrusion into New Mexico After the Pueblo Revolt of 1680." Catholic University, 1939.

Kurrelmeyer, Louis H. "Recent Developments in the Economics of the Potash Industry, With Particular Reference to Carlsbad, New Mexico." University of New Mexico, 1950.

Kyle, Clara Ethel. "The Reconquest of New Mexico, 1680–1698." University of California, Berkeley, 1924.

Leopard, Donald D. "Joint Statehood: 1906." University of New Mexico, 1958.

Lewis, Victor Truman. "Texas and the Nation, 1845–1860." East Texas State Teacher's College, 1940.

McCord, T. T. "An Economic History of the Mescalero Apache Indians." University of New Mexico, 1946.

Maddox, Charles E. "The Statehood Policy of Albert J. Beveridge: 1901–1911." University of New Mexico, 1938.

Naegle, Conrad K. "The History of Silver City, New Mexico, 1870–1886." University of New Mexico, 1943.

Paulus, Lena. "Problems of the Private Land Grants of New Mexico." University of Pittsburgh, 1933.

Reid, Billy G. "The Voice of New Mexico in the Seventy-third Congress." Eastern New Mexico University, 1956.

Reiter, Robert Louis. "The History of Fort Union, New Mexico." University of California, Berkeley, 1953.

Robinson, Mary L. "History of Roosevelt County, New Mexico." University of Texas, 1947.

Seman, John Paul. "The Administration of Governor Merritt Cramer Mechem (1921–1923)." University of New Mexico, 1953.

Sjoberg, Gideon. "Culture Change as Revealed by a Study of Relief Clients of a Suburban New Mexico Community." University of New Mexico, 1947.

Sluga, Mary Elizabeth. "The Political Life of Thomas Benton Catron, 1896–1921." University of New Mexico, 1941.

Sofford, Eugene V. "History of the Farwell, Texas Community." Eastern New Mexico University, 1955.

341

Tate, Alta Mae. "History of the Mescalero Apache Indian Reservation from the Time of its Establishment to 1954." Eastern New Mexico University, 1955.

Wilferth, J. W. "An Economic History of Harding County, New Mexico." New Mexico Normal University (Highlands), 1933.

II. Published Materials

1. Books and Pamphlets

Abernethy, Thomas Perkins. *The Burr Conspiracy.* New York, 1954.

Aiton, Arthur S. *Antonio de Mendoza, First Viceroy of New Spain.* Durham, North Carolina, 1927.

Armstrong, Patricia Cadigan. *A Portrait of Bronson Cutting Through His Papers, 1910–1927.* Albuquerque, Division of Government Research, University of New Mexico, 1959.

Arnold, Elliott. *The Time of the Gringo.* New York, 1953.

Athearn, Robert G. *William Tecumseh Sherman and the Settling of the West.* Norman, 1956.

Bailey, Jessie Bromilow. *Diego de Vargas and the Reconquest of New Mexico.* Albuquerque, 1940. See also dissertations.

Bailey, Vernon. *Life Zones and Crop Zones of New Mexico.* Washington, 1913.

Bancroft, Hubert Howe. *Arizona and New Mexico, 1530–1888.* San Francisco, 1888.

Bandelier, Adolph F. *The Delight Makers.* New York, 1890, 1947.

Barker, Ruth Laughlin. *Caballeros.* New York, 1931.

Barreiro, Antonio. *Ojeada Sobre Nuevo-México.* Translated and edited by Lansing B. Bloom. Santa Fe, 1928.

Benavides, Alonso de. *The Memorial of Alonso de Benavides of 1630.* Translated and edited by Peter P. Forrestal. Washington, 1954.

Bender, Avery B. *The March of Empire.* Lawrence, Kansas, 1952.

Billington, Ray Allen. *Far Western Frontier, 1830–1860.* New York, 1956.

———. *Westward Expansion.* New York, 1949.

Bingham, Edwin R. *Charles F. Lummis—Editor of the Southwest.* San Marino, California, 1955. See also dissertations.

Bolton, Herbert E. *Coronado, Knight of Pueblo and Plains.* New York, 1949.

————. *The Spanish Borderlands*. New Haven, 1921.

————. *Wider Horizons of American History*. New York, 1939.

Bowers, Claude G. *Beveridge and the Progressive Era*. New York, 1932.

Bright, Robert. *The Life and Death of Little Joe*. Garden City, 1944.

Brown, E. K. *Willa Cather, A Critical Biography*. New York, 1953.

Caiar, Ruth, with Jim White, Jr. *One Man's Dream: The Story of Jim White—Discoverer and Explorer of Carlsbad Caverns*. New York, 1957.

Calhoun, James S. *The Official Correspondence of James S. Calhoun*. Edited by Annie Heloise Abel. Washington, 1915.

Calvin, Ross. *River of the Sun*. Albuquerque, 1946.

————. *Sky Determines*. New York, 1934.

Carroll, H. Bailey, and J. Villasana Haggard. *Three New Mexico Chronicles*. Albuquerque, 1942.

Cather, Willa. *Death Comes For the Archbishop*. New York, 1927.

Chase, Gilbert. *America's Music: From the Pilgrims to the Present*. New York, 1955.

Chavez, Fray Angelico, compiler. *Archives of the Archdiocese of Santa Fe*, 1678–1900. Washington, 1957.

————. *Origins of New Mexico Families*, 1598–1693 and 1693–1821. Santa Fe, 1954.

Chittenden, Hiram Martin. *The American Fur Trade of the Far West*. 3 vols. New York, 1935.

Cleaveland, Agnes Morley. *No Life For a Lady*. Boston, 1941.

————. *Satan's Paradise*. Boston, 1952.

Cleland, Robert Glass. *From Wilderness to Empire: A History of California*. Edited by Glenn S. Dumke. New York, 1959.

————. *This Reckless Breed of Men: The Trappers and Fur Traders of the Southwest*. New York, 1952.

Climatological Summary of New Mexico. Technical Report Number Five. State Engineer's office, Santa Fe, 1956.

————. Technical Report Number Six. Precipitation 1849–1954. State Engineer's Office, Santa Fe, 1956.

Coan, Charles F. *A History of New Mexico*. 3 vols. Chicago, 1925.

Colton, Ray C. *The Civil War in the Western Territories*. Norman, 1959.

Coolidge, Dane and Mary. *The Navajo Indians*. Boston, 1930.

————, Mary Roberts. *The Rain-makers: Indians of Arizona and New Mexico*. Boston, 1929.

Craig, Reginald S. *The Fighting Parson: the Biography of Colonel John M. Chivington*. Los Angeles, 1959.

343

Cremony, John C. *Life Among the Apaches*. San Francisco, 1868.

Crichton, Kyle. *Law and Order Limited, The Life of Elfego Baca*. Santa Fe, 1928.

Curry, George. *An Autobiography*, 1861–1947. Edited by H. B. Hening. Albuquerque, 1958.

Dale, Edward Everett. *Indians of the Southwest*. Norman, 1949.

——. *The Range Cattle Industry*. Norman, 1930.

Davis, W. W. H. *El Gringo, or New Mexico and Her People*. New York, 1857.

Day, A. Grove. *Coronado's Quest*. Berkeley, 1940.

De Korne, John C. *Navaho and Zuñi for Christ*. Grand Rapids, 1947.

Diffie, Bailey W. *Latin-American Civilization*. Harrisburg, Pa., 1945.

Dominguez, Francisco Atanasio. *The Missions of New Mexico, 1776*. Translated and edited by Eleanor B. Adams and Fray Angelico Chavez. Albuquerque, 1956.

Donnelly, Thomas C. *The Government of New Mexico*. Albuquerque, 1947.

——, editor. Rocky Mountain Politics. Albuquerque, 1940.

Duffus, R. L. *The Santa Fe Trail*. New York, 1930.

Edwards, Frank S. *A Campaign in New Mexico with Colonel Doniphan*. Philadelphia, 1847.

Espinosa, J. Manuel. *Crusaders of the Rio Grande*. Chicago, 1942. See also dissertations.

Falconer, Thomas. *Letters and Notes on the Texan Santa Fe Expedition*. Edited by F. W. Hodge. New York, 1930.

Fenneman, Nevin M. *Physiography of Western United States*. New York, 1931.

Fergusson, Erna. *Murder and Mystery in New Mexico*. Albuquerque, 1948.

——. *New Mexico: A Pageant of Three Peoples*. New York, 1951.

Fergusson, Harvey. *Home in the West*. New York, 1945.

——. *People and Power—A Study of Political Behavior*. New York, 1947.

——. *Rio Grande*. New York, 1933.

——. *The Blood of the Conquerors*. New York, 1921.

Fitzgerrell, J. J. *An Open Letter to President Cleveland*. Broadside in Huntington Library, San Marino, California. Las Vegas, New Mexico, January 15, 1886.

Folmer, Henri. *Franco-Spanish Rivalry in North America, 1542–1763*. San Francisco, 1953.

Forbes, Jack D. *Apache, Navaho, and Spaniard*. Norman, 1960.

Ganaway, Loomis Morton. *New Mexico and the Sectional Controversy 1846–1861*. Albuquerque, 1944. See also dissertations.

Garrard, Lewis H. *Wah-to-yah and the Taos Trail*. Edited by Ralph P. Bieber. Glendale, California, 1938.

Gladwin, Harold S. *A History of the Ancient Southwest*. Portland, Maine, 1957.

Grant, Blanche C. *When Old Trails were New, the Story of Taos*. New York, 1934.

Gregg, Josiah. *Commerce of the Prairies*. Edited by Max Moorhead. Norman, 1954.

Hackett, Charles Wilson, editor. *Revolt of the Pueblo Indians of New Mexico and Otermín's Attempted Reconquest, 1680–1682*. Albuquerque, 1942.

Hafen, LeRoy R. *History of Colorado*, 3 vols. Denver, 1927.

Haines, Helen. *History of New Mexico from the Spanish Conquest to the Present Time, 1530–1890*. New York, 1891.

Haley, J. Evetts. *Charles Goodnight, Cowman and Plainsman*. Norman, 1949.

———. *The XIT Ranch of Texas and the Early Days of the Llano Estacado*. Norman, 1953.

Hallenbeck, Cleve. *Land of the Conquistadores*. Caldwell, Idaho, 1950.

Hamele, Ottamar. *When Destiny Called*. San Antonio, 1948.

Hamilton, Holman. *Zachary Taylor: Soldier of the Republic*. Indianapolis, 1951.

Hamilton, Winifred Oldham. *Wagon Days in Red River*. N. p., 1947.

Hammond, George P. *Don Juan de Oñate and the Founding of New Mexico*. Santa Fe, 1927.

Hammond, George P., and Agapito Rey, eds. and trans. *The Gallegos Relation of the Rodríguez Expedition*. Santa Fe, 1927.

———, eds. and trans. *Narratives of the Coronado Expedition*. Albuquerque, 1940.

Harkey, Dee. *Mean as Hell*. Albuquerque, 1948.

Harper, Allan G., and Andrew R. Cordova, and Kalervo Obert. *Man and Resources in the Middle Rio Grande Valley*. Albuquerque, 1943.

Harwood, Thomas. *History of New Mexico Missions*. 2 vols. Albuquerque, 1908.

Hayes, A. A., Jr. *New Colorado and the Santa Fe Trail*. New York, 1880.

Henderson, Alice Corbin. *Brothers of Light*. New York, 1937.

Hewett, Edgar L. *Ancient Life in the American Southwest*. Indianapolis, 1930.

Hicks, John D. *The American Nation*. Boston, 1945.

Hodge, Frederick Webb. *Handbook of Indians North of Mexico*. 2 vols. Washington, 1907, 1912.

Hollister, Ovando J. *Boldly They Rode*. Lakewood, Colorado, 1949.

Hough, Emerson. *Heart's Desire*. New York, 1905.

Horgan, Paul. *Great River*. 2 vols. New York, 1954.

Hughes, Anne Eugenia. *Beginning of Spanish Settlement in the El Paso District*. Berkeley, 1914.

Hughes, John T. *Doniphan's Expedition*. Cincinnati, 1848.

Hutchinson, W. H. *The Life and Personal Writings of Eugene Manlove Rhodes*. Norman, 1956.

Irion, Frederick C. *Selected and Annotated Bibliography on Politics in New Mexico*. Santa Fe, 1959.

———, editor. *New Mexico and Its Natural Resources, 1900–2000*. Albuquerque, Division of Government Research of the University of New Mexico, 1959.

James, George W. *New Mexico: The Land of the Delight Makers*. Boston, 1920.

Judah, Charles B. *Governor Richard C. Dillon: A Study in New Mexico Politics*. Albuquerque, Division of Government Research of the University of New Mexico, 1948.

Keleher, William A. *Fabulous Frontier*. Santa Fe, 1945.

———. *The Maxwell Land Grant*. Santa Fe, 1942.

———. *Turmoil in New Mexico: 1846–1868*. Santa Fe, 1952.

———. *Violence in Lincoln County: 1869–1881*. Albuquerque, 1957.

Kelly, J. R. *A History of New Mexico Military Institute, 1891–1941*. Albuquerque, 1953.

Kendall, George W. *Narrative of the Texan Santa Fé Expedition*. New York, 1844.

Kerby, Robert L. *The Confederate Invasion of New Mexico, 1861–1862*. Los Angeles, 1958.

Kurrelmeyer, Louis H. *The Potash Industry*. Albuquerque, Division of Government Research of the University of New Mexico, 1951.

LaFarge, Oliver. *Santa Fe: The Autobiography of a Southwestern Town*. Norman, 1959.

Laughlin, Ruth. *The Wind Leaves No Shadow*. Caldwell, Idaho, 1956.

Lavender, David. *Bent's Fort*. New York, 1952.

Lockwood, Frank P. *The Apache Indians*. New York, 1938.

Loomis, Noel M. *The Texan–Santa Fe Pioneers.* Norman, 1958.

Lummis, Charles F. *The Land of Poco Tiempo.* New York, 1897.

Luxán, Pérez de. *Expedition into New Mexico Made by Antonio de Espejo, 1582–1583.* Translated and edited by George P. Hammond and Agapito Rey. Los Angeles, 1929.

McKee, Irving. *"Ben Hur" Wallace—The Life of General Lew Wallace.* Berkeley, 1947.

McKee, James Cooper. *Narrative of the Surrender at Fort Fillmore.* Prescott, A. T., 1878.

Magoffin, Susan Shelby. *Down the Santa Fe Trail and into Mexico: The Diary of Susan Shelby Magoffin.* Edited by Stella M. Drumm. New Haven, 1926.

Major, Mabel, Rebecca W. Smith, and T. M. Pierce, editors. *Southwest Heritage: A Literary History.* Albuquerque, 1948.

Marriott, Alice. *María: The Potter of San Ildefonso.* Norman, 1948.

Meline, James F. *Two Thousand Miles on Horseback.* New York, 1867.

Miller, Joseph, editor. *New Mexico: A Guide to the Colorful State.* New York, 1940, 1953.

Minerals Yearbook. United States Department of Interior, Bureau of Mines, Washington, various years.

Montoya, Juan de. *New Mexico in 1602: Juan de Montoya's Relation of the Discovery of New Mexico.* Translated and edited by George P. Hammond and Agapito Rey. Albuquerque, 1938.

Moorhead, Max L. *New Mexico's Royal Road: Trade and Travel on the Chihuahua Trail.* Norman, 1958.

Moulton, Edward. *New Mexico's Future: An Economic and Employment Appraisal.* Albuquerque, 1945.

New Mexico Artists. New Mexico Artist Series No. 3. Albuquerque, 1952.

New Mexico, State of. *Biennial Reports of the State Engineer.* Santa Fe, various years.

Northrop, Stuart A. *Minerals of New Mexico.* Albuquerque, 1959.

Oglesby, Catherine. *Modern Primitive Arts.* New York, 1939.

Osgood, Ernest S. *Day of the Cattleman.* Minneapolis, 1954.

Otero, Miguel Antonio. *My Life on the Frontier.* 2 vols. New York, 1935–39.

———. *My Nine Years as Governor of the Territory of New Mexico, 1897–1906.* Albuquerque, 1940.

Parker, William Thornton. *Annals at Old Fort Cummings.* Northampton, Mass., 1916.

Pattie, James Ohio. *Personal Narrative of a Voyage to the Pacific and in Mexico, June* 20, 1824–*August* 30, 1830. Vol. XVIII of Thwaites' *Early Westen Travels, q.v.*

Pearce, T. M., and A. P. Thomason, editors. *Southwesterners Write.* Albuquerque, 1953.

Pike, Zebulon M. *Expedition.* Edited by Elliott Coues. 3 vols. New York, 1895.

Poldervaart, Arie W. *Black-Robed Justice.* Albuquerque, 1948.

Prince, L. B. *Concise History of New Mexico.* Cedar Rapids, Iowa, 1912.

Pringle, Henry F. *Theodore Roosevelt.* New York, 1931.

Raine, William MacLeod. *Cattle, Cowboys, and Rangers.* New York, 1930.

Raines, Lester. *More New Mexicao Writers and Writing.* Las Vegas, 1935.

——. *Writers and Writings of New Mexico.* Las Vegas, 1934.

Richardson, James D. *A Compilation of the Messages and Papers of the Pesidents,* 1789–1897. 10 vols. Washington, 1896–99.

Richardson, Rupert N., and Carl Coke Rister. *The Greater Southwest.* Glendale, California, 1934.

Salpointe, Most Reverend J. B. *Soldiers of the Cross.* Banning, California, 1898.

Sanchez, George I. *Forgotten People: A Study of New Mexicans.* Albuquerque, 1940.

Saunders, Lyle. *A Guide to Materials Bearing on Cultural Relations in New Mexico.* Albuquerque, 1940.

Segale, Sister Blandina. *At the End of the Santa Fe Trail.* Columbus, Ohio, 1932.

Siegel, Stanley. *A Political History of the Texas Republic,* 1836–1845. Austin, 1956.

Smith, William E. *The Francis Preston Blair Family in Politics.* 2 vols. New York, 1933.

Sonnichsen, C. L. *The Mescalero Apaches.* Norman, 1958.

Stanley, F. [Stanley Francis Crocchioli]. *Desperadoes of New Mexico.* Denver, 1928.

——. *Fort Union.* Denver, 1953.

——. *The Las Vegas Story.* Denver, 1951.

——. *The Grant That Maxwell Bought.* Denver, 1952.

——. *Socorro: The Oasis.* Denver, 1950.

Statistical Abstract of the United States 1961. Washington, 1961.

Steinberg, S. H., editor. *The Statesman's Year-book* 1961–1962. New York, 1961.

Bibliography

Sunder, John E. *Bill Sublette: Mountain Man.* Norman, 1959.

Thomas, Alfred Barnaby. *Forgotten Frontiers: A Study of the Spanish Indian Policy of Don Juan Bautista de Anza, Governor of New Mexico., 1696–1727.* Norman, 1932.

Thompson, Robert, and Charles Judah. *Arthur T. Hannett: Governor of New Mexico.* Albuquerque, Division of Government Research of the University of New Mexico, 1950.

Thwaites, Reuben Gold. *Early Western Travels.* 32 vols. Cleveland, 1904–1907.

Twitchell, Ralph E. *Old Santa Fe, The Story of New Mexico's Ancient Capitol.* Santa Fe, 1925.

———. *The Leading Facts of New Mexican History.* 5 vols. Cedar Rapids, Iowa, 1911–17.

Underhill, Ruth. *The Navajos.* Norman, 1956.

United States Bureau & the Census. *U. S. Census of Population: 1960.* Vol. I, *Characteristics of the Population.* Part A, Number of Inhabitants. Washington, D. C., 1961.

Verrill, Alpheus H. *The American Indian: North, South, and Central America.* New York, 1927.

Vestal, Stanley (Walter Campbell). *Mountain Men.* Boston, 1937.

Villagra, Gaspar Perez de. *History of New Mexico.* Translated by Gilberto Espinosa. Los Angeles, 1933.

Wallace, Ernest, and E. Adamson Hoebel. *The Comanches.* Norman, 1952.

Wallace, Lew. *An Autobiography.* 2 vols. New York, 1906.

Wallace, Susan E. *The Land of the Pueblos.* New York, 1888.

Ward, Robert DeCourcy. *Climates of the United States.* Boston, 1925.

Warner, Louis H. *Archbishop Lamy.* Santa Fe, 1936.

Waters, Frank. *People of the Valley.* New York, 1941.

Webb, James J. *The Papers of James J. Webb, Santa Fe Trader, 1844–1861.* Edited by Ralph P. Bieber. St. Louis, Washington University Studies, vol. XI, 1924.

Webb, Walter Prescott. *The Great Plains.* Boston, 1931.

Wellman, Paul I. *Glory, God, and Gold.* Garden City, 1954.

Wentworth, Edward Norris. *America's Sheep Trails.* Ames, Iowa, 1948.

Werner M. R., and John Starr. *Teapot Dome.* New York, 1959.

White, C. Langdon, and George T. Renner. *Human Geography: An Ecological Study of Society.* New York, 1948.

Whitford, William C. *Colorado Volunteers in the Civil War.* Denver, 1906.

349

William, Mary W. *The People and Politics of Latin America*. Boston, 1945.

Wissler, Clark. *The American Indian*. New York, 1950.

Wollman, Nathaniel. *An Appraisal of New Mexico Labor Legislation*. Albuquerque: Division of Government Research of the University of New Mexico, 1950.

Wylls, Arthur S. *A History of Arizona*. Phoenix, 1950.

Ximenes, Vicente T. *Natural Gas in New Mexico*. *New Mexico Studies in Business and Economics* number 3. Albuquerque, Bureau of Business Research of the University of New Mexico, 1954.

2. ARTICLES

Baldwin, Percy M. "Fray Marcos De Niza and His Discovery of the Seven Cities of Cibola," *New Mexico Historical Review*, Vol. I (April, 1926).

Bender, Averam B. "Military Transportation in the Southwest, 1848–1860," *New Mexico Historical Review*, Vol. XXXII (April, 1957).

Binkley, William Campbell. "New Mexico and the Texas–Santa Fe Expedition," *Southwestern Historical Quarterly*, Vol. XXVII (October, 1923).

———. "The Question of Texan Jurisdiction in New Mexico Under the United States 1844–1850," *Southwestern Historical Quarterly*, Vol. XXIV (July, 1920).

Blumenfeld, Arthur A. "Oil and Gas, Three-Letter Words for Progress in New Mexico's San Juan Basin," *New Mexico Business*, Vol. X (September, 1957).

———. "Some Aspects of Municipal Finance in New Mexico," *New Mexico Business*, Vol. XII (January, 1959).

Campo, Arthur L. "Piñon as an Economic and Social Factor," *New Mexico Business Review*, Vol. II (October, 1932).

Chavez, Fray Angelico. "The Penitentes of New Mexico," *New Mexico Historical Review*, Vol. XXIX (April, 1954).

Clendenen, Clarence E. "General James Henry Carleton," *New Mexico Historical Review*, Vol. XXX (January, 1955).

Dargan, Marion, "New Mexico's Fight for Statehood," *New Mexico Historical Review*, Vols. XIV, XV, XVI, XVIII (1939, 1940, 1941, 1943).

Dunham, Harold H. "New Mexico Land Grants with Special Reference to the Title Papers of the Maxwell Grant," *New Mexico Historical Review*, Vol. XXX (January, 1955).

350

Edgel, Ralph L. "Manufacturing Gains in New Mexico," *New Mexico Business*, Vol. X (November, 1956).

———. "Mining in New Mexico," *New Mexico Business*, Vol. XII (August, 1958).

———. "New Mexico Population: Its Size and Its Changing Distribution," *New Mexico Business*, Vol. XII (October, 1958).

Francis, E. K. "Padre Martinez: A New Mexican Myth," *New Mexico Historical Review*, Vol. XXXI (October, 1956).

Greever, William S. "Railway Development in the Southwest," *New Mexico Historical Review*, Vol. XXXII (April, 1957).

Hackett, Charles W. "Retreat of the Spaniards from New Mexico in 1680, and the Beginnings of El Paso," *Southwestern Historical Quarterly*, Vol. XVI (October, 1912). Part II appeared in *Southwestern Historical Quarterly*, Vol. XVI (December, 1912).

———. "The Revolt of the Pueblo Indians of New Mexico in 1680," *Texas State Historical Quarterly*, Vol. XV (October, 1911).

Haley, J. Evetts. "The Comanchero Trade," *Southwestern Historical Quarterly*, Vol. XXXVIII (January, 1935).

Hamilton, David. "Imperial Texas and its Satellite States," *Frontier* (August, 1959).

Kelly, Henry W. "Franciscan Missions of New Mexico, 1740–1760," *New Mexico Historical Review*, Vols. XV, XVI (1940, 1941).

"Los Alamos—Boom Town Under Control," *New Mexico Business*, Vol. VI (May, 1953). Reprinted, May, 1953, by Bureau of Business Research, University of New Mexico.

Love, Clara M. "History of the Cattle Industry in the Southwest," *Southwestern Historical Quarterly*, Vols. XIX, XX (April, July, 1916).

Marshall, Thomas M. "Commercial Aspects of the Texas–Santa Fe Expedition," *Southwestern Historical Quarterly*, Vol. XX (January, 1917).

———. "St. Vrain's Expedition to the Gila in 1826," *Southwestern Historical Quarterly*, Vol. XIX (January, 1916).

Meaders, Margaret. "Copper Chronicle: The Story of New Mexico's 'Red Gold,'" *New Mexico Business*, Vol. XII (May and June, 1958).

Mechem, J. Lloyd. "Antonio de Espejo and his Journey to New Mexico," *Southwestern Historical Quarterly*, Vol. XXX (October, 1926).

———. "The Second Spanish Expedition to New Mexico," *New Mexico Historical Review*, Vol. I (April, 1926).

Moorhead, Max L. "Spanish Transportation in the Southwest 1540–1846," *New Mexico Historical Review*, Vol. XXXII (April, 1957).

Nolan, Frederick W. "A Sidelight on the Tunstall Murder," *New Mexico Historical Review*, Vol. XXX (July, 1956).

Norvell, Stevens T. "New Mexico in the Civil War," *War Papers: Military Order of the Loyal Legion of the United States*," (January 7, 1903).

"Prosperity During Recession," *New Mexico Business*, Vol. XII (February, 1958).

Rasch, Philip J. "Exit Axtell: Enter Wallace," *New Mexico Historical Review*, Vol. XXXI (July, 1957).

———. "The Horrell War," *New Mexico Historical Review*, Vol. XXX (July, 1956).

Rodríguez, Arnold L., O. F. M. "New Mexico in Transition," *New Mexico Historical Review*, Vol. XXIV (July, October, 1949).

Scholes, France V. "Church and State in New Mexico," *New Mexico Historical Review*, Vols. XI, XII (1936, 1937).

———. "Civil Government and Society in New Mexico in the Seventeenth Century," *New Mexico Historical Review*, Vol. X (April, 1935).

———. "The First Decade of the Inquisition in New Mexico," *New Mexico Historical Review*, Vol. X (July, 1935).

———. "The Supply Service of the New Mexico Missions in the Seventeenth Century," *New Mexico Historical Review*, Vol. V (January, April, October, 1930).

———. "Troublous Times in New Mexico 1659–1670," *New Mexico Historical Review*, Vols. XII, XIII, XV, XVI (1937, 1938, 1940, 1941).

Spell, Lota M. "Music Teaching in New Mexico in the 17th Century," *New Mexico Historical Review*, Vol. II (January, 1927).

Stanley, F. (Stanley Francis Crocchioli), "O. P. McMains, Champion of a Lost Cause," *New Mexico Historical Review*, Vol. XXIV (January, 1949).

Walker, Charles S. "Causes of the Confederate Invasion of New Mexico," *New Mexico Historical Review*, Vol. VIII (April, 1933).

Wallace, William S. "Stagecoaching in Territorial New Mexico," *New Mexico Historical Review*, Vol. XXXII (April, 1957).

Watford, W. H. "Confederate Western Ambitions," *The Southwestern Historical Quarterly*, Vol. XLIV (October, 1940).

Winther, Oscar Osburn. "The Southern Overland Mail and Stagecoach Line 1857–1861," *New Mexico Historical Review*, Vol. XXXII (April, 1957).

Ximenes, Vicente Trevino. "Where the Money Comes From," *New Mexico Business*, Vol. XI (August, 1957).

Index

Mesilla Valley: 13
Methodists: 211, 217
Mexican Highland Section: 6, 9
Mexican War: 112, 118, 129, 142, 218
Mexico: 3, 23, 28, 49, 101, 110, 150, 207, 243, 256, 287; 1821 revolt, 105
Mexico City, Mex.: 20, 43, 62ff., 69ff., 73, 105, 119, 244, 280, 328
Michigan: 230
Middle Río Grande Conservancy District: 13
Miles, John: 308
Military Department, Ninth: 184
Mining: 242; gold, 244–48; silver, 248ff.; copper, 249; lead and zinc, 249ff.; coal, 250ff.; potash, 251ff.; uranium, 252; natural gas, 253
Miranda, Francisco de: 102
Miranda, Guadalupe: 175
Missions: 61, 90–93
Mission supply service: 62
Mississippi River: 11, 104
Missouri: 112ff., 256, 265, 278; traders from, 120; volunteers from, 135
Missouri Compromise: 147
Missouri River: 11
Mixtón War: 48
Mogollon (Mountains): 9, 14
Monroe, John: 142ff.
Montana: 232
Montezuma Hotel (near Las Vegas): 272, 295
Montoya, Pablo: 136
Moors: 39, 200
Moqui Indians: 93
Morada (Penitente meeting place): 220ff., 224
Mora, N. M.: 128, 136ff.
Mormons: 150, 211; Battalion, 218; establishment of missions, 218
Moslems: 39
Mountain Men: 102, 104–109
Mount Taylor–Río Puerco Region: 4
Mun, Jules de: 108
Murphy wagons: 112, 276
Murphy, Lawrence G.: 163ff.
Music: native, 205; Penitente, 224; recent tendencies, 331–34

Nacimiento Mountains: 8
Narváez, Pánfilo de: 41
Natchitoches, La.: 103
National Guard: 274

Natural gas: 253
Navaho Dam: 14
Navaho Indians: 28, 30, 32–37, 94, 121, 178, 183ff., 197, 252, 272, 291, 320, 330, 332 ; difficulty of conversion, 93; conquest of, 188–91
Navaho Section: 6, 8ff.
Negroes: free, 145; in New Mexico, 283
Neighbors, R. S.: 142
Netherlands, The: 61
New Deal: 274
New England: 319
New Hampshire: 163
New Mexico Cattle Growers' Association: 263
New Mexico: name, 3; size, 3; location, 3; terrain, 3; geology, 4; elevation, 6; vegetation, 9; water, 11; rivers, 11; climate, 14; precipitation, 17; wind, 18; dust storms, 19; restrictive natural influences, 20; Indians of, 23–27; exploration and conquest, 39–60; as a buffer area, 61; French threat to, 97–99; under Mexico, 119 ff.; invaded by Kearny, 129; boundary controversy with Texas, 140–44; Civil War in, 148–57; lawlessness in, 158ff.; land-grant problem in, 174–76; Indian menace to, 177ff.; volunteers, 189; native homes, 201; native food, 202; native clothing, 202; amusements, 203; nineteenth-century education, 206; church in, 212–18; Penitentes in, 218–25; quest for statehood, 226–41; mining, 241–54; sheep raising in, 255–57; cattle raising in, 258–62; agriculture in, 263–68; industry in, 269–73; labor in, 273–75; transportation in, 275–82; cities in, 282–95; politics, 296–315; literature of, 318–27; arts in, 327–31; music in, 331–34
New Mexico, State Museum of: 320, 333
New Mexico, University of: 289, 335; founded, 212; Press, 326ff.; Art Department, 328
New Mexico Highlands University: 295, 335
New Mexico Institute of Technology: 335
New Mexico Military Institute: 212, 292, 335
New Mexico State Hospital: 295

359

361

The text of *New Mexico* has been set on Linotype machines in Janson, a highly legible type face which originated in Europe in the late seventeenth century. Janson's modern qualities of distinctive design and ease of reading, together with its traditional historical associations, suggest that it is a harmonious typographic choice for this account of four centuries.

UNIVERSITY OF OKLAHOMA PRESS

NORMAN